The techniques and approaches fostered in the first half of this century by what was called the 'New Bibliography' have spread throughout the world, developing and expanding in association with bodies such as the Bibliographical Society. The essays specially commissioned for this book take 'New Bibliography' into the twenty-first century. They survey bibliographic and textual studies in some thirty fields, and include discussions of major issues and developments. Areas covered include manuscript studies and the analysis of handwriting; the physical characteristics of the book – its paper, type, and binding; enumerative and descriptive bibliography; incunabula, cartography, book illustration, book catalogues, and the Stationers' Company; bibliographical developments in the history of science, and in many countries – France, Germany, Italy, Scotland, Wales, Ireland, the British provincial book trade, Japan and the Orient, Australia and New Zealand; developments in the theory and practice of editing texts (including biblical texts); the history of the book; and the implications of the computer for bibliography.

An important feature of these essays is that each makes proposals for future research, ensuring the vitality of bibliography in the next half-century. Appearing at the time of the Bibliographical Society's centenary, the collection provides a landmark, taking stock of developments in what has become a vast and vital area of study, and mapping out its future parameters.

The Book Encompassed

The Book Encompassed
Studies in Twentieth-Century Bibliography

Edited by

PETER DAVISON

CAMBRIDGE
UNIVERSITY PRESS

Published by the Press Syndicate of the University of Cambridge
The Pitt Building, Trumpington Street, Cambridge CB2 1RP
40 West 20th Street, New York, NY 10011-4211, USA
10 Stamford Road, Oakleigh, Victoria 3166, Australia

© Cambridge University Press 1992

First published 1992

Printed in Great Britain at the University Press, Cambridge

A catalogue record for this book is available from the British Library.

Library of Congress cataloguing in publication data
The Book encompassed: studies in twentieth-century bibliography
edited by Peter Davison.
p.   cm.
Includes index.
ISBN 0 521 41878 x (hard cover)
1. Bibliography – Methodology – History – 20th century.   2. Book industries and trade –
Historiography.   3. Editing – History – 20th century.   4. Manuscripts – Historiography.
5. Books – Historiography.
I. Davison, Peter Hobley.
Z1001.3.B66 1992
010'.42 – dc20   91–45041CIP

ISBN 0 521 41878 x hardback

VN

Contents

Contents

Illustrations

ix

Contributors

ROBIN ALSTON: Professor of Library Studies, University of London (1990–   ) and Director of the School of Library, Archive and Information Studies, University College London (1990–   ). Editor-in-Chief, *Eighteenth-Century Short Title Catalogue*, 1976–1983; author of books on Old English and on bibliography; Compiler of the *Bibliography of the English Language, 1500–1800*, 22 vols. (of which 12 published to date). President of the Bibliographical Society, 1988–90.

NICOLAS BARKER: Deputy Keeper, British Library, since 1976, and Editor of *The Book Collector* since 1965. President of the Bibliographical Society, 1981–2, 1983–5.

TERRY BELANGER: Associated for twenty years with Columbia University of New York School of Library Service; directed the Rare Book School (which he founded in 1983) within the SLS; recently appointed University Professor and Honorary Curator of Special Collections, University of Virginia, where he will continue to direct the Rare Book School.

CHARLES BENSON: Keeper of Early Printed Books, Library of Trinity College Dublin, since 1988.

JOHN BIDWELL: On leave from William Andrews Clark Memorial Library, University of California, Los Angeles, to study bibliography at Oxford University. He has written a number of articles on American papermaking and related aspects of American printing history.

BARRY BLOOMFIELD: Latterly, Librarian, SOAS, 1974–8; Director, India Office Library and Records, 1978–90; Keeper, Department of Oriental Manuscripts and Printed Books, British Library, 1983–90; Director, Collection Development, Humanities and Social Sciences, British Library, 1985–90; President of the Bibliographical Society, 1990–2.

FREDSON THAYER BOWERS (1905–91): Joined University of Virginia in 1938 retiring in 1975 as Linden Kent Professor Emeritus of English. Founded *Studies in Bibliography*, 1948, which he edited; edited *Leaves of Grass*, and the works of Dekker, Hawthorn, Beaumont and Fletcher, Dryden, Crane, Marlowe, and William James. Rosenbach Lecturer, 1954; Sandars Reader, 1958; James Lyell Reader, 1959; Gold Medallist of the Bibliographical Society, 1968.

SEBASTIAN P. BROCK: Reader in Syriac Studies, University of Oxford and Fellow of Wolfson College. Interests include the text and early versions of the Bible, particularly the Greek Septuagint and Syriac Peshitta.

TOM DAVIS: Lecturer in Bibliography and Palaeography, University of Birmingham; practising forensic handwriting analyst since 1974 – cases include investigation of authenticity of interview notes taken by Midlands Serious Crimes Squad.

PETER DAVISON: Visiting Professor in English and Media Studies, De Montfort University; Professor of English, University of Wales, 1973–9, and of English and American Literature, University of Kent, 1979–82; editor of *The Library*, 1971–82; Vice-President, Bibliographical Society. Currently editing *George Orwell: The Complete Works*, 20 vols.

CHRISTOPHER DE HAMEL: Director of Sotheby's (which he joined in 1975) in charge of sales of illuminated manuscripts. Recent books include: *Glossed Books of the Bible and the Origin of the Paris Booktrade*, Woodbridge, 1984, *A History of Illuminated Manuscripts*, Oxford, 1986, and *Syon Abbey, The Library of the Bridgettine Nuns and their Peregrinations after the Reformation*, Roxburghe Club, 1991.

CONOR FAHY: Emeritus Professor of Italian, University of London, and Honorary Research Fellow, Department of Italian, University College London. Author of a volume of essays on textual bibliography in Italy and of a detailed study of the printing of the definitive edition of Ariosto's *Orlando furioso*. He has recently edited an account book relating to the publication of a Veronese edition of 1622, and is currently preparing an edition of an eighteenth-century Italian printing manual.

JOHN L. FLOOD: Deputy Director and Reader in German, University of London Institute of Germanic Studies. Recent books he has edited include: *Modern Swiss Literature, Unity and Diversity*, 1985; *Ein Moment des erfahrenen Lebens, Zur Lyrik der DDR*, Amsterdam, 1987; *Kurz bevor der Vorhang fiel. Zum Theater der DDR*, Amsterdam, 1990; *Common Currency? Aspects of Anglo–German Literary Relations*, Stuttgart, 1991; and *Die Historie von Herzog Ernst*, Berlin, 1992.

MIRJAM M. FOOT: Director of Collections and Preservation, The British Library. She worked for ten years with Howard Nixon and has published three books (with two more forthcoming) and well over sixty articles on the history of bookbinding. Joint Honorary Secretary, The Bibliographical Society, 1975–81; Honorary Secretary since 1981.

LOTTE HELLINGA: born and educated in Amsterdam; joined the staff of the British Library in 1976, where she is Deputy Keeper, Humanities and Social Sciences. Publications include: with W. Hellinga, *The Fifteenth-Century Printing Types of the Low Countries*, 2 vols., Amsterdam, 1966, and *Henry Bradshaw's Correspondence on Incunabula . . .*, 2 vols., Amsterdam, 1968–78; *Caxton in Focus: The Beginning of Printing in England*, 1982; ed., with John Goldfinch, *Bibliography and the Study of Fifteenth-Century Civilisation*, 1987.

BRIAN HILLYARD: Assistant Keeper, Department of Printed Books, National Library of Scotland, since 1977. Author of *Plutarch: De Audiendo*, New York, 1981, and of articles and reviews in classical and bibliographical journals. Editor of *Library Association Rare Books Group Newsletter*, 1983–9; and of *Edinburgh Bibliographical Society Transactions* since 1984.

TREVOR HOWARD-HILL: C. Wallace Martin Professor of English, University of South Carolina. Has compiled seven volumes of the *Index to British Literary Bibliography*, Oxford, 1969–   and has published on the text of *King Lear*, the Jacobean scribe, Ralph Crane, and early English dramatic manuscripts. His edition of *A Game at Chess*, Malone Society, 1990, is accompanied by a Revels edition and an account of the play's textual problems. Currently collaborating on the New Variorum *Two Gentlemen of Verona*.

PETER ISAAC: Emeritus Professor of Civil and Public Health Engineering, University of Newcastle upon Tyne; Vice-President, Bibliographical Society; Chairman, History of the Book Trade in the North; Chairman, British Book Trade Index; Chairman, Printing Historical Society, 1989–91; Liveryman, Worshipful Company of Stationers and Newspaper Makers; Sandars Reader in Bibliography, Cambridge, 1983–4.

WALLACE KIRSOP: Associate Professor of French and Chairman of the Centre for Bibliographical and Textual Studies, Monash University. Editor, *Australian Journal of French Studies*; first President, Bibliographical Society of Australia and New Zealand (1969–73); Sandars Reader in Bibliography, Cambridge, 1980–1; Fellow of the Australian Academy of the Humanities.

D.F. MCKENZIE: Professor of Bibliography and Textual Criticism, University of Oxford, and Fellow of Pembroke College. Sandars Reader in Bibliography, Cambridge, 1975–6; Panizzi Lecturer, British Library, 1985; Fellow of the British Academy, 1986; Lyell Reader in Bibliography, Oxford, 1987–8. President, Bibliographical Society, 1981–3; Gold Medallist of the Society, 1990. Publications include: ed., *Stationers' Company Apprentices, 1605–1800*, 3 vols., Oxford, 1961–78; *The Cambridge University Press, 1696–1712*, 2 vols., Cambridge, 1966; and *Bibliography and the Sociology of Texts*, 1986.

DAVID MCKITTERICK: Fellow and Librarian, Trinity College, Cambridge; Vice-President, Bibliographical Society; President, Cambridge Bibliographical Society. Publications include: *Cambridge University Library: A History. The Eighteenth and Nineteenth Centuries*, Cambridge, 1986; and, forthcoming, a three-volume history of Cambridge University Press. Editor, *Cambridge Studies in Publishing and Printing History*; joint editor, *A History of the Book in Britain*.

ROBIN MYERS: archivist and teacher; Hon. Archivist to the Stationers' Company since 1978; Hon. Librarian, Bibliographical Society. Co-architect of annual book-trade history conferences since 1979 and editor of their proceedings, *Publishing Pathways*, 1981–   . Publications include: *The British Book Trade: A Bibliographical Guide*, 1973; *The Stationers' Company Archives: A Companion*, Cambridge, 1990.

MICHAEL PERKIN: formerly Curator, Special Collections, Liverpool University Library; sometime Secretary of Liverpool Bibliographical Society. Publications include a bibliography of Abraham Cowley (Folkstone, 1977), and editions of *The Book Trade in Liverpool to 1850: A Directory*, 1981 and 1987. Now working on a part-time basis in Winchester Cathedral Library, Reading University Library and its Department of Typography.

MARY POLLARD: after a late start in Marsh's Library, was in at the setting up of the Department of Early Printed Books, Trinity College Dublin, 1968; retired in 1983; Lyell Reader in Bibliography, Oxford, 1986–7.

EILUNED REES: started her career as an Assistant Keeper in the Department of Printed Books, the British Museum. She was, for 27 years, in the National Library of Wales preparing a catalogue of pre-1820 Welsh books (published as *Libri Walliae*, 1987) and latterly serving as Conservation Co-ordinator. She retired in 1991.

JULIAN ROBERTS: Assistant Keeper, Department of Printed Books, British Museum, 1958–74, thereafter Keeper of Printed Books, Bodleian Library and subsequently Deputy Librarian. Fellow of Wolfson College, Oxford. Honorary Secretary, or Joint Honorary Secretary of the Bibliographical Society, 1961–81; President, 1986–8. Edited with Andrew G. Watson, *John Dee's Library Catalogue*, for the Society, 1990.

DAVID SHAW: Senior Lecturer in French and Computing, University of Kent at Canterbury. Specializes in the history of printing and culture in fifteenth- and sixteenth-century France. Co-editor, *The Cathedral Libraries Catalogue*, Vol. 1 (1984).

JENNY STRATFORD: Assistant Keeper, Department of Manuscripts, British Museum, 1962–71; her exhibition and catalogue, *Poetry in the Making*, 1967, was followed in 1974 by *The Arts Council Collection of Modern Literary Manuscripts, 1963–1972*. Joint editor since 1979 of the Newsletter of the SCONUL Advisory Committee on Manuscripts. Publications also include: *Catalogue of the Jackson Collection in the Royal Library, Windsor Castle*, 1981, and *The Bedford Inventories: The Worldly Goods of John, Duke of Bedford, Regent of France (1389–1435)*, Society of Antiquaries (forthcoming, 1992).

G. THOMAS TANSELLE: Vice President of the John Simon Guggenheim Memorial Foundation and Adjunct Professor of English and Comparative Literature, Columbia University, New York. Has been President of the Bibliographical Society of America, the Grolier Club, and the Society for Textual Scholarship. He has written extensively on bibliographical and textual matters.

SARAH TYACKE: Keeper of Public Records and Chief Executive, Public Record Office and formerly Director of Special Collections, British Library, where, from 1968–85, she was Deputy Map Librarian. She has written a number of works on the history of map-making and prepared several catalogues.

GWYN WALTERS: until his retirement, Assistant Keeper and Head of the Accessions Division, National Library of Wales; later, from 1983–8, Curator of the Old Library, St David's University College, Lampeter, during which time he was elected a Leverhulme Research Fellow in early book illustration. Fellow of the Society of Antiquaries.

MAGDA WHITROW: has worked in technical libraries and as a library consultant. Served on the Council and Publications Committee of Aslib and is a member of the Classification Research Group. Edited *Index to Theses* for Aslib, vols. II–XI; edited *Isis Cumulative Bibliography, 1913–1965*, six vols., 1971–84; in recognition of her work on this she was made an Honorary Member of the Académie Internationale d'Histoire des Sciences. She has published a number of papers on bibliographical subjects.

AKIHIRO YAMADA: Professor of English Literature, Meisei University, Tokyo. Awards include Fulbright Advanced Research Scholarship, 1966–7, Folger Shakespeare Library Fellowship, 1967, and Editological Society of Japan Prize, 1981. Publications include, in English, an edition of Chapman's *The Widow's Tears*, Revels series, Manchester, 1975; and, in Japanese, *Books and the Age of Shakespeare*, Tokyo, 1979; and an edition of *Richard III*, Tokyo, 1987.

Acknowledgements

The Council of the Bibliographical Society wishes to record its thanks to all those who devoted time and effort to preparing contributions for this book in order to mark the Society's centenary. The editor expresses his gratitude to them for responding to suggestions for changes and in particular for requests to work within what were often too-strict word limits. He also wishes to express his warm appreciation to Professor Tom Birrell for his wise counsel.

Abbreviations

The Bibliographical Society 1892–1942: Studies in Retrospect, the Society's volume celebrating its fiftieth anniversary (published in 1945), is referred to as *Studies in Retrospect.*

The following abbreviations have been adopted:

BC	*The Book Collector*
BMC	*Catalogue of the Books printed in the XVth Century Now in the British Museum*, 12 parts, 1908–85
BSA	The Bibliographical Society of America
BSANZB	*The Bibliographical Society of Australia and New Zealand Bulletin*
EBST	*Edinburgh Bibliographical Society Transactions*
ESTC	*Eighteenth-Century Short-Title Catalogue*
JPHS	*Journal of the Printing Historical Society*
Lib	*The Library* (followed by series number)
MLR	*Modern Language Review*
NCBEL	*The New Cambridge Bibliography of English Literature*
NLS	National Library of Scotland
PBSA	*Papers of the Bibliographical Society of America*
PH	*Publishing History*
PMLA	*Publications of the Modern Languages Association*
RES	*Review of English Studies*
RSTC	The Revised *STC*, begun by W.A. Jackson and F.S. Ferguson; completed by Katharine F. Pantzer; Oxford; vol. I, 1986; vol. II, 1976; vol. III, 1991
SB	*Studies in Bibliography*
SCONUL	Standing Conference of National and University Libraries
SOAS	School of Oriental and African Studies, University of London
STC	A.W. Pollard and G.R. Redgrave, *A Short-Title Catalogue of Books Printed in England, Scotland, & Ireland . . . 1475–1640*, Oxford, 1926.
TLS	*Times Literary Supplement*
Wing	Donald Wing, ed., *Short-Title Catalogue of Books . . . 1641–1700*, New York, 3 vols., 1945–51, 2nd edn 1972–88

Place of publication

The place of publication of books is London unless otherwise stated.

Introduction

PETER DAVISON

> Truth is not served by leaving out commas
> George Orwell[1]

There are a number of reasons for the publication of essay-collections. One side-effect of the expansion of tertiary education was the proliferation of collections of genuinely or allegedly scholarly essays. These, if one were reasonably charitable, might be claimed to make more readily available worthwhile contributions to students' (or lecturers') understanding, or, if one viewed them a touch cynically, to package mainstream information so that it might be reprocessed into acceptable student essays and so turn what might well be the dross of academe into the gold of someone's bank account. But, if its overuse, or even misuse, has made the essay-collection suspect, there are collections that justly celebrate the achievement of some individual or institution, or which bring together a great scholar's occasional work so that what might be overlooked can be brought into focus.[2]

---

1 Review of *Hunger and Love*, by Lionel Britton, *The Adelphi*, April 1931; *Complete Works of George Orwell*, ed. P. Davison (New York and London, due 1993), vol. x, item 99, p. 167.
2 Such essay-collections may be illustrated from the bibliographic field by the following, not otherwise mentioned in the pages that follow, all worthy of publication: *A.E. Housman: Selected Prose*, ed. John Carter (Cambridge, 1961), includes at least three essays which are essential reading for all studying bibliography: his 'Introductory Lecture' (1892); the Preface to *Manilius* I, 1903 (which likens an editor of no judgement, having a choice of two manuscripts, to a donkey standing between two bales of hay, who imagines that he will have his problem solved for him, and so cease to be a donkey, if one bundle is removed – p. 35); and 'The Application of Thought to Textual Criticism', 1921 (which likens the textual critic not to Newton investigating the motions of the planets but to a dog hunting for fleas, in which task mathematical principles would enable a flea to be caught only by accident: 'every problem which presents itself to the textual critic must be regarded as possibly unique' – pp. 132–3). Other notable collections of essays by individuals are those of W.W. Greg, *Collected Papers*, ed. J.C. Maxwell (Oxford, 1966), which includes 'What is Bibliography', read to the Society, 1912; 'The Present Position of Bibliography', read 1930; 'Bibliography – an Apologia', read 1932; and 'The Rationale of Copy-Text', read 1949; Fredson Bowers, *Essays in Bibliography, Text, and Editing* (Charlottesville, 1975); and G. Thomas Tanselle, *Selected Studies in Bibliography* (Charlottesville, 1979). The Bibliographical Society of America published *A Retrospective Collection* of thirty-nine essays (Charlottesville, 1980). Other particularly useful collections are: *Bibliography and Textual Criticism*, ed. O.M. Brack, Jr and Warner Barnes (Chicago, 1969); *Art and Error: Modern Textual*

Essay-collections of academic essays fall into two categories. There are those that reprint, sometimes shortened or up-dated, what has already appeared in a scholarly journal; and there are collections, fewer in number, which bring together specially written essays; of these, the *Festschrift* is the best (and noblest) example. The problem with the *Festschrift*, as those who have struggled with them know only too well, is bringing together a collection that has a *raison d'être* over and above the individual being honoured. How often has one dug out a single note from a large book otherwise unregarded?[3]

Fifty years ago, the Bibliographical Society produced a volume of specially written 'studies in retrospect' to mark its half-century.[4] Fifty years on, over thirty scholars, many members of the Society eager to celebrate the Society's centenary, have combined to survey the field of bibliographical studies. Inevitably – and properly – reference is made to what the Society has done and many contributors have looked back to *Studies in Retrospect*, to its assessment of those first fifty years, what was deemed the rôle of bibliography, and what that book passed over with little or no comment. The thrust of this book is different. *Studies in Retrospect* tended to look at what had been achieved by the Society, how, from Copinger's tentative proposal that a Society be formed – a suggestion he quickly seemed eager to withdraw – a flourishing Society was established which produced not only a quarterly journal but a remarkable series of specialist studies of which the most significant was what came to be known simply as 'the STC'. The focus was on the Society. This was done, one can fairly say, with a proper diffidence for, though there were other societies concerned with bibliographical studies, the Society could reasonably claim that, in bringing to birth 'The New Bibliography', it had accomplished a very great deal. Two of the ten contributions dramatically demonstrated the inward-looking direction in which the Society conceived its rôle. Chapter 8 devoted but sixteen pages to 'The Society's Contribution to Foreign Bibliography', and Chapter 10, which comprised only two pages of text, was entitled, 'The Study of Bibliography in America'.

The Book Encompassed, whilst not ignoring the past, has been concerned rather to build upon what has been achieved in various fields of study and to look ahead to suggest the direction research should go. Its subtitle might well have been 'Studies Celebrating the Centenary of the Bibliographical Society', but, in an

Editing, ed. Ronald Gottesman and Scott Bennett (Bloomington, Indiana, and London, 1970), showing some overlap with the former; and *Readings in Descriptive Bibliography*, ed. John Bush Jones (Kent, Ohio, 1974). A more broadly based collection, *Language & Texts: The Nature of Linguistic Evidence*, ed. Herbert H. Paper (Ann Arbor, 1975), includes Morse Peckham's 'The Editing of 19th-Century Texts', pp. 123–46, which opens with: 'It is my conviction that the current theory and practice of editing 19th-century texts suffers from a good many illusions.' Finally, a useful recent example of an essay collection on a single theme issued by a journal is that on the New Oxford Shakespeare, *Analytical and Enumerative Bibliography*, n.s. 4, no. 1 (1990).

3 Thus, E. Vinaver's useful essay, 'Principles of Textual Emendation', which appeared in *Studies in French Language and Medieval Literature Presented to Professor Mildred K. Pope* (Manchester, 1939).

4 *The Bibliographical Society 1892–1942: Studies in Retrospect* (Cambridge, 1945, for 1942). Referred to hereafter as *Studies in Retrospect*.

attempt to deal broadly with bibliographical work, its net has been cast more widely. In part this is because of the very success of the Society's pioneering endeavours. The Society is now but one of many such societies; *The Library* one among a number of important bibliographical journals; the Society shares its membership with those of other societies. To consider bibliography purely from the vantage point of the Society would be limiting and absurdly self-centred. The Society has, therefore, tried to take a world-view – hence the adaptation of the title of Sir Francis Drake's *The World Encompassed* (1629).[5] Even by tripling the number of contributions, it has not proved possible to cover every aspect of bibliographic endeavour nor to touch upon bibliography in every country.[6] Thus, medicine is only briefly mentioned (by Magda Whitrow in an extension to her main contribution), and contributions on music and the classics failed to materialize.

The chapters, deliberately, do not fall into obvious categories. It would have been simple to have commissioned some chapters on, say, enumerative bibliography, others on analytical bibliography, and the book as physical object, and to continue 'The Bibliographical Society's Contribution to Foreign Bibliography' on a broader scale – with, perhaps, an essay on foreign contributions *to* the Society. Essays on bibliographical studies in specific fields or countries are, of course, represented here but it was thought that it would be more interesting and more useful if contributors were given a freer rein (within a tightly controlled word limit) to offer what seemed to them most pertinent in their fields of special interest as the Society came up to its centenary. Each contributor was asked to look back over the past fifty years (quite briefly, if that was thought appropriate), to consider the present state of work in their subject, and, most importantly, to offer some guidance as to the direction of future research. It would be presumptuous to make the book's subtitle, 'Bibliographical Studies for the Twenty-First Century', but, in effect, that is what contributors have been encouraged to undertake. Apart, obviously, from the first contribution, they do not, as fifty years ago, pay particular attention to the rôle of the Society.

Within that framework, no attempt was made to force contributions to conform to a single style; variations in approach were encouraged and these are, in part at least, an expression of the different demands of individual disciplines and the ways in which the contributors interpret what seems to them to be at issue. Treatments of bibliographical studies in individual countries reflect the

---

5 Sir Francis Drake, the circumnavigator's nephew, was the author of *The World Encompassed*, printed by Nicholas Bourne, 1628. See also, *Francis Drake, Privateer: Contemporary Narratives and Documents*, selected and ed. by John Hampden (1972).

6 Drake, in his circumnavigation, did not, of course, touch on all the known world so that omissions of some countries and fields of studies in encompassing the book may be forgiven. The association with Drake may make the omission of Spain less offensive; Ireland, which probably suffered at Drake's hands in the massacre at Rathlin Island, deserves an apology of the opposite kind. Drake as pirate, however, is not out of place to bibliographers familiar with A.W. Pollard's *Shakespeare's Fight with the Pirates* (1917). And the extraordinary outcome of Thomas Doughty's quarrel with Drake (see Hampden, *Francis Drake*, pp. 147–50 and 222–9) may warn the contentious!

scholarly philosophy of those countries and, again, variation in the way contributors have approached their subjects has been encouraged.

Contributors' freedom has presented problems in arranging the essays. Some, dealing with manuscripts and handwriting, or paper, type, and binding, fall into natural groups; others do not. The arrangement adopted, suggested by the book's title and the book that inspired it, Drake's *The World Encompassed*, is designed to offer something of a world-view of bibliography, though no more than did Drake does it touch upon all countries. The book begins with an account of the Bibliographical Society's contribution to scholarship. Its range of publications (and not only *The Library* and *STC*) demonstrate the scope and vigour of that contribution; and its importance is touched on indirectly by Flood and Fahy when they remark that 'what impeded the healthy development of analytical bibliography in Germany was the lack of a unifying force such as the Bibliographical Society'. This chapter is, as it were, in the metaphor of the title, the 'home port'. Tanselle then discusses major issues in bibliography over the past half-century. The journey proceeds to a consideration of manuscripts and handwriting, and, via physical characteristics of the book, to what, broadly, might be considered enumerative topics. The bibliographical approaches of more than a dozen countries are discussed, and then we return to issues – the computer and the history of the book; finally there is an envoi that looks pointedly to the future. It will be apparent from even a cursory reading that what unites the chapters is a concern for the state of the field discussed and where its future lies rather than in similarities of treatment.

This journey started with issues and, although issues were never far from the concern of every contributor, we return to confront issues at the end of the book. The important word here is 'return', and the important image that of the world of scholarship encompassed. This is not a linear journey: like Drake's circumnavigation, it completes a circle and it should be a progressive (or radial) experience for the reader who proceeds from start to finish.

The recent death of Fredson Bowers sharpened perception of a change that had already become apparent in textual studies. If one associates the centuries before the Bibliographical Society and 'The New Bibliography' with, say, Erasmus, Bentley, Malone, Lachmann, Westcott and Hort, Headlam, and Housman, to select but a few names, the period covered by the Society's first fifty years might be said to be the age of Greg, Pollard, McKerrow, and the Wilsons (F.P. and J.D.). By the end of the Second World War, that generation of scholars was passing and for reasons scholarly and economic it was the United States that gave a lead to many aspects of bibliographical studies originally associated especially with the Society. Jackson took over the revision of *STC*; Bowers, Hinman, and Tanselle advanced textual studies with tireless energy; *Studies in Bibliography* became a force; and the Centre for Editions of American Authors was established, prompting a strong reaction from those who disagreed with what it did and how it did it. The energy motivating all this activity in North America dominated many fields of bibliography even though (as these essays show), the kind of bibliography initiated by the Society, spread rapidly from Europe and America to the Far East and Australasia. 'The New Bibliography' was no longer 'New' and it had, by the end of the Society's second half-century, spread world-wide.

It is sometimes assumed that a very high proportion of this work, especially in Anglo-American studies, was too narrowly devoted to textual analysis, in particular to isolating compositors, identifying types and running titles, and working out setting by formes, and the like, which, in the end, bore little fruit. Further, that this concentration of effort was at the expense of attention to studies in other fields.[7] Unless there is a central directing authority, it is extraordinarily difficult in a subject that by and large depends upon the goodwill, initiative, and even self-funding of scholars working independently to direct research in a balanced manner. Yet, a glance at John Feather's *An Index to Selected Bibliographical Journals 1971–1985* (Oxford, 1991) reveals that although he lists 84 articles under the heading 'Textual Criticism' published by the six British journals surveyed, there are 124 associated with printing, 34 with publishing, 96 on the book trade, 125 on bookbinding, and, perhaps a little surprisingly, 101 on manuscripts. This is a crude measure; it does not allow for the space devoted to each article, nor does it take account of the diplomatic editions and volumes of *Collections* produced by the Malone Society, but it does suggest that textual criticism did not receive quite such disproportionate attention as has been asserted. Nevertheless, in recent years there has been a turning away from the detailed analysis of what happened in the printing house as revealed by, or reconstructed from, extant printed copies of books, and a shift to what is usefully summed up as 'The History of the Book'. This in part stems from disenchantment with some of the products of textual analysis, and, in part, from admiration for the work of the *annales* school of economic historians.[8]

Erroneous conclusions based on detailed analysis of printing-house practice demand correction; that can prove difficult when a great mass of data must be sifted, corrected – and published – but such re-assessments are vital to the health of a subject.[9] Less commendable has been the acrimony that has sometimes

---

7 For a convenient account of what is considered by some to be the undue attention paid to textual criticism see John Feather, 'Cross Channel Currents: Historical Bibliography and *L'Histoire du Livre*', *Lib.* VI, 2 (1980): 1–15. Feather maintains that 'It is unfortunate that the world of bibliography has been swamped by textual criticism . . . The obsession with textual criticism has . . . led to the neglect of other fields' (p. 3).

8 Jerome McGann, in 'Theory of Texts' (*London Review of Books*, 18 February 1988: 20–1), a review-article of D.F. McKenzie's 1985 Panizzi Lectures, writes of a 'quiet yet profound change [that] has been taking place in literary studies during the past ten years or so'; the 'return to history is one signal' and McKenzie's suggestion that historical bibliography should be placed at the centre of the study of texts has, he says, far-reaching implications. He continues: 'The most immediate object of McKenzie's critique is that line of positivism which has underwritten most work in bibliography and textual criticism (properly so-called) during this century. McKenzie has Fredson Bowers particularly in mind here, whose position – that "historical bibliography is not, properly speaking, bibliography at all" – McKenzie stands opposed to.'

9 For a good example, see Peter W.M. Blayney, '"Compositor B" and the Pavier Quartos: Problems of Identification and their Implications', *Lib*, V, 27 (1972): 179–206.

accompanied reaction to the way scholarship is proceeding. But one can only welcome the energy devoted to harnessing different facets of scholarship that combine to make up the history of the book, with, in prospect, a major, multi-volume work devoted to this aspect of bibliography. What has come about is that change of emphasis in bibliographical studies, *vis à vis* textual criticism and *l'histoire du livre* (discounting for a moment all the other work being done), called for by D.F. McKenzie in 1969:

> if our basic premise is that bibliography should serve literature or the criticism of literature, it may be thought to do this best, not by disappearing into its own minutiae, but by pursuing the study of printing history to the point where analysis can usefully begin, or by returning – and this is the paradox – to the more directly useful, if less sophisticated activity of enumerative 'bibliography'.[10]

It may well seem that, in the post-Lachmann age, we have experienced first a McKerrow–Greg age; then a Hinman–Bowers age; and that these are now being succeeded by a period in which the history of the book, its social context (something scholars as different in temperament as Greg and Thomson would not find surprising), and its economic basis, will serve as a focus for bibliographical studies.[11] This could be not only a welcome broadening of scholarship, but a means whereby research in fields which have tended to remain independent of, or even aloof from, the main thrust of the textual criticism of 'The New Bibliography' might contribute productively to a much more broadly established understanding of bibliographical work, whether individual scholars continue (as they will) to pursue textual criticism, or research into printing and printing history, collecting, readership, and so on.

This is another world from that which Greg, sixty years ago, considered to be bibliography: 'essentially the science of the transmission of literary documents'.[12] Although Greg recognized that 'since bibliography is the study of books as material objects, it is bound to take cognizance of everything appertaining to them',[13] he went on in summarizing his position to give a caveat against interpreting bibliographical study as it is now advocated:

> while convinced that bibliography ranks as a serious study just in so far, and only in so far, as it relates to the essential function of books, namely the transmission of literary documents, I yet take a catholic view of our pursuits, and welcome light and guiding from every branch of bookish lore, only premising that the strictly bibliographical importance of these branches is

---

10 'Printers of the Mind: Some Notes on Bibliographical Theories and Printing-House Practices', *SB*, 22 (1969): 1–75; the passage quoted is from p. 61. McKenzie was not alone in asking awkward questions at that time. See for example, the pronouncements of the editors of the Ohio Browning; also James Thorpe, 'The Aesthetics of Textual Criticism', *PMLA*, 80 (1965) and his and Claude Simpson Jr's, *The Task of the Editor* (William Andrews Clark Memorial Library, 1969).

11 If the inspiration for the history of the book stems from the French *histoire du livre*, let us hope that this third period of 'The New Bibliography' is not *le troisième âge*.

12 'Bibliography – an Apologia', read to the Bibliographical Society, 21 March 1932; pub. in *Lib*, IV, 13 (1932): 113–43; reprinted in *The Collected Papers*, 239–66, from which this quotation is taken (p. 241).   13 *Collected Papers*, p. 242.

not always that which their devotees would claim for them. *A bibliotheca sum, nihil biblicum a me alienum puto.*[14]

We do not have to be bound by definitions of what was proper to bibliography over half-a-century ago, but the words of a scholar as wise and experienced as Greg are worth bearing in mind. Against that one might, in parallel with the history-of-the-book approach, set the work of Form Critics concerned with what influenced the transmission of gospel texts – the taking account of *Sitz im Leben* in its various manifestations.[15]

In an important aspect of textual criticism a deep division has developed. David Shaw, in his chapter here, '*La bibliologie* in France', neatly sums up this change in attitude:

The theoretical interests of French literary scholars have notoriously tended to structuralist criticism and its various offshoots, many of which have stressed the reader's rôle in re-creating the identity of a text as he reads it. There has been a bias against the notion of texts having an author who possesses some sort of textual right of ownership and there has been a consequent lack of interest in the concept of a 'correct' text restored through the study of the historical process of transmission.

As long ago as 1962, in an essay in Japanese which, in English, would be entitled 'The Principles of Variant Texts', Professor Shigehiko Toyama argued that the text of a literary work, whether oral or written, is always subject to change, undergoes variation giving birth to variant texts, debased or improved, and, if qualified enough to become a classic, transforms itself through a creative audience's idealization into something new and precious by its audience 'adding action', just as a pebble trapped in a shell is transformed into a pearl. Toyama went further, suggesting that the reader's 'added action' enabled the work to achieve classic status, and he argued that bibliography which was concerned to establish the original text representing the author's intention, *prevented* a work achieving classic status.[16] The concept of added action by an audience at a theatrical performance is well known to students of the drama and it may give meaning beyond that found in the written text. The catch-phrase, usually meaningless as it stands, provides a perfect example.[17]

---

14 *Collected Papers*, p. 246.
15 Examples of additions to manuscripts explicable by *Sitz im Leben* are given by Bruce Metzger in *The Text of the New Testament: Its Transmission, Corruption, and Restoration* (2nd edn, Oxford, 1968), p. 203; these reflect the increasing emphasis on asceticism in early Church society.
16 The article was reprinted in 1964 and again in 1969 in *Kindai Dokusha Ron* (Tokyo), from which edition Toyama's argument, as given here, was summarized by Akihiro Yamada in his paper, 'Text, Performance, and Bibliography: Shakespeare's Individual Talent *versus* Cultural Tradition', read to the 1991 Shakespeare Conference, Tokyo. Earlier, Yamada had argued against Toyama's thesis in '"The Principles of Variant Texts" and Bibliography' (*Eigo Bungaku Sekai*, August 1970, pp. 30–4). The editor is indebted to Professor Yamada for a copy of his conference paper.
17 When Hamlet ad libs after his instruction that the Clown speak no more than is set down for him in the Bad Quarto of 1603, he rehearses four catch-phrases (F2 lines 2–4). Whatever significance they once had – or which the audience gave them – is now lost. One, at least, is found elsewhere: 'your

Jerome McGann independently elaborates Toyama's theory of the reader's 'added action' in his review-essay of McKenzie's Panizzi Lectures.[18] McKenzie, he says, 'unfolds a profound truth about "the book" itself – and thence about every kind of possible text: that it is meaning-constitutive not simply in its "contained" or delivered message, but in every dimension of its material existence'; that includes its readership and, to adapt Toyama's phrase, the meaning added to what is read. McGann gives examples of spatial and radial (as opposed to linear) reading. He contrasts the reaction to the publication of the first two cantos of Byron's *Don Juan*, in quarto in 1819 for a restricted audience, and then in cheap, pirated duodecimos 'destined to fall into the hands of working-class readers'. Reviewers praised the quartos for the poem's wit and verve; the duodecimos they denounced as immoral, blasphemous, and seditious. These contrasting responses sprang from what 'the audience [the reviewers] perceive as present to and in the two texts, and in the general socio-historical context which those perceptions call attention to'. Further examples lead to a general conclusion: 'the entire socio-history of [a] work – from its originary moments of production through all its subsequent reproductive adventures – is postulated as the ultimate goal of critical self-consciousness', a goal McGann describes as unreachable.

It is clear that concern for the economic and social history of the book and of individual texts, and of readers' responses, is beginning to dominate bibliographical research. That has obvious virtues, but there are dangers lurking in every Eden. We dismiss the search for authorial intention in favour of economic and social contexts of publication and of reader expectation ('added action'), at our peril, attractive though that might seem in a liberal context. Erasmus, in his first edition of his New Testament, omitted the *Comma Johanneum* (1 *John* 5:7–8, King James version), which enunciates the concept of the Holy Trinity, because it did not appear in any authoritative text. Nor has such a text been discovered since and the passage is excluded from contemporary editions of the New Testament.[19] However, in the sixteenth century, such an omission was scandalous and soon a version was found which supplied what readers expected. This forgery gave physical form to the readers' 'added action' and restored 'classic status' to what had been regarded as a deficient (if authoritative) text. It also provided 'a text' to use against those who disagreed with the concept of the Trinity, placing them in penal and mortal danger. In a totalitarian regime, political or religious, it can be dangerous if reader-expectations 'control' the

---

beere is sowre' appears at the end of the first scene of *A Yorkshire Tragedy*, 1609 (line 85). The effect of the audience's added action can be well demonstrated from the reception given to a wartime catch-phrase, 'Can I do yer now, sir?' In a recording of the radio show, *ITMA*, made in 1941–2, the audience does not respond at all; the phrase, with its *double entendre* (and the character) are greeted with roars of applause on 13 January 1944, holding up the performance for ten seconds (Oriole disc, MG 20032). Though interesting in studies of audience reactions, whether such added action is of much relevance in establishing a text is doubtful.

18 'Theory of Texts', p. 21.

19 See Bruce Metzger, *The Text of the New Testament*, p. 101; and his *A Textual Commentary on the Greek New Testament* (United Bible Societies, London and New York, 1971), pp. 716–18.

transmission of texts. It does not require that books be burnt to subvert their 'intended meaning'. In our enthusiasm for a broader approach to the study of the book and the transmission of texts, and, indeed, the importance of readership studies, it would be unwise to dismiss too readily the concept of authorial intention: difficult thought that concept is, it may prove the surest guide to the truth so far as that can be ascertained.[20]

L'histoire du livre and new concepts of authorial intention and the rôle of the author[21] are but the more striking changes that have come about in the past decade or two in bibliographical studies, changes which will characterize work in the immediate future. It is important that the direction of this change should be seen, not as linear, but as circular – as feeding back into the origins of the subject rather than as destructive and confrontational. This is not a matter of propriety (which is not unimportant) but of simple utility. We cannot afford to exclude or diminish the ideas of the past, failures as well as achievements, for much is to be learned from the history of bibliography and especially in textual criticism. Curiously, the broadly inclusive history-of-the-book approach, and the all-embracing concept of authorship, might to advantage be turned back on to bibliography itself.

Jerome J. McGann, in *A Critique of Modern Textual Criticism*, argued that 'We need to become fully conscious of the history of scholarship . . . including the history of classical and biblical scholarship'.[22] He is correct, but writes, perhaps, as if this were a novel thought. Bibliography, and especially textual criticism, have been taught with an eye on the past. Thus, some twenty-five years ago, bibliography undergraduates studying English at the University of Birmingham were introduced to the nature of classical and biblical textual scholarship (at a modest level, of course) by scholars as distinguished as George Thomson and Sebastian Brock, and they were also introduced to, and examined on, the work of Karl Lachmann and Paul Maas.[23] Even more important (and possibly a trifle

20 Compare A.E. Housman on the primacy of the author: 'The indulgence of love for one manuscript and dislike for another inevitably begets indifference to the author himself', Lucan, *Bellum civile* (Oxford, 1926), p. VI.

21 Sarah Tyacke, in her chapter below, 'Describing Maps', makes a pertinent point when she notes that 'maps can and hace been judged for accuracy by measuring them against the world itself. The question of "authorial intentions" has, on the whole, seemed less important to map describers' than it does to letterpress bibliographers. Contrast D.F. McKenzie's argument that 'the land – not even a representation of it on a map, but the land itself – might be a text', which he illustrates from the significance to the Arunta of Australia of their traditional lands: 'every prominent feature of the landscape . . . is associated in tradition with some totemic group'. It is not simply that these are sacred objects 'but of their having a *textual* function' (*Bibliography and the Sociology of Texts* (1986), pp. 31–2).   22 Chicago (1983), p. 11.

23 This was briefly noted in my 'Science, Method, and the Textual Critic', *SB*, 25 (1972): 22. One of the student course lists carried as an epithet Erasmus's question to van Dorp in a letter of May 1515: 'What are we to say when we see that copies of this edition do not agree?' (For the original Latin, see *Opus Epistolarum Des. Erasmi Roterodami*, ed. P.S. Allen, vol. II (Oxford, 1910), p. 111, lines 790–1.) The article in *SB* also drew on Thomas S. Kuhn, *The Structure of Scientific Revolutions* (Chicago, 1962) on pp. 2–3, 23–4; on P.B. Medawar's *The Art of the Soluble* (1969) on pp. 5, 7–9; and on Housman's

dangerous), they were introduced to textual theories that had been found wanting. This was on the ground that a scholar of the knowledge and experience of, say, John Dover Wilson, deeply immersed in the problems of a text, might well have had ideas which, if not then applicable, were worth bearing in mind. It is wryly amusing, in the Age of Deconstruction, to mull over J.M. Robertson's arguments of some seventy years ago for the disintegration of Shakespeare's plays![24]

One now-discounted theory applied about that time to Shakespeare's plays was that of continuous copy. According to this, 'an author's original draft . . . became the official prompt-book, was annotated by the book-keeper, was cut or expanded according to the demands of circumstances . . .was freely revised and rewritten, sometimes in the margin, sometimes by means of inserted or substituted slips or leaves' and was eventually passed to some luckless compositor.[25] This theory attracted A.W. Pollard and Dover Wilson for a time; both they and Greg rejected it, though Greg did suggest that in *1 Henry VI* 'we seem to come nearer to Wilson's "continuous copy" . . . than in any other play'.[26] This was never more than a theory – a conjecture that did not convince. There was no physical evidence of such an occurrence in Shakespeare, but it remains an interesting idea, once thought worthy of serious consideration by very able scholars, and, like much else that did not find favour, deserves a small place in an education in textual criticism. And, of course, physical evidence has since been brought to light to demonstrate that continuous copy was practical, if idiosyncratically, and not in Shakespeare.[27]

F.P. Wilson reminded readers of *Studies in Retrospect*, that Dr Johnson spoke 'with greatest authority' when answering Pope on the dull duty of the textual editor: 'Conjectural criticism demands more than humanity possesses, and he that exercises it with most praise has very frequent need of indulgence.'[28] Forbearance in the Humanities is often, paradoxically, in short supply and bibliography has had its share of over-heated controversy that has done nothing to promote scholarship. This is not a recent phenomenon but it has in recent years become more strident. Confrontation which does not allow of forbearance does nothing to advance the discipline nor does it attract would-be scholars.

Selected Prose, all of which served as texts for the introductory study of bibliography at Birmingham. Coupled with them, as they appeared, were Peter S. Bennett, *What Happened on Lexington Green?* (Menlo Park, CA, 1970) – which proved particularly illuminating to English undergraduates studying bibliography; and M.J. Mulkay, *The Social Process of Innovation* (1972).

24 J. M. Robertson, *The Shakespeare Canon*, 4 pts. (1922–32); but see E. K. Chambers, *The Disintegrators of Shakespeare* (1924); repr. in his *Aspects of Shakespeare* (Oxford, 1933), pp. 23–48.

25 From Greg's succinct summary in *The Shakespeare First Folio: Its Bibliographical and Textual History* (Oxford, 1955), p. 102, Note H. He remarks that this theory would not have been pushed to such lengths were it not that the manuscript of *Sir Thomas More* had proved 'an unfortunate red herring in Shakespearian textual criticism' (pp. 102–3).

26 *The Editorial Problem in Shakespeare* (3rd edn, Oxford, 1954), p. 139.

27 See the sequence of annotations, reprintings, and paste-overs described and illustrated in 'The Annotations to Thomas Milles's Books in the British Museum and Bodleian Library', *Lib*, v, 16 (1961): 133–9 and Plate XI.   28 *Studies in Retrospect*, p. 134.

Bibliographical scholarship does not proceed as a strictly linear evolutionary process with the more fitting always surviving at the expense of rejected ideas of the past. The work of scholars such as Pollard and the two Wilsons, of McKerrow and Greg, Hinman and Bowers (to consider only textual scholarship in the Anglo-American tradition applied to texts in English) ought to be a part of our initial and continuing education. So should an awareness of the scholarship of earlier generations and related fields and traditions.

It is the Society's hope that this volume will encourage cooperative scholarship. It might be appropriate therefore to repeat what F.C. Francis said of A.W. Pollard in the Preface to *Studies in Retrospect*, fifty years ago. He wrote that it was Pollard's 'genius to bring into the Society's life a personal element, a sense of common adventure, which has been one of its most valuable features and which I hope will never disappear from it'.[29] For 'the Society' we can now read a whole world of scholarship. In repeating that hope for an adventure in common, perhaps as an epilogue one might offer this, from Drake's *The World Encompassed*:

> if any will not be satisfied
> nor believe the report of our experience and ey-sight,
> hee should be aduised to suspend his iudgement,
> till he haue either tried it himselfe,
> by his owne trauell,
> or shall vnderstand, by other trauellers,
> more particulars
> to confirm his mind herein.
> GI^r

29 *Studies in Retrospect*, p. vii.

The Bibliographical Society, 1942–1992

JULIAN ROBERTS

The Bibliographical Society's celebrations of its golden jubilee on 15 July 1942 were, understandably, muted. Although air-raids on London had lost some of their severity and it proved possible to restore meetings to their normal pattern of six a year by 1943–4, at the time of the actual anniversary public attention was upon the battles for Stalingrad, for Egypt, and in the seas round Australia.

Nevertheless, in January 1942 the Council decided to publish an anniversary volume, and this, entitled *Studies in Retrospect*, duly appeared in 1945, three years after the event. (It had indeed only lacked one chapter as early as September 1943.) Two features of the book stand out, of which the first is the elegance of its appearance, both in its austere wartime garb of 1945 and even more in the reprint of 1949; an elegance in printing of which the Cambridge University Press was and remains a master. The second quality is the enduring value of the contributions, all made by leading members of the Society, as statements of the function of historical bibliography. Only the brief contribution, 'The Study of Bibliography in America', by W.A. Jackson, a member since 1932 and Honorary Secretary for America since 1936, now strikes one as failing by its very brevity to do justice to its theme.

The first chapter of *Studies in Retrospect*, F.C. Francis's 'A Sketch of the First Fifty Years', was written with the benefit of access to both written and printed records of the Society's work. This successor sketch does not enjoy such advantages in full, since extensive searches have failed to locate the voluminous correspondence which one file, surviving by chance, shows must once have existed. From 1942 to 1962 the Society's historian must rely upon the Council Minute Books and upon printed records such as Annual Reports, Arrangements Cards, and Lists of Members preserved by the more archivally minded libraries. The Society's correspondence does, however, survive from 1962 onwards in a quantity and detail which call for the services of an archivist.

In his 'Sketch' at the outset of *Studies in Retrospect*, Francis noted that in addition to the hazards of war the Society had lost its three principal figures, R.B. McKerrow having died in 1940 and A.W. Pollard in 1943, while W.W. Greg no longer lived in London. Nevertheless, the impetus that these three had given enabled the Society to survive also the absence of its younger members on war service, to maintain at least in the later years of the war a regular 'slate' of meetings, to prepare at least one major publication, and to continue the production of *The Library*. What he left unsaid was that the integrity of bibliographical studies as a whole had been seriously compromised by the exposure of T.J. Wise, a former President of the Society, and that that integrity had only been saved by the use of bibliographical methods in the exposure and by the rapid rise to prominence within the Society of John Carter and Graham Pollard. It is also clear now that Francis's own presence at the British Museum during the war years was a major factor in keeping the Society going; he had joined McKerrow as Joint Honorary Secretary in 1938, and became sole Secretary on McKerrow's death in 1940, having previously taken on the editorship of *The Library* in 1937. He did not relinquish the latter office until 1953.

The Annual Report for 1945–6 lamented – a little unreasonably, some may think, in view of the state of Europe and the world at the time – that 'It is disappointing that the cessation of hostilities in Europe has not been speedily followed by the restoration of all available facilities for carrying on bibliographical research.' Nevertheless, the Rules and List of Members issued in 1947 reveal that bibliographical research was reasserting itself at least in the form of membership of the Society. In 1939 there had been 323 British Empire, 191 American, and 33 foreign members. There was an obvious spurt in 1944, and in 1947 the categories were 413, 209, and 17 respectively. The halving of the foreign membership was only to be expected, but it is surprising that the increase in British membership is proportionately so much greater than the American. Statistics of membership are, for various reasons, extremely unreliable, but the Society claimed 1,000 members in 1967 and 1,100 in 1975. Membership remained static for about five years thereafter, and at the time of writing (1991) is about 1,150. The most rapid increase coincided with the expansion of university and polytechnic education in the sixties and early seventies, and the slower rate of growth with the reduction in funds available both to public and university libraries after 1974. This has been offset to a certain extent by the greater interest in the Anglo-American approach to bibliography apparent elsewhere in Europe and in Japan. All these factors have, as will appear later, had a powerful effect on the Society's publishing policy.

The Society's objects as laid down in its Rules (and amplified a little in its Prospectus) are to promote and encourage bibliographical studies, and in particular: (a) to print and publish works concerned with bibliography, particularly those which are not likely to be commercially profitable; (b) to maintain a bibliographical library; (c) to hold meetings at which papers are read and discussed. The last three objects have always been considered as means of fulfilling the first, and the history of the Society during the last half-century may be very conveniently considered in the order in which they appear in the Rules.

This is not perhaps the place in which to consider what kind of bibliography the Society engaged itself to promote and encourage, since the topic was debated exhaustively at the Society's inception, at its golden jubilee, and indeed throughout its history, with the most challenging recent definition pronounced in the Panizzi Lectures for 1985 by D.F. McKenzie (President 1982–3).[1] However at the outset of our period the long intimacy, going back indeed to the early years of the century, between A.W. Pollard, R.B. McKerrow, and W.W. Greg, physically centred on the British Museum, focused the Society's attention on the bibliography of English books up to the seventeenth century and in particular upon the literary implications of bibliographical research. In addition, the eminence of Victor Scholderer as an incunabulist, of A.F. Johnson in early foreign bibliography, and of H.M. Nixon in binding studies (all of them based at the British Museum) ensured that these areas were prominent among the Society's concerns – a position strengthened by the physical and cultural isolation of Germany in the decade before 1945. But the principal concern was English and early English at that; there was nothing in *Studies in Retrospect* on the later-seventeenth-century English book. How the Society's preoccupations have altered as the result of the post-war establishment and flourishing of other societies and journals will be discussed later.

The Society not only promotes bibliographical studies, but rewards distinction by the award of a gold medal. The high and constantly increasing cost of gold has meant that most post-war medals have been of silver-gilt, since the medal fund established in 1929 by Eustace F. Bosanquet proved insufficient to meet the cost. The procedure under which the award is made was drawn up under the Presidency of Graham Pollard, himself considered (with John Carter) for a medal in 1935 after the publication of the *Enquiry into the Nature of Certain Nineteenth-Century Pamphlets*. Pollard finally received a medal in 1969 and Carter, posthumously, in 1975.

In retrospect, the Bibliographical Society's publishing has, since 1942, been dominated by four major projects.

W.W. Greg's majestic *Bibliography of the English Printed Drama to the Restoration* was begun before the Second World War, the first volume being issued in 1939 and the fourth and last twenty years later, in the year of its author's death. The seemingly effortless flow of its production, the complexity of its typesetting, the amplitude of its design and, above all, the lack of problems for the Society in its publication, mark it off as different from all subsequent projects undertaken. This point can best be illustrated, perhaps, by the Council's reception in 1948 of a proposal from Professor Fredson Bowers for a continuation of Greg from 1660 to 1700, on the same scale. The proposal was accepted, but only subject to the provision of half the cost by an American institution. That was not the last of the Society's qualms, for at a later meeting the Secretary (Francis) was instructed to investigate the possibility of replacing quasi-facsimile transcription by a facsimile. Francis was always interested in facsimile – indeed it was the subject of his own Presidential Address – and the investigation was perhaps his own idea.

In 1942 the Council received a request from Miss Margaret Hands to sponsor a

---

1 D.F. McKenzie, *Bibliography and the Sociology of Texts* Panizzi Lectures 1985 (British Library, 1986).

catalogue of books up to 1700 in the libraries of the Anglican cathedrals of England and Wales. In agreeing, the Society supposed, with the optimism habitual to such projects, that it would take first four, then six years, after which time a printed catalogue could be issued. A grant made for the purpose in 1944 by the Pilgrim Trust ran out in 1956, by which time Miss Hands had catalogued all but six of the libraries (among which, however, were some of the largest). The work remained in abeyance until 1962 when the Society resumed the initiative. In this it was aided by the interest displayed by universities in the resources of neighbouring cathedrals, an interest evinced as much by the new universities at York and Canterbury as by the older ones at Birmingham and Durham. Miss Hands (who had become Mrs McLeod upon marriage) returned to catalogue the library at Carlisle, but was unable thereafter to do more than editorial work on the catalogue cards which had been deposited at the British Museum. A new approach to the Pilgrim Trust in 1976 failed, but the British Library was able, under the far-sighted provisions of Section 1(3)b of the British Library Act (1973), to supplement funds provided by the Society and by a private member. The first volume, listing British books, was published jointly by the Society and the British Library in 1985, forty-one years after Miss Hands had begun work at Worcester. The Society's dependence on the British Library for finance and on the University of Kent for computer facilities and the help of its staff, notably Dr David Shaw, demonstrated how complex, and indeed how costly, the making and publishing of a union catalogue of early books had become. The second volume, listing foreign books – for which no reference works like *STC* and Wing were available – has not yet been completed.

The later stages of the *Cathedral Libraries Catalogue* were watched over by the Society's standing Ecclesiastical Libraries Committee, which now finds itself with a new and grave concern: that the reduction of government funding for universities is likely to jeopardize the care that university libraries have hitherto been able to give to neighbouring cathedral libraries.

While the *Cathedral Libraries Catalogue* has been long drawn out, and indeed is not yet completed, it cannot be said to have had a major impact on the whole course of the Society's activities. That, however, is certainly true of the revision of the *STC*, with which must be coupled the potent influence of the 'short-title' concept upon British enumerative bibliography as it covers, and perhaps goes beyond, the year 1800.

The reprint of the *STC* of 1926, authorized by the Council in 1946, was the first of at least four, required by the value to scholarship of the Society's best-known publication, and the unexpectedly long time needed for the production of a second edition.

The first volume (though the second published) of the revised *STC* carried, in its Preface by Nicolas Barker (President 1981–2 and 1983–5) a history of the project, which was the more useful in that it drew upon the files of correspondence among W.A. Jackson's own papers at Harvard which thus compensate for the absence of the Society's own papers (other than minute-books) before 1964. The story is well known of how the young Jackson, a student at the Chapin Library, Williams College, Williamstown, MA, bought a copy of the newly published *STC* in 1926, interleaved it and bound it into two volumes, into which he wrote the ever more complicated results of the fairly light-hearted Dibdinesque travels in England recorded in *Records of a Bibliographer*,[2] his work in the Pforzheimer Library, New York, and later as Librarian of the Houghton Library at Harvard, and finally his discoveries during more formal and carefully prepared visits to libraries after the Second World War. The agreement to the revision of *STC* came before the Society's Council on 24 September 1946; 'stenographic assistance' for Ferguson was also approved, but there is no evidence that he ever availed himself of it. Indeed the issue of F.S. Ferguson's expenses was the first to confront the incoming Joint Honorary Secretary in 1961. The fact that at the same Council meeting in 1946 the offer to continue Greg's *Bibliography*, mentioned above, was discussed, is perhaps evidence of the mood of post-war optimism that older members may recollect.

It is often said that Jackson intended the revised *STC* to act as an investment to subsidize the Society's other work. That it should in fact, after many years of travail, have proved so, is a measure of his foresight. His collaborator in the revision, F.S. Ferguson, alongside his work as an eminent scholarly bookseller with the firm of Bernard Quaritch, had been engaged for many years upon a publication for the Society, *Annals of Printing*, apparently a chronological rearrangement of *STC* by printer, and thus akin to the Society's original *Handlists* of 1895–1913. He was also working upon a revision of W.C. Hazlitt's *Collections and Notes* (5 vols., 1876–1903). When his papers came to the British Museum after his death in 1967, there was little evidence that either project had gone much farther than his detailed and valuable card-files. It was Jackson's ability to consult and indeed photograph these files on his annual visits that was to constitute the main result of their collaboration. Jackson also sent Ferguson the typed-up copy of his revision. These too came to the Museum (as did Miss Pantzer's continuation of them), but Ferguson seems to have made little use of them. Despite a collaboration which was thus not well matched and only indirectly productive, the first specimen of the revision was sent to F.C. Francis late in 1949, and received detailed consideration and, ultimately, approval. The revision proceeded and by 1955 Jackson expected that 'a decade at least' would be required for its completion. The reasons for the profound inaccuracy of his forecast may be found, not only in his own premature and unexpected death in 1964, but in the delays inherent in the very success of his work. In line with the general expansion of literary, and in particular of bibliographical, research in the United States and a little later in Britain, there came a greater awareness of, and ability to solve, bibliographical problems; widening access to libraries by scholars; and a growing readiness by booksellers to draw attention to bibliographical distinctions. But the spread of research and teaching initiated

---

2 *Records of a Bibliographer: Selected Papers of William Alexander Jackson*, ed. William H. Bond (Cambridge, MA, 1967).

both by Jackson himself and by his principal British correspondent, L.W. Hanson at the Bodleian Library in Oxford, was to bear valuable fruit, for when Jackson died in 1964 and Hanson equally suddenly in 1966, they had inculcated into others the knowledge to bring the revision to a successful end. How Jackson's latest assistant, Katharine F. Pantzer, took up the work after his death is set out in the Preface to volume I of the revised *STC*, and the whole project was successfully concluded in 1991 with the issue of the third volume containing the printers', publishers', and chronological indexes. In her acknowledgements in volume I Dr Pantzer paid generous and detailed tribute to those who had helped with the work of revision. There were also aspects of the revision which remained the concern of the Society's Officers, which in retrospect may seem to have affected the whole work of the Society, and can only be concluded with the issue of the third volume. These were the financing, jointly with Harvard, of the research of Miss Pantzer and her colleagues until the burden was ultimately shouldered by the National Endowment for the Humanities, and second the negotiations with the Oxford University Press for printing the work – and paying for that printing.

Jackson's original research on *STC* had been financed, from 1957, by a grant from the Ford Foundation, administered by the American Council of Learned Societies. This was discontinued after his death, and no money, other than that from Harvard College Library, could at that time be raised in America. The continuation of the work thus became the Society's responsibility. By great good fortune the President of the Society (1966–8) was Walter Oakeshott, Rector of Lincoln College, Oxford, both a friend of Jackson's and immensely influential in British academic circles. By appealing to Oxford and Cambridge colleges and to British trusts and foundations he raised enough money to ensure the continuation of the work until the anticipated date of completion. It was only when this date also proved over-optimistic that recourse was had to the National Endowment for the Humanities, whose grant, from 1975 onwards, firmly underpinned *STC* until its completion.

It had always been assumed that the Oxford University Press, printer of the original edition of 1926, and with which the Society had enjoyed close relations, would also print the second edition. A specimen and an estimate were requested in 1966; the fact that the author represented on the specimen was Robert Parsons the Jesuit was perhaps due to the extensive research into recusant printing – and thus to the number of insertions – since 1926. Since the revision of the second half of the alphabet was in a more advanced state than that in which Jackson had left the earlier letters, the Council decided to issue the second volume first. Sales would help to fund the publication of volume I, and the Society's members would be rewarded for their patience. This was accordingly done in 1976, on *STC*'s own 'golden jubilee'; the printing was paid for from the Society's reserves. These, however, proved insufficient to finance the printing of volume I, and a further and successful fund-raising campaign was undertaken by Nicolas Barker during his presidency. This, combined with a bequest by a member, Mr R.K. Smith, of his two cottages in Essex, made it possible for printing to go ahead.

Simple statistics, such as the inclusion of perhaps 10,000 more bibliographically distinct items than its predecessor, or the recording of copies, on a world-wide basis, in a far greater number of libraries (many of which did not exist in 1926), do little justice to the revised *STC*, any more than does the obvious fact that, with its three volumes, it is physically far larger than the pioneering work of 1926. It is the summation of a half-century of bibliographical work in a field which many for long, and not without reason, believed to be the Society's principal concern.

The success of the original edition of *STC* dictated much of the agenda for future bibliographical activity. The terminal date of 1640 had been imposed by the huge upsurge in printing associated with the Civil War. It was also thought that the British Museum's catalogue of the Thomason Tracts (1908) provided an adequate substitute for complete bibliographical coverage. These considerations – and the circumstances of war – prevented the Society's involvement in Donald Wing's continuation of *STC* from 1641 to 1700 (published in three volumes, 1945–51). Wing informed the Council at its meeting of 2 October 1939 that he had finished the continuation up to 1700, and asked for an assurance that the Society was not itself contemplating the publication of such a work; the assurance was readily given. Although many members have given considerable personal help with the revision of Wing – and some sit on the Advisory Committee – the Society has had no formal involvement.

While a number of works, if not specifically linked to *STC* yet contributing materially to research into early English books, were published during the thirties by the Society, the need was also felt for a printers' index and for a chronological index to the main work, linked to it by the numbers which had by now become standard reference points. The Society itself was unable to provide them and the need was met by Paul G. Morrison's *Index of Printers, Publishers and Booksellers*, issued by the Bibliographical Society of the University of Virginia in 1950; chronological access was provided for those libraries that needed it by a set of cards from the Folger Library. A work supplementary to, and closely linked to *STC*, was the *Index of Dedications and Commendatory Verses*, proposed by Franklin B. Williams as early as 1937. Williams, for many years the Society's highly efficient American Treasurer, finally issued his work under the Society's imprint in 1962.

Though the Society's attitude towards Donald Wing's continuation of *STC* was benevolently neutral, it was quite otherwise with the *Eighteenth-Century Short-Title Catalogue*, where it was the first organization to consider what might be involved in such a work. A Sub-Committee of the Council was set up on 25 October 1962, consisting of the President (Graham Pollard), Sir Frank Francis, L.W. Hanson, and D.F. Foxon. This Committee held ten meetings, and produced a report in the following year (unfortunately, perhaps, in view of its historic interest, on an office duplicator) which attempted to gauge the size of the century's literary output, and concluded that the task could be performed; the way forward was the production of a pilot list, based on the holdings of the British Museum and American holdings extracted from the *National Union*

Catalog. That nothing happened for another thirteen years was due to the series of crises in which the Society was subsequently involved; the death of W.A. Jackson in 1964, the need to support financially the 1475–1640 *STC*, and the death of L.W. Hanson in 1966. The report remained on the table until 1976, when the British Library convened a conference in London. Members of the Society played a leading part in the Conference, with the opening address by the Joint Honorary Secretary, Julian Roberts, and a memorable contribution by Graham Pollard. By then, however, the *Eighteenth-Century STC* (or *ESTC* as it was soon called) was perceived as a project which a society of relatively modest membership could only influence and bless, even if those members, British, European and American, had a prominent rôle in it, and in one instance the leading rôle, for the original editor (afterwards editor-in-chief) was Dr Robin Alston (President 1988–90). The initiative taken by the British Library was even more crucial than that taken by the British Museum (or more precisely by some of its senior staff) in 1918 with the original *STC*. The production of a 'pilot list' in the form of the British Library's microfiche *ESTC* very much followed the recommendations of the Society's 1962–3 Committee, though even that prescient group did not perhaps envisage a list on microfiches, nor could they have known how vital a bibliographical tool the computer was to become.

The fourth publishing project which has spanned many of the years under review is the publication of the Bowyer ledgers by K.I.D. Maslen of Otago University. The history of this project, like those above – perhaps even more so – encapsulates much of the Society's own history. It was originally conceived in 1962 as a limited exercise, the editing of the Paper Stock Ledger, which belonged to the Bodleian Library. It then emerged that seven further ledgers existed in the Library of the Grolier Club in New York. The form that the edition of these should take was debated at great length between the Publications Sub-Committee and Maslen. The view which prevailed, and in which Graham Pollard's views on the Society's publishing policy (discussed below) were decisive, was that the edition should consist of introduction and indexes together with a facsimile of the most significant parts of the ledgers. The facsimiles were to open up the ledgers to scholars (and not only to the editor). Pollard saw the introduction as coming, indeed, at the end of the publishing process. The Society assumed for many years that this pattern, perhaps in different order, thanks to Maslen's growing mastery of the information in the ledgers, would be followed. Escalating costs in the production of the facsimiles, and a decreasing ability to meet them, led to an agreement with the Bibliographical Society of America to share the costs and the edition. Nevertheless, the printed facsimiles had to be abandoned in favour of microfiches. The editorial introduction, together with a wallet of microfiches, was finally published in 1991.

The demands made by these four grand projects, and in particular the need to set aside a large part of the Society's income from subscriptions and sales for printing and even research costs, rendered the establishment and execution of a publications policy extremely difficult. A determined effort to move away from a position where the Society was merely a passive recipient of offers of publications, some of which might be of indifferent quality, was made by Graham Pollard during his presidency (1960–2). As early as 1939 he had complained in a letter to John Johnson, 'They [the Council] wait for people to put themselves forward instead of taking the initiative in securing important bibliographical work . . .The solution is to have a small sub-committee for each of these three functions: publications, invitations to read papers, and *The Library*.'[3] He had to wait for over twenty years and for his own presidency (and, perhaps, for a more malleable Secretary) for the opportunity to create these; only the Publications Sub-Committee was to endure. The correspondence with Johnson does not show what he wanted to see published, but by 1960 he was pressing for the publication of bibliographical sources, where possible in facsimile. The publication of the Bowyer ledgers was an example; he also offered an edition of *Liber A* of the Stationers' Company. This had been called for in the Introduction to W.A. Jackson's *Record of the Court of the Stationers' Company 1602 to 1640* issued by the Society in 1957. But despite such powerful backing, *Liber A* remains unpublished, though not unexploited. Pollard himself prepared an edition for the Society of *The Earliest Directory of the Book Trade by John Pendred (1785)*, issued in 1955 and a facsimile of W.H. Hodson's *Booksellers, Publishers and Stationers Directory* of 1855 (published by the Oxford Bibliographical Society in 1972). The latter volumes, together with D.F. Foxon's invaluable series *English Bibliographical Sources*, were a large part of the specialist contribution to the wave of reprint publishing which was so marked a feature of the academic publishing scene of the sixties.

The foundation of new universities, each needing a rapidly expanding library, and the staffing of these libraries with librarians who had usually undergone a professional training in which historical bibliography had been prominent, ensured that there was from about 1960 to 1973 a firm demand for the Society's publications, whether new or reprinted. It was found that the original print runs of major publications, for example, Greg, had been far too small. This was probably the result of the policy which obtained until about 1951, of distributing all publications, with the exception of *STC*, exclusively to members. Print runs in the sixties were accordingly calculated on a generous basis, often totalling 1,000 copies beyond the Society's membership. When retrenchment came after 1973 the Society was left with huge stocks, which its then agent, the Oxford University Press, faced with a similar problem on a far larger scale with its own publications, could no longer carry. Ultimately the Society appointed Mr Raymond Kilgarriff of Howes Bookshop as its agent, though the Press continued to distribute new publications.

Shrinking demand and rising cost in printing forced another change in the Society's publishing policy. It had long been customary to allot a publication to a particular year and to distribute it free to members who had paid a subscription for that year. The high cost, and the delays in publishing the first two volumes of *STC* made it necessary to allot these to as many as three years each. Even by

3 Bodleian Library MS. Pollard 394, fols. 47–8.

1973 the cost of producing *The Library* alone was more or less equal to the Society's subscription income, and the stagnant market for previous publications meant that new publications could not be financed from the profits on the old ones. The Council eventually decided in 1982 to publish on subscription. The first work financed in this way was *John Dee's Library Catalogue*, edited by Julian Roberts and Andrew G. Watson, and published in 1990. A series of Occasional Publications, which would be produced relatively cheaply and distributed to members in return for their subscription was inaugurated at the same time. The Council's decision to make *The Library* the first call upon the subscription income had been preceded by a change of printer; after a long association with the Oxford University Press, the Council entrusted the printing of *The Library* to W.S. Maney and Son Ltd. of Leeds. This was in 1979, and the Sixth Series of *The Library* was opened.

Such celebrations as were deemed possible in 1942 were planned by the Council at its meetings in the Rooms of the British Academy in Burlington Gardens, and it was there also that the Society held its meetings. Once the bombing of London eased, the Society resumed its pattern of having six meetings in the months from October to March, and this was maintained over the next fifty years, with the occasional addition of a seventh meeting in April if the number of papers on offer proved to be unusually generous. The Society has also arranged summer meetings, in London one year and outside it in the next. When the British Academy moved to its more spacious quarters in Burlington House the Society followed it for a few years. It was, however, unable to sustain this long-cherished relationship and finally moved its public meetings to University College. With fine impartiality, the Council (at the suggestion of Professor Julian Brown, President 1985–6) met thereafter in the Committee Room of King's College.

As with publications, the Society has generally relied upon offers in drawing up its programme of papers, rather than taking a more active role in inviting them. Graham Pollard's privately expressed dissatisfaction with this has already been noted; 'I could write a list of about twenty people who ought to be asked to read papers', he complained to John Johnson in January 1939.[4] Once he became President in 1960 he established a Programme Sub-Committee which would, he hoped, review bibliographical work in progress and invite papers from those engaged in it. The Sub-Committee did not long outlive his presidency. This happened also to another of his innovations: evening discussion meetings, which were usually held in the Library of London University. Nevertheless, over the past ten years, an increasing number of papers have been solicited, and the Society has two endowed annual lectures, one established in commemoration of Pollard himself, and another in honour of the late Homee Randeria.

The formation of a Bibliographical Library is the last of the Society's stated objects to be discussed, and it is despite the efforts of the present Honorary Librarian, one where only limited success has been achieved. At the outset of our

---

4 Bodleian Library MS. Pollard 394, fol. 51.

period, the Society's Library was housed in the Rooms of the British Academy in Burlington Gardens, the scene of both the Society's and the Council's meetings, where it was open to regular inspection and use by members. When the Academy moved, a new home was found for the Library in the newly acquired Foster Court buildings of University College, where it was at first well housed and displayed. A period of neglect followed, however, and in 1981 the Society removed it, concluding an agreement with the Stationers' Company for its accommodation close to the Company's own library in Stationers' Hall. Perhaps because of its remoteness from the Society's own meetings the Council has devoted very little money to keeping it up to date with the admittedly expensive books upon which much bibliographical research depends.

The state of bibliographical studies in various fields is of course the subject of other essays in this commemorative volume. One of the most striking features of the last fifty years is how often the Bibliographical Society has been paid the compliment of imitation; a compliment which had nevertheless sometimes had the effect of limiting or reducing the Society's rôle. On occasion the Council adopts a social guise in the form of its Colophon Club, one purpose of which is to entertain, twice a year, the session's speakers. Customarily toasts are drunk to the Queen, to the guests and to the other bibliographical societies. In 1942, enumeration of these last would not have been difficult, and the President would perhaps have named half a dozen, of which the societies at Oxford, Cambridge, Edinburgh, and Glasgow, and the Bibliographical Society of America might readily occur to him. A list published in the Library Association Rare Books Group's *Newsletter* in 1987 enumerated twelve in Britain alone, and the list was almost certainly incomplete. The welcome proliferation of such societies may be put down in part to the expansion of university education, mentioned above as an influence upon the Society's reprint and publication programme, though many of the 'provincial' societies are supported as keenly by public library staff and the local book trade as by university staff, and have a rôle, which the Society itself could never adopt, in the study of their local book trade. But a more important strand in the Bibliographical Society's history over the last fifty years has been the increased acceptance of historical bibliography as a part of the process of literary and historical research, particularly research as carried out in universities. Universities have established palaeographical and bibliographical studies as autonomous areas of research, and knowledge of them is often formally required of students embarking upon literary and historical research for higher degrees. Ironically the demolition of T.J. Wise's pretentious 'bibliophilic' edifice by John Carter and Graham Pollard, employing impeccable techniques of scholarship probably assisted in this process, though equally ironically, only one of these two men was, briefly, to hold a university post. Inevitably, increased professionalization has also led to increased specialization and to the rise of societies and journals to cater for these new needs. A portent was the foundation of the Bibliographical Society of the University of Virginia and the appearance, under the editorship of the late Fredson Bowers, of its annual *Studies in Bibliography* from 1948. Although textual bibliography, and in particular work involving compositor analysis of dramatic texts, is far from being the only theme of *Studies*, Bowers's own concern with textual bibliography has guided work in this area to *Studies* rather than to *The Library*. The foundation of the Printing Historical Society and the issue of its *Journal* from 1965, and the publication of *Publishing History* from 1977 have also had the effect of diverting work which might have come before the Society as papers or have appeared in *The Library*.

In the English-speaking world at least, the *Book Collector* is as essential reading for bibliographers as *The Library*. Founded in 1952, its first task was perhaps to purge bibliophily of its Wisean associations. Since precise bibliographical evidence had been used for this cleansing task, it was inevitable that such preoccupations should also be the preserve of the *Book Collector's* editorship, and many articles could as easily be placed in one journal as in the other.

This survey of the Society's history over the past fifty years is inevitably incomplete, representing as it does the view and recollections of someone who had little or no connection with it for the first twenty years of the period, and who has lacked the guidance of those (most of whom are dead) who were so involved. He has not been able to find the correspondence of the Society's officers for the time before he became Joint Honorary Secretary in 1962.[5] Not all the Society's publications are mentioned in this account; nor are the names of all those who served as Presidents, Honorary Secretaries, Honorary Treasurers (and their American and foreign equivalents), as Honorary Librarians, as Editors of *The Library*, or who were awarded Medals. Nevertheless, it must be said that the Society's Honorary Treasurer from 1967 to 1988, during the times that it raised money for research on STC, hoarded money for its printing, received a steady income from sales of new and reprinted publications, found itself with huge unsaleable stocks of these, and finally approached its centennial with healthy reserves, was Dr Richard Christophers.

The survey has also been written from the inside; someone who has been on the Council for thirty years, whether as Secretary, Vice-President, or President, does not know what the Bibliographical Society looks like from without. What is incontestably true, however, is that the Society has achieved in the half-century from 1942 to 1992, a corpus of publication in *The Library*, its monographs and its Occasional Publications – particularly the monographs whose genesis and construction, often intensely debated, has been discussed above – of weight and value appreciated far outside the Society's own relatively small community. It has participated in the expansion of bibliographical studies into the academic curriculum not only in Britain, America, and the Commonwealth, but into Europe and Japan. The STC concept, so tentatively sketched out by A.W. Pollard in the final years of the First World War has been taken over and enhanced for the recording of the book-production of Britain and its empires and colonies and of the spread of the English language up to 1800. The Bibliographical Society moves into its second century with an assurance born of achievement.

---

5 Somewhat freer rein is given to my views and reminiscences in a contribution, 'The Bibliographical Society as a Band of Pioneers', to Robin Myers and Michael Harris, eds., *Pioneers in Bibliography* (Winchester, 1988).

Issues in bibliographical studies since 1942

G. THOMAS TANSELLE

When the Bibliographical Society celebrated the fiftieth anniversary of its founding, it was in the position of having nurtured and brought to early maturity an entire discipline. The study of the structure of books, which had effectively begun in the 1860s with Henry Bradshaw's work on incunabula, was provided with a forum after 1892 in the Bibliographical Society's publications and meetings; and the repeated appearance in this forum of several great scholars gave further stimulation to the development of the field. One cannot recount the history of bibliography in its modern form without telling the story of the Bibliographical Society; and the Society's important fiftieth-anniversary volume, *The Bibliographical Society, 1892–1942: Studies in Retrospect*, was simultaneously an account of the Society and a survey of the field. Another half-century has now gone by, and the centenary of this Society is a natural occasion on which to think about what has happened to the field since 1942.

Unlike many anniversaries, that fiftieth birthday marked a real dividing line. It occurred in the midst of war, when scholarship, like everything else, was disrupted. Partly because of wartime difficulties, the jubilee volume did not appear until 1945, the year the war ended. The midpoint of the century was at hand, and the years ahead beckoned as a time of new beginnings, a time for rebuilding in every field of endeavour. This mood was caught by F.C. Francis in the last sentence of his historical sketch of the Society in the 1945 volume: 'If we feel we have come to the end of one generation of members, we know that we shall be able to use their work as the starting-point of our own, and their achievements will be the inspiration to carry us on to another fifty years of progress.' The passing of a generation was symbolized by the deaths, during the war years, of two of the three figures who had dominated the field during the previous half-century – R.B. McKerrow in 1940 and A.W. Pollard in 1944. The third, W.W. Greg, lived on until 1959 and embodied the transition that Francis predicted, for his *Bibliography of the English Printed Drama to the Restoration* (published 1939–59) was the monument that summarized the first half-century's achievements in descriptive bibliography, and his 'The Rationale of Copy-Text' (published 1951) served as the focal point for discussions of scholarly editing in the second half-century.

Among those returning to academic life after the war was Fredson Bowers, who immediately established his position as the dominant force of the new era by the inauguration of an annual publication, *Studies in Bibliography* (the first volume was dated 1948–9), and the completion of *Principles of Bibliographical Description* (1949). Bowers was clearly building on the work stimulated by the Bibliographical Society, but his principal forum became the new society he helped to establish at his own university, the Bibliographical Society of the University of Virginia, which was the publisher of *Studies in Bibliography*. This society has a central place in any history of bibliographical development in the second half of the century, for it is associated not only with Bowers's standards for bibliographical description but with the fostering (through the pages of *Studies in Bibliography*) of new techniques of analytical bibliography and new approaches to textual criticism. Indeed, the course of bibliographical discussion during the past fifty years has been shaped by the direction given to these three areas in the two decades after 1948 in *Studies in Bibliography* and in Bowers's own writings; and his death in 1991, almost at the end of the Bibliographical Society's second half-century, reinforces the present impulse for retrospection.

The questions that have been taken up over these years, however, are inevitable ones, which go to the heart of bibliographical endeavour. It could be said that this period has been characterized by vigorous – even, sometimes, rancorous – debates about fundamental issues, the kind of questioning of established viewpoints that marks a mature discipline. The first half-century, though not without its controversies, could be thought of as reflecting 'a sense of common adventure' (to use F.C. Francis's phrase for describing the genius of Pollard's contribution to the Bibliographical Society) – the shared excitement of exploring new uses for the physical evidence in books and of publicizing those discoveries. It is a measure of the success of those efforts that the resulting body of work had the substance and stature to be regarded in retrospect as the product of orthodoxy. Questioning established viewpoints and procedures can only follow their establishment, and the debates of the second half-century grew out of the work of the first. One way of summarizing the evolution of the field over the last five decades is to look at the principal issues that have concerned those working in descriptive and analytical bibliography and scholarly editing, and I believe that in each of these areas there is a single central issue that illuminates the development and present position of the discipline.

In descriptive bibliography the issue is whether bibliographies should be conceived of primarily as guides for the identification of particular editions and impressions or as full-fledged works of historical and biographical scholarship. Bowers's *Principles of Bibliographical Description* inaugurated the new half-century with a firm statement of the contours of descriptive bibliography as a scholarly discipline. In so doing, Bowers was building on the English tradition of Bradshaw, Pollard, McKerrow, and Greg, all of whom recognized the fundamental significance of book structure and set their minds to formulating concise and unambiguous ways of describing it. The *Principles* summarized procedures that had become relatively well established, largely through Bibliographical Society publications, among scholars dealing with fifteenth-, sixteenth-, and seventeenth-century printed books; but it was nevertheless a startling work, for never before had the rationale for bibliographical description been so comprehensively set forth or the implications of the procedures been so thoroughly enumerated. The importance of fully rounded descriptions of books, not limited to points considered necessary for identification, was made clear on page after page, by precept and by example; such descriptions put on record some of the details out of which printing and publishing history, as well as biography, can be built up, and they contribute to the process whereby new editions, printings, issues, and states are discovered. Descriptive bibliography, as presented in the *Principles*, was a demanding historical discipline. With this message, the book was an inspiration to some and a burden to others; but to all who wished to undertake a bibliography it was a presence that could not be ignored.

It may be wondered why, in the face of so rigorous a delineation of the field, anyone would try to defend the idea that a bibliography need record only the physical details that are required for identification and need not attempt a full description. But an alternative tradition already existed: the genre of guides for collectors, concentrating on points for identification, had developed from the last quarter of the nineteenth century, as nineteenth-century (and then twentieth-century) authors began to be popular subjects for collecting. The contrast between the two traditions led some people to think that books from earlier centuries necessitated fuller treatment than books from later times, and simultaneously that bibliographies for scholars had to be different from bibliographies for collectors. The fallaciousness of these notions was well understood as early as the 1920s by Michael Sadleir, whose bibliography of Trollope (1928) is a landmark in its explicit aim of contributing to book-trade history and its consequent recognition of the importance of analysing book structure, even for modern books. 'Bibliographia: Studies in Book History and Book Structure' was the title Sadleir gave to a series of books he edited in the 1930s, drawing on such like-minded members of the book trade as John Carter and P.H. Muir. When Sadleir came to write the essay on the nineteenth century for the 1945 Bibliographical Society volume, he asserted that an emphasis on publishing history was expected of descriptive bibliographies, a position that was reaffirmed soon afterward in Richard L. Purdy's bibliography of Hardy (1954). Bowers's inclusion in the *Principles* of a section on nineteenth- and twentieth-century books provided an even stronger endorsement of the view that the same standards are applicable to books of all periods. Yet the idea that nineteenth- and twentieth-century books can be given a simpler treatment than earlier books dies hard. Even Donald Gallup, whose well-known bibliographies of T.S. Eliot (1952, 1969) and Ezra Pound (1963, 1983) are excellent in some respects, has maintained that signature collation is unnecessary for twentieth-century books (as in *On Contemporary Bibliography*, 1970), and he thus carries over into relatively sophisticated work some traces of the old concept of recording only what is thought to be necessary for identification. There have been many other bibliographies since 1949 that – while perhaps following the *Principles* in some respects – reject the major lesson it has to teach.

A failure to grasp the full significance of this lesson – the status of descriptive bibliography as historical scholarship – lies at the heart of the various lesser questions relating to bibliographical description that have repeatedly been discussed, sometimes with great urgency, during the last fifty years. They are all symptoms of the one underlying problem, not major issues in their own right. For example, some people have objected to the formula for signature collation, codified by Bowers, as too technical and arcane. The most famous complaints of this kind came from Geoffrey Keynes, who believed (in the words of his 1981 autobiography, *The Gates of Memory*) that the recommended notation would have been 'incomprehensible' to the audience for his own long series of bibliographies – 'book collectors, booksellers, and even many librarians'. He added, 'I preferred to give readers less pedantry and more humanity.' Whether the system of notation can really be regarded as difficult is not the primary question. What is remarkable about his position is the resistance to scholarship that it seems to reflect. An open-minded acceptance of descriptive bibliography as a branch of historical scholarship – by virtue of being concerned with the study and classification of one category of artefacts – would lead to rather different conclusions. It would cause one to see that all readers of bibliographies, whether professional scholars or not (and there will be many in both categories) are on a scholarly mission, seeking accurate information about the past; that they are not well served if the research that has been undertaken is not reported with precision; and that precision need not rob the work of humanity. A view similar to Keynes's has been expressed by Herman W. Liebert, who stated in his Feldman Lecture, *Bibliography Old and New* (1974), that a proliferation of measurements in a bibliographical description makes the work more technological than humanistic. Such a position is not flattering to the humanities, suggesting that precision is foreign to them, and it clearly springs from a failure to think of bibliography as history. That people like Keynes and Liebert (each of whom served as president of a bibliographical society) could hold these attitudes is an indication of how powerful is the strain of thinking that links scholarship with a cold and inhumane professionalism, not recognizing that all work is a product of human striving and that the most satisfaction comes from striving on the highest attainable level.

Another area of debate concerns the relative proportions within a bibliography, the question of how to abbreviate the descriptions of books that can be regarded as less important than others. Following the publication of William B. Todd's bibliography of Burke (1964), in which the quantity of descriptive detail varied according to the perceived significance of the items described, there was an exchange of letters in the *Times Literary Supplement* about the so-called degressive principle, showing that it was still – after sixty years – a live issue. The most judicious discussion of the matter came shortly thereafter from Fredson Bowers, whose 1967 Bibliographical Society address, 'Bibliography Revisited', was his most important supplement to the *Principles*. His main point was that, although abbreviated descriptions can sometimes be justified for certain categories of material, the research underlying those descriptions cannot be abbreviated. He was saying, in effect, that variations in copiousness of detail should reflect the emphases of the bibliography, not the amount of work that the bibliographer has done. That this whole matter became an issue at all is another sign of how little bibliography has been thought of as historical scholarship. It is well understood that historians who write narrative histories will expand or contract their treatment of certain subjects, depending on the aims and focus of the accounts they are constructing; descriptive bibliographers must similarly shape their work into coherent accounts, since every historical reconstruction involves selection. Neglect of this point also underlies the controversy over whether photographic facsimiles of title pages can take the place of quasi-facsimile transcriptions. The best-known criticism of the practice of transcription occurs in David Foxon's pamphlet *Thoughts on the History and Future of Bibliographical Description* (1970), but his argument does not spring from a conception of a bibliographical description as a verbal historical account – which may of course be supplemented, but not in part supplanted, by illustrations. The decision whether or not to provide transcriptions would logically rest on the overall scope and proportions of a given bibliography and would be a separate question from the decision whether or not to include illustrations of title pages.

Although these several debates have sometimes seemed unproductive, the half-century as a whole does show a clear forward movement. Whereas scholars of incunabula and Renaissance books were largely responsible for establishing the foundations of descriptive bibliography, scholars of eighteenth-, nineteenth-, and twentieth-century books have since 1950 taken the lead in extending and refining the procedures. The best of their bibliographies have increasingly reflected a sense of descriptive bibliography as a form of biography, a view epitomized in the title of Dan H. Laurence's Engelhard Lecture, *A Portrait of the Author as a Bibliography* (1983). In a time of massive biographies, author bibliographies have also become full-bodied accounts of careers, told through the details of book production and distribution history. This development has been aided by the presence of three post-war publishing outlets for scholarly bibliographies – the Soho Bibliographies (originally published by Rupert Hart-Davis, and uneven in the early years; now published by Oxford University Press), which have contained David Gilson's bibliography of Jane Austen (1982), Dan H. Laurence's of Bernard Shaw (1983), and William S. Peterson's of the Kelmscott Press (1984); the Pittsburgh Bibliographies (University of Pittsburgh Press), in which have appeared J.M. Edelstein's bibliography of Wallace Stevens (1973) and C.E. Frazer Clark's of Hawthorne (1978); and the series (now called the Linton Massey Bibliographies) published by the Bibliographical Society of the University of Virginia, which has included the revision of B.C. Bloomfield and Edward Mendelson's bibliography of Auden (1972). The principle that concise descriptions must be based on thorough research has also been well illustrated in this period by several bibliographies of large scope, among them Jacob Blanck's *Bibliography of American Literature* (1955–91), David Foxon's *English Verse, 1701–1750* (1975), and Katharine Pantzer's revision of the *Short Title Catalogue* for 1475–1640 (the landmark publication of the Bibliographical Society's second half-century). At present the most innovative work in descriptive bibliography is, fittingly, coming from Bowers's successor as editor of *Studies in Bibliography*, David L. Vander Meulen, who has published some by-products of his major investigation of Pope. There is no better way to gain a sense of where descriptive bibliography now stands than to read his Engelhard Lecture, *Where Angels Fear to Tread* (1988). In it one recognizes that the goal Sadleir enunciated in the 1945 Bibliographical Society volume foreshadowed the direction of the next half-century.

If the central issue that illuminates the history of bibliographical description in the last fifty years relates to the fundamental nature of what a descriptive bibliography is, the central issue for analytical bibliography has been a questioning of its very existence. This challenge has come from two directions: one kind of criticism questions the validity of the conclusions that emerge from bibliographical analysis; the other asks what rôle those conclusions, if they can be established, have in the broader study of the way books have affected society. Analytical bibliography – or the examination of the physical evidence in books – is of course involved in the process of description, but many people have engaged in it without the aim of producing full physical descriptions, and it developed in the first half of the century as a distinct area of endeavour. The stage had been set by the earlier work of Bradshaw, Proctor, and Pollard on incunables; and the recognition by a few Renaissance scholars, early in the century, that bibliographical evidence was crucial to the editing of Elizabethan and Jacobean drama set the new direction for the field. By the time F.P. Wilson wrote his splendid essay on 'Shakespeare and the "New Bibliography"' for the 1945 Bibliographical Society volume, such landmarks as Pollard's *Shakespeare Folios and Quartos* (1909), McKerrow's *An Introduction to Bibliography for Literary Students* (1927), and Greg's *The Variants in the First Quarto of King Lear* (1940) had appeared, along with a number of articles that helped to give substance to the movement. What was 'new' about this approach was that it used physical clues present in each book as the basis for trying to identify compositorial stints, the method of proofreading, and other details of a book's printing history that would have a bearing on editorial decisions regarding the correctness of the text in it.

Two scholars who began to pursue this kind of work just before the entry of America into the war were Fredson Bowers and Charlton Hinman, and after the war they became its leading practitioners, each producing by the 1960s a major statement: Hinman's *The Printing and Proof-Reading of the First Folio of Shakespeare* (1963) was both an introduction to the method and a detailed case-study, explaining the various techniques of bibliographical analysis in the process of offering a page-by-page account of the printing of the Folio; Bowers's *Bibliography and Textual Criticism* (1964) provided a theoretical grounding for the examination of bibliographical evidence, assessing the degrees of certainty that could be expected of bibliographical analysis under varying circumstances and exploring its rôle in textual, and indirectly in literary, criticism. Bowers played a further rôle as editor of *Studies in Bibliography*, welcoming to its pages during the 1950s and 1960s analytical papers by such scholars as W. Craig Ferguson, Robert K. Turner, Jr., Alice Walker, George Walton Williams, and Philip Williams. Work of this kind was also appearing in *The Library* and the *Papers of the Bibliographical Society of America*, and the 1950s and 1960s can be seen in retrospect as its heyday.

Into this setting in 1969 came D.F. McKenzie's 'Printers of the Mind', published in *Studies in Bibliography*. This long essay examined a number of conclusions that had been drawn by analytical bibliographers about the way particular books were printed and in each case questioned the validity of those conclusions. The implication was that scholars might better spend their time making available the details to be found in surviving printers' records. That this effectively presented essay put a damper on what had become a major industry within bibliographical scholarship is undeniable. In one respect this result was desirable, for there had been some instances in which scholars, caught up in the general excitement, came too hastily to conclusions about the significance of patterns they had found in their data and were too quick to generalize on the basis of their findings. This danger is ever present in research, of course, but a reminder of the difficulties of dealing responsibly with inductive evidence was not out of place. That some people would form the idea that analytical bibliography was thereby discredited, however, is a depressing indication of how misunderstood the nature of bibliographical research can be. If books as physical objects are the subject of bibliographers' investigations, there is no way that the examination of those objects for clues to their own manufacture can be discredited. The examination may not always be conducted responsibly, but the search must go on, for the books themselves constitute the primary body of evidence about their own production. Printers' records and other documents external to the books should not be neglected, but they can offer only secondary evidence for this purpose.

More recently the value of analytical bibliography has been challenged in a different way, but the underlying cause is a similar failure to understand fully the significance of 'reading' the physical evidence in books as well as the texts in them (the texts, in fact, are also physical). In the last three decades, since the appearance of Lucien Febvre and Henri-Jean Martin's *L'Apparition du livre* (1958), a number of historians in the English-speaking world have been influenced by the French school of *histoire du livre*, and the study of printing and publishing as a force in intellectual and cultural history has become a prominent topic. Two of the best-known products of this approach, both appearing in 1979, are Robert Darnton's *The Business of Enlightenment*, based on the archives of the printer of Diderot's *Encyclopédie*, and Elizabeth L. Eisenstein's *The Printing Press as an Agent of Change*, dealing with 'cultural transformations' in the first two centuries of printing. Most of the historians working in this area, including these two, have had little acquaintance with bibliographical scholarship and tend to prefer archival evidence over the physical evidence present in printed matter.

There is sometimes the implication that analytical bibliography, seen as a key element of an Anglo-American school of printing history, is too narrowly focused and has little to contribute to the study of the rôle of the printed book in society. This kind of view is oblivious to the effect of the printing process on the transmission of texts and the consequent rôle of physical evidence in textual study. Such tedious work as the tabulation of recurring types and of patterns in the reuse of settings of headlines leads to the detailed reconstruction of the course of individual books through the printing process and the discovery of how certain features of the texts came to be what they are. A concern with the social repercussions of printing is ultimately a concern with texts – with what works, and what texts of those works, were disseminated through print at particular times. The study of variations in texts, and the reasons for them, is therefore basic to the broadest concerns of intellectual history; and analytical bibliography is thus fundamental not only to the history of printing but to 'book history' in its newest sense.

The challenges to analytical bibliography have received considerable attention, but all the while there have been scholars pursuing the work. Peter W.M. Blayney, T.H. Howard-Hill, MacD. P. Jackson, and Paul Werstine, for example, have recently been adding to the store of detail about English Renaissance printing. And although the bulk of the analytical work since 1942 has been devoted to Renaissance books, a good start has been made on books of other periods. William B. Todd's work on the eighteenth century has now been followed by David Vander Meulen's. The study of incunables has been enlivened by the analytical approach of Lotte Hellinga, Paul Needham, and Felix de Marez Oyens. And both Needham and Vander Meulen can be seen as successors to Allan Stevenson, whose work on the use of paper as evidence was one of the great accomplishments of analytical bibliography in the earlier part of this half-century. Analysis of nineteenth- and twentieth-century books, given spectacular encouragement in 1934 by John Carter and Graham Pollard's *An Enquiry into the Nature of Certain Nineteenth Century Pamphlets*, has thus far occurred mainly – and on a modest scale – in the pages of author bibliographies and scholarly editions. For background and methodology, the major effort – along with the basic books of Hinman and Bowers – is Philip Gaskell's *A New Introduction to Bibliography* (1972); it is indispensable as a guide to book-production history, despite the fact that it is no guide at all to most of the techniques of bibliographical analysis. (The scepticism about analytical bibliography that has marked recent decades is thus enshrined in a standard reference book.) High among other general treatments are two thoughtful essays by Peter Davison on the marshalling of bibliographical evidence and its rôle in editing. Although the details of printing history are of interest in their own right, analytical bibliography – as it has developed from the early days of the Bibliographical Society – has never been far from editorial concerns, and this conjunction is what truly distinguishes the Anglo-American approach to book history.

The issues in analytical bibliography have therefore had to be faced by editors, but the central issue for textual criticism has been the place of authorial intention among the goals of scholarly editing. This issue is essentially new: in the long history of textual criticism, the supremacy of authorial intention had scarcely been questioned before the middle of the twentieth century. Editors did sometimes emend a documentary text with readings more to their liking, but they usually justified their actions by believing that the emendations were what the authors must have intended. The idea of textual 'corruption' has regularly implied that the standard from which the corrupt form deviated was the form intended by the author. Certainly those who were developing modern analytical bibliography in the early decades of the Bibliographical Society agreed that the goal towards which they were working was the establishment of texts that would reflect the authors' wishes as far as surviving evidence permitted. What was at issue was not the goal but how best to achieve it – an issue that came down to the question of how large a rôle editors' judgement should have in editing. McKerrow, responding to what he regarded as the irresponsible eclecticism of his predecessors, displayed in his 1904 edition of Nashe a reluctance to trust editorial judgement very far. Some time passed before the editors of English Renaissance drama came around to the liberal view that A.E. Housman had been advocating from the early years of the century (as in his Manilius of 1903); but the movement during the first half of the century was in this direction, even though McKerrow's *Prolegomena for the Oxford Shakespeare* (1939), published at the beginning of the war, was still guarded (if less so than his earlier position) about the centrality of judgement in editorial procedure.

This situation abruptly changed after the war, with W.W. Greg's 1949 English Institute paper, 'The Rationale of Copy-Text'. In proposing that textual authority might be divided between two editions (an early one for punctuation and spelling, the 'accidentals', and a later one for verbal variants, or 'substantives'), he was also suggesting that editorial judgement was the key to distinguishing substantive variants that were authorial from those that were not. He did not maintain, as had frequently been done before him, that if one detected the author's hand in some of the variants of a later edition one had to adopt all the variants (except obvious errors) from that edition. This reliance on judgement, though it marked a new stage in the modern evolution of editorial procedures for English Renaissance drama, was not what made Greg's 'Rationale' become an issue of debate. The controversy arose, in the first instance, over the extension of Greg's approach to periods later than the Renaissance. In the 1964 volume of *Studies in Bibliography* Bowers showed how Greg's reasoning could be applied to nineteenth-century American authors, and the Modern Language Association of America set up a Center for Editions of American Authors (CEAA) with Greg's 'Rationale' as its guiding principle. Multi-volume editions of major American authors soon began appearing, and in this way Greg's 'Rationale' came to have an enormous influence. The idea that it had received institutional sanction was enough to cause some people to object to it, arguing that no one approach could fit all circumstances. Many of these arguments were misguided, for Greg's approach was not prescriptive, and in its extended form it was really only a framework for thinking about situations in which the evidence was not conclusive – as the variety of treatments in published CEAA volumes testifies. Greg had insisted that his rationale was not 'philosophical' or theoretical but practical: that choosing an early text as copy-text, relying on its readings whenever there does not appear to be convincing reason to alter them, maximizes one's chances of producing a text reflecting the author's intention. It is therefore not a criticism of Greg to argue that in a particular instance either an author's personal habits or the treatment of that author's texts by printers and publishers points away from an early text as the best choice, for Greg had not suggested that his general guideline should prevail except when the evidence is inconclusive.

A more productive line of argument, and a recurrent one from the late 1960s onwards, concerns the definition of authorial intention itself. Even those textual critics who accept as their goal the construction of authorially intended texts have often recognized that this goal requires further clarification. One issue has been whether an author's final manuscript or the first edition set from it is in general the preferable choice for copy-text when both exist. Bowers's logical extension of Greg's reasoning to periods from which authors' manuscripts more commonly survive favours the manuscript over its derivative printed edition. Other scholars, such as Philip Gaskell in some of the examples in *From Writer to Reader* (1978), have argued for the first edition on the grounds that authors expect certain kinds of alterations to be made in their manuscript texts during the publication process. The debate obviously turns on whether personal intention can usefully be defined to incorporate the expectation of actions on the part of others. Another issue has been whether, in cases of authorial revision, an author's first or last (or intermediate) intention should take precedence. Greg focused on 'final intention' at each point of revision, though he understood that sometimes early and late versions are best thought of as separate works, to be edited independently. A different viewpoint, held by a number of European textual theorists and publicized by some Shakespearean editors of the 1980s, emphasizes the evolution of texts and asserts that elements from different versions of a work must not be mixed; it often fails, however, to distinguish conceptually between a version of a work and the text that happens to be preserved in a particular document. Despite the flaws frequently present in efforts to promote one or another version of a work, these discussions have served to call attention to the fact that an author's textual intentions are not always static and that an editor is therefore obligated to try to distinguish revisions that refine the previous conception of a work (and thus do not produce a distinct version) from those that reflect an altered conception of a work (and thus result in an independent version).

Such questions, particularly those involving the relation of intention to expectation, lead directly towards the challenges made in the 1980s to the dominance of authorial intention as the goal of editing. The stage had been set at the beginning of the 1970s by Morse Peckham's 'Reflections on the Foundations of Modern Textual Editing' (in the 1971 volume of *Proof*), which criticized Greg's rationale for reinforcing what Peckham regarded as an unrealistic separation of the author from others involved in the production of printed texts. But the issue became more prominent in editorial debate in the 1980s as a result of the writings of Jerome J. McGann and D.F. McKenzie. In *A Critique of Modern Textual Criticism* (1983) and many other pieces, McGann argues that literature is a collaborative art, the result of a number of people working together, and that the editor who strives to segregate an author's uninfluenced intentions is working towards an artificial goal. In his view the alterations of publishers' editors are not corruptions of a pure authorial text but a natural part of the social process of bringing the text of a work to the public; the author's intentions, or even the author's expectations, are only one element in the combined intentions of the collaborative group. McKenzie's emphasis is different, but he, too, is interested in the social side of literary production, as the title of his Panizzi Lectures, *Bibliography and the Sociology of Texts* (1986), suggests. McKenzie is especially concerned with the physical presentation of texts as part of the social milieu in which reading takes place, and he examines the role of typography, layout, and format in affecting readers' responses. (Indeed, he argues that bibliographical studies as a whole should be regarded as 'a sociology of texts'.) Both McKenzie and McGann, despite lapses in the logic of their arguments, have performed a valuable service in encouraging readers to think about the importance of the wording and the formal presentation of the texts that were actually made available to people in the past. It is unfortunate, however, that they have considered their position to entail a criticism of authorial intention as an editorial goal. Texts as publicly distributed in the past and texts as conceived by the minds that initiated them are both, obviously, valid subjects for historical study; but they can rarely be accommodated by a single scholarly text. (The former interest can be served by facsimile editions, but the latter frequently necessitates editions with critically emended texts.) Failure to recognize that different kinds of editions may be required to satisfy different historical interests has weakened many of the editorial debates of the past half-century. But even if the criticisms of the Greg–Bowers approach have not always been cogent, the discussions stimulated by Greg's 'Rationale' throughout this period have unquestionably served to broaden our understanding of textual issues.

In each of these branches of bibliographical endeavour the pattern of the past five decades – and particularly of the past three – can be described as the questioning of what have been regarded as established principles and pro-cedures. Not infrequently during these years one has heard it said that bibliography is in a state of 'crisis'. But such alarmist language seems to me inappropriate for characterizing what has occurred. I would instead take these debates as a sign of the maturity of the field and as an indication of its vitality. They are not the debates of a formative period: what could be thought of in the 1940s as the 'new bibliography' is now approached as an orthodoxy. Disciplines move in and out of positions of centrality, and the kinds of discussions that have been taking place in bibliographical and textual study demonstrate that bibliography is moving closer to the centre of scholarly argument than it has been before. It is still far from being a basic element in the thinking of literary and historical scholars, but they are increasingly recognizing it – whether favourably or unfavourably – with a depth of feeling that reveals how fundamental its concerns are.

An age of literary theory, such as this half-century has been, might be expected to have produced an intellectual climate in which the insights into verbal communication that are inherent in bibliographical study would be more widely understood. Whether one is a New Critic, a structuralist, or a deconstructionist, whether one is interested in authors' (or publishers') intentions or readers' responses, one takes a position, implicitly if not explicitly, regarding the status of words on paper. What textual criticism, in its long history, has always implied is that the texts of documents are to be distinguished from the texts of works: since language is intangible, works made of language are intangible, and the tangible texts we find in written and printed documents are the potentially flawed attempts to transmit such works. Even literary critics not interested in historical approaches to literature must decide whether to accept texts as they stand in particular documents or to make alterations in them. Analytical bibliography, in turn, provides techniques for examining documents, so as to uncover physical evidence that may help to explain how the texts came to be constituted as they are; and descriptive bibliography offers a way to display this evidence along with external evidence, so as to provide comprehensive accounts of the production of particular documents. Although analytical bibliography and descriptive bibliography serve other purposes as well, their development has been largely fostered by their integral place in textual criticism.

Those who founded the Bibliographical Society a century ago would probably not have explained the unity of their field as stemming from the effort to grapple with the distinction between documents and works. But an understanding of that distinction, however formulated, was perhaps the dominant impulse behind their work and that of their successors. And it is what may eventually bring textual criticism and literary critics together. The issues that have dominated bibliographical studies in recent years are indicative of greater interaction between the two areas. Textual criticism, after all, involves literary judgement, and literary criticism – indeed, the act of reading – involves questioning the makeup of texts. The bibliographical way of thinking, as developed over the past century, not only underlies the reading of written and printed matter in all fields but also points the way to the study of all tangible records of works in intangible media. The announcement that this view has become an orthodoxy, however, must await a future anniversary of the Bibliographical Society.

Further reading

For a more detailed understanding of the approaches to these basic issues that characterized the past half-century, one might begin with the landmark works mentioned above, especially Fredson Bowers's *Principles of Bibliographical Description* (Princeton, 1949), supplemented by his 'Bibliography Revisited' (*Lib*, v, 24, 1969, and in his *Essays in Bibliography, Text, and Editing*, Charlottesville, 1975); Bowers's *Bibliography and Textual Criticism* (Oxford, 1964), along with Charlton Hinman's *The Printing and Proof-Reading of the First Folio of Shakespeare* (Oxford, 1963) and Philip Gaskell's *A New Introduction to Bibliography* (Oxford, 1972); and W.W. Greg's 'The Rationale of Copy-Text' (*SB*, 3, 1950–1, and in his *Collected Papers*, Oxford, 1966), supplemented by Bowers's 'Multiple Authority' (*Lib*, v, 27, 1972, and in his 1975 *Essays*). The best introduction to the nature of present-day descriptive bibliography is David Vander Meulen's *Where Angels Fear to Tread* (Washington, 1988), which can be supplemented by two other Library of Congress lectures, Dan H. Laurence's *A Portrait of the Author as a Bibliography* (1983) and G.T. Tanselle's *A Description of Descriptive Bibliography* (*SB*, 45, 1992, and a separate pamphlet), by Vander Meulen's 'The History and Future of Bowers's *Principles*' (*PBSA*, 79, 1985), and by G.T. Tanselle's 'A Sample Bibliographical Description with Commentary' (*SB*, 40, 1987), the latter three of which record much of the significant literature on the subject. For the debate about analytical bibliography, one might read D.F. McKenzie's 'Printers of the Mind' (*SB*, 22, 1969), followed by two essays of Peter Davison's – 'Science, Method, and the Textual Critic' (*SB*, 25, 1972) and 'The Selection and Presentation of Bibliographic Evidence' (*Analytical & Enumerative Bibliography*, 1, 1977) – and two of G.T. Tanselle's – 'Bibliography and Science' (in *SB*, 27, 1974, and in his *Selected Studies in Bibliography*, Charlottesville, 1979) and *The History of Books as a Field of Study* (Chapel Hill, 1981). In textual criticism, the key documents in the movement to emphasize the social nature of literature are Jerome J. McGann's *A Critique of Modern Textual Criticism* (Chicago, 1983) and D.F. McKenzie's *Bibliography and the Sociology of Texts* (1986). The various developments in textual criticism and editing during this period have been chronicled and analysed by G.T. Tanselle in *Textual Criticism since Greg* (Charlottesville, 1987), supplemented by his 'Textual Criticism and Literary Sociology' (*SB*, 44, 1991); and the distinction between documents and works has been elaborated in his *A Rationale of Textual Criticism* (Philadelphia, 1989).

Medieval manuscript studies

CHRISTOPHER DE HAMEL

There is a pleasant parlour game for one player taught me by a notable Oxford bibliophile. Sit among your books in the evening and imagine that by magic all volumes (or parts of them) produced after 1900 should suddenly vanish. What would you now see on the shelves? Then try for 1800, 1700, 1600, and so on, as the collection in one's fantasy becomes smaller and smaller until the last tiny incunabular or medieval scrap finally disappears.

One could play this diversion in a first-rate reference collection of books on medieval manuscripts. The most comprehensive in Britain are in Selden End of Duke Humfrey's Library in the Bodleian, and in the Palaeography Room of London University Library. Conjure everything printed after 1945 to disappear. Shelves of wonderful picture books of manuscript illumination would be gone, and palaeography would seem a duller subject. But the shelves would be remarkably well-stocked. There would still be quite enough books to allow serious pursuit of a good many research topics. Most of the great national catalogues of medieval manuscripts would be there, including Seymour de Ricci's *Census of Medieval and Renaissance Manuscripts in the United States and Canada*, compiled with W.J. Wilson (New York, 1935–40). The huge four-volume British Museum *Catalogue of Western Manuscripts in the Old Royal and King's Collections*, 1921, by Sir G.F. Warner and J.P. Gilson, would be there as a model of fact and readability. There too would be the first volumes of E.A. Lowe's *Codices Latini Antiquiores, A Palaeographical Guide to Latin Manuscripts prior to the Ninth Century* (Oxford, 1934, 1935, and 1938), covering the Vatican, Great Britain, and Ireland, and half of Italy, with a tantalizing promise of much more to follow. The folio shelves would also include complete sets of the facsimiles of the Palaeographical Society (1873–94) and the New Palaeographical Society (1903–30). The monumental palaeographical textbooks would be there: those of Ludwig Traube (*Nomina Sacra*, Munich, 1907), Edward Maunde Thompson (*An Introduction to Greek and Latin Palaeography*, Oxford, 1912), E.A. Lowe (*The Beneventan Script*, Oxford, 1914), and E.K. Rand (*A Survey of the Manuscripts of Tours*, Cambridge, Mass., 1929), and there would be Jean Destrez's *La Pecia dans les manuscrits universitaires du XIIIe et du XIVe siècle* (Paris, 1935), later described by Professor T.J. Brown as 'in many ways the most elegant and satisfying palaeographical work ever written'. There would not be as much colour reproduction as in the 1990s, but most of the Roxburghe Club books would be present, as would the portfolios of the Société française de reproductions de manuscrits à peintures, and good surveys of illumination by Eric Millar for English manuscripts, 1926–8, by Henri Martin for France, 1923, and by Adolph Goldschmidt for Germany, 1928. There would be the first publications of Walter Oakeshott, Neil Ker (including the slim first edition of his *Medieval Libraries of Great Britain*, 1941), Richard Hunt, and Roger Mynors. The empty spaces on the shelves caused by the magic trickery would allow the librarians to put back on open access – as they still should – Migne's *Patrologia Latina*.

If the disappearing trick were tried with a magic cut-off date of 1895, fifty years earlier, the bookcases would certainly need the *Patrologia* to help fill them. There would be a sound emphasis on topography and biblical scholarship. There would be the old-fashioned catalogues (mostly not superseded even today) of the library of the British Museum, as it then was; the first stout little blue-bound instalment (volume III, as it happened) of Falconer Madan's *A Summary Catalogue of Western Manuscripts in the Bodleian Library at Oxford* (Oxford, 1895), to supplement the old Quarto Series catalogues published from 1853; the folio (and best) volumes of the Historical Manuscripts Commission Reports; thirty-five volumes so far of the vast series of catalogues of the French provincial libraries, in two series, 1849–85 and 1886 onwards; and the beginnings of runs of catalogues for the Bibliothèque Nationale in Paris (1739), Florence (1774), the Vatican (1852), Munich (1858), Vienna (1864), Wolfenbüttel (1884), Trier (1888), and so on. There would be the inestimably useful L. Delisle, *Cabinet des Manuscrits de la Bibliothèque Impériale* (*Nationale* in later volumes) (Paris, 1868–81), and the two early editions of W. Wattenbach, *Das Schriftwesen im Mittelalter*, (Leipzig, 1871 and 1875; revised 1896). Both Delisle and Wattenbach are still prime candidates for desert-island textbooks. There would be little on manuscript illumination, which photography had not made as accessible as now, but there would be major studies by Comte Paul Durrieu identifying Loyset Liédet (1888), Jean Fouquet (1888–9), Jacquemart d'Hesdin (1889), André Beauneveu (1894) and other important medieval manuscript painters.

In 1895 the Bibliographical Society was newly founded and in that year too M.R. James published the first of his great catalogues of manuscripts in the college and museum libraries of Cambridge and of Eton. Montague Rhodes James (1862–1936), of King's College in Cambridge, had an intelligence formidable to his academic colleagues in those most intellectual decades of Cambridge scholarship, and an energy and single-minded industry which produced nearly ten publications a year for over thirty years, and a joyful delight in antiquarianism for its own sake which appears in his catalogues and in his still haunting ghost stories. 'As the twentieth century wears on', wrote Nicolas Barker, 'it seems increasingly certain that the name of M.R. James will dominate the history of manuscript book studies in this century, as substantially as Delisle the last century' (*BC*, 19 (1970): 7). He was an inaugural recipient of the Bibliographical Society's Gold Medal in 1929. James has been the subject of two recent biographies, remarkable for a subject whose most exotic adventure was a bicycling holiday in France. He was Director (if a not very active one) of the

Fitzwilliam Museum from 1893 to 1908, Provost of King's College from 1905 to 1918, and Provost of Eton from 1918 to 1936. His early publications were classical and theological but by the mid 1890s M.R. James had been drawn far enough into the raw materials of texts to set himself the task of identifying and dating the medieval manuscripts of the college libraries of his university. The Fitzwilliam catalogue of 1895 included a 23-page battlecry 'Points to be Observed in the Description and Collation of Manuscripts' which could still serve as a pattern for palaeographers and stands with N.R. Ker's sixteen points of method as explained in his *Medieval Manuscripts in British Libraries*, 1 (1960), pp. vii-xiii. Having set himself a formula and with a minimum of published aids to speed identification of texts, James brought out catalogues of Eton, the Fitzwilliam, Jesus, King's, and Sidney Sussex (all 1895), Peterhouse (1899), Trinity (1900–5), Emmanuel (1904), Christ's College, Pembroke, Queens', and Clare (all 1905), Gonville and Caius (1907–8), Trinity Hall (1907), Westminster Abbey (with J.A. Robinson), Magdalene, and Corpus Christi (all 1909), St John's (1913), and so on, becoming in the course of classifying the origin of manuscripts before him the principal authority on the sources for our knowledge of pre-Reformation libraries of Britain, as reflected in his studies of the long-dispersed libraries of Canterbury and Dover (1903), the Augustinians of York (1909), the Franciscans of Hereford (1914), and so forth.

James combined something of a Durrieu with a Delisle in that, though primarily a textual scholar and palaeographer, he delighted in illuminations ('postcard manuscripts', Dr M.B. Parkes would mutter dismissively). When James left the Fitzwilliam he was succeeded there by his friend Sydney Cockerell (1867–1962), the great English connoisseur and articulate advocate of manuscripts. Throughout his long life, Cockerell (knighted in 1934) exhibited manuscripts, collected manuscripts, studied manuscripts, wrote letters about manuscripts, published books about manuscripts, and talked and talked about manuscripts. He spread a spell of enchantment which is not yet dispersed. There has probably never been anyone quite comparable as a catalyst for promoting palaeographical scholarship. He convinced rich men to buy manuscripts and he inspired the publication of their collections, realizing (as is too rarely appreciated) that bibliophiles will always collect what some might have preferred to see in public libraries but that this can be turned to the scholar's advantage and the collector's delight by advising on the collections and then publishing them as research resources. It is a most agreeable practice, helping everyone at the expense of no one but the collector. Thus we have *Illustrations of One Hundred Manuscripts in the Library of Henry Yates Thompson*, I-VII (1907–18); Sir George Warner, *Descriptive Catalogue of Illuminated Manuscripts in the Library of C.W. Dyson Perrins, D.C.L., F.S.A.* (Oxford, 1920); E.G. Millar, *The Library of A. Chester Beatty, A Descriptive Catalogue of the Western Manuscripts* (Oxford, 1927–30); and J.J.G. Alexander and A.C. de la Mare, *The Italian Manuscripts in the Library of Major J.R. Abbey* (1969).

Cockerell had worked for both Ruskin and Morris and his initiation into manuscripts had not been by the usual nineteenth-century path of classics and theology but through the craftmanship of letterforms. His delight in calligraphy and in the penmanship of the Italian Renaissance was almost unique in the early twentieth century. The passion for recognizing individual hands of *quattrocento* scribes unfolded into an active palaeographical industry peculiarly English in its origin. Scribes who were medieval book historians and vice versa gave an informed and new impetus to Renaissance studies. The investigation of medieval script owes much to the practical experience of Edward Johnston (1872–1944), Stanley Morison (1889–1967), Alfred Fairbank (1895–1982), Berthold Wolpe (1905–89), and others, who all wrote beautiful hands themselves. Fairbank instructed E.A. Lowe in how to cut a quill: 'That was a very happy day', he recalled in 1969. The tradition is maintained today by Michael Gullick.

M.R. James and Sydney Cockerell achieved their greatest work in Cambridge, leaving there a passion for bibliophily echoed in A.N.L. Munby and for palaeography upheld there against all odds by T.A.M. Bishop, but they withdrew respectively to Eton in 1918 and Kew in 1937. Cockerell's intellectual heirs were of London, not of Cambridge: palaeographers of the Victoria and Albert Museum and of the Department of Manuscripts in the British Museum. James Wardrop (1905–57), scribe and librarian, author of *The Script of Humanism, Some Aspects of Humanistic Script 1460–1560* (Oxford, 1963), is to be remembered not least for the first identification of Bartolomeo Sanvito. Eric Millar (1887–1966) joined the Department of Manuscripts in the British Museum in 1912, just after Sir George Warner had retired as Keeper, and was intimate with both James and Cockerell. Millar's work on manuscript illumination included the two-volume *English Illuminated Manuscripts* (Paris and Brussels, 1928), cited above, and major studies of the Lindisfarne Gospels (1923), and Luttrell Psalter (1932) and, after an amazing discovery in 1938 when Lieutenant-Colonel D.E. Prideaux-Brune brought into the Museum a parcel of inherited drawings and manuscripts, *An Illuminated Manuscript of La Somme le Roy* (1953), and *The Parisian Miniaturist Honoré* (1959). He was joined in the Department in 1927 by Francis Wormald (1904–72). Wormald had begun his interest in manuscripts while a schoolboy at Eton under the provostship of M.R. James, he read history at Cambridge, and he retained his link with Cambridge by later accepting the honorary keepership of manuscripts at the Fitzwilliam. His work, like Millar's, centred on English manuscripts with important studies of Anglo-Saxon illumination and early English Calendars. In 1949 Francis Wormald was appointed as the first Professor of Palaeography at King's College, London. The establishment of a chair in palaeography marks a significant advance in the teaching of medieval manuscript studies. When Wormald retired in 1961 he was succeeded by another outstanding historian of English manuscripts at the British Museum, Julian Brown (1923–87) who had joined the Department of Manuscripts in 1950 after a training in classical archaeology in Oxford. Professor Brown was drawn further and further back into the origins of Northumbro-Irish manuscripts, and his redefinitions and classifications of insular books and script transformed our knowledge of our earliest books. At the time of his premature and final illness he was President of the Bibliographical Society. His research work is continued by Michelle Brown, of the Department of Manuscripts in the British Library.

The metaphorical mantles of M.R. James and Sydney Cockerell (the former doubtless scarlet and doctoral, the latter perhaps the Arab cloak in which he had been shipwrecked with Wilfrid Blunt in 1900 and which Cockerell later presented to Alec Guinness) thus passed to London, in the studies both of calligraphy and of illumination. London still has the only established chair of palaeography in Britain, the largest number of students of manuscripts, and by far the greatest collections. However, the focal point of manuscript scholarship has since 1945 been in Oxford. The absolute centre has been Duke Humfrey's library. Richard Hunt (1908–79) joined the Bodleian as Keeper of Western Manuscripts in 1945 and he retired in 1975. Every morning for thirty years, like a doctor doing a ward round, Richard Hunt appeared, latterly with a walking stick, and moved from reader to reader, looking, asking questions, dispensing shelfmarks, asking, muttering, asking, asking. It was an astonishingly effective technique. Hunt published little – well-turned articles on medieval learning – but gathered around the Bodleian a formidable confraternity of manuscript scholars.

It is worth pausing at this point to glance both to continental Europe and across to America. James was suspicious of foreigners, though he welcomed their artefacts safely in English museums. There is a patriotic pleasure in English manuscripts felt by many in this country but of course palaeography has always been an international science. There has been a chair of palaeography in Louvain since 1881. The rôle of the Belgians in defining the methodology of modern palaeography has been remarkable, and the fundamental scholarly journal *Scriptorium, International Review of Manuscript Studies*, was founded in Belgium in 1946. In Germany the rigorous discipline of recording manuscripts and their details before making conclusions (obvious enough perhaps, but still rare) was established in Munich by Ludwig Traube (1861–1907) and his successors Paul Lehmann (1884–1964) and Bernhard Bischoff (1906–91). The three great American palaeographers studied in Munich under Traube and Lehmann: E.K. Rand (1871–1945), working on early manuscripts of Tours, B.L. Ullman (1882–1965), and E.A. Lowe (1879–1969). Lowe was the greatest. He was of Lithuanian origin, emigrating to America with his parents at the age of four (his name was spelled Loew then). His joyful rediscovery of Beneventan script, the weird uniquely southern Italian cursive, first published in 1914, has led to a canonization of the script enthusiastically continued by his pupil Virginia Brown. In May 1960 Lowe addressed the Bibliographical Society on the origins of his *Codices Latini Antiquiores* project, the monumental scheme to publish a specimen facsimile and brief palaeographical commentary on every Latin manuscript earlier than the ninth century. The plan was conceived in 1916. Volume I was published in 1934. The last part, volume XII, *Supplement*, was published in 1971. It inspired a similar series for documents, *Chartae Latinae*

Antiquiores, edited by R. Marichal and A. Bruckner, (I–XIII, 1954–81), and the gigantic corpus of ninth-century Latin manuscripts in the final stages of preparation by Bernhard Bischoff.

1953 saw the establishment in Paris of the Comité International de Paléographie, a body which still flourishes, initially with the double aim of establishing a recognized vocabulary for medieval scripts and of publishing samples of precisely dated or datable manuscripts which must in the end be the only fixed criteria for assigning dates to the (great majority) of undated medieval books. The essay on vocabulary was published in Paris in 1954, *Nomenclature des écritures livresques du IXe au XVIe siècle* by B. Bischoff, G.I. Lieftinck, and G. Battelli. Catalogues of dated and datable manuscripts have issued at a great rate from many libraries of Europe. Those for England have been by A.G. Watson (British Library, 1979, and libraries in Oxford, 1984) and by P.R. Robinson (libraries in Cambridge, 1988).

It is in the context of this rigorous international palaeographical movement that one must see the Oxford group of academic manuscript historians gathering around Duke Humfrey's Library. The front-runner was certainly Neil Ker (1908–82), Reader in Palaeography in Oxford from 1946 to 1968, Gold Medallist of the Bibliographical Society in 1975. Improbable as it seemed to those who knew him, Ker too was an Etonian and had spent his schoolboy Sunday afternoons in the library there: 'Unlike James, I did not see the manuscripts', he recollected wistfully. His passion for manuscripts was formed at Oxford and channelled by C.S. Lewis into Anglo-Saxon literature. Probably his wisest book was the deceptively thin folio *English Manuscripts in the Century after the Norman Conquest*, the Lyell lectures for 1952–3, published in Oxford in 1960. Ker was always on the move. With string bag or rucksack, sometimes even with tent, he tramped England and Scotland taking rapid notes of manuscripts everywhere. Fruits included *A Catalogue of Manuscripts Containing Anglo-Saxon* (Oxford, 1957), and the multiple-volumed *Medieval Manuscripts in British Libraries* (1969 and continuing), which aims to describe concisely and comprehensively all manuscripts in public collections in Britain hitherto uncatalogued (and what a lot there were). It was a task almost too great for one man, even with Ker's energy and experience, and will be completed by Alan Piper. Ker's best-known work is edited from a card index. It is *Medieval Libraries of Great Britain, A List of Surviving Books* (1941), with much-expanded second edition in 1964 and *Supplement* edited by A.G. Watson in 1987. This too is a desert-island textbook. It can provide many hours of totally absorbing fascination. It lists alphabetically by monasteries and other medieval institutions all identifiable extant manuscripts from communal libraries suppressed at the Reformation. The manuscripts themselves are dispersed throughout the whole world. Ker's '*MLGB*' (as it is cited in innumerable footnotes) has transformed our knowledge of culture in medieval Britain. Inspired by this pioneering work, similar lists are being published for other European countries, most notably by Dr Sigrid Krämer for Germany.

When Ker and Hunt were to be seen taking tea together in the cafeteria of the New Bodleian or peering excitedly at a newly noticed erased inscription, there too probably would be one or more of a whole community of scholars. Professor Sir Roger Mynors (1903–89) was an early member of the team, editor of Bede and Erasmus, author of *Durham Cathedral Manuscripts to the End of the Twelfth Century* (Durham, 1939), with some of the finest plates ever reproduced by man, and of the *Catalogue of the Manuscripts of Balliol College, Oxford* (Oxford, 1963), with none at all. Mynors was a powerful figure behind the British Academy project for editing all English medieval library catalogues, a major undertaking encompassing many scholars and now in the care of Kenneth Humphreys and Richard Sharpe. Also to be seen in the Bodleian was Sir Walter Oakeshott (1903–87): his work on the supreme twelfth-century Winchester Bible spans from the elegant little *The Artists of the Winchester Bible* (1945), to the vast and beautiful *The Two Winchester Bibles* (Oxford, 1979). There too, after lunch, was Graham Pollard (1903–76) whose detective work on the medieval Oxford book trade circulated so widely in manuscript that it has never been published. Andrew Watson has become Ker's literary executor, and has recently retired from a personal Chair in Palaeography and Diplomatic in the School of Library Archive and Information Studies at University College in London, with a major track record of new work on the library dispersals of the Reformation. Distinguished too are Ian Doyle, formerly Reader in Bibliography at the University of Durham, eloquent scholar of English manuscripts and books, especially vernacular, and his sometime co-author Malcolm Parkes, poly-mathematical palaeographer who single-handedly has taught medieval manu-scripts to at least a generation of Oxford undergraduates and research students. Recruited from the Bodleian Library to fill the Chair of Palaeography in London, in succession to Wormald and to Brown, is Albinia de la Mare, London-trained and Oxford-practised historian of Italian Renaissance scribes, triumphantly and spectacularly out-pacing Cockerell and Wardrop and all others in the identifica-tion of individual hands and the reconstructing of careers and practices of very many scores of fifteenth-century scribes. In the vacations in Oxford old friends and pupils return: Richard and Mary Rouse, from Los Angeles; James Carley, from Toronto; Margaret Gibson, from Liverpool; Pamela Robinson, once from Belfast and now London; Peter Gumbert, from Leiden; Rodney Thomson, from Tasmania; and very many others. The academic publications of these alone would furnish a good library. They are welcomed now in the Bodleian by Bruce Barker-Benfield and Martin Kauffmann.

Oxford too acted as a magnet for historians of manuscript illumination. L.M.J. Delaissé (1914–72) was lured from Belgium with a Fellowship of All Souls in 1963, and became the father-figure for a squadron of active historians of fifteenth-century illumination, especially of Books of Hours and mainly in America: these include John Plummer, James Marrow, Douglas Farquhar, Sandra Hindman, Alison Stones, Roger Wieck, and many more. Until Delaissé, Books of Hours were despised by serious art historians (even M.R. James was apologetic) but now they are seen as the most comprehensive and most often localizable of all medieval artefacts. To Oxford too came the magisterial Otto Pächt (1902–88), retreating from the turmoil of Germany and Austria in 1936. He taught medieval art history at Oriel college, using manuscripts as the principal extant sources for pictorial art of the Middle Ages. In 1963 he returned again to his native Vienna. Otto Pächt probably revealed and linked more new medieval book illuminators than anyone since Comte Durrieu, a century ago. To have defined *The Master of Mary of Burgundy* (1948), is like having discovered Piero della Francesco or Jean Fouquet. With his pupil and collaborator Jonathan Alexander, Pächt devised and wrote the celebrated illustrated catalogues, *Illuminated Manuscripts in the Bodleian Library, Oxford* (I–III, Oxford, 1966–73), which have become (like Ker's *MLGB*) models being imitated in Vienna, under Pächt's direction, from 1974, in Paris, under François Avril's direction, from 1980, and elsewhere. Such catalogues are desperately needed to reveal the visual resources of the Morgan Library and, even more, of the British Library. In the meantime, Professor Alexander has gone on, in Manchester and New York, opening up new worlds of manuscript art from the late Roman empire to the illumination of incunables. He is general editor of another innovative series, also now being imitated in France and Germany, *A Survey of Manuscripts Illuminated in the British Isles* (Oxford), in six parts: I, sixth to ninth century, by Alexander himself, 1978; II, 900-1066, by Elżbieta Temple, 1976; III, 1066–1190, by C.M. Kauffmann, 1975; IV, 1190–1285, by Nigel Morgan, 1982–8; V, 1285–1385, by Lucy Freeman Sandler, 1986; and VI, from 1385, by Kathleen Scott, probably 1993. These bring together, chronologically and stylistically, with many plates, a first and eye-opening overview of medieval manuscripts illuminated in England. What Ker did for medieval English libraries, Alexander and his colleagues have begun for medieval ateliers.

If overall the objectives of palaeography have not changed greatly in the last century, it is because this is not a new science. We now speak of 'codicology' or the 'archaeology of the book' but Delisle or M.R. James or Traube would have understood the word palaeography to encompass much more than the simple history of script. Colour photography has certainly helped the study of manuscript illumination, and this is a topic more popular now than ever before. Relatively inexpensive facsimiles have made Books of Hours or the Book of Kells into household names. The objective of recording every extant medieval manuscript is still impossibly far off, but the work continues. Recent catalogues of American collections include the Beinecke Library at Yale (by Barbara A. Shailor, I, 1984, II, 1987), the Walters Art Gallery (by Lilian M.C. Randall, I, 1989), the Huntington (by C.W. Dutschke, I–II, 1989), the Newberry Library (by Paul Saenger, 1989). These are notable achievements, and many more are needed: a modern catalogue of the Morgan Library is the prime desideratum. If the standards of cataloguing are more exacting now than in the time of M.R. James, the resources available for identifying texts and scribes and provenances are now far greater. There are lists of *incipits* for texts in Middle English verse (Brown and Robbins, 1943, with supplements), commentaries on the Sentences (Stegmüller, 1947), Latin verse (Walther, 1959), scientific texts (Thorndike and Kibre, 1963), Latin sermons (Schneyer, 1965), treatises on the virtues and vices (Bloomfield, Guyot, Howard, and Kabealo, 1979), and so on; there are the indexes of signed colophons compiled by the Benedictines of Bouveret (1965–1982); there are monographs on authors, scribes, monastic scriptoria, stationers, illuminators, binders, readers, libraries, and collectors of manuscripts. M.R. James had little more than A.G. Little's *Initia Operum Latinorum* (Manchester, 1904), and M. Vattasso's *Initia Patrum* (Rome, 1906–8), and a prodigious memory. More catalogues are needed, and more aids to cataloguing. As the catalogues become more comprehensive, so the tools will become more refined, demanding more and more exactitude from the cataloguer. It will doubtless never cease. We shall never know enough about the books of the Middle Ages and no one will ever have seen them all. The twentieth-century's contribution to palaeography has been the attempt to record as much as possible of what survives. If all books about medieval manuscripts published before 1945 were to vanish magically, there would be a great deal still on the shelves, much of it very good indeed.

English literary manuscripts of the twentieth century

JENNY STRATFORD

W.W. Greg wrote in *Studies in Retrospect* (1945), 'the Bibliographical Society has always recognized that manuscripts came within its purview and encouraged some excellent work in this field', but no contributor wrote specifically on manuscripts in the Society's first retrospective collection. Rather than attempting to survey for the centenary the whole field of recent post-medieval manuscript studies, I have chosen to focus on English literary manuscripts of the twentieth century, that is, manuscripts of writers living after 1900, and almost entirely on the manuscripts of writers born in the United Kingdom or Ireland. There are two main reasons for this choice. First, much of the impetus for the study, and therefore the collecting and cataloguing of twentieth-century literary manuscripts, coincides with the years since *Studies in Retrospect* was published. This phenomenon depends in part upon the development in textual studies which took place during roughly the same period. Second, and this is a more personal reason, from the mid 1960s I have been privileged to be associated with a number of ventures to collect and to catalogue twentieth-century literary manuscripts, among them the manuscripts of living writers.

During the past twenty-five years, collecting the manuscripts of contemporary – recent and especially living – writers, which often used to be seen on this side of the Atlantic as a fringe if not quite lunatic activity, is now accepted as a natural responsibility of national and other public collections. As E.F.D. Roberts, then Director of the National Library of Scotland, wrote in *The Bibliotheck* in 1979, 'the special responsibility of a national library for preserving the literature of a nation in all its forms applies as much to manuscripts as it does to printed books, and as much to recent writing as to the earlier national traditions from which modern literature developed'.

Apart from having been collected recently and very rapidly, literary manuscripts of the twentieth century are not essentially different from literary manuscripts of other periods, especially those written after about 1700 when print finally displaced manuscript as a means of circulation. On the other hand, during the present century, the basis for collecting has changed and the term 'manuscript' has often been given an extended meaning. It refers primarily, as it always has done, to handwritten drafts or fair-copies of creative writing and to the letters of literary men: 'literary autographs' when they are in the hand of the

46

writer himself. But many other kinds of literary papers have come to be collected as 'manuscripts': every sort of document which illustrates the textual and intellectual evolution of a literary work up to the time of its publication, as well as letters, diaries, and other biographical materials which make up the 'archive' of a creative writer's life. These materials may be handwritten – autograph drafts, notebooks, or letters. They may also be typescripts, similarly corrected or revised, or versions produced by the word-processor and laser-printer, even if sale-room catalogues indicate that these are at present collected with reluctance. Equally they may be printed editions with manuscript marginalia, or proofs with autograph corrections or revisions, a form of textual witness which survives from the eighteenth century. By the twentieth century, examples are to be found in great numbers. Recent editions and studies have demonstrated the distinction between corrections and revisions and have shown how important proofs can be.[1] There are also memorabilia. The British Library has recently acquired, with the G.K. Chesterton archive, Chesterton's cloak, stick, and hat. The cumulative *National Union Catalog of Manuscripts*, produced at the Library of Congress, is an example of a standard reference work which lists all these kinds of material, as well as photographic reproductions, written archives of sound and television broadcasting, and tapes and films.

In what follows, I will first look briefly at the traditional field of literary autographs and will then consider the recent history of collecting; finally I will touch on problems of access and of cataloguing.

A.N.L. Munby's *The Cult of the Autograph Letter in England* (1962), written with characteristic wit and learning, embodies the text of his lectures in palaeography given at King's College, London, three years earlier. Although this is mainly a study of nineteenth-century autograph collectors, it contains a good deal which applies directly to T.J. Wise and to other collectors of the early twentieth century. Very little has been written about the handwriting, codicology, or other aspects of palaeography of the period after about 1650 and even less after 1800. T.J. Brown's 'English Literary Autographs', deceptively slight one-page commentaries with facsimiles of the autographs of fifty writers, published quarterly in *The Book Collector* between 1952 and 1964, are an exception. The autographs of writers whose careers extended into the first half of the twentieth century (Hardy, Bridges, Housman, Joyce, Wilfrid Owen, Yeats, and Shaw), were examined with the same care and according to the same principles as writers of earlier centuries. Scribal characteristics were carefully described and related to the works, life, and manuscript output of the writer. In 'The Detection of Faked Literary MSS' (1953), also printed in *The Book Collector*, Brown set out the principles which underlie the autograph series: investigation of provenance, contents, physical examination of materials (paper, structure, watermarks, ink),

---

1 See, for example, P. Davison, 'Editing Orwell: Eight Problems', *Lib*, VI, 6 (1984): 217–28 and the textual notes to his edition, *The Complete Orwell*, vols. I–XX (1984– , in progress); S.W. Reid, 'The First Editions of *The Secret Agent*', *Lib*, VI, 5 (1983): 237–53; Glen P. Wright, 'The Raverat Proofs of *Mrs Dalloway*', *SB*, 39 (1986): 241–61.

and handwriting. His inaugural lecture, 'Latin Palaeography since Traube' (1962), again emphasized that: 'Palaeography does not, in my view, end with the Renaissance.' The commentaries in P.J. Croft's two-volume *Autograph Poetry in the English Language* (1973) follow the same principles. Croft illustrated and discussed autographs of about 150 English, American, and Australian poets from the fourteenth to the twentieth century. Over forty of those chosen (some were quirky choices), died after 1900. When Croft's book came out, three of the poets, Auden, Graves, and Spender, were alive. It is perhaps now difficult to recall how original the inclusion of the manuscripts of living poets in a scholarly book then seemed to be.

Collections of English literary autographs often include twentieth-century material: Desmond Flower and A.N.L. Munby, *English Poetical Autographs* (1938), published by Cassell, also Croft's publisher, is an attractive anthology, with transcripts, but leaves the reader to make his own deductions about handwriting and other physical characteristics. Other collections which offer a basis for palaeographical study, but not the study itself, include James Thorpe, *Poems in Manuscript* (1970) and *Letters in Manuscript* (1971), from the Huntington Library. The second volume of the substantial two-volume set from the Pierpont Morgan Library (Verlyn Klinkenborg, Herbert Cahoon, and Charles Ryskamp, *British Literary Manuscripts* (1981), *Series I. From 800 to 1800*; *Series II, from 1800 to 1914*) is followed by an invaluable and updated checklist of British modern literary manuscripts and autographs dating from the sixteenth century to the present, which had been acquired up to the end of 1980.

Facsimiles of modern literary texts have multiplied in recent years. Users need to be aware of the distortions inherent in photographic reproductions of every kind. The discrepancies between facsimile and original were at the root of the controversial emendations in *Ulysses: the Corrected Text* (1986). Editors of facsimiles as well as textual critics, have sometimes refined techniques of physical examination. The infra-red image convertor and binocular microscope used to disentangle the 'exquisite difficulties' in the text of the poems of Gerard Manley Hopkins,[2] and the painstaking paper analysis which allowed three drafts of *Sons and Lovers* to be dated,[3] are two examples. A guide to recent work of this kind would be very useful.

I come now to the changes in patterns of collecting which have taken place during the present century. This is an absorbing subject and has already found many commentators – favourable and unfavourable – although there is as yet no comprehensive history. Once only a few private collectors were prepared to invest in the manuscripts of current writing; T.J. Wise and John Quinn are

---

2 Norman H. MacKenzie, 'Forensic Document Techniques Applied to Literary Manuscripts', *Bodleian Library Record*, 9 (1976), 234–40; 'exquisite difficulties', John Kelly, *TLS*, 7–13 December 1990, 1,323–4, reviewing *The Poetical Works of Gerard Manley Hopkins*, ed. Norman H. Mackenzie (Oxford, 1990) and *The Early Poetic Manuscripts and Note-Books of Gerard Manley Hopkins in Facsimile* (New York, 1990).

3 Helen Baron, '*Sons and Lovers*: The Surviving Manuscripts from Three Drafts dated by Paper Analysis', *SB*, 38 (1985): 289–328.

probably the best known. B.L. Reid's, *The Man from New York: John Quinn and his Friends* (1968), documented the ambitious extent of Quinn's manuscript collections drawing upon the Quinn correspondence in the Berg Collection, New York Public Library. After Wise had usurped Quinn as the collector of Conrad, Quinn bought between 1919 and 1922 drafts of *Ulysses*, piecemeal as it was written (the Rosenbach manuscript), and in 1922, at the time of publication, Eliot gave him the typescript and autograph draft of *The Waste Land* with Ezra Pound's notes and excisions. Until 1968, the whereabouts of the manuscript of *The Waste Land* was a mystery. It was then revealed to have been for the past ten years in the Berg Collection (where it ought to have been all along), its existence kept secret even from Eliot himself. The enduring interest of the manuscript and the changes made to it by Pound and Eliot is demonstrated by sales of the facsimile edition, edited by Mrs Valerie Eliot. In England alone, 23,350 copies were sold in the twenty years following its publication in 1971.[4]

Wise the manuscript collector is not yet as well known as Wise the forger. From 1918, Wise was steadily buying Conrad manuscripts and typescripts as they were written, but Wise's own catalogues of his Conrad and other manuscript collections show that his concerns remained to a considerable extent those of the autograph collector and bibliophile. Wise had been an active member of the short-lived Society of Archivists and Autograph Collectors (1893–1900). He was eager to acquire autograph fair copies of poems by Thomas Hardy, written out long after they had been printed, to make association copies for his Shelley and Swinburne collections,[5] and to bind up in 'ruby-red levant morocco by Riviere' Conrad's work in progress.[6] The concept of investigating the creative process through every stage in a text from manuscript to print then scarcely existed. What Philip Larkin once characterized as the 'magical value' of a contemporary writer's manuscripts was always recognized, but, with a few exceptions, not the 'meaningful' value.

During the economic depression of the thirties, few manuscripts of living writers reached the sale-rooms. Those which did were sometimes bought in, for example, Evelyn Waugh's *Decline and Fall* in 1930, and D.H. Lawrence's *The White Peacock* in 1934. The great research libraries only occasionally acquired a manuscript of a living writer. They could usually afford to wait until a writer was dead and his reputation secure. A 'representative' manuscript would then often be acquired by gift or bequest, not by purchase. The drafts of Wilfrid Owen's

4 Donald Gallup, 'The "Lost" Manuscripts of T.S. Eliot', *TLS*, 7 November 1968, 1238–40; Ezra Pound's preface and the editorial introduction to T.S. Eliot, *The Waste Land: A Facsimile and Transcript of the Original Drafts including the Annotations of Ezra Pound*, ed. V. Eliot (1971), [vii]–xxix. Mr John Bodley of Faber and Faber kindly supplied the sales figures.

5 'Shelley's Skylark', Ashley MS. 4164 (first published 1902), fair copy transcribed for Wise on paper watermarked 1913; 'A Singer Asleep', Ashley MS. 4467, annotated 'written at Max Gate, Dorchester, 1909', dated Bonchurch 1910, paper watermarked 1920. Hardy generally destroyed his working drafts and arranged fair copies for preservation.

6 Well illustrated by, e.g., T.J. Wise, *A Conrad Library: A Catalogue of Printed Books, Manuscripts and Autograph Letters* (London, privately printed, 1928), 24, description of 'The Crime of Partition'; see also, Michael L. Turner, 'Conrad and T.J. Wise', *BC*, 15 (1966): 350–1.

poems, presented to the British Museum in 1934 through the Friends of the National Libraries, are a typical example. There was no impetus to acquire a writer's whole literary 'archive'. Interest in publishers' archives, and in little magazines, had not yet developed.

The first signs of change came in the late 1930s. Charles D. Abbott, librarian of the Lockwood Memorial Library, Buffalo, New York, chronicled his search for worksheet materials in the introduction to *Poets at Work* (1948). Abbott wrote to poets to solicit donations, following up his letters by crossing to England in 1938 on the *Aquitania* for a three-month stay. Drafts came mainly as gifts, because few other libraries were interested in contemporary material. By the late 1950s everything had changed. Many North American research libraries had been founded or enlarged in the post-war decades. It was already next to impossible for the newcomers to build major collections of medieval or early modern manuscripts, while collections of nineteenth- and twentieth-century papers (literary and historical), good enough to add lustre to the university and to attract visiting scholars, could still be made. Buffalo paid the current market price when it acquired a substantial Robert Graves collection in 1959.

By 1960 the boom was publicly under way. At the London Library sale at Christie's, on 22 June 1960, the University of Texas at Austin emerged as the dominant purchaser of twentieth-century literary manuscripts, as it would remain to the 1970s. Texas rapidly built up an outstanding collection. Other libraries all over the United States and Canada competed to obtain modern literary materials, often whole 'archives', in the sale-room, by private treaty, by contract, and occasionally by gift. The tax arrangements in force to 1969 in the United States offered an incentive for donations in cash or kind; these donations were estimated for tax purposes at valuation, not at cost. John Carter, in an article published in *The Atlantic Monthly* in July 1960, summed up the current situation: 'practically all authors' manuscripts end up in American institutional libraries'.

Against this background, the leisurely and sometimes haphazard collecting policies of British libraries had to be reviewed. By 1960, A.N.L. Munby was deliberately fostering the modern literary collections at King's College, Cambridge. By 1962, the Arts Council of Great Britain had set up with the British Museum an ingenious scheme to collect the manuscripts of twentieth-century writers, the living as well as the dead. At first the scheme was limited to the manuscripts of poets (the Lockwood model), and to the British Museum. It was extended by 1970 to other libraries and to all kinds of imaginative writing. The scheme and the funding were on a modest scale, but first-rate material was collected: drafts or notebooks of W.H. Auden, Edwin Muir, Sylvia Plath, and Philip Larkin and the literary archive of Keith Douglas, in the early years. An exhibition, *Poetry in the Making*, which I was asked to organize and catalogue, was held in 1967. A second exhibition, *Modern Literary Manuscripts Acquired with the Aid of the Arts Council of Great Britain*, was organized in 1974, with an accompanying short catalogue. A full catalogue of the collection to 1972, *The Arts Council Collection of Modern Literary Manuscripts, 1963–1972*, was published at the time of the exhibition. The Welsh Arts Council implemented a similar but short-lived scheme, the Scottish Arts Council a third. These initiatives and the situation which demanded them were described by Philip Larkin in two influential papers. The first, 'Operation Manuscript', was written as an introductory essay to *Poetry in the Making*. The second, 'A Neglected Responsibility: Contemporary Literary Manuscripts', a talk given in 1979, was reprinted in Larkin's *Required Writing: Miscellaneous Pieces 1955–1982* (1983).

The scheme operated by the Arts Council in London foundered for political reasons in 1985, after some years of lingering half-life. A lasting effect has, however, been the continuing recognition by the national libraries and by a small but growing number of university libraries in Britain and Ireland, that modern literary manuscripts, including the manuscripts of living writers, ought to be collected. Acquisitions policies (quite outside the original Arts Council schemes), have been surprisingly successful, even in face of past competition and of present financial stringency in British and Irish universities. Among author collections are those of George Orwell at University College, London; Rupert Brooke, T.S. Eliot, and E.M. Forster at King's College, Cambridge; D.H. Lawrence at Nottingham; Philip Larkin at Hull; Samuel Beckett at Reading; William Plomer and Basil Bunting at Durham; Leonard and Virginia Woolf at Sussex. Most of these collections are still growing. The Brotherton Library, Leeds, and the Bodleian Library, Oxford, also hold impressive and growing collections. In the past five years, Trinity College, Dublin, has acquired literary manuscripts of Joseph Campbell (1879–1944), James Stephens (1880–1950), and the manuscripts of two novelists currently writing, John Banville and John B. Keane. The four national libraries report substantial additions to their modern literary collections almost every year. Publishers' archives are among large collections which have been recently acquired. The Macmillan Papers, which have been described as 'the finest publisher's archive in the world', are now divided between the British Library and the University of Reading.[7] Reading holds a strong collection of publishers' archives (some on deposit). They include papers of the Hogarth Press, Chatto and Windus, Bodley Head, Jonathan Cape, and Peter Owen, while the archives of Penguin Books are on deposit at Bristol University Library. However, it is to the original papers, not to the excellent series, *Archives of British and American Publishers*, published as microform sets by Chadwyck Healey, that searches for materials after about 1948 must be directed.

The National Heritage Memorial Fund (established in 1979), has made sizeable grants to libraries towards the cost of author and publisher collections of twentieth-century literary papers; the Victoria and Albert Purchase Grant Fund

---

7 See BL, Add. MSS. 54786–56035; 61894–6, and a further *c*. 50,000 letters, illustrations and art work at Reading University Library; *Archives of Macmillan & Company, 1854–1924: Part 1, Readers' Reports, 1867–1924; Part 2, Publishing Records, 1860–1921* (Archives of British and American Publishers, Cambridge, 1988), 8 and 65 reels, microfiche index; Warwick Gould, 'Selling the Macmillan Archive', *TLS*, 6–12 July 1990: 728; Sotheby's Sale-Catalogue, 19 July 1990 (now acquired by the British Library).

can sometimes offer a 50 per cent subsidy for purchase, as can the fund established in memory of Philip Larkin. For the papers of Henry Williamson in 1980, the existing 'acceptance in lieu of tax' arrangements were successfully brought into play. The University of Exeter Library now holds a fine collection of Henry Williamson manuscripts.

A cynical commentator might suggest that these successes are only relative, given the enormous amount of material which has already been exported. He might go on to say that the North American market has in any case declined in the last few years, although some libraries such as Texas have started to buy again after a fallow period, and that there is now much less really desirable material available anyway, especially of writers whose reputation was established before 1950 (witness the current sale-room catalogues compared with those of the 1960s). It remains possible – as it must – for a writer or his spouse to export literary papers without restriction. On the other hand, manuscripts have occasionally been bought back from the United States for British collections. The autograph draft of Siegfried Sassoon's *Memoirs of a Fox-Hunting Man* returned from America to the British Library in 1982. Review of British export-licensing regulations have successively reduced the age of manuscripts requiring a licence from a hundred years to seventy years in 1970 and to fifty years in 1979, although not to the thirty years for which some public bodies have pressed. Photographic copies of most exported literary manuscripts are deposited in the British Library. They are available for use at once unless the purchaser exercises his option to restrict access for seven years. Increasingly purchasers waive this right. Most institutions in the United States have moderated their belief, once widespread, that the value of the manuscripts in their collections lies in their 'virgin' or unpublished state. If access is free, the location of manuscripts is less important.

A fundamental problem of access to manuscripts, and one that is particularly acute in relation to modern literary papers, is the difficulty of discovering where they are housed. This is a problem which has been experienced by almost every editor of a scholarly edition and almost every literary biographer. Much current work in North America and in Britain is being devoted to finding more generally applicable solutions to this problem. Philip M. Hamer, *A Guide to Archives and Manuscripts in the United States* (1961), and the cumulative *National Union Catalog of Manuscript Collections* (NUCMC), which now covers collections reported between 1959 and 1984, both include literary manuscripts as part of a much wider brief. As yet, there is no specialized American guide to English literary manuscripts in North American collections. The *Location Register of Twentieth-Century English Literary Manuscripts and Letters: A Union List of Papers of Modern English, Irish, Scottish and Welsh Authors in the British Isles*, published in book form in two volumes (1988), was compiled during the 1980s at the University of Reading. The *Register* is a computer database and will be periodically updated. As published, it held about 40,000 records and represented a remarkably comprehensive coverage of British repositories large and small, listing manuscripts of writers who lived after 1900 on a name – author basis. It is already proving invaluable. A second project to list the manuscripts and letters of writers who lived between 1700 and 1899 is now in progress. The twentieth-century part of the *Register* is likely to be made available in the near future as an on-line file through an American host network, the Research Libraries Information Network of the Archives, Manuscripts, and Special Collections Group (RLIN-AMSC). In the longer term, there are proposals for two similar and compatible computer files covering related projects. These are, first, an updated version of the not wholly satisfactory *American Literary Manuscripts* (2nd edition, 1977), and, second, a new and very important project, *British Literary Manuscripts in North American Repositories*. It would be wrong to underestimate the difficulties of these undertakings. Their potential value means that during the next few years every possible effort should be made to bring them to fruition. In time it should prove possible to add records of collections housed both in mainland Europe and in other continents.

One of the most ambitious and successful bibliographical initiatives of recent years has been the *Index of English Literary Manuscripts*. The *Index* locates and describes surviving (and occasionally lost, but recorded) manuscripts of some 300 British and Irish writers from 1450 to 1900. Seven parts (each part in itself a sizeable volume), had been published by 1990. When complete, the series will consist of four volumes, each in several parts, chronologically divided. Volume I, *1450–1625, Parts 1 and 2* (1980), is so far the only volume completed. The remaining volumes, volume II, *1625–1700, Part 1, A-K* (1987), volume III, *1700–1800, Part 1, A-F* (1986), *Part 2, John Gay–Ambrose Philips* (1989), volume IV, *1800–1900, Part 1, A-G (1982), Part 2, Hardy–Lamb* (1990) are each about half finished. Volume v will provide indexes of titles, first lines, names, and repositories. The good reasons for the present closing date of 1900 are explained in the introduction to volume I. It 'avoids the need to assess contemporary writers, much of whose material has not yet reached a permanent location'. The 1800–1900 volume already includes two authors whose careers overlap well into the twentieth century: Hardy and Kipling. The textual approach of the *Index* to the manuscripts of major authors has proved its worth, making it an essential reference tool. In time, it should have a supplement extending into the twentieth century.

Neither location registers nor detailed textual studies, such as the *Index*, will ever fully replace the need for finding aids and catalogues of a library's own manuscript collections. Indeed location registers in particular depend to a very great extent on local finding aids, whether published or unpublished, and can usually only be as complete as their sources. More catalogues of modern literary manuscripts (as well as most other kinds of manuscript) are badly needed. The problem is acute where the pace of accession has greatly outstripped listing and indexing. On the other hand, the level of detail in descriptions cannot and need not be equal for all manuscripts. The most important aim must be to list and index collections as rapidly as possible, not to describe them in detail. It may make sense to look at *The Waste Land* under a microscope, however, for many large collections, well-indexed handlists (ideally indexing addressees of letters as well as writers), will probably do very well, provided that they include a brief mention of provenance and some physical description.

Cataloguing literary manuscripts in detail is rewarding, but very time-consuming, even if the end-product is concise. Drafts have to be identified in relation to published texts, often requiring a search of periodicals as well as books. Collected, uncollected, and unpublished works must be separately dealt with. The complications of the order in which a notebook was used may have to be explained, or perhaps the way in which measurements and watermark of the paper match drafts of the same work in another collection. For modern manuscripts the clearly established criteria which exist for the description of a medieval book are still lacking. Methods of arrangement and storage vary widely and it is by no means standard for a manuscript to be foliated. As the vast accumulations of the past thirty-five years come to be digested, we must hope that principles of description come to be settled, and that more catalogues will meet the level of the best.

Further reading

This is a very selective list. There is no standard reference work dealing with modern literary manuscripts; a bibliography of the many scattered articles and ephemeral publications, including exhibition catalogues, is badly needed. References to manuscripts often escape indexing in bibliographies and periodicals, see B.J. McMullin, 'Indexing the Periodical Literature of Anglo-American Bibliography', *SB*, 33 (1980): 1–17. Conservation (a key issue in relation to modern literary manuscripts), is too large a subject to be dealt with within the compass of this chapter. For an introductory bibliography, see A.D. Baynes-Cope, *Caring for Books and Documents*, 2nd edn (British Library, 1989). Paper and handwriting analysis are dealt with elsewhere in this book (see Bidwell and Davis).

Handwriting and codicology

Brown, T.J. 'English Handwriting after *c.* 1500', *NCBEL*, vol. 1, *600–1660*. Cambridge, 1974, col. 220
Croft, P.J. *Autograph Poetry in the English Language: Facsimiles of Original Manuscripts from the Fourteenth to the Twentieth Century*. 2 vols. 1973
Petti, Anthony G. *English Literary Hands from Chaucer to Dryden*. 1977

Facsimiles and reproductions

Eliot, T.S. *The Waste Land: A Facsimile and Transcript of the Original Drafts including the Annotations of Ezra Pound*, ed. V. Eliot, 1971
Joyce, James. *Ulysses: A Facsimile of the Manuscript*. 3 vols., ed. Harry Lavin and Clive Driver. London and Philadelphia, 1975
Kidd, John. 'An Inquiry into *Ulysses: The Corrected Text*', *PBSA*, 82 (1988): 411–584
Orwell, George. *Nineteen Eighty-Four: The Facsimile of the Extant Manuscript*, ed. P. Davison. London and Weston, MA., 1984
Tanselle, G. Thomas, 'Reproductions and Scholarship', *SB*, 42 (1989): 25–54

History of collecting: private collectors

Munby, A.N.L. *The Cult of the Autograph Letter in England.* 1962
Reid, B.L. *The Man from New York: John Quinn and His Friends.* New York, 1968
Wise, T.J. *The Ashley Library: A Catalogue of Printed Books, Manuscripts and Autograph Letters,*
    11 vols. 1922–36. See also review of the 1971 reprint, W.B. Todd, *PBSA,* 67 (1973):
    203–5

The market in modern literary manuscripts

Carter, John. 'What happens to Authors' Manuscripts?', *Atlantic Monthly* (July 1960): 76–80
Rota, Anthony. 'The Trade in Modern Literary Manuscripts', *Antiquarian Book Monthly*
    Review, 17 (1990): 482–93
Stratford, Jenny. 'The Market in Authors' Manuscripts', *TLS,* 24 July 1969: 817–8

Institutional collections

No attempt has been made to deal with the holdings of individual institutional libraries.

Bordin, Ruth B. and Robert M. Warner, *The Modern Manuscript Library.* New York and
    London, 1966
Duckett, Kenneth W. *Modern Manuscripts: a Practical Manual for their Management, Care and*
    Use. American Association for State and Local History, Nashville, TE., 1975
Kelliher, Hilton, and Sally Brown. *English Literary Manuscripts.* British Library, 1986
Larkin, Philip. 'Operation Manuscript', in *Poetry in the Making.* 1967: 14–21
    'A Neglected Responsibility', in *Required Writing: Miscellaneous Pieces, 1959–1982.* 1983:
    pp.98–108. (Introductory talk at the seminar on modern literary manuscripts, SCONUL,
    King's College London, 1979.)
Lewis, Jenny. *Poetry in the Making: Catalogue of an Exhibition of Poetry Manuscripts in the British*
    Museum, April–June 1967. 1967. With contributions by C. Day Lewis, T.C. Skeat, and
    Philip Larkin
Munby, A.N.L. 'The Acquisition of Manuscripts by Institutional Libraries', *PBSA,* 54 (1960):
    1–15
    'Viewpoint', *TLS,* 15 February 1974: 156. See also Bulloch, Penelope. *Modern Literary*
    Manuscripts from King's College, Cambridge: An Exhibition in Memory of A.N.L. Munby.
    Cambridge: Fitzwilliam Museum, 1976
Roberts, R.J. 'Rare Book Collecting: A View from Mid-Atlantic', *Long Room,* no. 6 (1972):
    7–16
Stratford, Jenny. *The Arts Council Collection of Modern Literary Manuscripts, 1963–1972.* 1974

Publishers' archives

Archives of British and American Publishers (microform sets with microfiche or printed indexes,
    Chadwyck-Healey, Cambridge), are listed in D.J. Munro, *Microforms for Historians: A*
    Finding-List of Research Collections in London Libraries. Institute of Historical Research,
    1990, nos. 1,079–90

Location registers and Union catalogues. Index of English literary manuscripts

Hamer, Philip M. (ed.). *A Guide to Archives and Manuscripts in the United States.* New Haven,
    1961

National Union Catalog of Manuscript Collections, 1959–1984 (1959– , in progress). For the
extent of coverage to 1984, see 'Geographical Guide to Repositories, 1959–84',
preceding the descriptions in the 1984 volume; *Index to Personal Names in the National
Union Catalog of Manuscript Collections, 1959–1984.* 2 vols., Alexandria, VA., 1988

Robbins, J. Albert (ed.). *American Literary Manuscripts: A Checklist of Holdings in Academic,
Historical and Public Libraries, Museums and Authors' Homes in the United States,* 2nd edn.
Athens, GA, 1977. See Broderick, John C. 'Finding (and Counting) American Literary
Manuscripts', *Review,* 1 (1979): 295–300

Sutton, David C. (ed.). *Location Register of Twentieth-Century English Literary Manuscripts and
Letters: A Union List of Papers of Modern English, Irish, Scottish and Welsh Authors in the
British Isles.* 2 vols. British Library, 1988

Index of English Literary Manuscripts. 5 vols. (in progress), especially volume IV, *1800–1900,
Part I, Arnold–Gissing* (1982), compiled by Barbara Rosenbaum and Pamela White and
Part 2, Hardy–Lamb (1990), compiled by Barbara Rosenbaum

Exhibition catalogues

Exhibition catalogues are a valuable but often elusive source of information about manuscript
collections; a specialized checklist would be useful. Apart from the catalogues themselves,
some materials exist, e.g. Marie Korey, 'Exhibition Catalogues', *PBSA,* 79 (1985): 543–66
(with a checklist of North American exhibitions, 1980–3); continued as 'Exhibition
Catalogues, 1984–1988', *PBSA,* 82 (1988): 113–22. Exhibitions held in England, Scotland,
Wales, and Ireland are normally listed in the *Newsletter of the SCONUL Advisory Committee on
Manuscripts,* 1978 (in progress).

The analysis of handwriting: an introductory survey

TOM DAVIS

When the founding fathers of modern bibliography defined the subject as they conceived it, the study of handwriting had a definite and considerable place. Greg, dreaming in 1914 of a university course in bibliography,[1] treated the study of manuscripts on equal terms with that of printed books and it is clear that he and his contemporaries regarded the monumental *English Literary Autographs*[2] as a crucial research tool. But something happened to this vision. The *Index to Selected Bibliographical Journals*[3] has no entries at all under 'handwriting' and only one under 'forgeries'. *The Library*, in its entire history, has published less than half a dozen substantial papers on handwriting. There *are* a number of articles and even books published on handwriting by bibliographers, but they are scattered, both physically and (as it were) intellectually: they lack a common and coherent rationale and methodology. They vary considerably in quality, shade off into other disciplines, and there seems to be a common feeling that the identification of handwriting is best left to experts, who sometimes do not seem to be obliged to state the reasons for their decisions. In the meantime, a great deal of work on handwriting in this century has been and is being done, not by bibliographers, but by forensic scientists, whose job it is, on a day-to-day basis, to identify holographs and analyse forgeries; their work, which is now very substantial, is hardly referred to in the bibliographical literature (and for that reason rather full notes are given for this chapter). It seems that a survey that attempts to draw together this scattered discipline, and in particular introduce the two halves of it, the forensic and the bibliographical, to each other, would be timely and useful.

I should begin by revealing where I come from: in particular, my biases and limitations. Although I spent much of three years reading Secretary hand for my research degree, and a further two at Yale reading eighteenth-century manuscript letters (both of these rather a long time ago), most of the work I have

---

1 W.W. Greg, 'What is Bibliography?' (1914) *W.W. Greg: Collected Papers*, ed. J.C. Maxwell (Oxford, 1966), 85–8.
2 W.W. Greg, *English Literary Autographs*, 1550–1660 (Oxford, 1925–32).
3 *Index to Selected Bibliographical Journals, 1933–1970* (The Bibliographical Society, 1982).

done on handwriting has been in the forensic area. I have practised as a forensic handwriting analyst since 1974, and have conducted or supervised a substantial amount of research in that field, much of it in the form of specific research projects funded by the United Kingdom Home Office. During this time I have done some work on the identification of literary handwriting, thanks to my early training, but not much, and of medieval handwriting – palaeography proper – I know almost nothing. These limitations therefore define not only the scope in time of this survey, but also the basis. Although the forensic analysis of handwriting is a science in its infancy, in that much of the theoretical and statistical work that needs to be done has not yet happened, it embodies a methodology that is clearly established, and has been tested countless numbers of times in the courts: there are many who are now in prison, or have been saved from going there, solely on the basis of handwriting testimony. I propose therefore to use the forensic analysis of handwriting as a constant reference point.

The study of handwriting is a discipline without a name. Forensic scientists call themselves 'Forensic Document Analysts', since their work includes the analysis of the physical characteristics of documents; when they talk of themselves specifically as handwriting experts, they use the term 'Forensic Handwriting Analyst'. Bibliographers, since the bulk of bibliographical study of handwriting centred upon Shakespeare's Secretary hand, which is certainly old, if not exactly ancient, have usually used 'palaeography'.[4] 'Calligraphy' has also been offered,[5] and there is some confusion with 'graphology', which is not particularly resolved by Tannenbaum's offering: 'graphiology'.[6] These names are all rather unsuitable, usually for etymological reasons. I wish to call the discipline simply 'handwriting analysis'. For two reasons: first because it is simple, and not confusing to those with any kind of classical education; and second because the term stresses the common ancestry and methodology between forensic and (as I shall call it, if the distinction needs emphasising) bibliographical handwriting analysis. Calligraphers are interested in the aesthetics of handwriting; graphologists attempt to discern character from handwriting; and palaeographers – may we agree? – study old handwriting. Whereas, I suggest, the timescale of handwriting analysis, like that of bibliography, as opposed to the study of incunabula, begins with the Secretary hand and continues to the present.

A second principle that I would wish to maintain is that the primary purpose of handwriting analysis is *identification*. In other words, it is based on the commonly agreed hypothesis that any piece of naturally occurring handwriting may, if it is sufficiently extensive, contain information that will enable its author to be identified, if it can be compared with suitable samples known to have been

---

4 The course I teach at Birmingham University is traditionally and unshakeably known as 'Bibliography and Palaeography'.
5 S.O.A. Ullmann, 'Dating Through Calligraphy: The Example of "Dover Beach" ', *SB*, 26 (1973): 19–36.   6 In his *Problems in Shakespeare's Penmanship* (New York, 1927).

written by that author.[7] This primary purpose subsumes a number of aspects of the study of handwriting: the two of greatest prominence in the bibliographical literature are the straightforward, if often difficult, task of decipherment and transcription, and the more theoretically interesting use of the analysis of variation in a known hand for the purpose of dating. A third principle follows from this: that bibliographic and forensic handwriting analysts are only distinguished by the nature of their subject matter: the former study literary and historical (and therefore usually older) documents, the latter contemporary material whose importance is that it is associated either with a crime or a civil dispute. Thus, in principle, forensically oriented research into, say, the hypothesis of similarity of the handwriting of close relatives would be equally useful for both sets of investigators.

The *method* of handwriting analysis, therefore, I take to be that used by currently practising forensic scientists. I will therefore now offer an (extremely) brief description of the state of the art of forensic handwriting analysis.[8]

The practice of forensic handwriting analysis is well established.[9] The *questioned writing*, as it is called, whether a signature or signatures or extended text, is compared with sample writing of known authorship from one or a number of hands. Both sets must be as contemporary as possible, and in the same kind of writing: signatures cannot normally be compared with text writing, a forgery with the forger's natural hand, or capitals with lower-case cursive. Care is taken to obviate the possibility of disguise in the samples. The two sets of documents are compared by means of a close examination of each letter in each. This comparison can be said to take place on two levels. The first level is that of the basic form of the letter, the *style characteristics* that the writer might share with others, but not all others. The second is the level of the *individual characteristics*, the identifying idiosyncrasies that do not derive from a taught style or an assumed fashion and are likely to be unique to that writer.

The examination is conducted on the basis of the following crucial assumption. Handwriting, particularly fast skilled cursive handwriting, is to some extent an automatic procedure and therefore contains elements that are not under conscious control of the writer. These elements will be those that tend to be ignored by an imitator for forgery or a disguiser for distortion; moreover, since both of those processes depend on conscious control, they will find it extremely

---

7 For an interesting qualification of this principle, see John J. Harris, 'How Much do People Write Alike?', *Journal of Criminal Law*, 48 (1958): 647–51.

8 I have given a much fuller description in 'Forensic Handwriting Analysis', *Talking About Text*, ed. M. Coulthard (Birmingham: English Language Research, 1986), pp. 189–207; there are also extensive accounts in the literature of forensic handwriting research, listed later.

9 It has been established for a long time, apparently: see Jean Gayet, 'The Expert Examination of Handwriting in the 17th Century', *International Criminal Police Review*, 169 (1963): 165–76. The technique described differs (in essentials) not at all from that practised today. See also the Hon. Edward Twisleton, ed., *The Handwriting of Junius Professionally Investigated by Mr. Charles Chabot, Expert* (1871), which contains what must be the most extensive published report of any handwriting analysis: it runs to over 300 substantial quarto pages.

difficult to imitate or suppress these unconscious physical actions. This is why what a document analyst will tend to look at first in a document is the *line quality*: the evidence in the pen-line for the speed of movement of the writing implement. The faster the pen is moving, the greater the proportion of unconscious to conscious control that is being exerted. So forgers, for instance, have a problem: if they attempt to imitate the speed of movement of the pen by maintaining the line quality of the original, they tend to miss the fine detail or even the gross outline of the letter-forms being imitated: even, in some cases, allowing their own unconscious idiosyncrasies to come through. But if they invest in careful rendition of the shapes of the letters, the pen tends to slow down, and the slowness of its movement relative to the imitated writing shows up in a comparison of the line quality.

Comparison of handwriting depends also on the view that each letter in each hand is only one instance of a range of ways particular to that hand of producing that grapheme:[10] adequate samples are those which can be expected to display this range for each letter in question, and adequacy in the sample therefore depends on the degree of variability of the hand. The sample writing is examined first, and referenced sketches are made in a work-book of each example of the range of typical realizations of each grapheme. The same is done for the questioned writing, and the two are then compared with reference to this analysis, which will then be augmented to point out significant matches or mismatches. Before a handwriting examiner gives a positive statement in a particular case, he or she would hope to find a significant match (or mis-match) in the samples with every letter in the questioned material. Anything less would result in a qualified, often severely qualified, report. Handwriting experts, it must be stressed, are *cautious*: they are very conscious of the significance of their opinion, not least to the person who may go to prison as a result of it. They are also, usually, trained as applied scientists, and are therefore deeply aware of the constant perversity of nature in refusing to conform to human expectations, and the fundamental evil of selecting only the evidence that corresponds to these expectations, in order to help the situation along a little. Since this evil is regarded as a perfectly normal and virtuous practice by literary critics, and even, on extremely rare occasions, by bibliographers, I have found my own training rather unhelpful in this respect, though very useful for the purpose of communicating with lawyers.

Once an opinion emerges, it is tested. Reports emanating in the United Kingdom from the three Document Laboratories used by the police are invariably double-checked internally, and any forensic handwriting analysis will usually be duplicated by an expert employed by the other side; the whole thing is tested again in court. There, the practice is certainly not to take the expert's word for it – not, that is, in any instance where the opinion constitutes important evidence. The handwriting analyst takes the court through the evidence for his or her opinion by means of detailed illustration in the form of

10 This useful term, which means, approximately, 'letter', is taken from graphic linguistics. See for instance Ernst Pulgram, 'Phoneme and Grapheme: a Parallel', *Word*, 7 (1951): 15–20.

enlarged photographs and sketches of significant features, and the court is invited to agree on the basis of evidence presented, which must, therefore, be presented in a way that is comprehensible, and convincing, to non-experts. And it is, of course, open to cross-examination, which can often be very detailed, penetrating, and stubborn. But handwriting evidence is, as a result of all of this care and testing, well respected: it has a good reputation in the courts, and the police, though they complain about the caution of handwriting examiners, are happy to get their evidence when it comes: it is as good, they say, as any other kind of solid forensic evidence, including, for instance, fingerprints.

In 1984 an Editorial appeared in the *Journal of the Forensic Science Society* (*JFSS*) entitled 'Watching, Doing, and the Black Arts'.[11] The 'Black Art' referred to was forensic handwriting analysis, and the clear implication was that this subject was rather more like witchcraft than a serious scientific endeavour. This caused quite a stir, since editorials in that journal are not normally controversial, and a stern letter from the then Director of the Metropolitan Police Forensic Document Laboratory[12] brought an apology from the editor: he was, he said, only talking about the way in which other forensic scientists tended to think about handwriting analysis, a view that was, he went on, contradicted by articles published in that very issue. Order was restored, but presumably the habits of thought of other scientists did not change. Bibliographers, including those who practise handwriting analysis, seem to agree with them. I doubt if the position has changed much since Giles Dawson made this statement, in 1942:

Axioms or truths can of course be recognized in this as in every other scientific pursuit, but they are in almost every case of limited applicability. Each individual problem presents new aspects and must be attacked in its own way, as I think I can show. It is advisedly that I call the attribution of manuscript material a 'scientific pursuit' rather than a science. It is not a science so much as it is a craft or art, for its exercise depends far less upon rules and instruments of precision than upon individual judgement, experience, and intuition.[13]

There is an awkward, palpable ambiguity as to whether handwriting analysis is in fact a science or not. Is it, or isn't it?

The answer lies in the development of the subject, as the editor of *JFSS* suggests. This can be said to fall into three periods. The early period, up to the beginning of this century, was chaotic. Handwriting analysis was practised by a variety of people: some produced reliable opinions, but many did not. The latter made unreliable or even partisan judgements that courts found unacceptable, and thus damaged the very basis of the subject.[14] There was also some confusion

11 *Journal of the Forensic Science Society*, 24 (1984): 155–6.

12 D.M. Ellen, 'Watching, Doing, and the Black Arts', *Journal of the Forensic Science Society*, 24.6 (1984): 559.

13 Giles E. Dawson, 'Authenticity and Attribution of Written Matter', *English Institute Annual*, (1942): 77.

14 See Antonia Sara, 'The Use of Handwriting as Evidence', *Birmingham University Working Papers in Handwriting Research* (1987), and Amanda Lumley, 'The History and Development of the Analysis of Handwriting', *Birmingham University Working Papers in Handwriting Research* (1983).

between handwriting identification and graphology,[15] the supposed study of character in handwriting. This association (since graphology, whatever one's view of its validity, has produced – to say the least – some deeply unserious work),[16] did nothing for the credibility of handwriting analysis.

Stage two, therefore, from the beginning of this century up to (rather arbitrarily) 1970, was concerned primarily with the professionalization of the discipline: with rescuing it from association with amateurs and graphologists. Forensic handwriting analysis is *important*: it cannot afford to make mistakes. The necessity was immediate and extremely practical: to establish an agreed and workable methodology, based on a set of relatively straightforward axioms. This method was developed and constantly tested and refined in the *practice* of forensic handwriting examination, and found to work. It is highly pragmatic: experience is a crucial component. So beginners learn the subject by serving a two-year apprenticeship, shadowing the work of their seniors, before they are allowed to give evidence in court. The aims of stage two have been obtained: the method is established, and with it the vital respect of the courts and the police.

But what is the basis of this method? It will be clear from my description that what the handwriting analyst actually *does* is to compare the elements of any piece of writing with an internalized database derived from observation of a great deal of handwriting; on this basis he or she will know what is or is not unusual, distinctive, or commonplace. They may or may not know, for instance, that a particular letter-form derives from a named style of handwriting taught in certain schools at a certain time, deriving from a specific set of published manuals; but they certainly will know that this form is a style characteristic, and therefore not as useful, potentially, as some less widely disseminated form. This is scientific in the sense that it is based on a rigorous methodology subject to constant testing, but pre-scientific in that it is not extensively theorized or based on published collections of data.

The literature of stage two demonstrates this primarily methodological and experience-oriented concern. The papers published on handwriting tended to be of two kinds: reports of unusual or interesting individual cases, that tested or were found to substantiate the often implicit principles of the method, and theoretical statements in the form of generalizations, based on wide experience, of what handwriting had been found to be like in practice.

It is to this period that the two extensive modern books on the subject belong. They date from within two years of each other, and were each produced by the

15 See Arthur J. Quirke, *Forged, Anonymous, and Suspect Documents* (1930), a (historically) interesting and certainly entertaining amalgam of the two disciplines.
16 For example, Jenny Halfon, *The ABC of Sex and Seduction: What Handwriting Reveals About Sexuality, Compatibility and Sensuality* (Wellingborough, 1986), to name but one. There is a very extensive literature of graphology, much of it unashamedly brash. For the more serious side of the subject see Baruch Nevo, *Scientific Aspects Of Graphology: A Handbook* (Springfield, 1986), and citations. The axioms of graphology have (in my view) been severely damaged by Abraham Jansen, *Validation of Graphological Judgments: an Experimental Study* (The Hague, 1973), which is a generous and sympathetic attempt to test the claims of graphology, and is all the more devastating for that reason.

leading authority in, respectively, the United Kingdom and the United States; the English book, Wilson R. Harrison's *Suspect Documents*, came out in 1958, and the American volume, Ordway Hilton's *Scientific Examination of Questioned Documents*, in 1956. Each of these reappeared in revised form, to take account of such crucial developments as the now almost universal use of the ball-point pen: Harrison's book in 1966 and Hilton's as recently as 1982. Both of them, however, still belong firmly to an earlier era of writing about handwriting analysis.[17] They are authoritative, extensive, and an excellent introduction to the subject, since no one would question the experience of either of those two writers, but they remain firmly experience based: the generalizations are based on knowledge, but not publicly accessible knowledge, and have an uncomfortably oracular quality.

Now that the discipline is established, however, those engaged in research in the field have become dissatisfied with this approach, and its 'black-art' connotations, and so the third generation of articles (but not, as yet, books) began to appear.[18] Thus, for example, Harrison's chapter on disguised handwriting (pp. 349–72) consists of a number of assertions that derive from his wide experience; recent work, however, has started to investigate these assumptions and attempt to test them against collections of data. A selection of titles makes the point clearly enough: 'Characteristics of 200 Awkward-hand Signatures', 'Disguised Handwriting; a Statistical Survey of how Handwriting is Most Frequently Disguised', and 'An Investigation into How Handwriting is Most Frequently Disguised'.[19]

In bibliographical handwriting analysis, the state of theory and practice seem to be that which pertained in the forensic field before the first stage of professionalization took place. A research student faced with a problem in the identification of handwriting would have a considerable problem in finding out even the rudiments of how to do it. There are two papers that offer general advice: one, 'The Detection of Faked Literary MSS', on forgery, and Giles Dawson's paper, already cited, on 'Authenticity and Attribution of Written Matter'.[20] Both of

17 Wilson R. Harrison, *Suspect Documents, Their Scientific Examination* (1966); revised edition: first edition 1958. A photographic reproduction of the first edition, scaled down but otherwise unchanged, was published by Nelson-Hall, Chicago, in 1982. Ordway Hilton, *Scientific Examination of Questioned Documents* (New York, 1982); revised edition: first edition 1956.
18 It is of course not possible to list here more than a very small selection of even recent articles on the subject. My database of handwriting references has 1,708 entries at the moment, and this is highly selective. Anyone who wishes to acquaint him- or herself with the subject is advised to read Harrison and Osborn, and then to browse backwards through the two main journals, the (English) *Journal of the Forensic Science Society*, and the (American) *Journal of Forensic Science*.
19 Viola Stevens, 'Characteristics of 200 Awkward-hand Signatures', *International Criminal Police Review*, 237 (1970): 130–7; E.F. Alford, Jr., 'Disguised Handwriting; a Statistical Survey of how Handwriting is Most Frequently Disguised', *Journal of Forensic Science*, 15 (1970): 476–88; Deborah Hubball, 'An Investigation Into How Handwriting is Most Frequently Disguised', *Birmingham University Working Papers in Handwriting Research* (1982).
20 T.J. Brown, 'The Detection of Faked Literary MSS.', *BC*, 2 (1953): 6–23; Giles E. Dawson, 'Authenticity and Attribution of Written Matter', *English Institute Annual* (1942): 77–100.

these are useful; Brown's piece on forgery is certainly a start, and offers some helpful advice, and Dawson's, though as we have seen he retreats immediately from theory into cases, nonetheless makes sensible and practical judgements about these cases. Most guides to scholarship, however, rather lamely recommend Harrison's forensic text;[21] it is clear that these articles simply do not go anywhere near far enough.

In casework the material is much more extensive, and it is possible to learn a great deal from it, though the quality is extremely variable. Let me try and describe the way it looks to one who stands somewhat outside it. There clearly are handwriting experts of considerable authority, and their work is impressive, but there is no explicit consensus. Dale Kramer, in 'A Query Concerning the Handwriting in Hardy's Manuscripts', rather plaintively asks that a 'handwriting expert' should look into the difference between Hardy's hand and that of his wife, but he does not seem to know how to find one.[22] Others, faced with similar problems, are reduced either to doing it themselves or to consulting those who may be familiar with the handwriting under consideration (textual editors, for instance) but who are not expert at handwriting analysis; in either case the handwriting evidence, which may be the key to the entire article, is often not given.[23] And there are errors, of a kind not seen in the courts (one fervently hopes) since the conviction of Dreyfus on (partly) handwriting evidence.[24] And, finally, the (to forensic scientists) vital disassociation from graphology has not been made; not even in the very best work in the field.[25]

I do not wish to dwell on these instances: what they show is not, I suggest, evil on the part of their authors but rather a lack of coherence and consensus in the discipline, which it is the purpose of this chapter to suggest ways of overcoming.

21 For instance, David V. Erdman and Ephim G. Fogel, *Evidence for Authorship* (New York, 1966).
22 Dale Kramer, 'A Query Concerning the Handwriting in Hardy's Manuscripts', *PBSA*, 57 (1963): 360.
23 For instance: 'Comparison with other examples of Sir Henry Savile's hand makes it clear that the writing of the Commonplace Book is always that of Savile', J.R.L. Highfield, 'An Autograph Manuscript Commonplace Book of Sir Henry Savile', *Bodleian Library Record*, 7 (1963): 74. See also (for instance) William Leigh Godshalk, 'A Sidney Autograph', *BC*, 13 (1964): 65; and J.S. Diekhoff, 'The Text of Comus', *PBSA*, 52 (1937): 726.
24 See R.S. Thomas and David McKitterick, 'John Donne's Kimbolton Papers', *TLS*, (1974): 870–3. The false ascription to Donne was refuted in a model handwriting analysis by Nicolas Barker, 'Goodfriday 1613: by Whose Hand?', *TLS*, (1974): 996–7. A similar false ascription to Marlowe was attacked, with rather less gentleness, by R.E. Alton, in 'Marlowe Authenticated', *TLS* (1974): 446–7. Not that forensic experts are incapable of error: see L. Michel and P.E. Baier, 'The Diaries of Adolf Hitler. Implication for Document Examination', *Journal of Forensic Science*, 25 (1985): 167–78.
25 'Here, if anywhere, the hand was the man: sensitive to the point of delicacy, but clear as running water and strong as iron at heart' (T.J. Brown, 'English Literary Autographs XIX: Thomas Hardy', *BC*, 5 (1956): 249). Even in P.J. Croft's otherwise admirable *Autograph Poetry in the English Language* (1973) there is frequently an uncomfortable feeling that the poetry, rather than the handwriting of the poet, is under discussion – e.g. 'It is certainly true that Byron's hand, while its individuality usually remains unmistakable, is particularly liable to temperamental fluctuations, and anything like consistency in its details is not to be looked for'. Any forensic scientist would wince a little at the following comment on Donne's handwriting, from Nicolas Barker's otherwise wholly convincing and authoritative 'Goodfriday 1613: by Whose Hand?', *TLS* (1974): 966–7: 'Everything he wrote bears signs of a strong individual intelligence applied to the formation of each word'.

Moreover, there are many examples in the bibliographical literature of identification of holographs and detection of forgery that forensic scientists would find completely acceptable, and our enquiring research student, if he or she were to search persistently enough, would find much to imitate and learn from. The handwriting of Shakespeare has attracted much nonsense, but also much that any forensic scientist would recognize as eminently correct procedure, including that of a practising Canadian forensic scientist,[26] and others scattered across the literary field, though clustering, like bibliography itself, in the vicinity of Shakespeare.[27] Two particularly evoke this kind of recognition: Giles Dawson's piece on John Payne Collier in *Studies in Bibliography*, which also has the discipline and comprehensive thoroughness which one associates with that journal at its best, and Maunde Thompson's analysis of the hand of Anthony Mundy from *The Library*. These and the others I have cited (and, without doubt, others that I have not found), belong firmly to the second stage of development of research in handwriting analysis.

In the remainder of this chapter I wish to sketch some directions for future research in this field. Some, that is, from very many: though much is known by experts in handwriting, very little is actually known in a public, stage-three, way. The topics I have selected are those in which the work already available is particularly useful and suggestive of further research.

It is accepted that normally the settled form of an individual hand will have developed after adolescence, and not usually change greatly thereafter. But some changes will take place: to what extent can one use these for the purpose of dating documents in which they occur? Here, rather refreshingly, all of the work so far has been done by bibliographers.[28] It is accepted by forensic scientists that there is a dating potential in changes in individual hands – hence, for one thing,

---

26 For instance R.C. Bald, 'The Booke of Sir Thomas More and its Problems', *Shakespeare Survey*, 2 (1949): 44–65; R.A. Huber, 'On Looking Over Shakespeare's "Secretarie"', *Stratford Papers on Shakespeare 1960* (1961): 52–70; Samuel A. Tannenbaum, *Problems in Shakespeare's Penmanship*, (New York, 1927); Sir Edward Maunde Thompson, 'The Handwriting of the Three Pages', *Shakespeare's Hand in the Play of Sir Thomas More*, ed. A. Pollard (Cambridge, 1923), pp. 81–112.

27 Hugh C.H. Candy, 'Milton Autographs Established', *Lib*, IV, 13 (1932): 192–200; P.J. Croft, *Autograph Poetry in the English Language*, (1973) *passim*; Giles E. Dawson, 'John Payne Collier's Great Forgery', *SB*, 24 (1971): 1–26; T.H. Howard-Hill, 'The Bridgewater-Huntington MS of Middleton's *Game At Chess*', *Manuscripta*, 28 (1984): 145–56; Sir Edward Maunde Thompson, 'The Autograph Manuscripts of Anthony Mundy', *Lib*, III, 14 (1915–17): 325–53; and the Nicolas Barker and R.E. Alton references, note 24.

28 Masahiko Agari, 'A Note on Milton's Trinity MS', *English Language Notes*, 22.2 (1984): 23–6; S.O.A. Ullmann, 'Dating Through Calligraphy: The Example of "Dover Beach"', *SB*, 26 (1973): 19–36; J.T. Shawcross, 'The Manuscripts of Comus: an Addendum', *PBSA*, 54 (1960): 293–4; J.T. Shawcross, 'Certain Relationships in the Manuscript of Comus', *PBSA*, 54 (1960): 38–56; J.T. Shawcross, 'Speculations on the Dating of the Trinity MS of Milton's Poems', *Modern Language Notes*, 75 (1960): 11–17; T.H. Johnson, ed., *Poems of Emily Dickinson* (Cambridge, MA, 1955), 3, xlix–lix; Madeline House and Graham Storey, ed., *The Letters of Charles Dickens*, I (1965): xxiv–xxv; II (1969): xiii; Helen Darbishire, 'The Chronology of Milton's Handwriting', *Lib*, IV, 14 (1933): 229–35; D.W. Cruickshank, 'Calderon's Handwriting', *MLR*, 65 (1970): 65–77.

the insistence that samples should be contemporary. But as far as I know no research has been done to substantiate the reliability of these changes as a dating method. Here, it seems to me, is an excellent instance of how examination of variation across time in collections of handwriting elicited from contemporary informants, together with interviews with the writers, using the methodologies proposed by the bibliographers cited below, could be used to reinforce the analysis of non-contemporary material, to the benefit of bibliographers and forensic scientists alike.

Handwriting analysis depends on the ability to recognize the difference between the taught style and the individual variations on that style. There are, in addition, styles that are common but not taught: the /i/ dot in the form of a circle is not in any taught style, but it is not re-invented by each of those who employ it. Handwriting analysts must have, for any period of time and writing community under examination, an extensive knowledge of these taught, individual, and 'underground' handwriting characteristics. At the moment much of this knowledge is intuitive but there are two areas of research that have made a beginning in rendering this knowledge publicly available: one of them from the forensic field, and the other from the bibliographical.

The first of these is our own work at Birmingham University.[29] This very extensive research has collected, analysed, and classified all the handwriting copy-books produced in the United Kingdom during the lifetime of any adult now alive, and related the results to geographical area and to time. Large samples of naturally occurring handwriting have been analysed, using this information, and a classification made of the underground styles found in them. As a result, it is now possible to make an informed statement about the taught and underground styles that influence the handwriting of any sample, and to relate the former to specific copy-books and thus to specific periods of time. A beginning has also been made in the investigation of these features in the handwriting of other European countries.[30]

Bibliographical research into the history of handwriting has been of two forms: an extensive analysis of the Secretary hand, largely for the purpose of aiding decipherment, and collections of samples of handwriting. The work on Secretary has, in one sense, been done. The list of works, and the extent of knowledge employed in them, is impressive.[31] However, the knowledge is

29 Frances Brown and Tom Davis, 'The Acquisition of Handwriting in the UK', Research Project for the Home Office (1984); Frances Brown, Tom Davis, and Richard Totty, 'The Acquisition of Handwriting in the United Kingdom' (in preparation); Frances Brown and Tom Davis, 'Evidence for the Learned Style in the Naturally Occurring Handwriting of Adults'; Paper presented to the Questioned Document Section of the Forensic Science Society, *Birmingham University Working Papers in Handwriting Research* (1986); Frances Brown, Tom Davis, and Sally Jellis, 'The Handwriting of Two Generations of Adults in a Small Village', Working Paper, Birmingham University Centre for Handwriting Research (1987).

30 Frances Brown and Tom Davis, 'Identification Characteristics of the Handwriting of Eight European Countries', Research Project for the Home Office (1989).

31 See for instance M. St C. Byrne, 'Elizabethan Handwriting for Beginners', *RES*, 1 (1925): 198–209; Giles Dawson and Laetitia Kennedy-Skipton, *Elizabethan Handwriting 1500–1650* (1968); L.C. Hector, *The Handwriting of English Documents* (1966); R.B. McKerrow, 'The Capital Letters in

normally what I have called stage-two knowledge: the results of exceptional experience, but not usually based on demonstrable evidence. A drawing of what the writer knows to be the characteristic forms of a particular letter in a particular period, as an attempt at the articulation and communication of essentially intuitive knowledge, and often with extraordinary powers of recall, can be of great value; but it is not enough.

With regard to later developments in English handwriting, from the Restoration to the end of the nineteenth century, there is nothing approaching even the stage-two level of analysis. The history of this handwriting has simply not been written. What we have is collections of samples.[32] These collections, which extend from the Renaissance to the mid-nineteenth century, have been made for a variety of reasons: to provide reference samples for identification, to give practice in decipherment, or simply to satisfy the pleasure that people feel in the contemplation of old, or beautiful, or famous handwriting. Sometimes they contain commentary on the hands, and sometimes, as in the case of P.J. Croft's remarkable book, this commentary is extremely interesting and informative. But as a history of handwriting, they are no more than the most initial raw materials, and the literary, historical, or aesthetic impulses behind the selection of the samples makes them necessarily unrepresentative.

The answer, it seems to me, is a synthesis of the methods that we have developed at Birmingham with the mass of material produced by bibliographers. In other words, the collection and rigorous analysis of large samples of handwriting, of published copy-books, and the relationship between the two. This, I suggest, is the way forward towards the yet unwritten history of English handwriting.

Finally, some reflections on a quotation.

The main basis for positing a young woman as the author of the holographs is the nature of the hand, an italic with long vertical strokes not present in the cramped corrections, which contain secretary elements. Though it possesses a certain elegance, it shows some features suggesting immaturity and lack of sophistication in writing more common to young women of the day than their usually better educated male counterparts: it lacks assured rhythm, it contains a large number of pen lifts; its ascending and descending strokes show uncertainty in direction.[33]

Elizabethan Handwriting', *RES*, 3 (1927): 28–36; R.B. McKerrow, 'A Note on Elizabethan Handwriting', *An Introduction to Bibliography for Literary Students* (Oxford, 1928), pp. 341–50; Samuel A. Tannenbaum, *The Handwriting of the Renaissance* (New York, 1930); Sir Edward Maunde Thompson, 'Handwriting', *Shakespeare's England*, 2 vols. (Oxford, 1916), I, 284–310.

32 T.J. Brown, 'English Literary Autographs 1–50', *BC*, I–13 (1952–64); W.S.B. Buck, *Examples of Handwriting, 1550–1650* (London and Chichester, Phillimore, 1973); Herbert Cahoon, Charles Ryskamp, and Thomas V. Lange, *American Literary Autographs from Washington Irving to Henry James* (1977); P.J. Croft, *Autograph Poetry in the English Language* (1973); Greg, *English Literary Autographs*, pp. 1–3; Hilda Grieve, *Examples of English Handwriting 1150–1750* (Essex Education Committee, 1954); Hilton Kelliher and Sally Brown, *English Literary Manuscripts* (British Library, 1986); Anthony G. Petti, *English Literary Hands from Chaucer to Dryden* (1977); Hilary Jenkinson, *The Later Court Hands in England from the Fifteenth to the Seventeenth Century* (Cambridge, 1927).

33 Mary Ellen Lamb, 'Three Unpublished Holograph Poems in the Bright Manuscript: A New Poet in the Sidney Circle?', *RES*, 35 (1984): 302.

Let me make it quite clear that I regard this as outrageous, and therefore amusing: it is precisely what handwriting analysis needed to be rescued from, nearly a hundred years ago. But such speculations are very useful: what, it asks one to ask, is the truth, if any, behind it? What is the difference between male and female handwriting? What are the influences of different kinds of education and social background upon handwriting – through history? What, for that matter, are the influences of alcohol, or physical exertion, or old age, or illness, or any kind of writing instrument, upon handwriting? We do not know; and we do not know how they are to be distinguished, one from another. Beginnings of an investigation have been made, in the modern period,[34] but there is much much more to be done, and in the period covered by bibliographical handwriting analysis there is everything to be done.

34 See, for instance, on gender and handwriting: David Essery, 'An Investigation into Differentiation Between Male and Female Handwriting', *Birmingham University Working Papers in Handwriting Research* (1989); J.H. Hodgins, 'Determination of Sex From Handwriting', *Canadian Society of Forensic Sciences*, 4 (1971): 124–32; R.N. Totty, R.A. Hardcastle, and J. Dempsey, 'The Dependence of Slope of Handwriting Upon the Sex and Handedness of the Writer', *Journal of the Forensic Science Society*, 23 (1983): 237–40. On alcohol: Robert G. Foley and A. Lamar Miller, 'The Effects of Marijuana and Alcohol Usage on Handwriting', *Forensic Science International*, 14 (1979): 159–64; O. Hilton, 'A Study of the Influence of Alcohol on Handwriting', *Journal of Forensic Sciences*, 14 (1969): 309–16. On old age: Tom Davis, 'The Handwriting of Old People', Research Project produced for the Home Office (1985); R. Doubrawa, 'Verä – derungren der Handschrift im Alter', *Zeitschrift für Gerontologie*, 10 (1977): 355–64. On education: Nils Sovik, *Developmental Cybernetics of Handwriting and Graphic Behaviour* (Oslo–Bergen–Tromso, 1975); Ching Y. Suen, 'Handwriting Education: A Bibliography of Contemporary Publications', *Visible Language*, 9 (1975): 145–58. On illness: Louis A. Gottschalk, 'Handwriting in Rheumatoid Arthritics', *Psychosomatic Medicine*, 11.6 (1949): 354–60; O. Hilton, 'Consideration of the Writer's Health in Identifying Signatures and Detecting Forgery', *Journal of Forensic Sciences*, 14 (1969): 157–66. On writing implements: O. Hilton, 'Effects of Writing Instruments on Writing Details', *Journal of Forensic Science*, 29 (1984): 806; J. Mathyer, 'The Influence of Writing Instruments on Handwriting and Signatures', *Journal of Criminal Law, Criminology, and Police Science*, 60 (1969): 102–12.

The study of paper as evidence, artefact, and commodity

JOHN BIDWELL

Paper plays a subsidiary role in book production. It is the basic substance of which books are made, yet almost never impinges upon their communicative function. It serves as a mute vehicle of text, rarely noticed except when it fails of its purpose, when defects inherent in its manufacture impede the transmission and preservation of printed information. What were once thought to be improvements in the composition of paper have sometimes caused its slow and inevitable decay, an irony of technological innovation that distresses library administrators as much as it mystifies conservation scientists. We have not yet learned to cope with the perilous expedients adopted by this craft while it was in the throes of becoming an industry. Even so, we know more about the craft of papermaking than about the craftsmen who worked in remote and isolated paper mills and the tradesmen who invested in these mills and forwarded their goods to market. Papermaking has been predominantly a rural occupation, sparsely and unreliably documented in regional archives, local histories, and genealogical publications. Despite these frustrations, paper deserves careful study for three compelling reasons.

First, close scrutiny of watermarks and other marks of manufacture can reveal bibliographical evidence that will help to date and localize a document or to interpret its significance. By examining paper, scholars have detected literary forgeries, discovered misleading dates in early imprints, and reassembled manuscripts in their proper order after the original sequence had been disturbed. They have developed investigative techniques applicable in many kinds of literary and historical research.

Second, paper survives in profusion, an identifiable artefact of an occupation older than European civilization itself. No other manufacturing activity has bestowed on scholarship such a vast quantity of its products, exhibiting its origins as a craft and its evolution into a modern industry. Conveniently catalogued, readily accessible, and fantastically abundant, the paper constituting early books and manuscripts stored in libraries easily outweighs the textiles and ceramics preserved in museums. Like other manufactures, papermaking

In preparing this chapter I am grateful for comments and criticism from Mark B. Bland, Andrea Immel, Paul Needham, R.J. Roberts, J.S.G. Simmons, and Michael L. Turner.

has generated records that historians can use to examine business practices, labour issues, economic trends, and technological developments. In addition, they can judge the outcome of these working conditions by inspecting early imprints or datable manuscripts composed of paper made at specific times or places. They can correlate data about the operations of the trade in paper with its visible and tangible results, an unparalleled opportunity to explain changes in style and design, and to consider how cultural influences and commercial incentives have affected the quality and appearance of the product.

Third, paper can be viewed as a bulk commodity linking the paper trade with the book trade, as merchandise entailing a significant expense to those who distribute texts in quantity. What we know about the economics of printing and publishing necessarily depends in part on what we can learn about the cost of paper, the sources of supply, the dynamics of the market, and the expectations of the consumer. Early printers bargained for a regular supply of paper as eagerly as papermakers schemed to obtain a steady income. The sale of paper to the book trade involved more than just a casual exchange of cash for goods. On many occasions it called for a detailed contract that fixed credit terms, set a deadline for delivery, and provided for payment by a variety of means, from sophisticated financial instruments to the simple barter of rags. Just as a publisher could become the major customer of a papermaker, so a papermaker could become the major creditor of a publisher. And yet, the close relationship between paper mill, paper warehouse, printing office, and publishing house has never been thoroughly explored. During the last half-century, scholars have made great progress in employing the bibliographical evidence available in paper and in appraising its significance as an industrial artefact. They have been less diligent in relating the artefact to the circumstances of its manufacture and least successful in learning how the commodity changed hands in the world of commerce.

Charles Moïse Briquet demonstrated that the study of paper could result in powerful bibliographical evidence with the publication of *Les Filigranes* (1907), a massive catalogue of more than 16,000 watermarks dating from the earliest known specimens of the late thirteenth century up to about 1600. Reprinted in 1923, and reprinted again with extensive addenda and corrigenda (Amsterdam, 1968), *Les Filigranes* remains the standard guide for the dating, localization, and identification of early European paper. Briquet not only collected watermarks – his catalogue reproduces only a fraction of the immense quantity he actually examined and recorded – but also documentary information about paper mills, which often corroborated his findings and sometimes enabled him to pinpoint the origin of the paper he described. Although some of his attributions have been challenged, and some of his methods have been superseded, his work still shows how paper studies can benefit research in other disciplines.

After Briquet, researchers adopted two divergent approaches to the study of paper for bibliographical evidence. Those who study watermarks – filigranologists – emulated Briquet's achievements by collecting and categorizing early watermarks as clues to dating and localization, or *identification*, while librarians and bibliographers formulated procedures and a nomenclature for *description*. These activities are complementary, of course, for description of paper occasionally culminates in its identification, but they tend toward different goals. Wisso Weiss neatly distinguished between these tendencies in a survey of watermark collections, noting that one collection of tracings had been formed more for *hilfswissenschaftlichen Zwecken* than for the cause of *Papiergeschichtsforschung*.

No guide to the identification of watermarks can claim to be as comprehensive as the *Handbuch der Wasserzeichenkunde* (Leipzig, 1962; reprinted 1983), written by Karl Theodor Weiss and revised by his son, Wisso, after his father died in 1945. It is a pioneering attempt to set standards for watermark research and to educate researchers in the rudiments of actual papermaking. Karl Theodor Weiss realized that it would be futile to study watermarks without understanding their origins and function, without knowing how paper moulds were made, how the watermark designs were fashioned with twisted wire fixed on the surface of the moulds, and how the translucent outlines they imparted to sheets of paper should be viewed in relation to *entire* sheets of paper. He was the first to forewarn researchers that variant watermarks are likely to be twins, since papermakers handled pairs of moulds during a stint at the vat. Weiss's recommendations for recording watermarks were already obsolete when the *Handbuch* appeared because he had been unable to complete his work and because its publication had been delayed for many years. Although updated by Wisso Weiss, the *Handbuch* had the misfortune to follow shortly after Allan Stevenson's *Observations on Paper as Evidence* (Lawrence, KS, 1961) and J.S.G. Simmons's report on 'The Leningrad Method of Watermark Reproduction', (*BC*, 10, 1961), which promised a practical means of applying Stevenson's more refined techniques.

Without a manual at hand, collectors of watermarks have not yet adopted the methods advocated by Stevenson, nor have they settled on any standard procedure, though they have ample precedent from which to pick and choose. Founded in 1948, the Paper Publications Society has sponsored an impressive series of watermark catalogues as well as histories of paper mills in various regions, including reproductions of watermarks attributed to those mills or prevalent in their locales. The Society's first major publication was Edward Heawood's *Watermarks, Mainly of the 17th and 18th Centuries* (Hilversum, 1950), the only attempt at a continuation of Briquet, less comprehensive of course, but still helpful in unexpected ways (such as in its prefatory notes on the bibliographical use of watermarks). Also noteworthy is the Society's 'New Briquet', a facsimile of *Les Filigranes* (1968) with corrections, supplementary remarks, and an extensive commentary. Some of the Society's monographs contain valuable information about trade practices. Others were intended mainly as reference guides for the identification of early papers. With that purpose solely in mind, the late Gerhard Piccard devised an elaborate classification scheme for the watermarks he reproduced in more than fifteen thematic *Findbücher* based on the holdings of the Wasserzeichenkartei Piccard im Hauptstaatsarchiv Stuttgart. The Staatliche Archivverwaltung Baden-Württemberg has overseen the publication of Piccard's tracings since 1961.

Librarians and bibliographers often describe paper more to place it in its historical context than to specify its origins. Instead of primarily collecting watermarks, they try to record all the relevant information about the paper they examine, noting the presence of a watermark (if there is one) in the context of other distinguishing features. While this form of evidence may supply only general answers to particular questions, it promises to resolve more problems in the long run and, in my opinion, bears greater relevance for historical studies. The thesaurus of paper terms recently compiled by Sidney E. Berger for the Bibliographic Standards Committee of the Rare Books and Manuscripts Section of the Association of College and Research Libraries provides a common nomenclature for signalling the special attributes of paper for the purposes of machine-readable library cataloguing; prudently, Berger did not attempt to standardize the names of watermarks. An article by G. Thomas Tanselle, *SB* 24 (1971), recommends a systematic procedure for recording the properties of book paper by taking a variety of measurements and by analysing its thickness, substance, colour, strength, opacity, and other salient characteristics. Philip Gaskell's *New Introduction to Bibliography* (Oxford, 1972; corrected reprint, 1974) has codified this approach and explains how it relates to the technology and business practices of the papermaking trade. In *SB*, 37 (1984), David L. Vander Meulen shows how to distinguish specimens of unwatermarked laid paper by taking precise measurements of wire lines, chain lines, and tranchefiles. Articles in *The Library* by R.W. Chapman (1926–7), Edward Heawood (1930–1 and 1947–8), Graham Pollard (1941–2), Herbert Davis (1951–2), Philip Gaskell (1957), and Rupert C. Jarvis (1959) have made it possible to describe paper used in England during the seventeenth and eighteenth centuries in contemporary terms, using the language of the stationers who dealt in paper and of the printers who consumed it. This distinguished series of articles is one of the Bibliographical Society's major contributions to the field of paper history.

Researchers in several fields can now learn to name the paper they encounter. Historians can read advertisements, business correspondence, publishers' ledgers, and other documents of the English book trade with a better understanding of the technical vocabulary of the time. They can explain more confidently what it is to write upon superfine wove hot-pressed quarto post, or why an author might request a few extra copies on royal to be presented with his compliments. They can infer what early watermarks actually meant, whether they designated a certain size of paper, its quality, or origin. A crowned fleur-de-lis, for example, should alert a researcher to the possibility that he is handling good-quality demy writing paper, a largish size more likely to be used in drawing up accounts than in writing correspondence. Bibliographers can indicate the size of a book in the same words as would have been used by its printer or publisher, by calculating the size of the sheet from the dimensions of an uncut leaf, determining what that size would have been called at a given time, and perhaps even verifying the results, if the book displays a typical watermark of its day. Those who consult bibliographies may need this information to identify books styled as foolscap folio, demy quarto, or with other such expressions of size and format occurring in early sources. In this regard, several recent bibliographies serve as important resources for the history of paper, most notably Philip Gaskell's bibliographies of the printing of John Baskerville (1959; reprinted with additions and corrections, 1973) and the Foulis Press (1964; reprinted with additions and corrections, 1986), Allan Stevenson's catalogue of eighteenth-century botanical literature (1961), D.F. Foxon's catalogue of English verse, 1701–50 (1975), and C. William Miller's remarkably thorough account of Benjamin Franklin's printing activities in Philadelphia (1974). These works testify that the study of paper need not be a haphazard pursuit, that it can be practised systematically on the basis of scientific principles, and that it can lead to reliable results.

This new-found scientific rigour has, however, sometimes discouraged practitioners of paper history, who have had to cope with the formidably high standards set by bibliographers like Allan Stevenson as well as the daunting example of self-taught, self-reliant researchers like Briquet. No one has extolled more convincingly than Allan Stevenson the scholarly benefits obtainable from the evidence of paper. He also devised techniques for the measurement and verbal description of watermarks, especially suitable for recording the names and initials of papermakers along with dates and other text worked into the main design or included in a countermark. A paper historian can employ this helpful shorthand to inventory large numbers of watermarks without having to undertake the labour of tracing them or the expense of ordering photographs. On the other hand, Stevenson insisted on absolute accuracy when comparing the various states of a watermark and demonstrated brilliantly what this precision can achieve in *The Problem of the Missale Speciale*, published by the Bibliographical Society in 1967. Photographs or (better still) beta-radiographs can tell the entire life history of a paper mould and of the wire profile that delineates watermarks in paper, by chronicling the movements of the wire profile across the mould and the progressive deterioration of that profile or outline during heavy use at the vat. Although tracings found in watermark catalogues might be useful clues, Stevenson showed that they cannot provide conclusive proof in many bibliographical applications. Furthermore, these tracings will often disappoint the bibliographer because they are usually derived from manuscripts in archives rather than from printed books, which are harder to examine. For the most part, Briquet's tracings are based on archival research, Heawood's on early imprints (but mainly those in the library of the Royal Geographical Society). Stevenson's method obliges his followers to seek filigranistic evidence on their own, to search as many books as they can find for analogous watermarks, and to record what they discover using expensive and unwieldy equipment. Only a few have mastered this method, and none, to my knowledge, has relied on it extensively except for the study of incunabula.

That is not to say that watermark research has languished because of Stevenson's formidable example. Scholars have obtained gratifying results from watermark evidence in the study of manuscripts as diverse as those of Mozart and Michelangelo. Jane Roberts's *Dictionary of Michelangelo's Watermarks* (Milan, 1988) describes and illustrates a multitude of anchors, birds, crossbows, and other sixteenth-century specimens, more than a hundred in all. She has been able to reunite two studies for the ceiling of the Sistine Chapel that may have been executed on the same sheet and has been able to date drawings made on paper that the artist also used for correspondence. By identifying watermarks, and measuring them if necessary, Alan Tyson has determined which papers Mozart used at various stages of his career. He has been able to redate some of Mozart's compositions and to explain in what order he wrote various portions of larger works such as *La Clemenza di Tito*. He has reconstructed the rondo for piano and orchestra (K. 386) and restored its original ending after discovering fragments of the manuscript, which had been broken up and dispersed during the nineteenth century. Portions of watermarks on the leaves he found and on others that survive reveal how they were once arranged and which ones are still missing. Tyson recognizes that watermarks are twins, that there is a crucial difference between the mould-side and the felt-side of paper, and that every part of the sheet must be accounted for, criteria still neglected by filigranologists despite the teachings of Allan Stevenson. His rigorous analysis of watermarks is just one reason why bibliographers should be grateful for his *Mozart: Studies of the Autograph Scores* (Cambridge, MA, 1987).

Nevertheless, neither Roberts nor Tyson can be said to have employed the methods exemplified in *The Problem of the Missale Speciale*, nor could it be expected in the specialist manuscript studies that serve the purposes of musicology and art history. The identification of different states of the wire profile on each mould of a pair and the comparison of those different states with similar stocks of paper used in other circumstances can only be accomplished by the examination of paper in quantity, which is most easily accomplished by the perusal of printed books. The beauty of Stevenson's proof lies in the abundance of his evidence and the variety of sources where he obtained it. Theoretically, bibliographers could employ his techniques with any book printed on handmade paper, but, for obvious reasons, they have preferred to use them only when the number of books in the sample can be delimited conveniently, such as in the early years of printing. The best recent examples of this approach and the best illustrations of its potential are articles on the dating of the *Catholicon* by Eva Ziesche and Dierk Schnitger in *Archiv für Geschichte des Buchwesens*, volume XXI (1980), and by Paul Needham in *PBSA*, 76 (1982).

Problems arising from the international traffic in paper may also dampen the zeal of bibliographers. The products of a paper mill sometimes travelled long distances and crossed several borders before reaching their intended market. Imported paper can figure more or less prominently in a country's printed output, depending on tariff barriers, the cost of transportation, the cost of manufacture at home and abroad, and the ability of domestic mills to satisfy local demand at competitive prices. At various times English printers relied on imports from Normandy, Brittany, Holland, and Genoa, just as American printers once depended on supplies shipped from England. A bibliographer who wishes to account for the influence of foreign trade may have to learn the business practices, manufacturing techniques, and technical languages of several different countries. This last obligation has been less of a burden since the publication of Emile J. Labarre's comprehensive, multilingual *Dictionary and Encyclopaedia of Paper and Paper-Making* (2nd edn, London and Toronto, 1952; supplement by E.G. Loeber, Amsterdam, 1967), but scholars still cannot turn to an adequate international bibliography of paper history, an obstacle soon to be removed by the efforts of the Deutsche Bücherei of Leipzig, which is preparing a four-volume compilation listing monographs, periodical literature, and manuscripts from the seventeenth century to the present day.

The bibliographical analysis of paper will rarely amount to much unless it is informed with a thorough knowledge of paper as an artefact, as the product of human labour at a given time and place and in certain historical and technological conditions. The more that is known about paper mills and their techniques, the more reliable will be the evidence of watermarks attributed to those mills. Conversely, the evidential value of watermarks diminishes in countries like the United States, where paper mills and papermakers have yet to be named and dated systematically. Very little can be said about the Italian paper favoured by printers in England and America during the eighteenth century, except that it is Italian, and probably shipped from Genoa. A growing appreciation of the artefact promises to remedy this state of affairs, preeminently with the publication of comprehensive histories of papermaking in various countries, but also with the organization of societies for furthering paper history, and with the formation of collections containing artefacts of the paper trade.

Some national histories reach out to an international audience, while others serve a more local clientele. Henk Voorn has recently completed his definitive three-volume history of paper mills in the Netherlands (1960–85), a model of its kind, and essential reading for those who seek information about Dutch imports into England and America. (Voorn's text is summarized in English.) The three-volume *History of Paper in Spain* (Madrid, 1978–82) by Oriol Valls i Subirà is sumptuously illustrated, fabulously expensive, and painfully necessary for studying the introduction of the papermaking craft into Europe. Alfred H. Shorter based his geographical survey of early paper mills in England (1957) on insurance policies, notices in newspapers, and other contemporary documents. Shorter also wrote a narrative history of English papermaking (1972), which can be used alongside the magisterial economic history of D.C. Coleman (1958; reprinted 1975), the technological history of Richard L. Hills (1988), and the remarkably perceptive view from within the trade by A. Dykes Spicer (1907). The most authoritative history of early American papermaking is Dard Hunter's sumptuous, large folio *Papermaking by Hand in America* (Chillicothe, OH, 1950), a *tour de force* of one-man bookmaking, set by the author in a handcut type and hand-printed on handmade paper manufactured at the author's own mill. As a further tribute to the artefact, the watermarks discussed in the volume were recreated in tipped-in samples, which can be viewed just like the originals.

Hunter spared no expense to record and evoke the paper mills of the preindustrial era. Substantial portions of his text reappeared in *Papermaking in Pioneer America* (Philadelphia, 1952; reprinted New York and London, 1981), a sensible alternative to the limited edition, which currently retails for about $6,500.

Several organizations have helped to co-ordinate the efforts of scholars by sponsoring conferences and by publishing journals. The journal *Papiergeschichte* (1951–76) appeared under the auspices of the Verein der Zellstoff- und Papier-Chemiker und -Ingenieure in association with the Forschungsstelle Papiergeschichte in Mainz until 1974, when the editorial offices were transferred to the Deutsches Museum in Munich. Founded in 1959, the International Association of Paper Historians has held twenty conferences and has published a biennial yearbook as well as a quarterly bulletin, *IPH-Information*, which completed its twenty-fourth volume in 1990. Both the bulletin and the yearbook have been indexed. In May 1990 it was decided to issue the yearbook annually and to replace *IPH-Information* with a new journal titled *International Paper History*, intended to reach a wider audience through the same channels as once used by *Papiergeschichte*. The recently founded British Association of Paper Historians convened its first annual conference in 1989. It publishes a quarterly newsletter as do the Friends of the Dard Hunter Paper Museum, who are planning a journal as well as a continuing programme of annual meetings.

Collections of artefacts contain the raw material of paper history. Some museums of papermaking not only display the instruments and methods of the craft but also preserve original samples of early paper selected and sorted for research purposes. Although an imaginative use of catalogues will reveal interesting specimens in libraries, only these specialist collections offer a coherent view of paper as the surviving artefact of certain mills or of the trade in certain countries. In the United States, for example, the American Antiquarian Society and the New York Historical Society have amassed substantial holdings of early American paper in loose sheets and tantalizing fragments, systematically arranged by the names, initials, and motifs of their watermarks. Germany appears to have the largest and most carefully organized collections, although various institutions in Holland, Sweden, and Great Britain have also gathered and classified significant amounts of early paper. At the John Johnson Collection in the Bodleian Library at Oxford, the advertising ephemera of English mills often occupies the same folders as the products they advertise, a juxtaposition rich in research potential. As restless as its founder, the Dard Hunter Paper Museum started in Cambridge, Massachusetts, then moved to Appleton, Wisconsin, and now resides somewhere in storage while waiting for the Institute of Paper Science and Technology to build its new quarters in Atlanta, Georgia.

Dard Hunter's tremendous energy, vast learning, and immense enthusiasm have influenced an entire generation of paper historians. With equal zeal he collected documentary evidence about the pioneering mills of America and recorded the traditional methods of village craftsmen in exotic lands. His *Papermaking: The History and Technique of an Ancient Craft* (2nd edn, New York,

1947; reprinted in 1978) remains the best general survey of the field, extending from the invention of paper in China to the nineteenth-century industrialization of the trade in Europe and America. An avid craftsman himself, and an avowed disciple of William Morris, Hunter frankly preferred handmade articles to mass-produced goods. He wrote more readily on the technology of papermaking than on sales and distribution, and more appreciatively of the skills of journeymen than of the wiles of capitalists and shopkeepers. He openly regretted the regimentation of labour in mechanized factories. This approach, which sometimes sentimentalized the artefact, coloured his view of the paper trade and narrowed the scope of the histories of paper written under his influence. American journals like *The Paper Maker* (1932–70) and *Hand Papermaking* (1986–) focus exclusively on craft techniques, the achievements of inventors, and the history of individual mills, with little or no interest in the fate of paper after it leaves the mill.

Quite independently of Hunter, some historians have discovered in papermaking a rich and largely unexplored body of information on economics, business, and technology. They can observe how the transition from craft to industry proceeded in paper mills just as clearly as in textile mills, which have usually served as their paradigm of the Industrial Revolution. At the end of the eighteenth century, some paper mills grew to be important, highly capitalized, labour-intensive concerns, whose operations have been well documented in ledgers, correspondence, legal records, and census reports. Here, historians realize, they can study the ferment of industrialization from a new vantage point, perhaps gaining new insight into the economic forces and social effects involved in becoming a big business. Their work avoids the nostalgia that suffuses historical writings in Dard Hunter's style as well as the technological determinism that pervades many accounts of the nineteenth-century trade. Judith McGaw recounts how small-town capitalists in western Massachusetts responded to the challenge of industrialization, and how the men and women they employed adapted to different living and working conditions, in *Most Wonderful Machine: Mechanization and Social Change in Berkshire Paper Making* (Princeton, 1987). Leonard Rosenband analyses the patterns of production in a large eighteenth-century manufactory, where masters intent on modernizing their facilities strove to discipline employees who still clung to their casual routines and customary privileges. After a bitter struggle, the masters supplanted the traditional rights of journeymen with an implacable factory regimen vividly described in Rosenband's Princeton doctoral dissertation, 'Work and Management in the Montgolfier Paper Mill, 1761–1804' (1980). Günter Bayerl maintains that a series of inventions contributed to the industrialization of the paper trade, a gradual process that Bayerl dates back to the Middle Ages. Drawing on a vast quantity of early technical literature, aptly cited in his *Die Papiermühle: Vorindustrielle Papiermacherei auf dem Gebiet des alten deutschen Reiches* (Frankfurt am Main, 1987), Bayerl argues that many paper mills had streamlined their production lines and were already mechanized in some department before the advent of the Hollander beater and the papermaking machine. If more rigorous, these histories of papermaking are no more concerned with the marketing and sale of paper than those that take the old-fashioned, arts-and-crafts approach. Paper was meant to be sold, they concede, yet once it becomes a commodity it seems as if it had suddenly left their realm of technology and entered a foreign territory best explored by others.

Paper could be a retail commodity, sold over the counter in various ways of interest to art historians as well as bibliographers. Based on an exhibit at the Victoria and Albert Museum, John Krill's *English Artists Paper, Renaissance to Regency* (1987) shows how the special properties of drawing papers and plate papers influenced the techniques of artists and the taste of amateurs, who, Krill reveals, could buy their art supplies as retail merchandise, as novelties packaged and promoted to catch a passing fancy. Regrettably, there is no equivalent study of early nineteenth-century writing papers, which were also elaborately packaged and fulsomely advertised to lure consumers partial to the latest fashions. Gaudily decorated quire wrappers attest to the merchandizing efforts of stationers and manufacturers, whose business methods and distribution networks surely deserve further enquiry.

Printing paper was a wholesale commodity, destined to be sold in quantity to printers through middlemen in the book trade who officiated in various capacities at various times. In many cases the route that paper took from the paper mill to the printing office still remains a mystery. No one has attempted to consolidate and interpret the stray data about the sale of printing paper that can be found in book-trade correspondence and publishers' ledgers. If paper represents half the manufacturing cost of books in the Elizabethan period, as Allan Stevenson says, then it behoves bibliographers to learn what its prevailing prices were, and who set them. In his *Golden Compasses* (Amsterdam, 1969–72), Leon Voet was able to name many of the suppliers of the Plantin Press, where paper consumed a third of the total investment in the firm. In 1566, for example, Plantin's purchases amounted to 4,529 fl. $18\frac{1}{2}$ st., a formidable portion of his total year's expenditure of 13,041 fl.

Figures for the seventeenth century are not yet at hand, but it should be possible to compare the cost of printing and of paper during the eighteenth century by analysing the accounts of William Strahan and William Bowyer, proprietors of two of the largest printing shops in London at that time. Regular customers usually supplied their own paper, as might be expected when the price was high, but many preferred to buy their paper from the printer, and these transactions occurred frequently enough and were recorded in sufficient detail to provide a good statistical sampling. On the basis of 471 entries in the Strahan ledgers, Partricia Hernlund asserts that half of the total cost of printing could be attributed to paper in her 'William Strahan's Ledgers, II: Charges for Papers, 1738–1785', *SB*, 22 (1969). A similar situation may have prevailed in the Bowyer printing shop, judging from a spot check of ten entries in *The Bowyer Ledgers* (1991), edited by Keith Maslen and John Lancaster and published conjointly by the Bibliographical Society and the Bibliographical Society of America. Jacques Rychner reports in *The Library* (1979) that the Société

Typographique de Neuchâtel recorded paper purchases and production costs for about 500 works printed from 1769 to 1789; an analysis of its ledgers should help to determine the price of paper and its effect on the price of printing in eighteenth-century Switzerland.

Paper was still a vital ingredient of bookmaking during the early nineteenth century, when major publishers such as Carey & Lea of Philadelphia and the Longman firm of London customarily assigned a third to a half of their manufacturing costs to the paper they requisitioned in large lots and at great expense. Bibliographers can infer and extrapolate these price figures even more confidently than before, having learned to identify the name, size, and quality of many early printing papers.

Historians of the book schooled in the French tradition can apply what they know about the structure of the book trade, and its economic context, to the study of paper as a commodity. In this spirit, Annie Parent devoted the first chapter of her *Les Métiers du livre à Paris au XVIe siècle* (Geneva, 1974) to the paper trade of that city, composed of licensed papermakers, paper merchants, and *libraires marchands*, each fulfilling a specific role in a complex hierarchy sanctioned by the University. Paper merchants became so rich and powerful that they could buy the entire output of one or more outlying mills for as much as two years in advance. They might keep in stock as many as 800 or 1,000 reams, to be sold as needed to the major booksellers of the city, who in turn supplied the printers who worked in their behalf. Likewise, paper merchants owned the means of production in sixteenth-century Genoa. Master papermakers pledged to them a certain quantity of their annual output in return for rags and manufacturing facilities, a submissive relationship attested by notarial contracts and elucidated by Manlio Calegari in his *La Manifattura genovese della carta (sec. XVI–XVIII)* (Genoa, 1986).

The London paper trade deserves a similar analysis. D.C. Coleman has identified some of the most prominent wholesale stationers of the eighteenth century and has described their relations with their suppliers and their customers. They too accumulated enormous wealth, which they could invest in paper mills and other manufacturing enterprises. A parliamentary commission of 1837 was informed that the stationery firm of Henry and Sealy Fourdrinier cleared £14,000 a year in profits before engaging in the development of their papermaking machine. Some stationers dealt in rags, and a few even entered the publishing business. Coleman also sought out invaluable information on credit terms and payment methods, such as the bill of exchange, which a papermaker might draw on a stationer and make payable to a rag merchant. More information of this kind is needed to understand the practices of the London trade and to learn about the rôle of wholesale stationers in other publishing centres. As a first step, we could register the names of wholesale stationers through the compilation of book-trade directories.

There are many more questions that need to be answered about the consumption of paper by the book trade. In what circumstances would a papermaker sell through a consignment house instead of a wholesale stationer?

Were publishers ever compelled to stock paper, or did they always purchase just enough for the books currently in press? Presumably, they would not want to tie up precious capital. What considerations moved them to contract with several mills to supply a single publication? How did the paper requirements of periodical publishers differ from those of book publishers? What grades of paper were deemed most appropriate for certain literary genres and publishing formats? Just as literary historians might like to know more about the meaning of eighteenth-century fine-paper copies – such as an author would distribute to friends and patrons – so cultural historians might want to survey the market for mass-produced fine-paper copies during the nineteenth century. Even then readers coveted the subtle distinctions that superior paper could confer on a book and its owner.

But these publications for a bibliophile market were exceptional. Nineteenth-century papermakers strove for a strict uniformity in weight, texture, and colour, and nearly achieved it with the introduction of mass-production technology. Chemical additives and mechanical improvements enabled them to manufacture a regular, reliable, and anonymous product. Regrettably the anonymity of machine-made paper has deterred bibliographical research in nineteenth-century papermaking. Historical research also suffers because of an emphasis on the technology of the machine, which has diverted attention from its economic impact as well as the economic circumstances that made it necessary. R.H. Clapperton's *The Paper-Making Machine: Its Invention, Evolution, and Development* (Oxford, 1967) contains fascinating details about patents, technological challenges, and engineering breakthroughs, with barely a word about the products of the first machines, and only a cursory mention of how they were sold to the papermaking trade. The story has yet to be told of the Fourdriniers' frantic attempts to remain solvent while building and testing the machinery that would bear their name. Unbeknown to Clapperton, they indulged in financial chicanery and desperate speculations that hastened their descent into bankruptcy. Their attempts to protect their investment, and the efforts of their creditors to cover their losses, greatly influenced the diffusion of machine technology in England. Next to nothing is known about the motivations of the papermakers who bought and installed the first Fourdrinier machines and who paid large licensing fees to the patentees in the expectation of tremendous profits from the sale of mass-produced goods.

What goods were manufactured on these early Fourdriniers also needs to be investigated. Contemporary observers praised the machines' proficiency in making newsprint, copperplate papers, and speciality products like pottery tissue, but said little about the profitability of these wares or their effect on the market. It would be useful to know when book publishers began to rely on machine paper, and whether they looked for superior printing qualities or merely a cheap and plentiful supply. If they sought to economize, then an enquiring paper historian might try to reckon how much they were able to lower the unit cost of their publications, and how much of their cost benefits were passed on to the consumer. With these figures at our disposal, we would be in a better position to interpret the downward spiral of book prices during the nineteenth century and to understand the role of cheap printed matter in the development of a mass reading public.

The information is at hand in papermakers' archives, publishers' ledgers, and in the books themselves. Despite the daunting uniformity of mass-produced paper, the products of some early machines can be identified. Among other distinguishing features, the stitching that joined the two ends of a machine's wire web left a characteristic mark, not unlike a watermark though less conspicuous, less predictable, and occurring far less frequently. A sewing mark can be as good as a papermaker's signature should a document come to light that names the manufacturer of the paper where that telltale sewing appears. The proprietors of the first machine in America experimented with several different stitching techniques, which help to date their mass-produced paper and to ascertain who purchased it and for what purposes. Mathew Carey, Philadelphia's most enterprising publisher, bought large quantities for a variety of publications: atlases, scientific treatises, law reports, reprinted fiction, and, appropriately, a plea for the protection of domestic manufactures.

This is only one example of how the analysis of evidence in paper can lead to a better understanding of its status as an artefact and its role as a commodity. Likewise, a knowledge of manufacturing techniques and trade practices can dispel some of the mysteries encountered in the evidence. The Bibliographical Society has witnessed a striking demonstration of these three approaches to paper studies, and of their interdependence, in the work of Sir Walter Greg. Just a year after the publication of *Les Filigranes*, Greg employed Briquet's techniques to explain perplexing similarities exhibited by a group of ten Shakespearian quartos variously dated 1600, 1608, and 1619. A tabulation of watermarks proved that all ten were actually printed in 1619 to form a collection published by Thomas Pavier, who had reasons of his own for not being entirely frank about this venture. *The Library* published Greg's findings in 1908 along with supplementary remarks partly intended to answer queries of A.H. Huth, who wondered why the measurements of certain watermarks appeared to differ in different copies. Greg himself was puzzled by the 'mixture' of so many different watermarks in these plays. As Allan Stevenson has shown, Greg was hard pressed to account for these anomalies because he could not say how the paper moulds were made nor how the paper was supplied to Pavier's printer.

Curiously, the technical and commercial knowledge that would have clinched Greg's arguments did not, in his opinion, belong within the precincts of bibliography. Greg, one of the first to exploit the evidence in paper, hesitated to admit within his chosen field other aspects of paper studies that might have supported his conclusions. His presidential address before the Bibliographical Society in 1932, published in *The Library* during that year, has become famous for its narrow definition of bibliography, which demarcated the discipline – and thus by implication, the Society's activities – so as to exclude all bookish pursuits that were not directly related to the transmission of literary texts. Studies of type and bookbinding were admissible in so far as they helped to date and identify early books. A history of paper mills or a study of papermaking technology would not qualify by his definition, although worthy enough in other respects. Yet no one would begrudge the title of bibliographer to Allan Stevenson, whose expertise outside the professional limits set by Greg enabled him to vindicate Greg in two articles contributed to *SB*, 4 (1951–2). Yes, explained Stevenson, the Pavier watermarks differ in dimensions because watermarks are twins, and they are twins because the team at the vat handled pairs of moulds. Yes, the Pavier quartos contain a multitude of watermarks, not a common phenomenon but nevertheless explicable if, as Stevenson suspected, French merchants bought from the mills of Normandy and Brittany small batches of variously water-marked paper to be sorted through and batched together, come what may, in large lots for export to England. Thus a history of French paper mills and a time-and-motion study of the interchange between vatman and coucher might participate in the 'serious science' of bibliography.

Currently, the study of paper extends across many disciplines, opening new fields of research in some and consolidating the achievements of others. In none, however, has it reached the point where its methodology has fully matured, where its relevance is immediately obvious. This leaves intriguing possibilities, particularly for learning about book production. If, in Greg's words, bibliography is 'the study of books as material objects', then the fundamental material of books should be esteemed as something more than a vehicle of text or a source of evidence.

Further reading

Coleman, D.C. *The British Paper Industry, 1495–1860: A Study in Industrial Growth*. Oxford, 1958

Hills, Richard L. *Papermaking in Britain, 1488–1988: A Short History*. 1988

Shorter, A.H. *Paper Making in the British Isles: An Historical and Geographical Study*. Newton Abbot, 1971

Spicer, A. Dykes. *The Paper Trade: A Descriptive and Historical Survey of the Paper Trade from the Commencement of the Nineteenth Century*. 1907

Stevenson, Allan H. 'Briquet and the Future of Paper Studies', in *Briquet's Opuscula* (Briquet's complete works other than *Les Filigranes*). Hilversum, 1955

Typographic studies

NICOLAS BARKER

The word 'serif' is odd. Its form suggests an Arabic origin, but it does not appear in print until the beginning of the nineteenth century, and then only in the context of the absence of that which it describes, the transverse stroke at the tips of letters. What is more, the multiplicity of spellings applied to this phenomenon, 'sans serif', 'seriffe', even 'surryph', suggest that the typefounders who first printed the word did so from oral tradition. The late Harry Carter, looking for an explanation, noted that typefounders were the only people who needed regularly to refer to the minutiae of letter forms, and that English typefounders, before William Caslon introduced the first native or vernacular types, got their matrices from Holland. The Dutch word *schreef*, a sharp or bounding line, might, he thought, have been rendered as 'serif' by an English tongue, and this, with a fashionable French privative, achieved a complex, but not Arabic, etymology for 'sans serif'.

This reminds us of an important factor in the study of printing types and letter forms in general, viewed historically. Making things, buildings, works of art, and *a fortiori* letters, is not something usually thought worth describing by those who make them or their contemporaries, even if the artefact itself is noticed. Moxon's *Mechanick Exercises* (1683–4) is a remarkable expection to this rule. The study of letters is thus a mainly archaeological discipline: it can only restore the crucial fact, the process by which letters were made, and the hand of the man who made them, by observation and comparison after the event. The history of printing types has mainly been reconstructed by this means, rarely assisted by documentary evidence of any sort. But, as such, they form the one strand that is common to the study of books and printed documents of all sorts (bibliology, I like to call it, rather than bibliography, a complex word corrupted by too many different usages). All such documents have a common characteristic: they are made up of letters.

How can the student of letter-forms build up an organic picture of the history and development of printing types, and how – if at all – does it relate to the

This text is, in part, an abridgement of material presented in my Presidential Address to the Bibliographical Society, 20 April, 1982, under the title 'Bibliography and Letter-Forms: The Study of Script, Type and Digital Letter-Formation', and in the Hanes Lecture for 1989, 'The Future of Typographic Studies'.

contemporary progress of written letters? Harry Carter provided the answer in *A View of Early Typography*, in a few clear comprehensive words: 'I had rather name typefaces by the conventional body that would best fit them, Pica, Long Primer, Minion, and such, than by numbers', and 'much the best indication of the character of a face of type is the name of the person who cut it'. To which he added, 'Concentrated in that is all manner of information as to place and time, circumstances and relationships on which a history can be built: the knowledge of who cut it enables one not only to describe a face of type, it makes it worth describing – it fits it into the whole scheme of things.'[1]

Now this may seem a tall order, especially in early times before type-body 'names acquired fixed meanings' and punch-cutting for types was a recognized profession, with named professors. But in the course of a study of fifteenth-century Greek types, I have, I think, established that in Italy, at least, and perhaps elsewhere, types were cast on bodies which stood in proportion to each other. This in turn, in Italy, depends on a metric scale, corresponding with the old Byzantine Imperial scale, uniform throughout the Levant. This will not surprise anyone who has worked in a printing house and knows the importance of proportion in making up pages of types of different body, and in the use of furniture cut to multiples of a pica. What is interesting, however, is that the same metric scale seems to have been used in determining the intervals between lines in the ruling of manuscripts, again at least in Italy and in the fifteenth century.

Measurement is essentially a mechanical affair. What Carter aptly calls the 'character' of a face of type, and the same word could as aptly be applied to written letters, is a more subjective business. It does not reside in easily definable differences in the shape of individual letters (the palaeographer's stand-by) but in the identification, the naming, of the person who cut or wrote or otherwise framed it. Fifteenth-century scribes could write what we now call different formal scripts with such virtuosity, such self-conscious accuracy, that to distinguish one from another one must look behind the shapes for the character of the man who framed them. The same character can be seen in the hand of the engraver who produces letters of quite different forms for the printer. If his name is rarely known, in the fifteenth century at least, his work is none the less identifiable. The very different types cut by Francesco Griffo all bear his mark of a common hand, as visible a sign of the artificer's personality as written script can be of the scribe's.

One of the questions discussed in *A View of Early Typography* was the nature of the models used for the first printed letters. Carter advanced the view that 'what was conceived of as better was found in the past, in an old model'. This 'backward look' undoubtedly contributed to the acceptance of the oldest letter of all, the antique Roman capital to which the geometry of Feliciano seemed to give an ideal symmetry, freed from the imperfection of the human hand. In the same way the B36 and B42 textura types, the I31 and I30 script types, are idealized

1 H. Carter, *A View of Early Typography up to about 1600* (Oxford, 1969), p. 23.

forms, and the ability to produce models for them may have been Peter Schoeffer's special contribution to the partnership of invention. Actual traces of the models used are, in the nature of things, unlikely to be found. Such pieces of script perish once their purpose is served; the intervening processes, a rough sketch of a curve, or verbal instructions, written or oral, or rejected punches, are still less likely to be found. Still, I think that it is possible to prove that the model for Aldus's first Greek type was a piece of writing by Immanuel Rhusotas, and that the five variant forms of lower-case in the *De Aetna* roman type also cut by Francesco Griffo for Aldus are as clear evidence of a model as they are of his intention to reproduce in metal the elasticity and variability of script.[2]

In turn, the Aldine model became the canon for roman type: for italic too, fused with the alternative Arrighiesque model that followed twenty years after, Aldus's model gained general currency. The great French punch-cutters of the 1530s, Garamont, Simon de Colines, Augereau, lent it their authority. Granjon and Haultin carried it abroad. Christoffel van Dijck adapted it for the innovatory demands of Dutch printing in the seventeenth century. This in turn became the model for Caslon's roman and italic, the vernacular English 'old face'. Garamont's *gros romain* roman itself was advertised for sale as late as 1799 by the Zatta typefoundry in Venice.

By this time, far-reaching changes had taken place in the shape of letters, both written and printed: both processes had mutually left their mark on each other. The formal script, both upright and sloped, of the late sixteenth-century writing masters, notably Giovanfrancesco Cresci, adopted the characteristics of roman and italic type, as well as evolving the *corsivo* script that led to the English 'roundhand'. The capitals of Cresci's disciple Luca Horfei, engraved on stone or copper plate, had a vertical stress that was further accentuated by Nicolas Jarry and the calligraphers of Louis XIV. This script, rationalized by geometry and further modified by Philippe Grandjean's graver, led to the prototype 'modern face'. Baskerville turned his experience as a writing-master and engraver on stone into further typographic innovation. François-Ambroise and Pierre-François Didot, in creating the first modern face types, did not ignore current calligraphy: the italic reflects the style of Montfort, D'Autrepe, and the like with a grace that recommended it to Stanley Morison as the model for the italic for the Times New Roman, an unlikely but successful match with Granjon's *gros cicero*.

I have tried to point to one or two cross-channels of influence between different modes of creating letters in four centuries. It would be equally possible to extend the scope of 'influence' to include the vast range of pressures, social and economic, artistic and mechanical, which shape any visual expression of human activity. Something of this sort would be necessary to explain the proliferation of letter-designs that followed the Industrial Revolution. Letters became plainer (and were imitated with ever more – for those anxious to identify

---

2 G. Mardersteig, 'Aldo Manuzio e i caratteri di Francesco Griffo da Bologna', *Studi di bibliografia e di storia in onore di Tammaro de Marinis* (Verona, 1964), III, 105–47; N. Barker, *Aldus Manutius and the Development of Greek Script and Type in the Fifteenth Century* (Sandy Hook, NJ, 1985).

them – agonizing fidelity), and also more exotic. The return to historicism that followed the invention of the automatic punch-cutting machine in 1885 by Linn Boyd Benton, and its dependent type-casting systems, the Monotype and the Linotype, is an interesting and significant repetition of what took place during and after the invention itself.

The transition from hand-set to machine-set type had just begun when Bradshaw at Cambridge began to correspond with Holtrop, his great counterpart at the Royal Library at the Hague, and began the practice whose theory of the 'backward look' was formulated in the passage just quoted. From that correspondence, and its immediate products, J.W. Holtrop's *Monuments typographiques des Pays-Bas au Quinzième Siècle* (The Hague, 1856–68) and William Blades's *Life and Typography of William Caxton* (1861), the modern study of printing type can be dated. How much of that history had already been written can be derived from Stanley Morison's essay, 'On the Classification of Typographical Variations', originally published as an introduction to the first fascicle of *Type Specimen Facsimiles* (1963). Its title is somewhat misleading, for it was, in effect, a compelling if idiosyncratic account of the historiography of type. Led by a natural sympathy, Morison gave rather more than their due to Blades and his other hero, Talbot Baines Reed. But he was right to seize the importance of two practical men, Blades the printer and Reed the typefounder, as an important moderating influence on the academic research of librarians like Bradshaw and Campbell, and to point out the significance of the Caxton Exhibition of 1877 and the foundation of the St Bride Printing Institute with its library as landmarks.

Morison was also right to see the critical importance of visual evidence in this history. He drew attention to the pioneering work of Joseph Ames's *Typographical Antiquities* (1749), with its plates, and also to that of Dom Placidus Braun, librarian of the monastery of SS Ulrich and Afra at Augsburg, who printed a catalogue of its books (1791–6) with plates, among them illustrations of sixty types, showing complete alphabets (no easy task to compile), of early printed books. Laire and Panzer simultaneously emphasized the importance of letter forms, and the latter reinforced the practice of assigning unsigned books to printers on the basis of types used in signed books by reference to reproductions. Braun's plates were singled out for praise by England's first scientific bibliographer, Adam Clarke. Morison himself noted in Blades's *Caxton* the 'infinitely (the word is not too strong) more subtle means of reproduction than those available to earlier scholars', the lithographic plates of G.I.F. Tupper, closely supervised by Blades himself. Holtrop's work, equally, was illustrated with careful reproductions of type.

Blades's plates possessed a quality that none since has attained: Tupper, no doubt instructed by Blades, reproduced the exact image of the types; that is, without the distortion of ink-spread. In typefounders' terms, these were the equivalent of 'smokes', carbon proofs of punches. The inaccuracy of photographs of printed pages has complicated the path of palaeotypography ever since. Still, photography had its immediate uses. Holtrop (1856) was followed by

Blades (1861), Thierry-Poux (1890), and Konrad Burger (1892), who successively initiated 'the production of facsimiles on a national basis' for Holland and
Belgium, France, and Germany and Italy.

The importance of visual evidence came of age, so to speak, at the end of the
nineteenth century in the use of photography. The lantern-slide lectures given
by Emery Walker on 'Printing' to the Arts and Crafts Exhibition Society at
Burlington House (1888) and by Reed on 'Old and New Fashions in Typography'
at the Royal Society of Arts (1890), gave it an immediate impact: William Morris
was not the only, if the most famous, convert; both lecturers took the whole
history of typography as their subject. This period is full of landmarks for us. In
1886, Henry Bradshaw's *Collected Papers* (Cambridge) were published, and
Edward Gordon Duff began cataloguing the Bodleian incunabula, thus inaugur-
ating an original career to which the early history of English typography owes
much. In 1891 the new edition of Hain's *Repertorium Bibliographicum* (Leipzig)
was published with Konrad Burger's much improved *Index*, which provided for
the first time not only a list of fifteenth-century printers but a chronological
list of their works. In 1892 the Bibliographical Society was founded, with
W.A. Copinger as its first president, whose own work was to supplement and
improve that of Hain and Burger. In the same year Robert Proctor was appointed
to the British Museum and began the meteoric career crowned after his death
with the inception of its *Catalogue of the Books Printed in the XVth Century Now in
the British Museum* (1908), in which photographic illustrations of type appeared,
an innovation due to the series of plates issued by the Type Facsimile Society
(1900–9), themselves modelled on those illustrating medieval handwriting of
the Palaeographical Society (1873–94). The pioneering work of George Dunn of
Woolley Hall, whose photographs materially assisted the progress of *BMC* and
are still preserved at the British Library, deserves to be recorded.

'In the early days of the Bibliographical Society', wrote Pollard, 'while Proctor
was alive, our Presidents were mostly fifteenth-century men.' The study of
fifteenth-century types dominated early twentieth-century typographic his-
toriography. Besides those named, mainly in England, Voulliéme and Haebler in
Germany, Fumagalli, Fava, and Bresciano in Italy, Claudin, Pellechet, and
Polain in France, all extended knowledge of early typography. It is perhaps
unnecessary to single out from these pioneers the work of Konrad Burger and
Konrad Haebler, since Victor Scholderer emphasized its importance in *Studies in
Retrospect*. Pollard was uncharacteristically dismissive of Burger's work:
Scholderer, more familiar with the German background, rightly saw it as 'still
the backbone of all attempts to assess output and determine first and last dates' of
the fifteenth-century presses. There is – and again Scholderer suggests the
reason – no proper biography of Burger. Haebler has been more fortunate in this,
as in life itself. Born in Dresden in 1857, his early career was spent in the then
Royal Library there. At this time his interests lay in the history of Renaissance
Spain and Portugal (an interest he never deserted), and a visit to Spain in
1897–8 led him to the books printed there in his period. It was then that he
devised the method of identifying the work of the different presses by building up

not just alphabets, but the full lay of the case for each fount used, an improvement on Braun. He learnt of Proctor's *Index* and had a leading part in the inception of the *Gesamtkatalog der Wiegendrucke* (Leipzig etc., 1925–   ), and directed it from 1907 to 1921. Scholderer, again, has summed up the importance of his own great work, the *Typenrepertorium der Wiegendrucke*, published in Leipzig between 1905 and 1924, in terms that need not be repeated here. The use of capital M for Gothic types and Qu for roman proved an analytic device of lasting, though not universal, value. The *Handbuch der Inkunabelkunde* (Leipzig, 1925), translated into English in 1933, is a universal guide. The last fourteen years of his bibliothecal career were spent in Berlin; in his long retirement he returned to Dresden, to bookbinding history, medieval Spanish, and the Dresden Maya codex; he died in 1946.

If I have emphasized the importance of German scholarship, it is in no way to diminish the British contribution. The publication in 1898 of Proctor's famous *Index to the Early Printed Books in the British Museum* was, as Scholderer put it, 'somewhat comparable to that of the launching of HMS *Dreadnought* in 1906'.[3] It was, to alter the metaphor, the first reliable world map, in which all the different founts of type used by fifteenth-century printers were organized into a co-ordinated pattern. Subsequent scholarship has filled in a few blank areas, added geographical detail, corrected locations. In this, the British Museum *Catalogue of Books Printed in the XVth Century*, the work of Victor Scholderer's lifetime, has had a central part, in particular its plates, which, with those issued by the Gesellschaft für Typenkunde (1907–   ), have provided the vital *visual* appendix to the work of Burger, Proctor, and Haebler.

Visual comparison, the ability to compare a reliable image of printing types with another, has thus been the underlying and growing element in typographic studies that has been responsible for the major part of its progress over the last century. What Braun foreshadowed has been brought about by the application of steadily improved photographic techniques to modern print, and the universal availability of photocopies. Where deviations from that progress have taken place – the revival of the ancient Coster–Gutenberg controversy between the wars and, more recently, the sad conflict over the *Missale Speciale* – it is because visual evidence has been neglected or misunderstood. More important, it has brought about a reversal of the incunabulist's practice (but one still consistent with Bradshaw's theory). Instead of pursuing each type variant to its ultimate form, the tendency is to look back to the original form of each fount, or rather to the matrices from which each was cast. The matrices lead to the typefounder, and thence even to the punch-cutter. The importance of pursuing the general from the particular was adumbrated by Ernst Consentius in *Die Typen der Inkunabelzeit: eine Betrachtung* (Berlin, 1929), and finally exemplified by Wytze and Lotte Hellinga's *The Fifteenth-Century Printing Types of the Low Countries* (2 vols., Amsterdam, 1966).

3 V. Scholderer, 'Early Printed Books', *The Bibliographical Society 1892–1942: Studies in Retrospect*, ed. F.C. Francis (1945), p. 135.

Proctor's early death had a by-product equally unfortunate. It had been his intention to 'bring post-incunabula into line with their predecessors'. The year 1500 as a terminus for the study of early typography was canonized in the seventeenth century, and made absolute a division, scholarly, bibliothecal, and bibliopolic, which has no reality in terms of printing history. True, Proctor's *An Index to the Early Printed Books in the British Museum* (1898–1902, continued by Isaac, 1938) extended to 1520, and his successors in the compilation of *BMC*, A.W. Pollard and Victor Scholderer, and elsewhere, notably Frederick Goff and Curt Bühler in the United States, wandered easily into the next century, but the wall was there. Indeed, it was Pollard, the first editor of *BMC*, who did most to keep alive interest in later printing types. The series of ten short illustrated articles on different printing types that he wrote in the *Caxton Magazine* in 1901–2 concentrated attention on individual founts and gave body to the aesthetic preferences – another strong *visual* influence on the history of typography – expressed in William Morris's Kelmscott Press types. His reviews in *The Library* reveal the catholicity of his interests, which extended to early promotion of the work of Bruce Rogers.

But Pollard's most influential contribution to subsequent work in this field was a piece of casual journalism, the article, 'The Story of Printing: Gutenberg to Morris', that he contributed to *The Times*'s special 'Printing Number' on 10 September 1912. Stanley Morison read it, and it struck him with the blinding force of revelation. The light never left him, throughout a career that did more to illuminate both the history of typography and the face of modern printing than that of anyone else in this century. History and practical printing were indissolubly entwined in his life, and that influence, if not always beneficial, has proved a necessary counterbalance to the 'theoretical' approach of in-cunabulists.

Oddly enough, Morison, *vox clamantis* at first, found his warmest echo across the Atlantic. Theodore Low De Vinne (1828–1914) was the most accomplished printer in the western hemisphere, and the collector of a great library on the history of printing (a subject curiously ignored by that other giant of the American printing-trade and book collecting world, Robert Hoe). The building that De Vinne put up on Lafayette Street in New York City was a temple to the art; the books that he wrote, in New York, also both practical and historical, were deeply influential in creating a sense of printing history as a continuum. His library passed on his death to the American Type Founders' Company, and thence, with its curator Henry Lewis Bullen, to Columbia University. De Vinne found an apt disciple in Daniel Berkeley Updike, whose *Printing Types: Their History, Forms, and Use* (Cambridge, MA., 1922) was, and remains, the only full-length history of the subject. Originally developed as a series of lectures at the Graduate School of Business Administration at Harvard, this book was still unpublished when Morison and Updike began writing to each other; their correspondence provides the most vivid picture of the birth of the history of post-incunabular typography. From it stemmed Morison's two great folios of reproductions, *Four Centuries of Fine Printing* (1924) and *Modern Fine Printing*

(1925). Note the accent on 'fine', not repeated in Morison's third and last volume, *German Incunabula in the British Museum* (1928).

Up to this point, we might trace three different impulses in the historic study of type: that which arose from the trade and the desire by printers and typefounders to record the work of their predecessors; the scholarly or bibliothecal desire to record and tabulate the products of that work; and what might be loosely called the aesthetic approach, the desire to identify and attribute to their designers the types themselves independently of the trades that employed them, or the books or prints that were their most extensive monument. Aestheticism has a bad name, and there were those who, like William Morris, looked at past printing and judged it merely by what pleased their eye. Morison and Updike, however, shared an ascetic and scientific approach that has given their work a more lasting importance. Not denying the eye and its ability to distinguish one letter or design from another, they put history and taxonomy first. This led to an important development in the study of post-incunabular types that has come to have an increasing influence on it.

Before embarking on this, however, we must note two other factors, institutional rather than personal, which underlie and influence all individual work, then and now. First, there are the old-established printing houses, where ancient types and the equipment for making them have been preserved. Second, there are the specialist libraries where documents relating to these repositories and the trade generally have similarly gathered together. Sometimes the two become one. Both the Oxford University Press and the Plantin-Moretus Museum in Antwerp have had this dual function. There is no longer an active press in either place now, the extinction of printing at Oxford following a century and a quarter after its cessation at Antwerp. C. Ruelens and A. De Backer's *Annales Plantiniennes* (Brussels, 1865) initiated a series of studies at the latter, notably those of Max Rooses (Amsterdam, 1882–1914) and latterly of Leon Voet and H.D.L. Vervliet (*The Golden Compasses: A History and Evaluation of the Printing and Publishing Activities of the Officina Plantiniana*, 2 vols., Amsterdam, 1967 and 1972; and *Sixteenth-Century Printing Types of the Low Countries*, Amsterdam, 1968; and also, L. De Voet with Jenny Voet-Grisolle, *The Plantin Press (1555–1589): A Bibliography*, Amsterdam, 1980–), which were based on the sorting and ordering of typographical material miraculously preserved like flies in amber, and on relating it to inventories, ledgers, correspondence, and other documents, whose preservation, if more ordinary, was none the less rare.

At Oxford, Horace Hart (1840–1916), Controller of the University Press and later Printer to the University (1883–1915), embarked on a similar campaign of sorting historic and ordering new material. His findings were published in *Notes on a Century of Typography at the University Press, Oxford, 1693–1794* (Oxford, 1900). R.W. Chapman and John Johnson, Hart's successor, engaged Morison's interest in 1925; at intervals over the next forty years, type, matrices, and punches were finally sorted and identified, and the details of their acquisition and use recovered from documents. The result was *John Fell: The University Press and the 'Fell' types* (Oxford, 1967). In this great book the full story of the

University's seventeenth-century investment in types already old was set out, and the types themselves displayed and attributed to the great punch-cutters of the sixteenth century.

Among other printers whose resources have furthered typographic history, the firm of Johannes Enschedé en Zonen is first in both time and importance. Its historic types were first displayed by Johannes Enschedé, a substantial collector as well as an observant printer, in the *Specimen des caractères typographiques* (Haarlem 1768); the organization and historic research which he then undertook finally bore fruit in Charles Enschedé's *Fonderies de caractères et leur materiel dans les Pays-Bas, du XVe au XIXe siècle* (Haarlem, 1908), in which the work of early native engravers, Hendric Lettersnider and Hendric van Keere and others, mainly French, who worked in the Low Countries, was distinguished, and the relative merits of Van Dijck and Fleischmann defined; for the first time, the importance of the Egenolff-Luther foundry, in history and as a source of historic evidence, was given its due value. Finally, the Imprimerie Nationale, the repository of historic types going back to the seventeenth, if not the sixteenth century, was developed and extended in the eighteenth century, when the *roman du roi* was canonized as the progenitor of modern face types, and in the nineteenth century, when it pioneered the development of exotic types, Arthur Christian, in *Débuts de l'Imprimerie en France; L'Imprimerie Nationale; L'Hotel de Rohan* (Paris, 1904), exemplified these resources, each chapter being set in a different and appropriate historic type. The impetus of this, as of the work of Rooses, Enschedé, and Hart, in showing historic types in *use*, rather than as obsolete relics, had a powerful influence on Morison and Updike, and through them on further work in Europe and America.

The second factor in the development of these historic studies was the existence of specialist libraries, whose resources provided the vital documentation of what the eye could see and distinguish. At Leipzig, the Börsenverein, the centre of the German book trade, built up in the latter part of the nineteenth century an extensive and important collection of books on printing, as part of a library on the book trade as a whole. The collection of De Vinne, as augmented during its sojourn with the American Type Founders' Company by Bullen, fulfils an equal role in the United States at Columbia University library. The St Bride Printing Institute, founded in 1892, provided a repository for the collections of Blades and Reed, to which the Passmore collection was added; its augmentation ever since (and the loss or inaccessibility of the Leipzig collections) has made it the best specialist library of its kind in the world. Its duplicates, with Updike's collection, make the Providence Public Library collection of major importance. Finally, the Bibliothèque Nationale at Paris possesses, in the Anisson–Duperron collection, documents, in the shape of type-specimens and the working papers of printing firms, going back to the sixteenth century, whose full wealth (despite Coyecque's catalogue) remains to be explored.

These two factors, the resources of these historic printing firms and libraries, had a marked effect on the development of typographic studies after the First World War. The foundation of *The Fleuron* by Oliver Simon in 1922 provided a natural forum for Morison, Beatrice Warde, and others, in which successive discoveries in quarters were revealed. It was, however, anticipated by the Leipzig *Archiv für Buchgewerbe* (1988–   ), earlier titled, revealingly, *Archiv für Buch-druckerkunst* (1864–99), while the *Gutenberg Jahrbuch* (1926–   ) provided an outlet for typographic studies, not only of incunabular types. It was in the *Archiv für Buchgewerbe* in 1907 that Gustav Mori (1872–1950) published an article on the Luther typefoundry at Frankfurt, in which he reproduced the 1592 type-specimen, printed for Conrad Berner, successor to Christian Egenolff. The Egenolff–Berner specimen, doubtless intended for printers coming to the Frankfurt book fair, ascribed the types in it to the punch-cutters whose names 'sold' them. For the first time, documentary evidence of the independent work of Claude Garamont, Robert Granjon, and others in the sixteenth century was available.

Mori was an isolated and solitary person, and it was some time before the importance of his discovery was realized. A lawyer who had married the last descendant of the Luther family, he became fascinated by the historic documents which came to him by inheritance. A full-size facsimile of the Berner specimen followed in 1920, followed by *Das Schriftgiessereigewerbe in Frankfurt am Main und Offenbach* (Frankfurt, 1926), which reproduced it again with thirty-one other specimen sheets from 1592 to 1770s. It is hard to over-emphasize the importance of this discovery, or of the facsimiles that accompanied it. It led to the realization by Morison, Updike, and others that the specimens of typefounders had an unique importance as the means of identifying, attributing, and – ultimately – classifying printing types. Mori corresponded sporadically with Morison. The material in his hands was exhibited in 1926 at the Kunstgewerbe-Museum at Frankfurt for a brief month, under the auspices of the Third Kreisverein of the Verein Deutscher Schriftgiessereien, of which the full catalogue, *Schriftproben Deutscher Schriftgiessereien und Buchdruckereien aus den Jahren 1479 bis 1840* (Frankfurt, 1926), is still useful.

The most immediate result of his work, however, can be seen in Birrell and Garnett's *Catalogue of Typefounders' Specimens: Books Printed in Founts of Historic Importance; Works on Typefounding, Printing and Bibliography* (1928). This was the work of Graham Pollard (1903–77). It contained printers' specimens as well as those of typefounders, 'books printed in founts of historic importance and archival works that document the activities of printers and typefounders'. It emphasized the importance and filiation of founders' specimens; it was 'the first work to define the scientific value of the several categories of surviving documents'. Pollard had early made Morison's acquaintance, and the *Catalogue* was a cooperative enterprise; it was reviewed in the last volume of *The Fleuron* in terms which, if not uncritical, recognized its importance.

The closure of *The Fleuron* created the need for a further forum where matters typographic, ancient and modern, could be published and discussed. *Signature*, also founded by Oliver Simon, provided this need, its two series being interrupted by the Second World War. Ellic Howe and A.F. Johnson were among those who contributed, and Johnson collaborated with W. Turner Berry, the St Bride's

Librarian, in the *Catalogue of Specimens of Printing Types by English and Scottish Printers and Founders 1665–1830* (1935). This work represented not only an advance on previous knowledge of the native (as opposed to imported) sources of type, but also a methodological advance. The bibliographical description of the specimens was combined with a listing of the typographic contents and locations of surviving copies. Although not perfect, still less complete, this work provided a standard for similar works in English. It represented a considerable contrast to Marius Audin's *Les Livrets typographiques des fonderies françaises créés avant 1800* (Paris, 1933). Covering roughly the same period, Audin was less concerned with bibliographical description than with changes in the ownership of firms and their stock in trade. Though harder to use as a means of identifying individual specimens, it is a more reliable guide to the transmission of types.

It was a long time before typographic studies recovered from the war. Updike died in 1941; Morison's books and papers were destroyed in the same year. Presses and libraries were more concerned with immediate survival than with the further exploitation of their heritage. The first sign of revival was the new series of *Signature* in 1946. The new edition of Reed's *History of the Old English Letter Foundries* compiled and published by A.F. Johnson in 1952 gave that classic work new readers, confused though they were by the absence of any distinction between old and new text. In 1957 André Jammes in his catalogue, 'Typographia Regia', gave a foretaste of the scholarly insight into typographic history revealed in his majestic folio *La Réforme de la typographie royale sous Louis XIV: le Grandjean* (Paris, 1961). In the following year the long awaited portfolio of *Type Specimen Facsimiles* appeared. As long ago as 1942, a group of signatories had written to *The Library*, listing all known type specimens, defined as 'any piece of printing which contains an indication of the origin of the type design in which it was printed' (a Pollardian phrase), with the aim of reproducing them. Now the first series drew together the notable *fonds* which Mori had first discovered with other related sheets connecting the Frankfurt foundry with its Dutch successors. It also contained the essay by Morison 'On the Classification of Typographical Variations' (a curiously formed misnomer) alluded to above. Faithful reproductions were accompanied by notes identifying the types by various hands, of which Harry Carter was the chief.

Now archivist to the Oxford University Press, Carter had already, before the war, published a translation of P.S. Fournier le jeune's *Manuel typographique* (Paris, 1764–6).[4] He had learned to cut punches, and there was a practical rigour about his approach to the identification and description of type. His work on *Type Specimen Facsimiles*, of which the second volume, covering the Plantin *fonds* and specimens, appeared in 1972, was an accompaniment to his large share in the completion of Morison's *John Fell*. He completed another study begun by Morison, in his translation and edition of *The Le Bé Memorandum* (privately printed for André Jammes, Paris 1967), unique memorials of the punch-cutters and typefounders of the sixteenth century by three generations of

---

4 *Fournier on Typefounding* (1930; new edn, with supplementary bibliography, New York, 1973).

the Le Bé family, whose material descended to the Fourniers in the eighteenth century, a rare window on the reality, rather than the theory of the making of type. In his work on the translation of Charles Enschedé's *Fonderies de caractères*, he extended his knowledge to the identification of the wealth of old typographical material at Haarlem. A lifetime spent on this work was distilled in his 1968 Lyell lectures, published as *A View of Early Typography*, in which he addressed the problems of determining how type was made in the century after the invention with the same sense of the practical expressed with terse clarity. He also contributed the text to a facsimile of the type specimen of Delacolonge (1773), one of a series published by Menno Herzberger and A.L. van Gendt (Amsterdam, 1965–72). The large and elegant books in the series published by Il Polifilo have included several devoted to matters typographical.

Although in no way limited to such, W.Gs Hellinga's *Copy and Print in the Netherlands* (Amsterdam, 1962) dealt with material of great value to the typographic historian, as well as opening up discussion of such matters as the layout of printed matter and its correlation to illustration. It was followed in 1966 by Wytze and Lotte Hellinga's *The Fifteenth-Century Printing Types of the Low Countries*, already noted. This work not only represents a revival of the comprehensive interest in a national body of printing types of the incunabular period that engaged the heroic figures of the nineteenth century; it is also the realization in full of Bradshaw's 'natural history' method. Each fount of type is accurately defined, character by character, dated and attributed to the printer or printers who used it, and traced back to its first use, which may suggest where, and by whom, its punches were cut; the full bill of fount is illustrated. Beyond this, the book encompassed all the evidence on every edition and every copy of it brought to light in over a century of intensive research on all aspects of book production in the Netherlands in the fifteenth century, including much evidence on typography *per se*. 'HPT', as it is known, shows what can be done in a period when there are no type-specimens to guide research, and it is a criterion by which to measure future studies of later typography, to which founders' specimens will provide a guide. Another link with the past was the translation of Charles Enschedé's *Type Foundries of the Netherlands from the Fifteenth to the Nineteenth Centuries*, based mainly on an account first published in French in 1908. This had passed through the hands of Jan van Krimpen, and was translated with revisions and notes by Harry Carter, with the assistance of Netty Hoeflake, and edited by Lotte Hellinga (Haarlem, 1978); the resultant text was of some complexity, although, unlike Reed-Johnson, new material was clearly indicated. There was thus much that was new, as well as the original text now available in English and printed from handset new Dutch type, perhaps the last of its kind and thus itself a historic monument.

The founding of the Printing Historical Society in 1964 represents another coming of age, so to speak, in typographic history. Although devoted to the history of all aspects of printing, a strongly technological base has tended to direct interest towards the mechanical improvements of the later period, the eighteenth and nineteenth centuries. This has resulted in the publication of useful facsimiles of later specimen books, as well as important articles in the Society's *Journal*, edited by James Mosley, librarian of St Bride's, and himself a notable exponent of the history of letter forms in general, and author of *British Type-Specimens before 1831: A Handlist* (Oxford, 1984).

No account of recent type-historical literature would be complete without mention of György Haimann's monograph on *Nicholas Kis: A Hungarian Punch-Cutter and Printer 1650–1702* (San Francisco, 1983). The extraordinary circumstances by which a Hungarian schoolmaster came to fill the vacuum left in Amsterdam by the death of Van Dijck, providing a distinctive advance upon the Aldine-Garamont roman and italic – in which the seeds of modern face can be seen – and whose punch-cutting skill gained not him but his types a reputation that stretched from Georgia to Sweden, from Italy to America – all this demands, and has found, a study which will commend itself to the historian of type as surely as to the Hungarian patriot. It has a further importance to us here. It is the first full-length biography of a punch-cutter. The engraving of steel punches is the *fons et origo* of type. Kis's own autobiography, shortly to be published in English, has the same importance as *The Le Bé Memorandum*.

What of the future? When Morison wrote the essay prefixed to *Type Specimen Facsimiles*, 1, his title reflected an increased absorption with the transmission of written to printed letter forms, and also with the much-vexed question of nomenclature. Nomenclature is a will-o'-the-wisp that has diverted palaeographers, historians of print, and modern type-designers equally. Each group has responded in its different way: the first prefers descriptive words; the second a Carterian 'common name'; the third allusive appellations. This troubled Morison. *The Library*, once open to every aspect of the history of books, had in his lifetime become increasingly preoccupied with textual bibliography. True, the Bibliographical Society's monograph series, which had early included Duff's *Early English Printing* (1895) and Proctor's *The Printing of Greek in the Fifteenth Century* (1900), persevered with Colonel Frank Isaac's patient extension of Duff's work, *English and Scottish Printing Types 1501–35, 1508–41* (Bibliographical Society, 1930), but left his *English Printing Types of the Sixteenth Century* (1936) to be published in the same series as Berry and Johnson's *Catalogue of Specimens*. The focus of the Society's interests had moved away, and Morison regretted it, viewing the publication of Bowers's *Principles of Bibliographical Description* (Princeton, 1949) as a limitation, rather than an extension, of bibliographical investigation. It was, he conceded, 'a bright, finished performance', but sadly limited as to printing type. Yet Bowers put his finger on the main point: suggesting that the main text type of any book described should be identified, he wrote 'when possible this type should be identified . . . but for books at this period [that of hand-press printing] precise identification is usually difficult'. Morison saw the difficulty:

There is no 'Descriptive Principles of Typography' as an equivalent to Professor Bowers's 'Descriptive Principles of Bibliography'. We do not even have a monograph on the body sizes of type, or the faces cast upon them, in the sixteenth century and later; we know little of the origin, and still less of the history, of the habit of casting a large face on a small body, that is, what the Germans called Grobe and the French Gros Œil. We have no documentation on the development of type-design consciously viewed as a means of reducing the real space occupied by the letters while maintaining their appearance; no study of the competition, expressed in terms of type-design, in the Bible trade of the sixteenth and seventeenth centuries. The creation of types for the use of newspapers (as distinct from newsbooks) has not been investigated. We need to know the precise sources from which matrices for the types, or the means by which parcels of cast type, reached London and the universities in the Elizabethan period. The steps by which 'black-letter' was abandoned in favour of 'Roman' have not been traced. These are only some of the typographical and historical questions that await treatment.[5]

All this is still true. The real reason why letters have not been studied, as they should be, as *organic* structures, is that they are so hard to identify, let alone define. It needs a trained eye, equipped to see the similarities and differences (perhaps a single letter in a fount of over a hundred) that connect or distinguish types. Blades had such an eye, as his Caxton plates prove. So did Morison, vividly demonstrated in his analysis of the characteristics (the individual 'f', 'j' and '?') that distinguished 'Clay's Long Primer No. 3' and condemned the forgeries of Forman and Wise. Few people combine such optical sensitivity with historical awareness.[6] But help is on the way. Charles Bigelow has published a series of articles called 'Technology and the Aesthetics of Type' and 'The Principles of Digital Type'. His objective is to define the problems (and their solutions) of converting traditional letter forms, framed by hand and eye, into mechanized images of acceptable clarity. What Bigelow writes, with admirable thoroughness and clarity, is about contemporary letter-design: it can as easily be applied to the identification of letter forms of the past. The means in both cases is the same: the combination of modern optical technology with the computer, the use of lasers to convey the shapes of letters to an electronic database with such refinement that the minutest details can be picked out and adjusted or studied. The further ability to return from the minute to the general offers both disciplines further, entirely novel, opportunities.

The problem is simply stated:

Until recently, our familiar letter-forms have all been analog designs, formed by continuously varying smooth contours. This is true not only for printing types, but for handwriting, calligraphy, stone inscriptions, and other forms of lettering art. These analog forms must be converted into mosaics of discrete elements to be usable in digital display and output devices . . . Ideally, each pixel should be small enough to unambiguously represent a point on the letter, or a point off the letter. We don't want to leave anything out, nor do we want to put anything else in. Each pixel is a small sample of the picture area. It tells whether part of a letter is there or not. Thus analog-to-digital conversion requires a sampling process.[7]

5 *Type Specimen Facsimiles*, ed. J. Dreyfus, 1 (1963), p. xxviii.

6 Harry Carter was one, and his *View of Early Typography* takes up the challenge implicitly laid down by Bowers.

7 Charles Bigelow, 'Aesthetics v. Technology', *The Seybold Report*, 11, no. 11 (1982): 5.

Sampling means going back to the familiar record of regular cyclical change through time, whether audible or visual, the sine wave. Fourier analysis – that is, an accurate picture of the band-wave, without 'aliasing' (errors due to faulty sampling) – provides this record. But a full 'bit-map' is complex. A short cut is needed, an algorithmic representation: at simplest a run-length code, better a vector code, or best of all an arc-and-vector code or spline.

A number of systems have been developed which offer different methods of spline restoration. Ikarus (Karow-Hell, Hamburg), Metafont (Knuth, Stanford University), ELF and Logos (Kindersley-Wiseman, Cambridge University), all offer synthetic systems of letter-analysis and representation, and no doubt further refinements are on the way. The possibility of refining a printed image so that we can get at the engraved shape, unencumbered with ink-spread, is not, in engineering terms, a chimerical hope. By these means it will be possible to record and compare the essential shape of written and printed letters, and to demonstrate similarities and differences, not only letter by letter, but also stroke by stroke and fount by fount, and not subjectively (that is, based on the dubious assumption that two pairs of eyes will see and record an identical image) but objectively, by reference to an image built by independent optical and electro-mechanical means. What is more, such a system offers more than identification of a particular letter form: it can help us to get at the personality of the man who formed it.

We believe that the evolution of computer-aided design systems into fully functioning synthetic letter design tools will allow the creation of what we call 'macrofonts'. A macrofont is a kernel design which is expandable into a complete range of digital representations by a set of rules created with the original image. A macrofont therefore has a deep structure consisting of abstract descriptions of the design and a set of transformations for generating series of possible surface structures, realized as digital bit maps for given output rasters. This is not something as simple as a spline-outline sampled at different frequencies – which inevitably invites sampling problems – but an alphabet description with built-in intelligence about the necessary structure of letter images.[8]

Bigelow is writing about modern letter-design, and the problem of retaining an 'essential character' throughout a range of small and large, condensed or expanded, upright or sloped, light or bold, letters. But the same principles could be reversed. One would not only be able to distinguish Sanlecque's *Saint Augustin* roman from Garamont's: put together thus, all the types of one or other engraver, roman, italic, even Greek or Hebrew, and you could extract from it *his* 'essential character' or personality, which would distinguish his work from the same composite picture of another man's work.

One could not only distinguish the three post-1550 Garamontesque *gros canon* romans, one could prove whether or not it was Garamont who engraved the 1530 prototype. Applying the same process to a scribe's work is even easier to imagine. One last picture from Bigelow:

8 *Ibid.*, no. 12 (1982): 17.

The possible forms of a macrofont are subject to the raster restrictions on diversity discussed earlier. We can imagine a potential macrofont as an inverted pyramid. At the low resolutions of the bottom point, only a few different alphabet designs are possible. At the highest resolutions of the broad base, all analog forms are possible. Any actual macrofont will take the form of a branching tree within the myriad potential designs of the pyramid. As with real trees, the trunks of most macrofonts will resemble one another, because only a few simple forms are realizable, but the leafy crowns will show the vast diversity of form, pattern, and texture possible at the high resolutions.[9]

I like that. It is an image of letter-design itself. The 'leafy crowns' may be made up of myriad leaves, but the botanist will not be deterred by their quantity from tracing beyond them twig, bough, and trees. Henry Bradshaw was the first to apply the natural-historical analogy to the study of types.[10] We can at least imagine how his vision may one day be realized; then the true value of letter-forms, 'the oldest, largest and most complex set of abstract visual features produced by human culture', will be seen.

9 *Ibid.*, no. 12 (1982): 18.
10 H. Bradshaw, *Collected Papers* (Cambridge 1889), p. 221; cited by A.W. Pollard, *Catalogue of Books in the British Museum Printed in the XVth Century*, 1 (1908), p. xii.

The future of bookbinding research

MIRJAM M. FOOT

In *Studies in Retrospect* (1945) E.Ph. Goldschmidt compared the history of bookbinding to the history of costume, thereby encapsulating in a single phrase the state that the research in this subject had reached fifty years after the foundation of the Bibliographical Society, its lack of status, and its incompleteness. Although during those fifty years the study of bookbinding had moved from the aestheticism of the arts and crafts, the 'Cult of Beauty and Good Taste', into the field of bibliography, from the book beautiful to the book as an historical clue, it remained the history of the book's costume, the study of its appearance and – first and foremost – of its decoration. A further fifty years on, the history of costume is still with us, although during the latter decades of this period some have looked behind the costume, removed the clothes and found an emperor worth studying.

When Goldschmidt wrote his *Gothic and Renaissance Bookbindings* (1928) – one of the first books to give academic respectability to a subject hitherto largely the domain of the amateur and the connoisseur – the subject was still in its infancy. The debt we owe him and early scholars such as W.H.J. Weale, G.D. Hobson, and J.B. Oldham, followed by H.M. Nixon and Graham Pollard – to name only the giants – is incalculable. Nevertheless, with the exception of Pollard, they occupied themselves largely with the observation and interpretation of binding decoration, with the attempts to identify decorative tools, to postulate groups of tools into workshops and – here Nixon and Pollard were particularly successful – to attribute these workshops to binders, real men and women with names and addresses.

It is not surprising that the study of decorative tools proved both the most attractive and the most fruitful way to further the subject and increase our knowledge of this aspect of the book trade. Its attraction needs no explanation, for anyone with an eye for colour and form will be struck by the rich glowing colours of leather, the creamy smoothness of vellum at its best, the grandeur of velvet and the shimmering of silks and satin; by the brilliance of gold, the variety of coloured threads, spangles, seed pearls, and the near-vulgarity of paint. The elegance of line, the intricacy of intertwined ornament and the charm of picturesque display will appeal to the observer's visual sensibility. Moreover, the scholar can isolate facts by painstaking comparison, can identify individual tools and groups of tools in attempting to create order out of aesthetic pleasure. The study of tools and combinations of tools is the surest way to identify individual workshops and it is this aspect of binding research that has been most successfully pursued over the past forty years. This kind of work takes time and patience, but it can be done and – provided that the raw material is extensive – it is complex but not difficult. Or is it? How solid are the facts? The tool itself – hand-engraved in brass – is a fact,[1] but what do we know about its maker, its use, its life?

Before the nineteenth century very little is known about tool cutters. We know that, by the seventeenth century and probably earlier than that, in France the trade was divided into forwarding and finishing and that consequently books bound by a variety of forwarders could be finished in the same shop and vice versa. Was the *relieur du roy* the finisher? Or the binder (forwarder)? Or was he the mastermind directing both operations? Whatever the nature of his involvement, are we right to link the names of the successive *relieurs du roy* with the tools found on royal bindings? The same problem arises in the eighteenth century. Is the name on the binder's ticket that of the entrepreneur, the forwarder or the finisher? In England this particular problem seems less acute, since the trade was organized differently, and forwarding and finishing were carried out by the same person or – at least – in the same shop. But were tools borrowed? Did they on occasion belong to the publisher or – even – to the owner of the book? Were they farmed out with the unbound books to a number of shops? The disposition of the royal insignia on the bindings for Henry Prince of Wales, for example, suggests that the blocks belonged to a central source but were allocated – with the books – to a number of binders.

Tools were inherited and sold. They could move from binder to binder and from shop to shop. Their life span would have been dependent on how frequently they were used and how carefully they were treated. It is not exceptional to find the same tool occurring over a period of thirty to fifty years, sometimes in combination with different sets of other tools. We postulate a fire, a death, a wedding gift – but do we know? Moreover, how reliable are groups of tools? There is some evidence that in the seventeenth, eighteenth, and nineteenth centuries journeymen finishers (with their own sets of tools) would travel round the country looking for work. Some would be employed in a country house to gild the backs of the books in the library. The result, uniformly decorated spines lining the walls, can be seen in several big houses, but it would be dangerous to link the tooling of the covers with that of the spine as the two operations may have been carried out by different binders at different times.

And even when groups of tools can be identified, when they turn up in the same combination over a period of thirty to forty years, when the provenance of the books they decorate points to the same place of origin and the bindings can

---

1 S. Fogelmark, *Flemish and Related Panel-Stamped Bindings* (New York, 1990), argues, with a great deal of force, that panels were cast and not engraved, thereby throwing doubt on the validity of earlier literature on this subject. Cast panels would have existed in a multiplicity of identical copies and can therefore not be used to identify the work of an individual binder or binder's shop.

with some confidence be attributed to a locatable and datable workshop, the question arises how to link such a group of bindings with the men (and occasionally women) who produced them. Finding their names in archival sources is hard work, needing perseverance and devoted pursuit, but it can be done on occasion as Pollard, Nixon and, most recently, Paul Christianson,[2] have proved. But to link these names with the products for which they were responsible needs more than perseverance: it needs insight and – dare I say it? – luck. To hit on an inventory or bill where the books listed can be identified as individual copies, to find an inscription linking a specific copy with its binder, to quarry from extant accounts specific dates and specific products needs luck, but also the intelligence to recognize what luck has laid before us, as well as the knowledge and insight necessary to use it.

Linking named binders with their output is one element in the history of a book. Linking the binder and his product with the person who ordered it to be bound is another. In some cases the publisher or the printer may have commissioned the binding, either for presentation to the patron or dedicatee of the book or to some other suitable grandee, or to have a limited number of a readily saleable title bound up for stock. Authors or editors also ordered presentation bindings: Lord Herbert of Cherbury comes instantly to mind,[3] but there are many other examples. The famous collectors who had their names, mottoes, or armorial bearings tooled on their bindings can be identified with greater or lesser ease, but those whose devices are less explicit, at least for later historians, are more difficult to trace and it is remarkable how successful Anthony Hobson has been, not only in identifying important patrons, but in placing the production of manuscripts and bindings in its cultural context.[4]

During the second half-century of the Bibliographical Society's existence much valuable work has been done in identifying tools and workshops, in locating, dating, and attributing them to named individuals, and in discovering by whom they were patronized. Some of this work was done by the Society's members, and at least five of its past Presidents, two current Vice-Presidents, and a number of past and present Council members have made their name in this field. Those parts of F.A. Schmidt-Künsemüller's *Bibliographie zur Geschichte der Einbandkunst* (Wiesbaden, 1987) that list what has been published on the history of bookbinding over the past fifty years make impressive reading and there is no need to repeat that considerable achievement here.[5] However, the

---

2 P. Christianson, *A Directory of London Stationers and Book Artisans, 1300–1500* (New York, 1990).

3 See M.M. Foot, *The Henry Davis Gift*, 1 (1978), pp. 50–8.

4 A.R.A. Hobson, *Apollo and Pegasus* (Amsterdam, 1975); and *Humanists and Bookbinders* (Cambridge, 1989).

5 F.A. Schmidt-Künsemüller, *Bibliographie zur Geschichte der Einbandkunst von den Anfängen bis 1985* (Wiesbaden, 1987) contains most of the important bookbinding literature published before 1985. Especially of the older literature the author has left very little unlisted. Some gaps can be found among the more recent literature.

Most of the authors referred to in this article can be found in Schmidt-Künsemüller's *Autorenregister* which lists their pre-1985 work.

time has come for a change of direction, to extend research into areas beyond the study of decoration. It is time both for more detailed study of the object, its materials and its structure, to move towards archaeology and engineering, and to branch out into still wider fields: into social history, into the history of education, of learning, of the intellectual development of mankind. The humble aspect of the book trade, the history of bookbinding, has much that it can contribute here.

Let us begin with the need for the detailed and the specific. Over the past thousand years or so binders – and sometimes observers – have described, more or less accurately and explicitly, the technical processes involved in the binding of books. These manuals, whether they served as *aides-mémoires* or as a set of instructions, were largely written by and for craftsmen. They present the practice at a given time in a particular place and they can be of great use to the historian, however frustrating and incomprehensible they often turn out to be to the uninitiated. A list of *Early Bookbinding Manuals* was compiled by Graham Pollard, continued by Esther Potter, and published by the Oxford Bibliographical Society (1984), and several early manuals, such as those by Anselme Faust (1612), Dirk de Bray (1658), J.V. Capronnier de Gauffecourt (1763), Hendrik de Haas (1806), and the anonymous *Whole Art of Bookbinding* (1811) have been recently re-published.

The retrospective, historical observation and detailed description of the nature and use of materials and the changes in technical practices is something else. Only in recent decades, a few scholars such as Roger Powell, Bernard Middleton, Christopher Clarkson, Nicholas Pickwood, Michael Gullick in the United Kingdom and Jean Vézin, Janos Szirmai, Guy Petherbridge, and others in Europe and America, have started to study the materials that constitute a binding and the techniques that were employed to create it. They observed, with attention to minute detail, all the constituent parts of a binding or, where the original structure is defective, such traces of it as remain, and they have begun to explain how binders worked, how they used their instruments, in some cases, what those instruments were, and how they obtained the results we now have before us. In most instances this work has concentrated on the earlier periods and binding archaeology is becoming a real and advancing subject. A recent initiative, started in Cambridge, to compile a census of medieval bookbindings in Britain is based on the study of their structure. Similar initiatives are developing in Germany, Italy, and France. Once these ambitious projects get under way they will, in due course, provide us not only with a map of the existence of remaining specimens, but with a much greater knowledge of medieval techniques and materials. They may also – incidentally – encourage owners and librarians to show greater respect for historical relics. So often, well-meaning attempts to repair or replace an older binding structure by binders, acting on the instructions of owners and librarians, destroy evidence that would be of great value to the binding historian. Neglect is often a better ally than intervention, although there are signs that a more enlightened conservation policy is becoming more widely understood and accepted.

The pioneer work by Graham Pollard[6] was followed by Middleton and Pickwoad. They have shown that it is not only medieval binding structures that are of interest, and their work on the history and development of the use of materials and the practices of techniques during the sixteenth to nineteenth centuries has encouraged the study of trade bindings, a subject that has hitherto received far too little attention. Yet it is the simple, plain trade binding that provided the binder's daily bread. It was the trade binding that was ordered, produced, and used in quantity, and that forms the solid rock and foundation on which the trade was built. The splendidly decorated presentation bindings, works of art made for discerning owners, were exceptional, the icing on the cake of more ordinary work, but it is the icing that has hitherto received more attention than the cake itself.

In this need for the study of detail and of the ordinary, we are hampered by a lack of an agreed and generally understood vocabulary. Most disciplines in the humanities have developed their terminology alongside their subject. The history of bookbinding suffers from a lack of an explicit, unmistakable, generally understood and generally accepted terminology. This terminology is most sorely needed when technical processes are described, although the lack of a common vocabulary for the description of the decorative aspects of binding has meant that literature without illustration is of little use. Several attempts have been made – in America, in Europe, and now also in Britain – to establish a terminology, but so far with limited success. Terms are either vague and open to a multiplicity of interpretations, or so inflexible that only their author fully understands their meaning. An internationally agreed vocabulary, including descriptive terms for the component parts of a binding, and terms for every step of the various binding processes – elaborately illustrated – written by binders, restorers, and historians is what is now most urgently needed.

I am uncertain how far such a vocabulary can extend to the definition of ornament. Can one specify when to call a vase an urn or a pot? It may be helpful to try and describe more or less naturalistic flowers as roses, lilies, pansies, tulips, daisies, or marguerites, but how significant is the term 'four-petalled formal flower' and, worse, what objective meaning can be attached to the word 'fleuron'? Description of ornament without illustration remains a highly subjective exercise and time would be better spent in compiling illustrated tool catalogues for individual binders or groups of bindings. Much good work of this kind has already been done but more is needed – however tiresome it is to compile accurate same-size reproductions of a binder's stock of tools.[7]

Standards of description also vary with each author and each publication. Guidelines on how bindings should be described, what should be observed,

6 G. Pollard, 'Changes in the style of bookbinding, 1550–1830', *Lib*, v, 11 (1956): 71–94.
7 A few recent examples are J. McDonnell and P. Healey, *Gold-Tooled Bookbindings Commissioned by Trinity College, Dublin in the Eighteenth-Century* (Leixlip, 1987); D. Carvin, *La Reliure médiévale* (Arles, 1988); C. Federici and K. Houlis, *Legature Bizantine Vaticana* (Rome, 1988); M. Tidcombe, *The Doves Bindery* (1991).

which elements recorded, to what degree of detail and in what way, could be developed alongside the compilation of an agreed terminology. It should not be forgotten that what needs to be described varies with the binding under consideration and with the purpose of the description. Complex records for their own sake are a luxury that can be ill afforded.

It is tempting to let the study of the specific become an aim in itself. The questions – how books were bound, with what materials, which techniques were employed, what tools were used and in what way, when and where materials, instruments, and methods used first and last, by whom and for whom – are all fascinating and crying out for solution, but this is not enough. The history of bookbinding is only one aspect of the history of book production and of the history of the book trade, which in turn is only a small aspect of the history of civilization. How does the binder fit into the chain of author, patron, scribe or printer, publisher, bookseller, buyer, and reader? The relationship between the binder and all others involved in the production and marketing of books, as well as that between him and the owners of the books, has changed over the centuries, but our knowledge of the exact nature of these relationships and how and when they altered lacks precision. What was the relationship between binders and other decorative artists, how did they relate to the leather workers for example? Before the end of the eighteenth century, divisions between branches of similar crafts were not so distinct, and finishers would not have limited their skills to the decoration of bindings only; they also tooled boxes, containers, covers and cases for telescopes and other instruments, and furniture, in the same way as cut-leather artists applied themselves from time to time to book covers. What exactly was their role outside the book trade, how were they regarded in the arts, crafts, and business hierarchies? The majority of binders were no doubt craftsmen who played a useful, even an indispensable rôle in the production of a book, but some were artists and some were entrepreneurs and businessmen. On the whole their social status was fairly humble, even within the book trade, but some moved in exalted circles. The rôle of the binder in society over the centuries deserves more attention than it has received thus far.

The relation between the binders and the tool cutters also needs further explanation and so do the tool cutters or tool engravers themselves. Extremely little is known about them; they were metal workers, who cut dies for seals, coins, and medals, as well as binders' finishing tools and printers' ornaments, and even punches for typefounders; they may also have made clasps and metal corner and centre pieces for bindings, but exactly what their business consisted of and how widely their skills ranged we do not know. Nor do we know where they got their patterns from. It is thought that much ornament derives from a common source. Some binders' tools can clearly be traced back to manuscript illumination, to book illustration or title-page designs, to carving, to sculpture, to ceramics, and to architecture. Some finishing tools have close affinity with printers' ornaments and with patterns for embroidery, but who specified the designs for these tools? In the eighteenth and nineteenth centuries tool cutters issued pattern books or pattern sheets for binders to choose from. Patrons, such as Thomas Hollis, commissioned the designs for the tools that were to decorate the bindings he ordered.[8] Roger Payne took great interest in the designs of his tools and may have specified them, but the legend that he cut them himself has no firm basis. How close was the cooperation between patron, binder, and tool cutter and how did it develop or change with time? Some binding historians, notably G.D. and Anthony Hobson, have attempted to trace binding and tool designs to their source of inspiration, and Anthony Hobson has studied the meaning of certain emblematical tools with most interesting results, but much more work needs to be done in this field both by art historians and by bibliographers. The history of binding decoration not only needs a place in a wider art-historical context; the history and development of binding structure, particularly as it applies to everyday, run-of-the-mill bindings and trade bindings, needs also to be considered as part of the history of collecting, of reading, and of education. A fair amount of work has been done on the collecting of fine bindings and on binding patronage, although it would be interesting to know more about the individual patrons' degree of involvement in the specification for and production of the bindings they acquired.

For most book buyers and book collectors a binding is essentially a way to keep together and protect a text, although binding collectors consider it an object desirable in its own right. In certain cases, bindings were seen to have greater significance. Splendidly decorated bindings encasing the word of God empha-sized the value and importance of what they contained and their production and use can be seen as an act of worship. Some medieval treasure bindings were used as reliquaries and became objects of veneration in their own right. Lavish presentation bindings could indicate the esteem in which the recipient was held by the donor and might hint at the *noblesse* that obliged the granting of preferment in return. Bindings as objects, why they were made, for whom, and with what purpose, can teach us much about the culture of their time. Roberts and Skeat[9] demonstrated that different book structures denoted usage for different purposes: tablets were used for ephemeral jottings, scrolls for publish-able texts. The spread of learning, increased education for a different and wider public, changes in readership, the changes in methods of book production and its continuous growth, are all reflected in the changes in style and techniques of bookbinding. There are various periods in the history of bookbinding when a greater demand for books led to changes in binding structures. Examples of this are plentiful and a search for cheaper materials and less time-consuming practices, a cutting of corners in order to cut costs and speed up production, can be seen throughout the history of the craft, culminating in its mechanization during the 1820s and 1830s.

8 W.H. Bond, *Thomas Hollis, of Lincoln's Inn* (Cambridge, 1990).
9 C.H. Roberts and T.C. Skeat, *The Birth of the Codex* (1987).

The time has come to extend our knowledge of bookbinding into the more obscure and hidden corners of the run-of-the-mill bindings and their structure, from the first development of the codex format onwards; to establish a better defined methodology, backed up by a more precise and internationally usable terminology; to pursue binding ornament back to its source, to discover more about the tool cutter and to establish his relationship with the binders and their patrons, and to use this knowledge to increase our understanding of the history of the book and its place in the history of society at large.

Incunabula 1942–1992: from type to text

LOTTE HELLINGA

It is a curious coincidence that while Victor Scholderer was writing his survey of incunabula studies of the period 1892–1942 for *Studies in Retrospect*, the Bibliographical Society was about to issue a monograph which more than any other single work indicated the new direction that the study of incunabula was to take in the next half-century. E. Ph. Goldschmidt's *Medieval Texts and their First Appearance in Print* (1943) [Supplement to the Bibliographical Society's Transactions No. 16, Bib. Soc. publication for 1940, issued to members 1943], was the work of one of the most experienced incunabulists of his generation. Having served his apprenticeship in incunabula as a member of the editorial team of the Kommission of the *Gesamtkatalog der Wiegendrucke* (Leipzig etc., 1925–) with responsibility for recording the collections in Austria, Goldschmidt was deeply versed in the methodology of the identification of fifteenth-century printing materials by their types, steeped also in the extensive form of bibliographical description developed for the *Gesamtkatalog*. Goldschmidt's talents, however, extended far beyond impeccable technique. In his relatively brief study he leaves the confines of a well-established methodology to explore questions of survival and dissemination of texts, contemplating the obstructions raised by cataloguing traditions which often block the way to complicated materials, and suggesting new systematic approaches. Even now, when modern technology makes such departures from the orthodoxy of cataloguing rules more feasible, Goldschmidt's daring approaches have not been carried out on the scale he suggested. But his themes of survival, transmission, distribution, and modern access remain central to the study of incunabula. Meanwhile, cataloguing in the old tradition remains an important preoccupation of the incunabulist.

Victor Scholderer had been one of the protagonists of 'incunabulizing' (as he called it) for almost the entire period he reviewed. He had joined the British Museum in 1904, filling the vacancy left by Robert Proctor's death, and was thus engaged almost at once on the *Catalogue of Books Printed in the XVth Century Now in the British Museum* (*BMC*) which was to occupy him not only until his official retirement in 1944, but until his death in 1970. The ten volumes of *BMC* which appeared in his lifetime, eight under his editorship, are a lasting monument to his vast knowledge, his scholarship and his determination. The last volume to appear under Scholderer's sole editorship was that devoted to books printed in France, which appeared in 1949. It was mainly prepared in Aberystwyth, where he spent the war years together with the collections which had been evacuated to escape the dangers of the Blitz. *BMC*'s later volumes (the Netherlands, the Iberian peninsula, a supplementary volume to Italy) are a continuation of this spirit, and were prepared by L.A. Sheppard, G.D. Painter, and D.E. Rhodes. The volume for England still awaits completion, and it is hoped that before long preparations for a volume devoted to Hebrew incunabula will be taken in hand.

Scholderer was therefore particularly well fitted to provide the survey of fifty years of incunable studies, and he delivered himself of this task admirably, in a concise essay that is still one of the best introductions to the subject. Scholderer wrote his essay at precisely the time of a watershed, for the emphasis of most work on incunabula was to change after the Second World War. The fifty years he surveyed has been a period of ambitious projects in the cataloguing of early printed books, often conceived on a national basis, and vulnerable to the fates affecting nations. The history of incunable bibliography bears therefore its share of scars marking the political upheavals of the twentieth century. The First World War caused the national project for the recording of collections of incunabula in France to founder, after the publication of the third volume bringing the project to the entry *Gregorius*; but France's loss became Belgium's gain, for from then on the editor of the French project, M.-L. Polain, concentrated on the Belgian collections, a task which he successfully completed in 1932. Important as the French national union catalogue was in its concept, it had to cede priority of place to the *Gesamtkatalog der Wiegendrucke* (GW), the initiative for which was taken in 1904, only a few years after the beginning of the French project (vol. I of which was published in 1897). Publication could not start until after the First World War, but then, from 1925 on, a steady stream of volumes was produced until fate intervened again in 1940, when the GW had reached the entry no. 9730: Federicis, Stephanus de. By that time a constellation had established itself with the GW as undisputed centre, and the BMC as most important secondary enterprise. It was confidently expected that the whole of fifteenth-century printing would be accessible in only a few more decades. Meanwhile other projects continued on an only slightly smaller scale: the United States maintained a tradition of a regular account of its expanding collections of incunabula with the publication in New York in 1940 of Margaret B. Stillwell's *Second Census*. In 1942 the first volume of Italy's national census, the *Indice Generale degli incunaboli delle biblioteche d'Italia* was published, which without major interruptions made steady progress until the completion of a supplementary volume in 1981.

Until the outbreak of the Second World War the editors of the two projects in Berlin and in London had been in frequent contact with one another, constantly cross-referring and with mutual reliance on expertise and willingness to support. The Second World War and its aftermath put an end to the GW's very efficient progress. Its editors, now in East Berlin, were separated from the collections of the former Preussische Staatsbibliothek and it was a long time before the Deutsche Staatsbibliothek was able to fund a small team. Nevertheless, in 1961 it was announced at the IFLA conference that the *Gesamtkatalog* would resume publication. A team of editors was assembled, who with great courage decided to maintain the pre-war standards, but with innovations on some points. The first issue of the post-war *GW* came out in 1972 and a publication programme has been maintained, but production by printers in the German Democratic Republic was beset with difficulties, and progress has been slow. The reaction in England following the announcement in 1961 of the resumption of the work on the *GW* was to initiate a project that would support it. The Bibliographical Society agreed to sponsor a census of incunabula in the British Isles to be carried out by C.A. Webb of the National Central Library; after his early death this was continued by D.E. Rhodes at the British Library.

Gradually, as the library world recovered from the Second World War and it was realized that it could no longer rely on the rapid completion of the *GW*, libraries, large and small, took their own initiatives to catalogue their collections. These initiatives were often partly undertaken to support the progress of the *GW* but also to serve local, more restricted, interests. A very substantial number of national union catalogues was produced on a short-title principle, referring for more extensive descriptions of editions to existing bibliographies and catalogues. It should never be forgotten that most of the (estimated) 30,000 editions of the fifteenth century have been described *somewhere*, in the extensive literature on the subject. The progress of cataloguing was surveyed in 1979 when the *GW* celebrated its seventy-fifth birthday in a special issue of the *Zentralblatt für Bibliothekswesen*, 93 (1979), entitled 'Der internationale Stand der Inkunabelkatalogisierung'. This is therefore not the place to repeat that information. Of the national union catalogues, one should be singled out: F.R. Goff's *Incunabula in American Libraries: A Third Census of Fifteenth-Century Books recorded in North-American Collections* (New York, 1964), the successor to Stillwell's *Second Census*; this is the basis for an automated database of fifteenth-century printing, about which more below.

Meanwhile the number of catalogues published by large and small collections continued to increase, many in short-title form with the addition of more or less extensive records of early owners or of other particulars of the copies described. The description of the printed book as individual copy reveals a series of different aspects of the book, which a catalogue entry confined to particulars common to the entire edition cannot reveal: about its distribution, its readers, its subsequent movements through collections and the book trade. Catalogues of this sort provide the basic building materials from which to construe a history of the book in the widest sense. One of the earliest of the post-war catalogues, which set a pattern followed by many, is J.C.T. Oates's *A Catalogue of the Fifteenth-Century Printed Books in the University Library Cambridge*, published in Cambridge in 1954. Of the other large collections in the United Kingdom, the Bodleian Library's catalogue, still unpublished, was prepared by L.A. Sheppard after his retirement from the British Museum, and follows the pattern of the Cambridge catalogue. For a list of the very many catalogues of large and small collections in many countries which have appeared in the past half-century, reference should be made to the survey undertaken in 1979 by the *GW*. Since then the first volume of a much more comprehensive bibliography has appeared; S. Corsten and R.W. Fuchs (eds.), *Der Buchdruck im 15. Jahrhundert: Eine Bibliographie* (Stuttgart, 1988). The appearance of the index volume is expected shortly. Mention should also be made of the two catalogues which are now in progress and record collections which, with the British Library, are the world's largest: the Bibliothèque Nationale (first issue in 1981) under the editorship of Ursula Baurmeister, and the Bayerische Staatsbibliothek (vol. 1 1988; vol. 2 1991) which is the responsibility of Dr E. Hertrich. Both catalogues, independent and critical, testify to a consistent, steady progress in the refinement of methodology and the broad interpretation of the responsibilities of the discipline.

In cataloguing, finally, two new categories have been developed. The generous catalogue of a private collection is of course not a new concept, but lately we have been presented with several particularly lavish examples which show great depth and explanatory talent in demonstrating the underlying principles of the collections: the Otto Schäfer collection in Schweinfurt, catalogued by Manfred von Arnim (1984) and the Bibliotheca Philosophica Hermetica in Amsterdam, catalogued by Margaret L. Ford (1990). An outstanding catalogue of a private collection of a different kind is that of the Durazzo collection in Genoa compiled by A. Petrucciani (1988). This collection was brought together in the second half of the eighteenth century, and the catalogue draws on the account books and other documentation preserved in the collection to analyse the purchase of each item, thus presenting an unparalleled document for book collecting in that period. A new genre, however, is the very extensive and luxuriously illustrated auction catalogue. The first catalogue of incunabula on this scale was that of the Estelle Doheny collection (Christie's, New York, 1987), an example followed by the George Abrams collection (Sotheby's, London, 1989).

With this proliferation of catalogues, added to the extensive literature which had grown since the eighteenth century when incunabula became a subject of concentrated interest, the need to make this material more accessible became urgent. As it multiplied, incunable literature has become more and more impenetrable to all but a few initiates. These are mainly to be found among librarians and as a result this rich source of material remains painfully under-exploited by other disciplines. One way to improve access to this material can be found in modern electronic technology which facilitates indexing in many more cross-sections than is ever possible in manually compiled catalogues. In 1980 the British Library started to prepare an automated database modelled on that successfully developed for *ESTC*, which had by then proved successful. With the generous permission of Dr F. R. Goff and of the Bibliographical Society of America, the British Library began by converting the 13,000 entries in Goff's *Third Census* into machine-readable form. This, the largest national union catalogue, with admirably organized and consistent entries, was an ideal starting point for the system. By adding the records of collections in the United Kingdom, in Italy, Belgium, the Netherlands, and (less systematically) from other major catalogues the *Incunabule Short-title Catalogue* (or *ISTC*) has to date grown to some 25,000 records. It has enjoyed the generous help of many colleagues, and is now the basis for two other major national projects, the census of incunabula in public collections in Germany and in Italy. Since 1984 it has been available on-line, and this service encourages its use by others than specialist incunabulists, although these in particular are putting the database increasingly to new and imaginative uses. The *ISTC* is conceived as having a supplementary function to that of the *GW*. It already covers over twice the number of editions so far recorded in *GW*, and it updates the information of the early *GW* volumes, but the information contained in the records is not intended even to approximate the detailed information provided in the *GW*. The application of the system to the recording of collections which is now increasingly taking place encourages the belief that a reasonable overview of fifteenth-century printing will be within the grasp of the present generation of incunabulists. It will then be for them to decide in what ways, and for what purposes, the system (which can be amended *ad infinitum*) should be refined.

As far as cataloguing is concerned, which remains the preliminary to all other activities concerning printed materials, the last fifty years can be summed up as a phase of diversification, in the first place due to the change in function of the *GW*. But there are further changes to be noted, as a result of other developments in the discipline. The basic methodology of the study of incunabula was based, since Bradshaw, Holtrop, Proctor, and Haebler, on the identification of printing types. Features, characteristic for each printer, could be established in practically all typefaces used in the fifteenth century, and these were used to build up the well-known system for the identification, and to a lesser extent the dating, of all material printed in the incunable period. Once the documentation for this method was established by bibliographers, mainly for their own benefit, historians of typography, notably Ernst Consentius in his *Die Typen der Inkunabelzeit: eine Betrachtung* (Berlin, 1929), queried to what extent a system, based exclusively on the images printed on pages, reflected the historical realities of type design, typefounding, and the trade in printing types. It is difficult to provide other than a very general answer to this – no more than 'very little' – since direct evidence on the manufacture of types and their trade barely exists for the fifteenth century. In more recent studies of fifteenth-century typography there is, however, a greater awareness of the underlying procedures and techniques, and the various channels and connections by which types reached printers. In *The Fifteenth-Century Printing Types of the Low Countries* (Amsterdam, 1966), Wytze and Lotte Hellinga attempted to set out these factors systematically in a work that was primarily intended to identify all printing types used in one well-defined cultural area. While their point of departure was the bibliography of printing in this area, Harry Carter surveyed in his Lyell lectures of 1968 related questions from a purely typographical point of view. This pioneering study appeared with the title *A View of Early Typography up to about 1600* (1969).

Technical developments have made it possible to extend the basis for material evidence. Identification and dating of paper has been practised in a fairly crude fashion since the publication of Charles Moïse Briquet's large collection of tracings, *Les Filigranes* (1907; reprinted with supplementary material, Amsterdam, 1968) but when photographic techniques took the place of tracing much refinement of reproduction became possible. Allan Stevenson pioneered new methods in the 1950s and 1960s, progressing from images made with photo-sensitive paper to betaradiography. He applied these techniques in general studies, for example, of the Dutch block-books, early Cologne printing, Caxton's paper, but most spectacularly in a study of the controversial *Missale Speciale*. This resulted in the publication of the Bibliographical Society monograph in 1967, *The Problem of the Missale Speciale*. Paper evidence decisively proved that the *Missale* was printed *c.* 1473–4, instead of at the very dawn of printing in the 1450s, as had been surmised before. Paper evidence took precedence over the typographical evidence, which in this case was ambiguous.

The development of Stevenson's researches shows an analogy with typographical studies in that he demonstrated the importance of the effect of production methods on the state of the watermarks as observed in the paper. As marks move, deteriorate, are taken off, and resewn on the wires, it is possible to establish a chronology of paper manufacture.

Since Stevenson's work, further progress has been made in technique, notably the experiments with electron radiography in the Bundesanstalt für Materialprüfung in Berlin; this method which enables a large number of high-definition images to be produced in a short space of time, was applied to early printed books, in particular to the Mainz *Catholicon*, confirming that in the production of this book paper was used which was manufactured at various times. The methodology of paper research was also at the centre of the researches of Gerhard Piccard and Th. Gerardy, who worked extensively on fifteenth-century material, Piccard having compiled and partly published an enormous collection of tracings in the State Archives in Stuttgart. Finally, Paul Needham is engaged on large-scale projects in which paper-evidence and typographical evidence of fifteenth-century books are considered in relation to one another.

Paper, used in such large quantities in book-production, clearly requires a methodology hitherto not applied either to paper studies or to printed materials. Similar difficulties are encountered in the newly developed Proton Milliprobe analysis of printing ink, which generates an avalanche of data for interpretation. This method has been pioneered by Richard Schwab supported by a team of physicists at the University of California at Davis. Initial experiments have been confined to very limited material, due to the high cost and elaborate organization required to investigate early materials under the appropriate safe conditions. Results have shown that the data, if difficult to interpret, can reveal production procedures which would otherwise go unobserved. A European project using the same techniques is now under discussion. Although showing promise, this line of investigation is still in its infancy.

The bibliographer's observations can nowadays be aided by other equipment adapted for his purposes from the standard requirements of any modern research laboratory. In the first place there are relatively simple visual aids: fibre optics which provide piped light to be deployed to throw into relief even very slight differences in height, such as caused by indentation of printing types; the spectrum of lighting from infra-red to ultra-violet, and luminescence, combined in one machine, the Video-Spectral Comparator (one is available in the British Library). The Hinman collating machine of the 1950s has been further developed to enhance electronically the differences between superimposed images, and showing them on a screen, thus enabling it to achieve a degree of objectivity which was impossible with its predecessors. Unfortunately, at the time of writing this form of collating machine is not yet available in any library in the United Kingdom. Scrutiny with the microscope can be useful for establishing the order of what was written or printed on paper or vellum, especially when used with low magnification, and it can provide a first step in the analysis of the materials used. However, all this sophisticated equipment can do no more than provide data, or images, for interpretation. Presenting this evidence to an audience by photographic means is quite another matter, and can present very considerable difficulties, not to speak of the high costs involved. For example, it did not take very long to detect traces of printing ink, and some offsets of Caxton's printing types, when I examined the Malory manuscript, now British Library Add. MS. 59678, but it was extremely difficult to make these faint traces visible in photography or to enhance the visual differences between the two kinds of ink, water-based writing ink and oil-based printing ink, in a photographic image. (They can be seen in 'The Malory Manuscript and Caxton', in T. Takamiya and D. Brewer (eds.), *Aspects of Malory*, Arthurian Studies 1 (1981): 127–41.)

More than merely demonstrating the application of forensic research techniques to early materials, the Malory manuscript can serve to introduce another aspect of the study of incunabula which has developed in particular over the last two decades. This is the study of textual bibliography, so widely and successfully applied to English-language materials and only very gradually to other Western languages. The significance of the offsets of Caxton's printing types in the Malory manuscript is that they are the only tangible evidence for the presence of the manuscript in Caxton's workshop. Textual historians had decided that the (undated) manuscript and Caxton's *editio princeps* of 1485 were independent witnesses for Malory's text, and that Caxton's edition could not derive from the Malory manuscript. The offsets indicated that although the manuscript was not cast off as printer's copy, it had been used by Caxton, and that this should lead to a re-assessment of the textual variants Caxton's edition shows in relation to the manuscript. Could it, after all, be a direct descendant, with variations introduced by Caxton himself when he edited the text, and by his compositors when they set the text from a manuscript prepared for them, presumably by Caxton?

A definitive answer to this question cannot be attempted without comparison with other instances of literary manuscripts in vernacular languages used in the same period in a printer's workshop or in a comparable transmission process. Such instances are few and far between, but the increased interest in textual transmission in the fifteenth century has caused more examples of printer's copy to be recognized in recent years. Moreover, instances which reveal procedures of textual transmission, and the purposes and methods of editing and publishing in the period, need not be confined to manuscripts used as printer's copy. Early proofs with correctors' marks, even rarer, can be equally revealing. Once some understanding is obtained about procedures, derived from the direct evidence found in manuscripts marked by printers and compositors, it can be applied to investigate the reprinting of books. A printed book would be marked up and used by compositors in the same way as a manuscript. As more examples have come to light it has become clear that there is considerable textual variation possible between *exemplar* and the work produced from it. Furthermore, there is great variation in practice, due undoubtedly to variation in standards between printers, also varying with the nature of the texts, and not least due to variation in technique which in the first decades of printing was still in full development. By the end of the century this had consolidated to a degree where particular expectations may be justified, but for the early years much remains to be explored.

Among the first to study materials used in printing houses in the fifteenth century was Gavin Bone with an important article in *The Library*, IV, 12 (1932) in which he discussed several manuscripts used by printers in England in the fifteenth century. After Percy Simpson had given due attention to these manuscripts in his *Proof-Reading in the Sixteenth, Seventeenth and Eighteenth Centuries* (1935), the subject did not receive much further attention for some twenty years. In the 1950s some important examples were brought to light, notably the Traversanus manuscript used by Caxton, discovered in the Biblioteca Apostolica Vaticana by Mgr José Ruysschaert (see *Bulletin of the John Rylands Library* 36, 1953/4) and the Plimpton manuscript of Bartholomaeus Anglicus, discussed by Robert W. Mitchner in *The Library*, v, 6 (1951). However, the connection between printing-house practice as inferred from such instances and the production of text was put in a much broader context of the history of book production by W. Gs Hellinga in *Copy and Print in the Netherlands* (Amsterdam, 1962), which was a deliberate attempt to apply the methods and ideas of the 'New Bibliography' of the English bibliographers of the turn of the century to another area and to other periods.

For incunabula this has since then been much extended. For example, my own work on printer's copy, reprinting and early examples of proof-correction, which was, of course, a direct continuation of W. Hellinga's work; A.C. de la Mare's discovery of the *exemplar* used for the first book printed in Oxford; and Paul Needham's discovery that the Cambridge University Library's copy of the Gutenberg Bible had served as printer's copy for one of Heinrich Eggestein's Bible editions. Massimo Miglio has discussed and illustrated some manuscripts used by Italy's prototypographers Conrad Sweynheym and Arnold Pannartz (Milan, 1978). Mention should also be made of Adrian Wilson's study (Amsterdam,

1978) of the layouts for the Nuremberg Chronicle (1493), also a form of printer's *exemplar*.

Slowly, very slowly, a body of evidence is thus coming together which, in spite of the rarity and random survival of such materials, begins to give fundamental insight into the nature of textual transmission in the fifteenth century. This understanding is an ideal formulated by A.W. Pollard in 1908 in his introduction to the first volume of *BMC*, but not realized by him since his interest shifted to Elizabethan and Jacobean texts, where the literary rewards to be reaped were much more immediate and infinitely greater. In the intervening years his influence and that of the contemporaries he inspired can be felt in the work of many incunabulists: not only his successors in the British Museum, Victor Scholderer, L.A. Sheppard, George D. Painter, and Dennis E. Rhodes, in many of their studies devoted to specific problems, but also in other countries, in particular in the publications of Curt F. Bühler and Jeanne Veyrin-Forrer, both fortunately collected. Madame Veyrin-Forrer's collection bears the title *La Lettre et le texte* (Paris, 1987), words so apposite to sum up the development of this century, that they simply had to be borrowed to head this piece. It seems therefore appropriate to end with pointing out the parallel between Pollard's methodology for the study of English printing and the slower development of the study of incunabula: the overall survey of book production, provided by the *STC* was the background which was a prerequisite for any authority in the study of printing-house practice, which in turn was a prerequisite for an understanding of the procedures of the transmission of texts. It is not surprising that the larger and more complicated field of incunabula studies has taken the best part of a century to get this objective into its sights.

Stationers' Company bibliography, 1892–1992

ROBIN MYERS

The publication between 1875 and 1894 of Edward Arber's transcript of the Stationers' Company Registers[1] focused bibliographical attention on the records. Although the early registers had been used for the study of English literature since the eighteenth century, when scholars first verified the dates of early printed drama from them, members of the newly founded Bibliographical Society were quick to realize the potential of the Stationers' records for bibliographical research and to seize upon Arber's work as providing them with a text which superseded the various, unreliable, and piecemeal transcriptions of earlier editors. It was one of the reasons why, during the first decades of the Society's existence, Stationers' Company bibliography was more or less tied to the records before 1640 which, for the first time, Arber made so widely available. The addition of English to the university curriculum at the turn of the century was a contributing factor – its syllabus was dominated by early literature, above all Shakespeare and his contemporaries. The pioneers of the new bibliography, A.W. Pollard, W.W. Greg, and R.B. McKerrow, whose influence on bibliography, not least Stationers' Company bibliography, cannot be over-estimated, were particularly concerned with Elizabethan and Jacobean drama. Although neither Pollard nor McKerrow published very much directly on the Stationers' Company, they knew the early records inside out, and based many of their studies on them. Pollard, in particular, advised the Company on publication over the many years that he was secretary of the Society, and compiled the *STC* with Arber at his elbow, so to speak, even to taking Arber's end date of 1640 for the termination of *STC*.

C.R. Rivington, the Stationers' Clerk, a founder member of the Society and its Council, fostered cooperation between the Company and the Society by encouraging the Court of Assistants to sanction further publication of the records and he led the way by engaging H.R. Plomer to transcribe the registers for 1640–1708, which were published on the eve of the First World War. Although Eyre & Rivington, was, in Greg's words, 'nothing like as trustworthy as Arber', it is a fitting climax to the work of editing the Company's records in the Society's first twenty-one years.

Greg's influence dominated Stationers' Company bibliography from the

---

1 Full titles of works referred to are given in Further reading (pp.120–1).

beginning of the century until some years after his death in 1959. He was quick
to see that the early records were integral to a study of the book trade and a key
source for the bibliography of pre-Restoration printed drama. Two papers in *The
Library*[2] preceded his edition of the *Records of the Court . . . 1576–1602* (1930),
which was, in his words, 'a first instalment' in filling the gaps in publication of all
the records to 1700. However, he was unable to complete work on the
seventeenth-century registers because he needed to push on with his bibliography of printed plays for which study of the records was preparatory; but he went
on working on the Stationers' Company to the end of his life and his working
notes on press licensers to 1640 and his calendar of documents in Arber and
elsewhere were published posthumously. His Lyell Lectures on London publishing from 1550 to 1650 embodied half-a-century's accumulated knowledge of
the Elizabethan and Jacobean book trade. The first of the four volumes of *A
Bibliography of the English Printed Drama* (1930–59), lists all the play entries in
the Stationers' registers to 1616; it is more accurate than Arber and easier to use
because it employs modern transcriptional conventions and a less idiosyncratic
typography.

From the eighteenth century the early registers had been searched by students
of ballad literature. In the early 1920s, E. Hyder Rollins used Arber and Eyre &
Rivington to extract all the ballad entries in the registers (1557–1709). His
index supersedes John Payne Collier's suspect extracts from the registers, which
were, in Rollin's words, 'honeycombed with misstatements, forgery and vague
references'. Rollins is still an indispensable tool for students of the popular
printed literature of the period.

Greg's wish to see all the records to 1700 in print has never been realized, but
in 1938 the Society appointed W.A. Jackson, its American secretary, to continue
Greg's work and fill the last gap left by Arber. Jackson's initial interest in the
Stationers' Company was for the study of Elizabethan literature and for his work
on the revision of the *STC*, but like Arber and Greg before him, he became more
and more enthralled by the workings of the Company and the structure of the
Jacobean trade. His edition of the Court Books, 1602–40, was published in 1957
to coincide with celebrations to mark the 400th anniversary of the grant of the
Company's royal charter in 1557. His introduction gives a lucid account of the
English, Latin, and Irish Stocks and other patents assigned to the Company in
this period, an area which had hitherto been little considered.

Cyprian Blagden, an historian by training, a publisher by profession, and a
Liveryman of the Company, did much to free Stationers' Company bibliography
from its dependence on literary studies. His research into the history and
workings of the Company was undertaken for its own sake and in less than ten
years he produced what the Court had been talking about, off and on, for more
than a century. His *History of the Stationers' Company, 1403–1959*, was the
scholarly, coherent narrative which bibliographers and the Company alike had

---

2 'Some Notes on the Stationers' Registers', *Lib*, IV, 1 (1927); 'The Decrees and Ordinances of the
   Stationers' Company 1576–1602', *Lib*, IV, 2 (1928).

been waiting for. Blagden, like Graham Pollard for the earlier period, used the Company's records in order to work out the structure of the trade at large and provide a yardstick by which the records could be evaluated. He disproved the long-held belief that the Company's records ceased to have any bibliographical relevance after 1695 and showed that the eighteenth-century records were also important for research, even if they were no longer the only major source for study of the book trade, which, for this period, includes the surviving ledgers of several large printers such as the Bowyers and the Strahans. Blagden's numerous separate papers, published between 1954 and 1960 in *The Library*, *Studies in Bibliography*, *The Book Collector*, and other journals, are masterly studies of aspects of the Company's activities and its various patents in the second half of the seventeenth and in the eighteenth century. In particular, his work on the English Stock shows that the Company, principally in defence of its valuable literary property, continued to wield considerable power over the trade long after it lost its statutory control.

Graham Pollard's interest in the Company began in 1936 when he and John Johnson were planning a series of Oxford Books on Bibliography. In time he came to be the Court's and the Council's unofficial adviser on publishing the records, and he encouraged and helped Jackson, Blagden, Ellic Howe, and many younger scholars by passing on to them a number of the discoveries he made among the records as well as advising and supporting them in their research. His rôle in Stationers' Company bibliography is much more important than the volume of his published work would suggest – his two papers on the Company before incorporation were a major contribution to a sparsely tilled field.

From time to time the membership records had been used for the study of sixteenth-century books, but their potential was not realized until bibliographers began to turn serious attention to the composition of the early book trade. Gordon Duff's *A Century of the English Book Trade . . . 1457 to 1557* (1905) was the first of the Society's dictionaries of the trade. Although he was never a member of the Society, Duff published a number of papers on early printers in the *Transactions*. 'The English Book-Trade before the Incorporation of the Stationers' Company', *Transactions* 8 (1905) (reprinted in *A Century of the English Book Trade*) was a pioneer study of the period between the formation of a book-trade brotherhood in 1403 and its incorporation by royal charter in 1557. H.R. Plomer's *Dictionary . . . 1641 to 1667* followed Duff's in 1907, and, with others, he completed the years 1557 to 1640 in 1910. The last two of the dictionaries, spanning the years 1668–1775, were published by the Society in 1922 and 1932. An ambitious plan to revise them in the 1950s had to be abandoned but in the meantime the Society reprinted the existing dictionaries in a single volume in 1977. Taking 1666, the year of the Fire, and 1723, the date of publication of Negus's list of printers, as his terminal dates, Michael Treadwell has been working for many years on a directory of London printers which the Society will publish in due course and which will supersede much of Plomer's dictionary for 1668 to 1725. D.F. McKenzie combined the various interlocking registers of members of the Company and, by also drawing on the Court Books, pension lists and various English Stock records, he provided easy access to a complete record of the Stationers' apprentices from 1605 to 1800. Michael Turner is compiling a computerized register of members of the Company (1801–30). He and Christine Ferdinand are currently engaged in combing the Company's records and other sources of book-trade membership (1557–1800) to provide data for the contributors to the projected Cambridge History of the Book in Britain. Work on the trade outside London has been going forward for many years – Peter Isaac's Book Trade Index has co-ordinated most of the work on the regional book trade – Mary Pollard's account of the Dublin trade to 1800, given as the Lyell Lectures for 1987, drew on the Stationers' records for the relationship between the Dublin and London trade. A directory of the Dublin trade in the same period, on which she has been working for many years, is nearing completion. It is hoped that all published and unpublished work on membership of the book trade will eventually be amalgamated in a single database.

In 1951 the Court of the Stationers' Company gave permission for University Microfilms to film most of the records to 1800 for the use of the University of Southern Illinois, and copies were later supplied to a handful of other national and university libraries. This opened up the eighteenth-century records just when that century had become a fashionable field of research. Scholars began to realize that book-trade studies were an important source for the study of literature of the period. Blagden's work on the English Stock also contributed to a change in attitude to the later Stationers' records and David Foxon's many years of study of the eighteenth-century records threw new light on Pope studies, much of which he incorporated in his Sandars and Lyell lectures.

The 1951 microfilm proved to be the shape of things to come, though few realized it at the time. When publishing costs shot up in the early 1970s, large-scale editions of the records became a thing of the past but technology now offered a viable, if unaesthetic, alternative in machine-readable microform facsimile. One result of this was that the onus of making the records accessible to scholars passed from the Bibliographical Society to the Company itself when, in the mid eighties, the bulk of the archive, 1554–1920s, was microfilmed for the Company by Messrs Chadwyck-Healey. At time of writing, this is available in some forty-five libraries round the world; it was followed by a companion volume to the archive (1990) compiled by the present author, which included a complete catalogue of the records, 1554–1984.

The history of copyright is an area where the Company's records have still to be thoroughly mined. R.C. Barrington-Partridge's FLA thesis, published in 1938, broke new ground in the specialist area of legal deposit; it is still the only comprehensive account written by a layman for bibliographers, although J.C.T. Oates published key studies of legal deposit in Cambridge University.

In the last thirty years there have been fewer published studies of the records themselves and their analysis and interpretation is more often to be found embedded in literary criticism, printing history, the economics of the book trade, copyright, history of science, London history, musicology, and much besides, as numerous footnotes in scholarly publications testify. What of future research? Most of the Stationers' archive is freely available on microfilm, and the Company makes the originals more readily accessible to bona fide scholars than was once the case. There remains a small amount of unfilmed material still to be examined, while the large quantity of miscellaneous documents (available on film for the first time), including recently acquired family papers of several members of the trade who were closely connected with the Company, have yet to be researched. Nor have the waste books, available on film for the first time, been fully explored, and there is work to be done on the nineteenth-century registers, both those at Stationers' Hall (and on microfilm) and those from 1842 (unfilmed) now at the Public Record Office at Kew. A quantitative study of the nineteenth-century trade, using the Stationers' register as a major source, is already under way under the direction of Simon Eliot and David McKitterick. As the rôle of the Company in the nineteenth century is re-assessed, so the registers, the Court Books, English Stock records and other nineteenth-century records will be explored by bibliographers and others. In time the Company's twentieth-century records will also become the subject of bibliographical research and the records of the voluntary registry which replaced the statutory copyright registers in 1923, will receive scholarly scrutiny. The Company's records remain a key source for the study of the book in Britain.

Further reading

Arber, Edward. *A Transcript of the Registers of the Company of Stationers of London 1554–1640 A.D.* 5 vols. Privately printed, 1875–94

Barrington-Partridge, R.C. *The History of Legal Deposit throughout the British Empire*. Library Association, 1938

Blagden, Cyprian. *The Stationers' Company, a History, 1403–1959.* 1960

Eyre, G.E. Briscoe and C.R. Rivington. *A Transcript of the Registers of the Worshipful Company of Stationers: from 1640–1708 A.D.* Roxburghe Club, 3 vols. 1913–14

Duff, E.G. *A Century of the English Book Trade . . . 1457 to the incorporation of the Company of Stationers in 1557.* Bibliographical Society, 1905

Greg, W.W. *Some Aspects and Problems of London Publishing between 1550 and 1650.* Oxford 1956

Licensers for the Press . . . to 1640. A Biographical Index based Mainly on Arber's Transcript. Oxford Bibliographical Society, 1962

A Companion to Arber, being a Calendar of Documents in Edward Arber's Transcript of the Registers, ed. I.G. Philip. Oxford 1967

Greg, W.W. and E. Boswell. *Records of the Court of the Stationers' Company 1576 to 1602 from Register B.* Bibliographical Society, 1930

Jackson, W.A. *Records of the Court of the Stationers' Company 1602–1640.* Bibliographical Society, 1957

McKenzie, D.F. *The Stationers' Company Apprentices, 1605–1800,* 3 vols. Oxford Bibliographical Society, 1960–78

Myers, Robin, ed. *Records of the Stationers' Company, 1554–1920.* 115 reels of microfilm. Chadwyck-Healey, 1986, with printed caption list, reprinted in *Book Trade History Group Newsletter,* 6 February 1988

The Stationers' Company Archive, 1554–1984: An Account of the Records. Winchester, 1990

Oates, J.C.T. 'The Deposit of Books at Cambridge under the Licensing Acts, 1662–79, 1685–95', *Transactions of the Cambridge Bibliographical Society*, 2 (1957)

Plomer, H.R. *A Dictionary of the Booksellers and Printers . . . in England, Scotland and Ireland from 1641 to 1667.* Bibliographical Society, 1907

Plomer, H.R., with H.G. Aldis, Robert Bowes, E.R.McC. Dix, E. Gordon Duff, Strickland Gibson, G.J. Gray, R.B. McKerrow, and Falconer Madan; general editor R.B. McKerrow. *A Dictionary of Printers and Booksellers in England, Scotland and Ireland, and of Foreign Printers of English Books 1557–1640.* Bibliographical Society, 1910

Plomer, H.R., with the help of H.G. Aldis, E.R.McC. Dix, G.J. Gray, and R.B. McKerrow; edited by Arundell Esdaile. *A Dictionary of the Booksellers and Printers . . . 1668 to 1725.* Bibliographical Society, 1922

Plomer, H.R., G.H. Bushnell, and E.R. McC. Dix. *A Dictionary . . . 1726 to 1775.* Bibliographical Society, 1932

Pollard, Graham. 'The Company of Stationers before 1557', *Lib*, IV, 18 (1937)

'The Early Constitution of the Stationers' Company', *Lib*, IV, 18 (1937)

Pollard, Mary. *Dublin's Trade in Books 1550–1800.* Oxford, 1989

Rollins, E. Hyder. *An Analytical Index to the Ballad-Entries in the Registers of the Company of Stationers of London.* Chapel Hill, 1924; new edition, with introduction by Leslie Shepard, Hatboro, PA, 1967

Enumerative and descriptive bibliography

T.H. HOWARD-HILL

In 1959, the year of his death, Sir Walter Greg completed his *Bibliography of the English Printed Drama to the Restoration*, the first volume of which had been published twenty years before. Fredson Bowers, the author of the equally influential *Principles of Bibliographical Description* (Princeton, NJ, 1949), considered that Greg's first volume 'set a standard for descriptive bibliography that has not been equalled' and he ranked the demonstration 'of the adaptability and simplicity of his comprehensive system' of bibliographical description as 'perhaps the greatest' of Greg's achievements.[1] This tribute is significant for the history of bibliography because Greg's career itself supported Bowers's aphorism that 'A true bibliography is primarily an analytical bibliography' (*Principles*, p. 34), the product of bibliographical analysis rather than of simple enumeration, and his claim that a descriptive bibliography provided essential preparation for textual and literary investigations. Scarcely anything Greg wrote after the compilation of his *List of English Plays before 1643 and Printed before 1700* (Bibliographical Society, 1900) was not related to the task for which the *List* was an essential prelude.[2] The 'Introduction' published in volume IV (1959) codified the descriptive practices Greg had developed from Madan, McKerrow, and others during the first half of the century. However, although he hoped that the descriptive methods he had found serviceable in his own work might prove of wider use (p. v), he had not set out to write a comprehensive guide to bibliographical description. Greg had, however, benefited from reading Bowers's *Principles* in typescript, but, he remarked, 'Professor Bowers and I do not always see eye to eye' (p. iv).

This was scarcely surprising, for, as John Carter put it, *Principles* issued from 'a powerful – indeed an autocratic – intelligence, addicted to formula and impatient of imprecision, at large in an area whose bibliography is still in a highly fluid, and therefore vulnerable, state'.[3] Acknowledging by his dedication

1 'Walter Wilson Greg, 9 July 1875–4 March 1959', *Lib*, v, 14 (1959): 172.
2 Reviewing vol. IV, David Foxon completely misread Greg's career when he wondered 'how much energy has been squandered on this bibliography that might have been spent in writing more of the historical and critical works which we would have gladly had from Greg's pen' (*PBSA*, 55 (1961): 356).
3 'Some Bibliographical Agenda', *Nineteenth-Century English Books: Some Problems in Bibliography* (Urbana, IL, 1952), p. 80.

Greg's influence upon his work, Bowers set out a rational, consistent yet adaptable method of bibliographical description that could be applied equally well to both hand- and machine-printed books. It was 'the basic function of a descriptive bibliography to present all the evidence about a book which can be determined by analytical bibliography applied to a material object' (*Principles*, p. 34). The rigour and amplitude of Bowers's method provoked objections on the one hand from those who contended that the value of analytical or descriptive bibliography lay principally in its contribution to the study of literary texts and, on the other hand, from those who argued that the principal object of a descriptive bibliography should be to illuminate the history of the book and serve book collectors and booksellers. But, as David Vander Meulen later commented, 'one of the major contributions' of *Principles* was that Bowers 'had stressed the *multiple* functions of bibliographical description, including that of providing a full historical record'.[4] *Principles of Bibliographical Description* in effect asserted the primacy of descriptive bibliography to all intellectual studies grounded on the printed book.

Principles, 'at once a landmark and a challenge' (John Carter, *Books and Book-Collectors* (1956), p. 186) both identified the crucial issues and provoked their discussion. In recent years, in a series of influential essays G.T. Tanselle has elaborated Bowers's statements of descriptive problems and solutions in the light of subsequent reaction to them and their employment in bibliographies of modern as well as earlier works. For instance, quasi-facsimile transcription of title-pages became common from Falconer Madan's advocacy of the practice in the 1890s so that, Tanselle judged, 'it must by now be one of the most widely employed conventions of bibliography' (*SB*, 38 (1985): 47). Notwithstanding, using Greg's *Bibliography* for primary data, David Foxon found in his *Thoughts on the History and Future of Bibliographical Description*[5] that the collation and only a 'straightforward transcription of the title in roman type' (p. 19) were usually sufficient to distinguish editions. However, as Tanselle mentioned, the title-page transcription was part of the description of the 'ideal copy' of a book, not merely a means of identification (p. 57). The labour and expense of printing quasi-facsimile transcriptions and the improvement of photographic techniques have prompted, for instance, the Pall Mall Bibliographies and the Pittsburgh Series in Bibliography from 1972 to reproduce photographs of title-pages and other printed material (e.g. copyright declaration pages) in place of title-page transcriptions. There is little consistency in the provision of photographs in bibliographies even if only for illustrative rather than descriptive purposes. For example, Philip Gaskell's *John Baskerville* (Cambridge, 1959) gives both title-page transcriptions and photographs of some items, but his *A Bibliography of*

---

4 David Vander Meulen gives a fuller description and assessment of *Principles* than can be given here in 'The History and Future of Bowers's *Principles*', *PBSA*, 79 (1985): 197–219. He discusses its reception and analyses the issues raised, and supplies a useful account of the literature of and developments in descriptive bibliography since 1949.

5 Where only titles or journal references are given, full details will be found under Further Reading.

the Foulis Press (1964) in the Soho Bibliographies series has none (and lacks a contents page). On the other hand, David Gilson's *A Bibliography of Jane Austen* (Oxford, 1982) in the same series under *'Title'* simply refers the user to a title-page facsimile; half-titles, spine labels, and half-title imprints are also reproduced photographically. However, photography without transcription effectively transfers the burden of description to the reader. As David Vander Meulen wrote reviewing Gilson's bibliography (*PBSA*, 79 (1985): 435–42, see especially 438–9), the uncritical provision of evidence from a single copy must leave the reader in doubt in many instances. In fact, title-page transcription and the provision of photographs, Tanselle judged, served different purposes; 'these approaches are complementary, and one does not necessarily obviate the other' (p.53).

Objections to the replacement of transcriptions by photographs depend on the underlying principle of descriptive bibliography at which Greg (*Bibliography* 4: cxlviii) and Bowers arrived independently: 'The collational formula and the basic description of an edition should be that of an ideally perfect copy of the original issue' (*Principles*, p. 113). Since a bibliographical description 'aims to provide a standard against which individual copies can be measured' (Tanselle, *SB*, 30 (1977): 21), it is necessarily dependent on the number of copies of each work a bibliographer has managed to examine. (David Shaw has calculated the probabilities that a certain number of copies will reveal all variations within an edition – *Lib*, v, 27 (1972): 310–19.) Necessity to distinguish editions, impressions, issues, and states has led increasingly to the use of optical (usually) collating machines. The first and most important of these was the Hinman Collator used for Charlton Hinman's *The Printing and Proof-Reading of the First Folio of Shakespeare* (Oxford, 1963), one of the most intensive bibliographical analyses of a single English book in this half of the century. The first application of the Hinman Collator to the works of a nineteenth-century author, Warner Barnes's *A Bibliography of Elizabeth Barrett Browning* (Austin, TX, 1967) resulted in the discovery of 'a variant state or concealed impression' (p.9) for every one of the first English editions collated in an average of six copies for each book. Admiring Barnes's bibliography, John Carter (*BC*, 19 (1970): 101–4) was quick to proclaim the challenge of his innovation for bibliographers and book collectors. In fact, substantially through the use of collating machines, editors rather than bibliographers have sought variant states assiduously, and descriptive bibliographers have followed in their footsteps. ('The truth is, modern textual criticism has progressed so far beyond descriptive bibliography as to be an aid to description, not the reverse', Bowers, *Lib*, v, 24 (1969): 116.) The preface to the second edition of Warren Roberts's *A Bibliography of D.H. Lawrence* (Cambridge, 1982) records, for instance, that 'Textual research with the Hinman Collator has revealed that many important textual differences exist in printings or issues which are not described in separate entries' (pp. xi-xii) of the 1962 edition of his bibliography.

The variations revealed by collation of multiple copies of titles led to re-examination of the fundamental descriptive categories, edition, impression, issue, and state (*Principles*, 37–113). Citing contemporary confusion in the use of the term 'issue' in descriptions of modern books, James B. Meriwether and Joseph Katz ('A Redefinition of "Issue"', *Proof*, 2 (1972): 61–70) suggested distinguishing the printing and the publishing history of a book; 'state' would then be reserved for the printing, 'issue' for the publishing history. Tanselle, however, objected that the proposed distinction would sometimes make it impossible to use a single term to describe the book as a physical object: 'The book itself, which cannot be torn apart into its printed and its published aspects, remains unclassified' (*PBSA*, 69 (1975): 34–5). He proposed definitions of 'issue' and 'state' to complement *Principles* (pp.65–6). On the other hand, prompted by the proliferation of variants of books printed by offset or relief methods between around 1840 and 1970, James West proposed an extension of Bowers's systematic terminology, 'the term *plating* as a step between *edition* and *impression*' (p. 257), which has been employed in bibliographies of American authors.

Bowers's *Principles* was generally understood to lay a heavy burden on anyone who undertook a descriptive bibliography according to its standards and some reviewers considered that it was not necessary to apply full descriptive techniques to all classes of printed material. On the other hand, the apparently scanty treatment *Principles* gave to the problems of describing nineteenth-century and later books suggested to some (see John Carter, 'Nineteenth-Century English Books', *Books and Book-Collectors*, 1956) that Bowers subscribed to Madan's degressive principle that required merely a short bibliographical description of modern books. Bowers put this misconception to rest in 'Bibliography Revisited', *Lib*, v, 24 (1969), 84–128: he concluded that 'the kinds of variation are likely to alter from period to period, and thus the details of description must remain appropriate to the problem by altering in conformity' (p.114). The importance of the issue for the descriptive bibliographer is that 'he should guarantee the same standards of methodical investigation both in respect to scope and to minuteness of examination for all entries listed under the descriptive sections of his bibliography' (p. 127). Very few bibliographies, however, are consistently descriptive.

Nevertheless, the best modern bibliographies exceed their earlier counterparts in at least two significant respects, in comprehensiveness and in uniformity of formulary and terminology. And yet, that's not much; despite *Principles*, some bibliographers still devise personal solutions to descriptive problems already resolved, and the generally agreed desirability of standardized descriptive methods based on *Principles* contends with the constant quest for precision and clarity. Little consistency exists even in such a simple matter as the designation of the recto or verso of a leaf, or the representation of an initial unnumbered page in a pagination. Tanselle's articles discuss modern innovations and controversies on points of descriptive detail too numerous to survey here. For the general improvement in descriptive standards Greg and Bowers share credit with the flourishing modern bibliographical societies, of course, but more with a distinctive realignment in the market for or readership of bibliographies. The post-war growth of university education and the associated development of literary studies redirected the descriptive bibliographer's principal goal to provide a handy means of identification for book collectors towards the provision of a fuller account of an author's literary production which included its pre-publication stages and post-authorial publication history. This development was driven by editors who sought to reconstruct textual histories from the evidence of the physical forms of authors' works.

On the other hand, compilers of author bibliographies have been criticized for their failure to locate individual titles within the wider context of printing and publishing history. Nevertheless, information about the book trade is not yet widely or uniformly available. A descriptive catalogue or bibliography of the output of a press (printer or publisher) is as onerous to compile as the bibliography of a prolific author. It is not surprising then that examples are few.[6]

Also influential in the recent history of descriptive bibliography are a number of publishers' series of bibliographies of greater and lesser scope. The Soho Bibliographies, published by Sir Rupert Hart-Davies (1951–72), is the most extensive series and the most important. (From 1976, the bibliographies were published by the Clarendon Press, Oxford.) The majority of the Soho Bibliographies were on modern authors.[7] W.S. Peterson's *Kelmscott Press* (1984), provides a welcome innovation. The preeminence of the Soho series and its concentration on more modern subjects suggests a certain uniformity of treatment, a 'Soho recipe' as a *TLS* reviewer termed it (25 October 1963). However, he could mention a host of descriptive details which varied in individual Soho volumes, and differences in the treatment of publishing history, an issue still debated. To B.C. Bloomfield ten years later, the 'general style seemed a little antique' (*Lib*, v, 28 (1973): 76) but recent volumes chart inexorable progress towards consistent and ample bibliographical description.

In the arrangement, however, the Soho Bibliographies established a convention widely adopted but as frequently varied. From the 1953 Slocum-Cahoon Joyce bibliography, sections were distinguished by capital letters, with different forms of numerical subordination. Usually the arrangement was 'A. Books and

6 Allen Hazen and J.P. Kirby's *Strawberry Hill Press* (New Haven, 1942, 1973), Philip Gaskell's *Baskerville* (Cambridge, 1959, 1973) and *Foulis Press* (1964), D.F. McKenzie's *Cambridge University Press, 1698–1712* (Cambridge, 1966), Otto Streptow's *John Siberch* (Cambridge, 1970), Margret Suchard's *John Ogilby and William Morgan* (Bern, 1975), Christina D. Stewart's *Taylors of Ongar* (New York, 1975), Stephen Parks's *John Dunton* (New York, 1976), J.H. Woolmer's *Hogarth Press* (1976, 1987), C.C.F. Morbey's *Charles Knight* (Birmingham, 1979) and W.S. Peterson's *Kelmscott Press* (Oxford, 1984) are prominent examples.
7 Allan Wade's *Yeats* (1951, 1958, 1968); John Carter and John Sparrow's *Housman* (1952), rev. by W. White, St Paul's Bibliographies (1982); J.J. Slocum and H. Cahoon's *Joyce* (1953); Cecil Woolf's *Douglas* (1954), and *Rolfe* (1957, 1972); Leon Edel and Dan Laurence's *Henry James* (1957, 1961, 1982); B.J. Kirkpatrick's *Virginia Woolf* (1957, 1967, 1980), *Forster* (1965, 1968, 1985), and *Blunden* (1979); Richard Fifoot's *Sitwells* (1963, 1971); Warren Roberts's *D.H. Lawrence* (1963, 1982); Miriam K. Benkovitz's *Firbank*, (1963, 1980, 1982); and Dan H. Laurence's *Shaw* (1983). Earlier authors are W.B. Todd's *Burke* (1964, 1982); Sir Geoffrey Keynes's *Berkeley* (1976); D.J. Gilson's *Austen* (1982); R.L. Green and J.M. Gibson's *Conan Doyle* (1983).

pamphlets', 'B. Contributions to Books', 'C. Contributions to Periodicals' and so on, but a fuller sequence is so far from being established that, for instance, Roberts's *Lawrence* (1982) did not get so far as section G, which is 'Letters' in Gilson's *Austen* (1982): in the Bloomfield and Mendelson *Auden* (1972) section G is 'Odds and ends', and O-Q is omitted in the arrangement. Nevertheless, the beginning sections are now generally adopted so that James L.W. West could assume standardization in suggesting additional refinements ('"Section B" and the Bibliographer', *Analytical and Enumerative Bibliography*, 7 (1983), 31–6). Similar topics and Craig S. Abbott's proposal for 'A System of Bibliographical Reference Numbering' (*PBSA*, 69 (1975), 67–74) are considered by Tanselle (1984), the more valuably because *Principles* contains little on the arrangement of bibliographies.

No account of enumerative and descriptive bibliographies in this century would be complete without notice of the unequalled achievements of Sir Geoffrey Keynes. Beside a wide range of other literary publications (notably on the study of William Blake), Sir Geoffrey compiled a long series of bibliographies,[8] many of which remain the fullest or only bibliographical treatment of their respective subjects. In terms of descriptive methodology, as R.C. Bald's review of the 1958 *Donne* makes clear (*Lib.*, v, 14 (1959): 54–8), Keynes was the last great exponent of a style of bibliography exemplified by the earlier bibliographies compiled by T.J. Wise.

The second edition of Keynes's *Hazlitt* was published by St Paul's Bibliographies (Winchester) which, like the Pall Mall series (1972–7), continued a line of author bibliographies that included J. Howard Woolmer's *Lowry* (1983) and *The Poetry Bookshop, 1912–1935* (1988), Michael Collie and A. Fraser's *Borrow* (1984), William LeFanu's *Jenner* (1985) and *Nehemiah Grew* (1988), Harold B. Carter's *Banks* (1987), and Marjorie Moon's *Mary Belson Elliott* (1987) and *John Harris* (1976, 1987). The series reflected a broader tendency in including Ray Desmond's *British Gardens* (1984) and C. Philip's *Fireworks Books* (1985). Many descriptive catalogues or bibliographies appeared in the *Book Collector*'s long-running 'Some uncollected authors' series and in bibliographical journals like *The Library* (e.g. F.F. Madan's 'A bibliography of George Bate's *Elenchus Motuum Nuperorum in Anglia*', v, 6 (1951): 189–99) but despite their value, they are too numerous even to mention here. However, the rôle of bibliographical societies, particularly the Bibliographical Society, in sponsoring the publication of checklists and descriptive bibliographies should not be neglected. Setting aside such monuments as Greg's *Bibliography* and *STC*, the Bibliographical Society's publications, for instance, have ranged from Occasional Papers (e.g. Thomas R. Adams's *The Non-Cartographical Maritime Works Published by Mount and Page*,

---

8 Austen (1929), Berkeley (Oxford, 1976), Blake (New York, 1921), Boyle (1932), Bright (1962), Brooke (1954, 1959), Brown (Cambridge, 1924, 1968), Donne (Cambridge 1914, 1932, 1958, 1973), Evelyn (Cambridge, 1937), Harvey (Cambridge, 1928, 1953, 1989), Hazlitt (1931, 1981), Hooke (Oxford, 1960), Lister (Winchester, 1981), Petty (Oxford, 1971), William Pickering (1924, 1969), Ray (1951), and Sassoon (1962).

1985) through more extensive listings: Folke Dahl's *Bibliography of English Corantos and Periodical Newsbooks* (1952), Brian Morris's *Cleveland* (1967), W.C. Smith's *John Walsh* volumes (1948, 1968; 1968), and Joel Wiener's *Descriptive Finding List of Unstamped British Periodicals* (1970).

Other publishers' series (e.g. Gale, Garland, Greenwood, G.K. Hall, Kent State, Mansell, Scarecrow, St Martin's, Whitston) established around the seventies have produced 'a flurry of unfortunate author bibliographies and checklists' (G.T. Tanselle, 'The State of Bibliography Today', *PBSA*, 73 (1979): 299) which gives no sign of diminishing. Nevertheless, this largely American phenomenon serves as reminder that all descriptive bibliography proceeds from the necessary prerequisite of enumeration, and that even in its simplest form bibliographical compilation involves skills and demands standards of performance that challenge the tyro. Standing far from such annotated author checklists is a superb example of a descriptive catalogue which employs the methods of descriptive bibliography within a deliberately restricted scope, David Foxon's *English Verse, 1701–1750; A Catalogue of Separately Printed Poems* (Cambridge, 1975).

Looking to the future, it seems that a general advance to the standards of description advocated by Bowers and Tanselle will be slow. The extensive collation demanded by the best modern practice necessarily extends the time of analysis, and the range of collateral evidence about publication which students of literature require in author bibliographies greatly enlarges the scope of the bibliographer's task. Dan Laurence's claim that the bibliographer creates 'a portrait of the author as a bibliography' (*BC*, 35 (1986): 173) is not likely to be confuted by bibliographical practice. On the other hand, students of the book trade expect a corresponding enlargement of the information descriptive bibliographers can supply about the physical means of book production in relation to a printer's overall output and about the mechanics of distribution, requirements difficult to fulfil given that only a small number of printers and publishers have been given even minimal bibliographical treatment. The relatively easy access to imprint information which computer databases give cannot conceal that bibliographical analysis of prolific book producers is laborious and time-consuming. *Ars longa . . .* Nevertheless, the continuing vitality of the bibliographical societies and such newer organizations as the Book Trade History Group promises well for descriptive bibliography.

Further reading

Bowers, Fredson. *Principles of Bibliographical Description*. Princeton, NJ, 1949
   'Purposes of Descriptive Bibliography, with Some Remarks on Methods', *Lib*, v, 8 (1953): 1–22
   'Bibliography Revisited', *Lib*, v, 24 (1969): 89–128
Buhler, Curt F., J.G. McManaway, and L.C. Wroth, *Standards of Bibliographical Description*, Philadelphia, 1949

Colaianne, A.J. 'Aims and Methods of Annotated Bibliography', *Scholarly Publishing*, 11 (1980): 321–31

Foxon, David F. *Thoughts on the History and Future of Bibliographical Description*, School of Library Service, Los Angeles, and School of Librarianship, Berkeley, University of California, 1970

Gaskell, Philip. 'Bibliographical Description', *A New Introduction to Bibliography*, Oxford, 1972; corrected 2nd printing, 1974, pp. 321–35

Greg, W.W. 'Introduction', *A Bibliography of the English Printed Drama*, vol. IV, Bibliographical Society, 1959, pp. i-clxxiii

Harner, James L. *On Compiling an Annotated Bibliography*, MLA, New York, 1985

Howard-Hill, T.H. 'Bibliographical Description and Arrangement', *British Bibliography and Textual Criticism: A Bibliography*, Oxford, 1979. (Index to British Literary Bibliography, IV), pp. 9–16. (See also 1970–1979 *Supplement*, 1992)

 Bibliography of British Literary Bibliographies, 2nd edn revised and enlarged, Oxford, 1987. (Index to British Literary Bibliography, I)

Jones, John Bush (ed.), *Readings in Descriptive Bibliography*, Kent State University Press, Kent, OH, 1974

Krummel, D.W. *Bibliographies, their Aims and Methods*, 1984

Pearce, M.J. *A Workbook of Analytical & Descriptive Bibliography*, 1970

Shaw, David. 'A Sampling Theory for Bibliographical Research', *Lib*, v, 27 (1972): 310–19

Tanselle, G. Thomas. 'A System of Color Identification for Bibliographical Description', *SB*, 20 (1967): 203–34

 'Tolerances in Bibliographical Description', *Lib*, v, 23 (1968): 1–12

 'The Bibliographical Description of Patterns', *SB*, 23 (1970): 71–102

 'The Bibliographical Concepts of "Issue" and "State"', *PBSA*, 69 (1975): 17–66

 'Descriptive Bibliography and Library Cataloguing', *SB*, 30 (1977): 1–56

 'The Concept of "Ideal Copy"', *SB*, 33 (1980): 37–92

 'The Description of Non-Letterpress Material in Books', *SB*, 35 (1982): 1–42

 'The Arrangement of Descriptive Bibliographies', *SB*, 37 (1984): 1–38

 'Title-Page Transcription and Signature Collation Reconsidered', *SB*, 38 (1985): 45–81

 'A Sample of Bibliographical Description, with Commentary', *SB*, 40 (1987): 1–30, see bibliography, pp. 3–5

Vander Meulen, David L. 'The History and Future of Bowers's *Principles*', *PBSA*, 79 (1985): 197–219

West, III, James L.W. 'The Bibliographical Concept of Plating', *SB*, 36 (1983): 252–66

Describing maps

SARAH TYACKE

The recently published volume of the *History of Cartography* takes as a definition of maps that they are graphic representations which facilitate a spatial understanding of things, concepts, conditions, processes, or events in the human world.[1] This definition is somewhat at odds with the more conventional view of a map held by Samuel Johnson, as a geographical picture on which lands and seas are delineated according to their longitude or latitude.[2] The difference between the two demonstrates the new and helpfully expanded perception of maps by scholars (including practising cartographers) of what maps are, and of how they have been made in the past. This new definition embraces all maps and map-like objects: charts, diagrams, sketches, plans, views, imaginary maps, as well as new forms of maps. The most recent form – digitally held maps or digital maps – is causing a futher debate about definition to take place within the field of cartography. An awareness is now evident of the difference between the visual map, i.e. the actual graphic product on a screen (an 'electronic display' map) or in printed form, and its ordered but 'unseen' existence in a topologically structured database, which has the potential for various display or printed outputs.[3]

'What is a map?' remains high on the agenda of the International Cartographic Association (ICA) which has established a working group on cartographic definitions. The present proposal of the working group is that a map is a 'holistic representation and intellectual abstraction of geographic reality intended to be communicated for a purpose or purposes, transforming relevant geographical data into an end product, which has visual, digital, or tactile output'.[4]

I should like to thank the late Brian Harley, Ian Willison, Donald Hodson, Tony Campbell, David Woodward, Andrew Cook, Donald McKenzie, and Thomas Tanselle for reading this in earlier versions and for helpfully criticizing its contents. The views expressed are mine (as are any misunderstandings).

1 J.B. Harley and David Woodward (eds.), *The History of Cartography*, vol. I: *Cartography in Prehistoric, Ancient and Medieval Europe and the Mediterranean* (Chicago, 1987), p. xvi.
2 S. Johnson, *Dictionary* (1755).
3 M. Visvalingam, 'Cartography. GIS Maps in Perspective', *Cartographic Journal* 26 (1989): 26–32.
4 Report by the chairman, Christopher Board, on the Working Group on cartographic definitions in the *Cartographic Journal* 26 (1989): 175–6. Indeed the definition of cartography, i.e. the activity cartographers do, is itself being reviewed. The British Cartographic Society has prepared two definitions, the first for use in communication with the general public – 'cartography is the art, science

J.B. Harley has taken issue with the inclusion of 'digital' as a map output, as a map is, if nothing else, an 'image' and 'digits' are not.[5] Even so the artefact, which cartobibliographers and others list, catalogue, or otherwise describe, is no longer necessarily the conventional piece of paper showing where places are, and cartobibliographers of the future will have to accommodate these developments.[6] The databases from which maps may be printed or otherwise produced are analogous, in my view, to the copperplate or type form; that is, they are the physical source from which maps are produced. At the same time they are manipulatable in ways which the earlier forms were not, and may be considered end-products in their own right; these characteristics have obscured their relationship to maps and confused them with maps themselves. They have a life of their own as 'Geographical Information Systems' (GIS) which is different from that of maps. This difference of form is recognized by the necessity to provide for separate, if similar, ways of description. In the United Kingdom, for example, the Economic Science Research Council database research centre at Essex University and the British Library published in 1989 a guide, which included a section on describing spatial or geographic datafiles.[7]

Although the problem of defining what is and what is not a modern map, and then of describing such maps may seem unconnected to past preoccupations, the underlying principles of description do not seem to be very different from those necessary to describe earlier maps. In the long history of map production from manuscript, woodcut, copperplate, lithography, photo-lithography, and digital databases, the relationship between the method of production and the map itself has been the stuff of cartobibliographical study and controversy; as have the shifting views of what cartobibliographies are, as against catalogues, location registers, union catalogues, and facsimile atlases and the like.[8]

When R.A. Skelton gave the first Nebenzahl Lectures in 1966 on the history of map collecting and its study, he provided the first systematic view of the subject since Lloyd Brown's *The Story of Maps* published in 1949.[9] His remarks were confined to early maps, however defined, and it is salutary to see what he suggested was still required to be done and what has occurred subsequently.

---

and technology of making maps'. The second, for practising cartographers – 'cartography is the science and technology of analysing and interpreting graphic relationships, and communicating the results by means of maps'.

5 J.B. Harley, 'Cartography, Ethics and Social Theory', *Cartographic*, 27 (1990): 1–23.

6 The coining of the term 'cartobibliography' dates from 1914 and seems to have been invented by H.G. Fordham, although he does not discuss its introduction, as far as I am aware. See H.G. Fordham's *Studies in Cartobibliography* (Oxford, 1914). The use of the term was presumably an attempt to distinguish map bibliography from bibliography, sometimes now called 'letterpress bibliography'.

7 M. Taylor, *Bibliographic Control of Computer Files: The Feasibility of a Union Catalogue of Computer Files*. British Library Research paper 89 (British Library, 1990).

8 See G.T. Tanselle's account of 'Descriptive Bibliography and Library Cataloguing', in *Selected Studies in Bibliography* (Charlottesville, 1979), pp. 38–92.

9 Lloyd A. Brown, *The Story of Maps* (New York/Boston, 1949). R.A. Skelton, *Maps, A Historical Survey of Their Study and Collecting* (Chicago, 1970). Given as the first Nebenzahl Lectures in 1966.

This may serve as a base-line for what follows. Referring to the need to build up a corpus of information about early maps he judged that

The activity of individual students has not slackened, rather it has increased and intensified as to both volume and variety. This activity rests on no agreed methodology or standards, it is poorly sustained by catalogues of resources and other aids, so that comparative studies run the hazard of incompleteness, and it can be criticized by a geographer as being out-of-balance. The volume of this activity indicates a healthy energy; but it is not enough to raise the whole edifice of cartographic history, which would be built on intensive and extensive study of surviving examples, with analysis emerging in synthesis and leading to generalization on the evolution of the form and content of early maps.

It will be obvious that Skelton took it as axiomatic that there was a purpose beyond the describing of maps *per se* and that the purpose was the construction of a history of the evolution of the form and content of early maps. In this view he would, presumably, have agreed with Gaskell that 'bibliography, and by extension cartobibliography, means primarily the study of all documents, manuscript and printed, . . . and any document, disc, tape or film where reproduction is involved'.[10] He would have approved of a view of cartobibliography, as Gaskell does of bibliography, as the transmission of documents, i.e. maps in this case, the relationship of variant texts, and the evolution of particular texts in the process of their compilation and reproduction. But he would not have agreed with the view that, like bibliography, cartobibliography's 'overriding responsibility must be to determine a text in its most accurate form'.[11] This seems to be one of the most fundamental differences in purpose between some map describers hitherto and letterpress bibliographers, and reflects the nature of maps as perceived by their describers. In a sense the difference is explainable very simply: maps can and have been judged for accuracy by measuring them against the world itself. The question of 'authorial intentions' has, on the whole, seemed less important to map describers, whose interests tend towards describing how the view of the physical world changes over time.[12]

This has sometimes been a 'progressive scientific' view,[13] and at other times a less deterministic view giving due weight to contemporaries' own view of the world. This latter view, I suppose, may be construed as a form of 'authorial intention', as applied to maps as 'text'. Map describers are interested in

10 P. Gaskell, *A New Introduction to Bibliography* (Oxford, 1985), p. 1. The nature and purpose of bibliography provides for the discussion of the differences between map describers and bibliographers in this paragraph.
11 See Gaskell, *New Introduction*.
12 R.W. Karrow, 'Cartobibliography', *A.B. Bookman's Year Book* pt. 1 (1976), pp. 49–50. Here Karrow addresses the problem of what in map terms reconstructing a correct text is, this being the objective of textual criticism to which bibliography is the mainstay. He concludes that this is not a characteristic of cartobibliography. The cartobibliographer is not confined in his endeavours by a text. His text, against which he may wish to judge a map, is the world or portion of it, which can be reconstructed by historical and other means.
13 See M.J. Blakemore and J.B. Harley, 'Concepts in the History of Cartography. A Review and Perspective', *Cartographica* (1980) (17) and J.B. Harley's ''Deconstructing the Map', *Cartographica* 26 (1989): 1–20, where the cumulative progress of the accuracy of maps is questioned (p. 15).

identifying particular stages in the evolution of a map or set of maps through time, not the establishment of a definitive text against which others may be judged. The map comes in many versions and needs to be ordered and described, but it is not normally edited.[14]

Perhaps it should be? The map bibliographer finds great difficulty in understanding the significance of the concept of 'final authorial intentions', not least because sometimes the map 'author' is a composite of map draughtsman, engraver, and publisher and the map itself is a compilation of knowledge of the world at any given time. I do not want to dwell on this difference too much, but it may explain partly the divergence of opinion which occurred in the 1970s between some map describers and letterpress bibliographers, and amongst the bibliographers themselves who are debating the purposes of textual criticism.[15]

In 1966 Skelton noted that the first task to improve the situation he had described was the establishment of the basic critical principles, methods, and practice to be observed in studying an early map. He pointed out the need for a description of the map in a form intelligible to other students and permitting comparison with other maps described in the same form. 'Appropriate and agreed terminology is to be prescribed. For this first task, a conference between specialists, or consultation will be necessary so that the principles adopted are in step with general usage outside cartography, for instance by students of graphic art.' This has not proved possible as yet, as there is no agreed usage in the graphic field although the term 'state' in all its manifestations is the most common term used by print cataloguers. Anthony Griffiths has attempted to clarify the position in his *Prints and Printmaking*.[16] The initiative on this front has come from the map field itself. Skelton continued, 'the end product will be a series of compact manuals of guidance. I put this task first because work is going on all the time, and the sooner we have a common language of analysis, identification, and description in which to speak to one another the better.' He was of course referring here to map specialists' needs, not to an all-embracing descriptive language for maps and other documents, which all could use. His second task

14 See Alan L. Manford, 'The Texts of Thomas Hardy's Map of Wessex', *Lib*, VI, 4 (1982): 297–306, where he argues that it is possible to reconstruct the authoritative copy-text of the map, i.e. a map most closely following what we know of the 'author's final intentions'.

15 It is not yet clear whether the present debate over the purpose of textual criticism in the literary field will contribute anything to cartobibliography, but see J.J. McGann, *A Critique of Modern Textual Criticism* (Chicago, 1983); G.T. Tanselle, 'Historicism and Critical Editing 1979–85', *Textual Criticism since Greg: A Chronicle 1950–1985* (Charlottesville, 1987), pp. 109–53, and D.F. McKenzie *Bibliography and the Sociology of Texts* (The British Library, 1985), p. 28.

16 Definitions of 'State' and 'edition' are to be found in A. Griffith's *Prints and Print Making* (1980), but while 'State' follows a definition or a series of them depending on the practices of the period concerned, 'edition' has not been a matter of interest to the print cataloguer whose interests tend to lie in minutely cataloguing single-sheet prints, thus avoiding the use of the word and its definition. The fields of printed botanical drawings and of musical scores have, however, contributed much to the development of standards in the description of printed images. See W.D. Margadant, 'Descriptive Bibliography Applied to Botany' *Early Bryological Literature* (1968), pp. 1–33; D.W. Krummel, 'Musical Functions and Bibliographical Forms', *Lib*, V, 31 (1976): 327–50.

was the recording of map resources, with locations, without which a sure foundation for the study of maps could not take place. Much had been done, but it had been sporadic along national lines, as for example, the facsimile atlases of F.C. Wieder – *The Cartography of the Netherlands in the Seventeenth Century* – and of Armando Cortesão – *The Cartography of the Portuguese from the Fifteenth to the Eighteenth Centuries*.[17] Although called facsimile atlases these types of works included full descriptions of the maps as well as reproductions – a form well suited to the graphic nature of maps. The descriptions were not according to any generally accepted formula and furthermore the majority of the maps described were manuscript, where the genealogical problems of manuscript copies were, and still are, a challenge for cartobibliography.[18]

If we agree that in the matter of description Skelton's tasks were a correct assessment of the work to be done, then how far have we got? The ambiguity of terminology has not disappeared, and, seemingly, will not go away. This problem is not confined to maps but affects art history, music, and, of course, illustrations in books. Tanselle has recently drawn his fellow bibliographers' attention to the necessity of considering illustrations in books as an integral part of any book's description, and has also commented adversely on the lack of a common acceptance of bibliographical terms across all bibliographical fields: these terms he views as more or less relevant to map descriptions of whatever sort, and he is certainly right to point out the lack of awareness by cartobibliographers of the commonality of problems which bibliographers, of whatever sort, have to solve.[19]

This point has been further stressed by J.B. Harley in his provocative review article, 'Cartobibliography and the Collector'.[20] Tanselle specifically criticizes Coolie Verner for this unfortunate state of affairs in map bibliography on the basis of the contents of one article, but the reasons for it are far more complex than the effect of Verner's undoubtedly seminal article of 1974.[21] Without the realization that maps are physically produced in a different way from letterpress books, the implications of which were either ignored or considered of no great importance to earlier practitioners, no real advance in the understanding of maps and how to describe them could take place.

This was what Verner supplied; an insight into the production of copperplate maps. From his point of view, as copperplate maps were produced differently from books they should be described differently. This does not, as Tanselle has

17 F.C. Wieder, *Monumenta cartographica* (The Hague, 1925–33). A. Cortesão and A. Teixeira Da Mota, *Portugaliae Monumenta Cartographica* (Lisbon, 1960–2).

18 For a discussion of the problem of applying printed cartobibliographic principles to manuscript maps see D. Hodson, *Maps of Portsmouth Before 1801* (Portsmouth, 1978).

19 G.T. Tanselle, 'The Description of Non-Letterpress Material in Books', SB, 38 (1982): 1–42.

20 J.B. Harley, 'Cartobibliography and the Collector', Imago Mundi, 39 (1987): 105–10.

21 C. Verner, 'Cartobibliographical Description: The Analysis of Variants in Maps Printed from Copper-plates', *The American Cartographer*, 1 (1974): 77–87, and 'Cartobibliography', *Western Association of Map Libraries Information Bulletin*, 7 (March 1976): 31–8, reprinted and revised as 'The Study of Early Printed Maps', A.B. Bookman's Weekly, 58 (12 July 1976): 194–206.

rightly pointed out, have to be the case, and indeed can be confining descriptively; although some terms may be more useful in some fields, and thus used more often by one set of bibliographers than by another. In the map field, I would think that 'edition' would probably be more useful for describing atlases than for separately printed maps, where 'state' is normally sufficient to identify the item accurately and place it in relevant sequence.

Robert Karrow, writing in 1976,[22] considered that, although Verner had attempted a systematic vocabulary for detailing the relationships between copperplate maps and for classifying the variants that occur, no rules had been agreed. Karrow wrote 'but before we get a "Principles of cartobibliography" we need an empirical study of the kinds of variations that have actually been observed and recorded in cartobibliographies'. In 1991 we are still observing these variations and the formulation of rules is still awaited.[23] These should indeed relate to the physical evidence of the artefact, but establishing the terminology of description cannot wait until all is known about map production, as our knowledge of it is continually improving and changing. The cartobibliographer should ensure that a map or atlas is actually being described in its printing or publication context, rather than applying a formula which can obscure those actual processes and thus misleads the reader of the cartobibliography as to the true identity of the map or atlas. The classic problem in terminology here is the misuse of the word 'edition' which has been used to order sequentially, for example, *factice* or composite atlases, and multi-sheet maps. Thus, to take an early example from Whitaker's *Catalogue of County Atlases, Road-Books etc.*,[24] Whitaker refers to 'another edition, 1720' of Christopher Saxton's maps by George Willdey. The use of 'edition' here is misleading, as each Willdey atlas is different in content and can only be described accurately as an 'example' of an atlas.[25]

For modern maps the situation has been altered by the publication of the International Federation of Library Association's (IFLA) *International Standard for Bibliographic Description (Cartographic Materials) (ISBD) (CM)* in 1977, followed by the *Anglo-American Cataloguing Rules*, second edition *(AACR2)* in 1978. These were followed in 1982 by *Cartographic Materials: Manual of Interpretation for AACR2*, which was published by the American Library Association, the Canadian Library Association, and The Library Association.[26]

---

22 See Karrow, 'Cartobibliography'.

23 See, for example, D. Woodward 'Analytical Cartobibliography of Sixteenth Century Maps Printed in Italy', an unpublished discussion paper at the History of Cartography Conference at Ottawa, 1985, where he writes, 'There is really *not* a continuum between levels of bibliographical description, from checklist, catalogue, cartobibliography to analytical cartobibliography (recognizing that these terms still remain to be properly defined).' He then divides his scheme of cartobibliographical description into physical (i.e. plate, ink, paper, etc.) and bibliographical content (e.g. design features).

24 H. Whitaker, *The Harold Whitaker Collection of County Atlases, Road-Books etc. Maps presented to the University of Leeds* (Leeds, 1947), p. 17.

25 See below, pp. 137–9, for further discussion of the problem.

26 Hugo L.P. Stibbe (ed.), *Cartographic Materials: A Manual of Interpretation for AACR2* (Chicago, Ottawa, London, American Library Association (etc.), 1982).

This manual took chapter 3 of *AACR2* (the chapter devoted to maps), defined and refined the terminology more securely, and gave examples of applications and advice on how to catalogue maps. Combined with the advent of automated cataloguing in the English-speaking world, which necessitated precise rules to make the machine-readable catalogues work, formulation of rules for the cataloguing of modern maps accelerated as never before.

Elsewhere, notably in the Netherlands and France, similar rules were devised allowing for the exchange of records. None of this activity seems to have had any effect on the establishment of a terminology for earlier maps, at least formally; unlike the book world, published work on the rules for description for older maps did not occur. In practice, however, *Cartographic Materials* did offer guidance in a number of descriptive cases for older maps; for example, title, edition, co-ordinates, publication, dates of publication and situation as shown on the map, physical description areas, and notes. The authors of the manual specifically state that the rules do not cover in detail the description of early or manuscript cartographic materials, although they can 'furnish a sufficiently detailed description for the general library catalogue.'[27]

Why is it that guidelines for older maps have not been forthcoming? Following Verner, the physical nature of maps as artefacts has been emphasized by regarding the history of the woodblock or copperplate (to refer to only two possibilities of manufacture) as the subject of cartobibliography. This means that the 'plate', that is, the copper-plate itself, is the artefact being described by inference rather than the map. In order to record its history, impressions pulled from the plate are put in order and recorded by the use of the word 'state', that is, state of the plate. Thus the plate is the constant base in the evolution of a map's history. A prime example of this approach is Verner's account of John Smith's *Map of Virginia 1606*.[28] In this article he showed the power of visual analysis to determine the map's history. He remarked that the publishing sequence of Smith's map had plagued scholars for a century. To paraphrase his work, in 1854 Norton's *Literary Gazette* published an identification of two states of the plate which had been followed by Charles Deane's identification of four states.

In 1955 Hind re-examined the matter and settled on nine states. Verner thereupon isolated twelve states, using the physical evidence from the various surviving examples to do it.

Physical evidence from state 8 of Smith's map

Geographical   Three new names have been added:
Featherstone/Baye etc.

Bibliographical   Page 41/Smith has been added in the lower right-hand corner. Numerous mountains . . . have been re-engraved so that the shading on the north side is now formed by closely parallel diagonal lines rather than finely sculptured shading as found in earlier states.

---

27 Whitaker, *The Harold Whitaker Collection*, p. 6.
28 C. Verner, *Smith's Virginia and its Derivatives*, no. 45 (1968).

This emphasis on the engraving and printing side of map description was seemingly at odds with the more traditional way of bibliographical description based on the act, however defined, of publication. He also noticed the use of re-engraving of features which had become worn, a phenomenon rarely noticed hitherto, and not mentioned in cartobibliographies. Similarly in his work on the atlas, *Captain Collins' Coasting Pilot*, he drew attention to the presence of 'ghosts' or the re-emergence of features late in the life of a copperplate, which had been concealed on the copperplate by beating the plate on the back to remove features from the printing surface, and which had then subsequently re-emerged.[29]

A diagram (below) of the two basic points of view may clarify the issues apparently dividing cartobibliographers amongst themselves, and dividing them from some bibliographers:

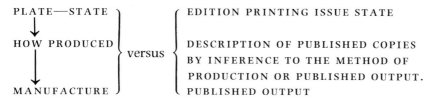

```
PLATE—STATE   ⎞        ⎛ EDITION PRINTING ISSUE STATE
     ↓        ⎟        ⎜
HOW PRODUCED  ⎟        ⎜ DESCRIPTION OF PUBLISHED COPIES
     |        ⎬ versus ⎨ BY INFERENCE TO THE METHOD OF
     ↓        ⎟        ⎜ PRODUCTION OR PUBLISHED OUTPUT.
MANUFACTURE   ⎠        ⎝ PUBLISHED OUTPUT
```

As Andrew Cook has pointed out, this polarization of approaches has been noted and criticized by Tanselle in his 1982 article on the description of non-letterpress material in books (see note 19) and Cook proposes that a second look be taken at the applicability of bibliographical terms to maps, especially 'edition', 'impression' (following Tanselle he prefers 'printing' to the word 'impression'), 'issue' and 'state' when applied to atlases, which combine letterpress and engraving, that is, text and maps, each of which may have its own separate history as well as a contextual history as part of an atlas.[30]

Since the late 1960s a number of cartobibliographies have been published whose authors have pointed out the necessity to understand map production and publication in all its physical manifestations. A meticulous example of this is Donald Hodson's continuation of Skelton's *County Atlases of the British Isles*, 1704–63.[31] This work is relevant in demonstrating the present pragmatic approach of some cartobibliographers and illustrates an awareness of issues not considered until very recently by letterpress bibliographers. Hodson writes in his introduction, 'during the time that an atlas was on sale it was common for the publisher to carry out revisions to the plates: thus the atlas can be seen to evolve'. Small stocks of made-up atlases, plus stacks of loose maps, were kept in the map-publishers' shops. As it was their practice to use on occasions newly printed sheets with old ones as they came to hand, many atlases exhibit 'instability' to such an extent that a word like 'edition' ceases to be adequate

29 C. Verner, *Captain Collins' Coasting Pilot*, Map Collectors' Series, no. 58 (1969).
30 A.S. Cook, 'Edition, Printing, Issue, and State as Terms in Cartobibliography', given at 13th International Conference on the History of Cartography, Amsterdam, 29 May 1989.
31 Donald Hodson, *County Atlases of the British Isles Published after 1703: A bibliography* (Tewin, Welwyn (Herts), 1989).

without some definition of what it should or could cover. In Hodson's work the word is used when:

1   There is a significant change to the title or imprint.
2   Pages of text are added or removed; or a significant part of the text is reset.
3   There is a significant revision of the maps.

Here we have a re-definition of the word 'edition', when applied to eighteenth-century atlases: but why did the term fall out of favour? At this period many atlases are merely 'examples' or varying versions of collections of maps, often without a title page, and it is their evolution which matters to cartobibliographers. The term 'edition' implied some regularity of characteristics, which cartobibliographers could not see in the collections of maps (i.e atlases) they were describing. Once this became apparent, as it did as more work was done on seventeenth- and eighteenth-century atlases in particular, a rejection of the term set in. The peculiarities involved may be exemplified by the atlas *factice* which is an atlas made up of maps, partly from a publisher's own stock and partly from others. The evolution of such an atlas may even contain regressive elements, that is, much older maps. Atlases in general are a very unusual sort of book and therefore the use of book terms without a great deal of thought will mislead, by giving a false sense of understanding to the reader. Even so it is evident that the word 'edition', if sensibly applied, is still useful. Hodson continues: 'When an alteration however small has been made, the plate is said to be in a different state; all the individual maps or impressions printed from the same state constitute a single edition, although the actual printings may have been spread over many years over half a century.' In this he follows Harvey in *The Printed Maps of Warwickshire*.[32] The dispute as to whether an edition corresponds to a printing or an impression from a copperplate (in the same way that a book edition corresponds to a printing from a forme of type rather than from a particular state of that plate) continues. The balance however seems to be coming down in favour of defining the word 'plate' as the equivalent of a book 'edition'. Atlases, at their worst from a bibliographical point of view, are a largely meaningless collection of individual printings of maps in various states; often only the title and text are the identifiers of some new stage in their history, and even they can fox the unwary, being, for example, earlier than the maps. It is hardly surprising therefore that by and large the full evolutionary history of atlases does not feature in the various short-title catalogues produced for books of the sixteenth, seventeenth, and eighteenth centuries. Instead there have been some monumental examples of separate atlas cartobibliographies, notably Koeman's *Atlantes Neerlandici* and more recently Pastoreau's *French Atlases of the Sixteenth Century*.[33] In the English context the publication of county

---

32 P.D.A. Harvey and Harry Thorpe, *The Printed Maps of Warwickshire, 1576–1900* (Warwick, 1959).
33 C. Koeman, *Atlantes Neerlandici*, 5 vols. (Amsterdam, 1967). M. Pastoreau, *Les Atlas français, XVIe-XVIe siècles* (Paris, 1984).

bibliographies has continued, notably for Sussex and Berkshire,[34] in which the methods of Harvey and Hodson have been followed.

If before the nineteenth century one is rarely dealing with an 'edition', what other terms are available? Hodson chooses the words 'variant' and 'example'. However he still needs to order these atlas manifestations chronologically, in so far as it is possible. Hodson does this by using all the types of evidence he can find, for example, newspaper advertisements; he then adopts a simple ordering sequence. Thus, for the *Speed (Overton Atlas)*, he describes it in chronological form as:

ATLAS	I	CIRCA 1713
ATLAS	2	POST 1716
ATLAS	3	CIRCA 1720
ATLAS	4	1743

Where it is obvious that the word 'edition' should be used he uses it; normally the more book-like products are amenable to this: for example, Herman Moll's *A New Description of England and Wales* . . . (1724) which went through five editions, according to his criteria, until 1753.

From this type of cartobibliography it is now clear that in order to make sense of the apparent chaos at this period of atlas production, the printing, publication, and selling processes must be understood, so that the bibliographical terminology is extended to fit the realities of production and can be used as precisely as possible.

Having considered atlases at one period of their production I now turn briefly to recent work on other types of maps; much work has been done, for example, on woodcut maps, notably by Tony Campbell[35] and David Woodward.[36] The terminology available to cartobibliographers, as Campbell points out, was mainly developed in the context of copper engraving, but woodcuts demand different words. They require ways, for example, of saying 'removal' when bits of wood fall off the woodblock! The advance in woodcut map description may be demonstrated by the difference in the identification of two woodcut maps: in 1952 when Marcel Destombes's catalogue of fifteenth-century maps came out,[37] the Rüst and Sporer maps were regarded as 'brothers off the same "block"'. Close comparison revealed that the two maps, looking the same, were from different blocks. The types of evidence available for a study of woodcut maps now include such factors as lettering which was produced by punches, or by movable type in recesses cut into the block, or else by stereotypes, or even by overprinting with letterpress. These types of physical phenomena were not identified before the work of Woodward and other woodcut cartobibliographers.

34 D. Kingsley, *Printed Maps of Sussex 1575–1900*. Sussex Record Society, vol. 72. (Lewes, 1982); E. Burden, *Printed Maps of Berkshire 1574–1900*, unpublished draft (1988).
35 Tony Campbell, *The Earliest Printed Maps, 1472–1500* (British Library, 1987).
36 David Woodward, 'The Woodcut Technique', *Five Centuries of Map Printing* (Chicago, 1975).
37 M. Destombes, *Catalogue des cartes gravées au XVe siècle* (Paris, 1952).

With woodcuts, some of the evidence is accidental – for example, damage to the woodblock – but, accidental or not, it provides evidence for the order of the printing of the maps. Although Campbell prefers not to use the word 'state', a definition of state which included accidentals would probably be helpful, provided the circumstances were made clear to the reader: what it is that has changed it physically. So in the case below of the Breydenbach map of Palestine we have, instead of a deliberately changed state, progressive stages of deterioration of the woodblock giving rise to a series of changes in the printed map.[38]

1488   Three letters have a piece missing
1490   Alexandria is incomplete, lacking part of the *r* and the complete *i*.
1498   The name 'Geth' has disappeared.

The more critical visual examination of atlases and the earliest woodcut maps, both those in books and those published as separates, has been matched by further consideration of the copperplate map and of the lithographic map. Again, following on from Verner, the emphasis has been on the physical means of reproduction but has also included consideration of other physical attributes of the map, notably watermarks, which can help determine the order of editions, states, etc., as well as the likely date of publication. David Woodward has most usefully used watermarks in his studies of sixteenth-century map and atlas production in Italy: from his investigation of watermark radiography[39] to his most recent catalogue of the maps and prints of Paola Forlani, where watermark evidence and that of the offsets on the backs of maps casts light on the context of their publication in the 1560s.[40]

The present expansion of cartobibliographical terminology, although it is not consistent nor universally agreed, is a necessary investigative stage in improving our understanding of how maps were made, printed, published, and distributed and has altered the use of previously accepted bibliographical terms, by modifying them to cover particular classes of maps and atlases. Without, however, a consensus on the meaning of the more commonly used terms, it will become increasingly difficult to discuss cartobibliographic problems within their area of study, and with other bibliographers in the book, print, music, and other image and text fields. In the past, little experience has been exchanged at a practical level. Within cartobibliography itself we should begin to codify both the production and publication terms which have been used pragmatically over the past thirty years and relate them more firmly to the practices of other bibliographers. Most important, we should understand clearly what the bibliographical terms mean in production and publication costs and use them appropriately, but avoiding them when they would mislead.

38 Campbell, *Earliest Printed Maps*, p. 95.
39 David Woodward, 'Watermark Radiography at the Newberry Library' *Mapline*, 15 (1979): 1–2.
40 David Woodward, *The Maps and Prints of Paola Forlani: A Preliminary Catalogue*. (Wisconsin – Madison, 1990), p. iv.

More generally cartobibliography has also to respond to the great changes which have occurred during recent decades, for example, in the production of maps in digital form; the creation of catalogue records, both for modern and earlier maps, by automated means; the establishment of cataloguing rules for modern maps; the publication of volume 1 of the *History of Cartography*; and the publication of a number of innovative cartobibliographies. This means establishing standards for machine-readable and conventional hard-copy formats. The discipline should not be inward looking, but should relate more to general historical and bibliographical frameworks.

Thus, the agenda is much the same as in the 1960s but has different emphases: we need to establish descriptive standards for earlier maps, but now in the light of machine-readable record formats; we need to construct combined cartographic record databases of groups of maps – for example, Dutch, French, and English mapping of the sixteenth, seventeenth and eighteenth centuries – so that maps can be studied in a wider context than hitherto and we can provide systematic evidence for historians of cartography and other scholars; we also need to recognize that current mapping and mapping of the immediate past is a legitimate concern of cartobibliography, if the continuum of the subject is not to be lost sight of in unrelieved antiquarianism.

Developments in the study of book illustration

GWYN WALTERS

'Consciousness of the illustrated book', wrote Frank Weitenkampf in 1938, 'has in recent years become acute.' Despite the note of urgency in this observation no iconographic matters infiltrated the contents list of The Bibliographical Society's *Studies in Retrospect*. But Victor Scholderer was one contributor who saluted Alfred Pollard's early and consuming passion for illustration, and paid tribute to the 'lightening' of bibliographical text by facsimile image in Claudin's *Histoire de l'imprimerie en France* (Paris, 1900–14). After 1945 a flood of literature engulfs the student, and emanates from catchment areas which are in turn the preserve of the manuscript scholar, the art historian, the print collector, the bibliophile, the bibliographer, the typographer, the literary historian, and others. Much of it is listed in Vito J. Brenni's *Book Illustration and Decoration: A Guide to Research* (Westport, CT, 1980), which carries an ambitious title and is certainly wide-ranging, but the avoidance of qualitative annotation invalidates the titular claim to guidance. In the short compass allowed here, a highly personal attempt is made to chronicle and evaluate some of the significant studies which consider the evolution of the West European illustrated book.

Weitenkampf's *The Illustrated Book* (Cambridge, MA, 1938) was matched, in that year, by Lawrence C. Wroth's editing of *The Dolphin*, no.3. It included a chapter on book illustration by Philip Hofer which remains a model of compression and analysis. A welcome and remarkable feature of the post-war general surveys by David Bland (1958), Norma Levarie (New York, 1968), John Harthan (1981) and indeed, Hendrick D.L. Vervliet's editing of the composite, *The Book through Five Thousand Years* (1972), was the assessment of the roots of illustration in the manuscript book. In terms of national survey the French are to the fore with the superlative Frantz Calot, L.M. Michon, and J.P. Angoulvent's *L'art du livre en France* (Paris, 1931), followed in 1947 by André Lejard's editing of *The Art of the French Book*. Edward Hodnett's *Five Centuries of English Book Illustration* (1988) extends further his primary concern for 'interpretive' literary illustration first outlined in the case studies of his *Image and Text* (1986). Complementing national surveys are those of individual presses. Characteristic of this genre is the Bibliothèque Nationale's *L'Art du livre à l'Imprimerie Nationale*

(Paris, 1973) where such relevant chapters as 'Le Cabinet du Roi' and 'Les livres de fêtes' lead up to the press's modern involvement in the *livre d'artiste*.

While in Britain the resources of the Victoria and Albert Museum are a byword for the arts of the book, it is impossible to ignore American institutional preeminence in amassing collections. The Rosenwald, Spencer, Hofer, and Mellon collections at Washington, New York, Harvard, and Yale respectively have no British and scarcely a European equivalent. The need for general surveys will no doubt continue to characterize publication trends, but if one must register a particular privation it would be to say that the illustrated printed book awaits the treatment accorded the illuminated manuscript in A.N.L. Munby's *Connoisseurs and Medieval Miniatures* (1972). That is to say we require a critical history of the attitudes of past patrons, collectors, and bibliophiles to book illustration.

The complexities which characterize the patterns of illustration in books and manuscripts from late Gothic to Renaissance exercise the minds of scholars in a wide spectrum of disciplines. The major bibliography of literature on incunables is certainly that assembled by Kurt Hans Staub and his team, *Der Buchdruck im 15. Jahrhundert* (Stuttgart, 1988), where the several entries under 'illumination' and 'rubricators', for example, demonstrate the potency of the manuscript age. Yet, to escape the surfiet of Staubian citations, and to epitomize the period in one work of noble proportion and aesthetic appeal, it would be necessary to look back to the first decade of the present century. The Pierpont Morgan Library's *Catalogue of Manuscripts and Printed Books* (1907), superbly printed at the Chiswick Press in four volumes, highlighted the libraries of William Morris, Richard Bennet, Ashburnham, and others. A.W. Pollard, taking pride in the catalogue's integration of illustration and text, saw the work as an exercise in 'visualising the fifteenth-century book in its finest riches'.

Neither can early twentieth-century imprints be ignored in national or regional studies. For Italy, Kristeller on Florentine cuts (1893) and the Prince d'Essling on Venetian illustration (Florence, 1907–14) are such, and have been followed by Sander's general Italian catalogue (Milan, 1942) and the now classic exposition – Ruth Mortimer's catalogue of sixteenth-century books at Harvard (Cambridge, MA, 1974). Scaling down the field Begey and Dondi unmask sixteenth-century Piedmont (1961–6), and George D. Painter examines a single volume, the *Hypnerotomachia* of 1499 (1963). Virtually the same pattern emerges for France. The illustration of incunables in Claudin's history (Paris, 1900–14) stretches liberality to massive proportions, as does Hugh Davies's catalogue (1910) of the Fairfax Murray library. Mortimer's majestic catalogue of Italian books was preceded (Cambridge, MA, 1964) by her French catalogue, while Robert Brun's listing (Paris, 1969) is more comprehensive if very much more taut. Konrad Haebler (Leipzig, 1923) and James Lyell (1926) are the expositors of early Spanish books, while the catalogue of Portuguese books edited by H.M. King Manuel, and printed by the University Press at Cambridge (1925–35), is a work of exceptional grandeur. The post-war years have seen the completion of Vindel's *El arte tipografico* (Madrid, 1945–51) and

Anne Anninger's catalogue of Spanish and Portuguese books in the Harvard collections (Cambridge, MA, 1985).

The Low Countries have benefited, despite the inaccessibility of the library of the Dukes of Arenberg, from the pioneer studies of woodcuts of the incunable era by W.M. Conway (Cambridge, 1884) and later by M.J. Schretlen (1925). Wouter Nijhoff's *L'Art typographique dans les Pays-Bas* (The Hague, 1903–35) is the base from which Dutch and Belgian scholars examine typography and illustration in H.D. Vervliet (ed.), *Post-Incunabula in the Low Countries* (The Hague, 1978), a work of considerable critical appeal. Early German illustration is featured in the facsimiles which characterize the work of Richard Muther (Munich, 1884), Wilhelm Worringer (Munich, 1912), and the Fairfax Murray catalogue (1913), and it found unbridled expression in the nineteen volumes of Albert Schramm's *Der Bilderschmuck der Frühdrucke* (Leipzig, 1924–36). Ferdinand Geldner's study (Stuttgart, 1968–70) included German printers 'abroad', while that of Horst Kunze (Leipzig, 1975) is a highly specialized introduction to incunable illustration. A truly fundamental advance was the study of manuscript layouts of Latin and German exemplars in Adrian Wilson's *The Making of the Nuremberg Chronicle* (Amsterdam, 1976). The yield from exemplars was heightened by Wilson's discovery of preliminary sketches for illustrations found in the endpapers of a Koberger Bible.

Much of the post-war critical literature on incunable and Renaissance illustration unveils the techniques of the manuscript age, and their adaptation or rejection in the printed book. The opening salvo was fired by E.Ph. Goldschmidt in his *The Printed Book of the Renaissance* (Cambridge, 1950). His thesis, stated baldly, is that the book with illustrations deriving from textual narrative was a medieval conception. The Renaissance, he argued, evolved a new-style 'picture-book', where the work of the artist no longer served as narrative explication or mnemonic function as in manuscript illumination. Of comparable influence was Curt F. Bühler's *The Fifteenth-Century Book* (Philadelphia, 1960) which disclaims simple autonomous categories for books and manuscripts in a new world of pictorial cross-fertilization. In order to avoid unscientific sampling he suggests the intensive study of a 'cohesive group' such as decorated Florentine incunables; it would now be possible to propose a further fruitful collation with the relevant research in Annarosa Garzelli's *Miniatura fiorentina del Rinascimento* (Florence, 1985).

The true successor to Goldschmidt and Bühler is *Pen to Press: Illustrated Manuscripts and Printed Books in the First Century of Printing* (College Park, MD, 1977) by Sandra Hindman and J.D. Farquhar. They accept Bühler's advocacy of Florence as a centre to be studied from the dual standpoint of illumination and printed illustration, but also advance the claims of Ghent and Bruges, Paris, Nuremberg, and Venice. Moreover, using Boethius as a sample author, they unfold the factors determining a variant contemporary iconography of the same text. Complementing such studies are the modern research trends revealed in the edited versions of two major conferences. First, the Library of Congress's *The Early Illustrated Book: Essays in honor of Lessing J. Rosenwald* (Washington, DC,

1982) allows eleven papers to focus on three important subject groups: Dutch and Flemish imprints; landscape depiction; and the illustration of the texts of Virgil. In the same year came a Warburg Institute colloquium, *Manuscripts in the Fifty Years after the Invention of Printing*. One of its papers of outstanding significance was that by Lilian Armstrong, demonstrating that the cycle of illustration established for Pliny manuscripts in the Gothic period continued to be used in printed books, although a classicizing iconographic variant developed in Venice.

Clearly the investigation of comparable classical cycle-models is an exciting prospect. The theme is further developed in Armstrong's *Renaissance Miniature Painters and Classical Imagery* (1981), and with some verve in Glasgow University Library's *The Glory of the Page: Medieval and Renaissance Illuminated Manuscripts* (1987), edited by Nigel Thorpe. The foundation for comparable Dante studies has been laid in massive detail and scholarship in *The Illuminated Manuscripts of the Divine Comedy* (Princeton, NJ, 1964) by Peter Brieger, Millard Meiss, and Charles S. Singleton. Other major studies in medieval secular illustration, but awaiting comparable and complementary studies in early printed books, are Hugo Buchtal's *Historia Troiana* (1971) and D.J.A. Ross's *Illuminated Medieval Alexander-Books* (Cambridge, 1971).

Philip Hofer noted that in general surveys of book illustration it is the practice to pass quickly over the seventeenth century. 'Someone who is enthusiastic', he wrote, 'should rediscover Baroque books.' An indulgent smile may have accompanied these words, for his *Baroque Book Illustration* (Cambridge, MA, 1951), based on his own collection, is the first general explication of the field. Indeed it became a Baroque touchstone.

National surveys of the Baroque have taken divergent paths, but certainly no account can afford to omit the attention given to the German illustrated broadsheet. While the single-leaf format prompts the attention of the print historian, the progression from *Andachtsbilder* to Renaissance *Bilderbogen* and Baroque *Neue Zeitungen* is in reality one of increasing textual proportion. The essentially pictorial catalogues of Geisberg and Strauss are admirable, but more thorough scholarship was displayed in William A. Coupe's study (Baden-Baden, 1966–7) for the 'Bibliotheca Bibliographica Aureliana' series. Coupe's elucidation of a surprisingly complex symbolism is massively bolstered by the reproduction of the resources of Wolfenbüttel, Darmstadt, and Strasbourg by Wolfgang Harms and his team (Munich, 1980–   ), while John Roger Paas has initiated (Wiesbaden, 1985–   ) the more thematically circumscribed study of the political broadsheet.

If Emma Pirani's work for Italy in the seventeenth century is only suggestive (Rome, 1956), that of Diane Canivet (Paris, 1957) for French fictional and poetic imagery is a notable addition to earlier surveys by Mornand (Paris, 1931) and Duportal (Paris, 1914). English illustration becomes distinctive for the first time in this century. Arthur Hind's *Engraving in England* (Cambridge, 1952–   ) has been extended, in collaborative volumes, to the Jacobean and Caroline periods;

and his engraver-orientated work is now supplemented by Alexander Globe's *Peter Stent* (Vancouver, 1985), a large-scale study of a single publisher, a natural progression anticipated by Leona Rostenberg's *English Publishers in the Graphic Arts 1599–1770* (New York, 1963). Edward Hodnett's *Francis Barlow* (1978) places that master's work in the wider context of English engraving.

It is only possible to be selective in noting important work on individuals. The coincidence of tercentenaries for Hollar and Ogilby (1976–7) prompted notable exhibitions and monographs on each, the latter written by Katharine van Eerde (Charlottesville, VA, 1970 and Folkestone, 1976). The early catalogues of Jacques Callot by Meaume (Paris, 1860) and Lieure (Paris, 1924–7) have been followed up by the work of Bechtel (New York, 1955), Schröder (Munich, 1971), and Ternois (Paris, 1962). Rubens's illustrations and title-pages for Balthaser Moretus are excitingly registered by facsimile, catalogue, notes, and correspondence in *Corpus Rubenianum Ludwig Burchard* (1978). A characteristic Baroque manifestation which prompted exotic contemporary record was the festival. Gabriel Mourey's pioneer *Les Livres de Fêtes françaises* (Paris, 1930) is now complemented, for the Low Countries, by Landwehr's *Splendid Ceremonies* (Leiden, 1971).

The metaphoric language of emblems brought a creative tension to both graphic and verbal arts. The foundation laid by Mario Praz (1938) has been soundly augmented by Landwehr's listings in the Utrecht 'Bibliotheca Emblematica' series, while the setting up of a major 'Index Emblematicus' at Wolfenbüttel in the late 1970s – influenced by the 'Iconographic' and 'Christian Art' indexes at the Warburg Institute and at Princeton – has resulted in the admirable *Andreas Alciatus: I. The Latin Emblems* (Toronto, 1983) by Peter Daly and others. A quintessential application of emblematic art was the illustrated title-page and the frontispiece. If Rubens, as practitioner, is well documented by the *Corpus Rubenianum*, Pepys, as collector of the genre, is now equally served by volume III of Robert Latham's *Catalogue of the Pepys Library at Magdalen College* (Woodbridge, 1981). Margery Corbett and Ronald Lightbown in their *Comely Frontispiece* (1979) set a new standard of critical introduction and detailed examination of English baroque imprints. Different in chronological span is Francesco Barberi's *Il frontespizio nel libro italiano* (Milan, 1969) which covers the manuscript, incunable, and Renaissance book, and provides a further dimension to the investigations of Hindman, Armstrong, Garzelli, Bühler, and others into the complex inter-relationships of manuscript and printed book in the century after Gutenberg.

It would not be exceptional to think of the eighteenth century as a placid interregnum between the vigour of the baroque and the experimentation of the nineteenth century. The Goncourts saw it as the 'century of the vignette' as opposed to the earlier baroque frontispiece, but such neat labelling is often subverted by extraordinary forerunners or the later persistence of modes characteristic of an earlier age. Thus the art forms of the High Rococo, 1750–80, were prefigured by Romeyn de Hooghe, while the baroque festival book cast forward long shadows into the Napoleonic era.

The court of first reference for France is now *The Art of the French Illustrated Book 1700–1914* (New York, 1982) by Gordon N. Ray, for on bibliophilic, literary, and artistic grounds it is a model. English-language sources for critical works are few, and in the case of Owen E. Holloway's *French Rococo Book Illustration* (1969) of a commendably idiosyncratic nature. When not immersing himself in Ray the student would do well to browse in Maggs's exceptional catalogue, *A Collection of French Eighteenth-Century Illustrated Books* (1930), where bindings by Derome, Padeloup, and others vie with plates of rococo illustration in epitomizing the French art of the book.

Christie's catalogue of 19 June 1981 presents the literary images of Venetian eighteenth-century books in the Saks collection. The primacy of Venice in Italian illustration is also attested by the studies of Morazzoni (Milan, 1943) and Lanckoronska (Hamburg, 1950). German illustration has always, as in France, followed a literary pattern. Thus Arthur Reumann's standard survey (Strasbourg, 1931) notes important German editions of Milton, Pope, Sterne, and Richardson alongside the expected Lessing, Goethe, and Haller. Chronicling a wider arc of German, Austrian and Swiss illustrations for the Frankfurter Bibliophilen-Gesellschaft (Frankfurt, 1932–5) are the three handsome and informative volumes which constitute the joint labours of Lanckoronska and Oehler. However, their once-useful citations for locations in German libraries may be of little use today.

No work on the English eighteenth-century scene has rivalled the authority of Hans Hammelmann's critical and biographical dictionary (New Haven, CT, 1975). Edited and completed by T.S.R. Boase for the Paul Mellon Centre, it follows Hodnett's concern for interpretive literary illustration. The preface recalls the author's work in an 'intractable' field, where the British Museum and Bodleian catalogues 'could not be relied on to state whether or not a volume held plates'.

The nineteenth century is without doubt the most formative and varied in the whole history of illustration. The English achievement is now considerable and it will be the more useful here to assess the modern literature centred upon the English scene. But, as suggested in the earlier oversight of incunable and Renaissance printing, the student must not deny himself the indulgence of sampling reference works imbued with the richness of a more leisured age. Howard C. Levis's *Descriptive Bibliography . . . of Engraving* (1912), magnificently printed at the Chiswisk Press, is such a work, and refers, even at that early date, to a large extant literature. Even so, Gavin Bridson and Geoffrey Wakeman's *Printmaking and Picture Printing* (Oxford, 1984) is a bibliography with such abundant reference to a vital trade literature of processes that any lack of familiarity with Levis is somewhat alleviated. The new garment, so to speak, has the character and warmth of the old.

Modern surveys have been varied in approach. Philip James (1947) invited readers to share William Morris's 'endless pleasure' in the illustrated book. Different in tone and purpose, Michael Twyman's *Printing, 1770–1970* (1970) exposed 'uncharted' areas as harbingers of new concepts of graphic design; and Percy Muir's *Victorian Illustrated Books* (1971) was impatient with the historical docketing of the sixties and nineties as periods of unity, and with the neglect of Turner as book illustrator. In many ways Wakeman's *Victorian Book Illustration: The Technical Revolution* (Newton Abbot, 1973) was the most radical and intelligent interpretation of factors in the transition from autographic to photomechanical processes.

A forthright salute to English achievement was Gordon Ray's *The Illustrator and the Book in England 1790–1914* (New York, 1976), based on the Pierpont Morgan Library exhibition. Pointers by Ray to new reaches of research are the large presence, in his entries, of artists' drawings, engravers' proofs, and autograph letters. Simon Houfe's large-scale dictionary (Woodbridge, 1978) for the same period helpfully notes the location of collections at libraries and galleries. At the other end of the scale are the studies of individual illustrators, where Rodney Engen's volumes on Housman and Doyle are examples of a significant reassessment of Victorian artists which beckons researchers. The literary form which commands special attention is the novel, and here Olmsted and Welch's checklist of studies (1979) has supplemented John R. Harvey's general survey (1970). The particular value of Harvey was his outstanding analysis of complementary influences of text and image. John N. Hall's *Trollope and his Illustrators* (1980) was preceded by John Buchanan Brown's successive studies of 'Phiz', Thackeray, and Cruikshank (Newton Abbot, 1978–80), while Gerald Finley, using the Cadell Papers at Edinburgh, explored, in his *Landscapes of Memory* (1980), the unsullied field of Turner as illustrator to Scott.

Concern with process is the subject of many of the more memorable modern studies. Antony Dyson in *Pictures to Print* (1984) establishes the eclectic nature of the metal engravers' work, and the focus of craftsman-engraver is also central to Basil Hunnisett's dictionary and historical studies of English work in steel, no less than Rodney Engen's dictionary of metal engravers, etchers, and lithographers (1979). Nor has work on wood been neglected. Eric de Maré's *Victorian Woodblock Illustrators* (1980) gives artists and engravers full rein in a work of enormous style, and Engen's *Dictionary of Victorian Wood Engravers* (1985) rectifies the inadequacies of listings in standard sources. Lithography is fortunate in having the authoritative history of Wilhelm Weber in English translation (1966). Michael Twyman's now classic *Lithography 1800–1850* (1970) is very much in the modern research mode of emphasizing the importance of the professional draftsman. The topographical genre in Britain and France is what Twyman chose to explore in order to exemplify techniques.

Work in colour applied, at one time or another, to all the processes of illustration. Martin Hardie's *English Coloured Books* (1906) is still of much value as a panorama. Special appendices on Baxter, Ackermann, Rowlandson, and Alken contrast with Ruari McLean's attention, in his *Victorian Book Design and*

Colour Printing (1972), to the neglected Shaw, Jones, Humphreys, and Cundall. Wakeman and Bridson's *Guide to Nineteenth-Century Colour Printers* (Loughborough, 1975) is a pioneering list of great potential and two major exhibitions celebrated the cause of colour printing. The 1978 exhibition at Yale's Center for British Art was documented in Joan Friedmann's *Color Printing in England 1486–1870* (New Haven, CT, 1978), where Vizetelly, Jones, and Humphreys are singled out for their work in formalizing a new concept of book design. The IPEX 80 catalogue, *British Coloured Books 1738–1898* (1980), pays tribute to 'conceivably the greatest assembly of British coloured books ever shown' as the preface puts it, and was notable for featuring the hand-coloured aquatint. Major J.R. Abbey's collections of aquatinted and lithographic books are beautifully exposed in catalogues representing *Scenery* (1952), *Life* (1953), and *Travel* (1955–7) in those media for the period 1770–1860; while Colin Franklin's *Themes in Aquatint* (San Francisco, 1978) asserts that 'the dust has not settled upon established taste'.

To pass judgement on the twentieth century is perilous, but there can be little doubt that the best general survey is John Lewis's *The Twentieth-Century Book* (1967). The author emphasizes that his dictum for book collecting is that illustration and design must show evidence of a 'directing intelligence'. A similar intelligence fashions the dimensions of his own work.

In this new century the categories of illustration which engage attention are delimited on aesthetic and stylistic grounds, rather than by process of printing. Three dominant groups, the *livre d'artiste*, the art nouveau book, and 'fantastic' literature, all have nineteenth-century roots, German expressionist illustration responding to later impulses. Major exhibitions, with their attendant catalogues, are frequently the best reflection of the modern age. Thus the New York and Boston *livre d'artiste* exhibitions of 1936 and 1960, with catalogues respectively by Monroe Wheeler and Eleanor M. Garvey are now standard reference sources. Based on exhibitions of his own collections, W.J. Strachan's *The Artist and the Book in France* (1969) educated English audiences in the work of French ateliers and their autographic processes. Harvard's contribution to the 1960 exhibition at the Museum of Fine Arts, Boston, is supplemented by its own splendid *Turn of the Century 1885–1910* exhibition and catalogue (Cambridge, MA, 1970) of the art nouveau mode. Reference must be made to John Russell Taylor's incomparable *The Art Nouveau Book in Britain* (1966), with its elegantly aggressive style and argument. Equally outspoken is Lothar Lang's *Expressionist Book Illustration in Germany 1907–27* (1976), an attempt to 'salvage the heritage' of books uncommon in the book trade. The larger context of modern German illustration is treated in Schauer's respected survey (Hamburg, 1963) and more sumptuously in Wolfgang Tiessen's more specialized volumes (Neu-Isenburg, 1968–72). 'Fantastic' or visionary subjects, which are so peculiarly an English manifestation, have been outlined by David Larkin (1974) and Brigid Peppin (1975), while Diana L. Johnson consolidates the theme with a catalogue (Rhode Island, 1979) of the exhibition of this 'uncharted territory' at The Rhode Island School of Design.

The progress and critical assessment of graphic art in the various national traditions is beyond the bounds of this chapter. While it is doubtful if English illustration can cling to its nineteenth-century primacy, there are extravagant avenues to explore, none more appealing than Rigby Graham's *Romantic Book Illustration in England 1943–55* (1965). More critical than others of the resurgent English wood engraving was A.C. Sewter (Manchester, 1962), whose Whitworth Gallery catalogue refers to English work as 'a backwater off the great stream of modern art'. Albert Garrett's *British Wood Engraving of the Twentieth Century* (1980) is in every respect the most satisfactory exposition to date, and is now nicely complemented by the wider embrace of Peppin and Micklethwait's *Dictionary of British Book Illustrators: The Twentieth Century* (1983).

Several lacunae will be apparent in this digest, most noticeably perhaps private press illustration, the work of the Limited Editions Club, the American illustrators, childrens' illustrated books, and the ever-evolving new frontiers of interest – periodical and cover illustration, for instance. What is certain is that the literature of book illustration is inexorably assuming a dominant rôle in the book arts.

Bibliographical developments in the history of science

MAGDA WHITROW

The advent of the computer has revolutionized all bibliographical work. Not that the work of the bibliographer has lessened, for quality still governs the efficiency of the mechanized procedures, but the latter have been made so much easier. The latest plans for Supplements to the *Isis Cumulative Bibliography*, 1913–65, the publication of which was a landmark in the bibliography of the history of science,[1] envisages the use of a hard-disk computer with a database consisting of the entire ten years of annual bibliographies. I shall first consider several publications and then monographs, handbooks, and guides, concluding with a brief account of the arrangement of references.

As a discipline the history of medicine[2] is older than the history of science, which may be said only to have come into existence in this century. It is not surprising then that it was a historian of medicine, Karl Sudhoff, who was first responsible for the compilation of a bibliography of the history of science. He included in the first volume of his *Mitteilungen zur Geschichte der Medizin, der Naturwissenschaften und der Technik*, published in Leipzig in 1902, abstracts of papers on the history of science in addition to a bibliography on the history of medicine. Not until March 1913 did the first number of *Isis*, an international review devoted to the history of science and its cultural influences, make its appearance. From its first issue one of its principal features was a bibliography of the history of science. Its founder, and its editor for nearly forty years until 1952, was George Sarton who, although preceded in his endeavour by Karl Sudhoff, may be considered the real father of the bibliography of the history of science. During his editorship no fewer than seventy-nine bibliographies appeared, containing over 100,000 notices. *Isis* has remained the most important periodical in the field and now contains an annual bibliography of well over 3,000 entries, many of which carry brief abstracts or annotations. There is an index of names and authors, but no subject index. It is in classified order.

I am grateful to John Neu, Editor of the 'Isis Critical Bibliographies', Graeme Fyfe, of the Science Museum Library, and Veronica Higgs, of Mansell Publications, for suggesting additions to this chapter.

1 A previous survey of the subject by the present editor of the 'Isis Critical Bibliography', John Neu, was published in *Library Trends* (Bibliography: Part 2), 15 (1967): 776–92.
2 The bibliography of the history of medicine is only touched on in this survey – see p. 158. There is extensive literature on the subject.

Beginning with the 1989 issue, the 'Isis Critical Bibliography' will be renamed the 'Isis Current Bibliography of the History of Science and its Cultural Influences' and will no longer be a fifth issue of *Isis* but a separate annual publication.

At present the most important bibliography of a serial nature, apart from the 'Isis Critical Bibliography', is the *Bulletin Signalétique* (formerly *Bulletin Analytique*) published quarterly since 1952 by the Centre National de la Recherche Scientifique. Like *Isis* it is international in scope. It is in classified order and many references are followed by brief annotations. Entries in Slavonic languages, sometimes even those in German, are given in translation. There are detailed subject, name, and author indexes and a keyword index.

Both Sarton, the editor of *Isis*, and François Russo, the editor of the *Bulletin Signalétique*, published articles setting out their programme for a successful bibliography of the history of science. Sarton, in a paper in *Isis* (3 (1920–1): 159–70), explained his ideal of a 'selective', as opposed to an 'analytical' bibliography. It should be critical and constructive and include every publication which is important. He reverted to the subject in an article in *Archives Internationales d'Histoire des Sciences* (6 (1953): 395–419), in which, after a short history of the field, he dealt with the methods of selecting items. He believed that completeness was an infantile idea; it was utility that mattered most. Bibliography should be *raisonné*. Russo set out his programme in the same journal (12 (1959): 253–66). He believed that the field should be limited essentially to the history of science and technology, although relations with other fields were important.

None of the other serial bibliographies of science is as comprehensive as the 'Isis Critical Bibliography' and the *Bulletin Signalétique*, nor as international in scope. *Mitteilungen zur Geschichte der Medizin, der Naturwissenschaften und der Technik*, which in the early days of the discipline was the second major bibliography, ceased publication in 1942, during the Second World War. Only two volumes have since been published: the first, edited by W. Artelt, *Index zur Geschichte der Medizin, Naturwissenschaften und Technik*, covering the years 1945–8 (Munich and Berlin, 1953), the second, edited by J. Steudel, covering the years 1949–52 (Munich and Berlin, 1966). In the first only a third of the entries deal with the history of science; in the second they are restricted to the biological sciences only.

The Comité Belge d'Histoire des Sciences issued *Notes bibliographiques* in typed form at irregular intervals until 1971, listing books, reviews, and articles in author order with subject indexes. In 1970 Roger Calcoen edited *Notes bibliographiques* from 1946–1968, containing entries published during those years. This publication is now being continued as *Technologia* (formerly *Technologia Bruxellensis*). An important classified bibliography of work in Russian on the history of science is *Istoriia Estestvoznaniia, Literatura, opublikovannaia v SSSR* (Nauk, Moscow). The first bibliography in this series, covering the years 1917–47, was published in 1949. The eighth volume in the series appeared in 1985.

The Swedish journal *Lychnos* published a bibliographical section, mostly containing entries in Swedish and/or dealing with topics in the history of Swedish science from 1962, but the 1967–8 volume seems to be the last to contain a bibliography. A general register, covering the years 1936–62, lists 3,159 references with author and name index that appeared during those years. *Scientiarum Historia*, a periodical which first came out in Antwerp in 1959, published annually a bibliography of the history of science in the Netherlands, but seems to have ceased publication in 1963.

However, new bibliographies published serially have been added to the list of publications in the history of science. *Bibliografia Biezaca Historii Nauki i Techniki*, a quarterly publication in Polish, was first published in 1971 by the Polska Akademia Nauk. It is now published in loose-leaf form inserted in the periodical *Kwartalnik Historii Nauki i Techniki*. An Italian bibliography, *Bibliografia Italiana di Storia della Scienza*, is published by the Museum of the History of Science in Florence. It first came out in 1982. It contains mostly references to Italian publications and works by Italian authors. A *Bibliography of the History of Australian Science* began to appear annually in *Historical Records of Australian Science* (Canberra) in 1981. The Japanese periodical *Kagakusi Kenkyu* ('Journal of History of Science, Japan') also publishes an annual bibliography.

Two serial guides to bibliographies of a more general nature, but including bibliographies of the history of science, are (1) *Bibliographic Index*, a cumulative bibliography of bibliographies published by H.W. Wilson since 1938, and (2) the German *Bibliographische Berichte*, published annually by the Deutsches Bibliographisches Kuratorium since 1959. In the first, bibliographies of the history of each branch of science can be found under a subdivision 'history'. There are no subsections of this kind in the second.

As far as technology and the special sciences are concerned, *Technology and Culture* began in 1962 publishing annually a current bibliography in the history of that subject. It is classified by subject and there are brief annotations. An earlier bibliography of the history of engineering and technology was published in the *Transactions of the Newcomen Society* annually from 1921 to 1947. Its first three issues included only periodical literature, but for the rest of its existence books were added. The quarterly journal, *Historia Mathematica*, first published in 1974, contains abstracts of references to the history of mathematics. A bibliography of the history of astronomy has been sponsored by Commission 41 (History of Astronomy) of the International Astronomical Union since 1960. It was published annually in Moscow and was prepared by Mrs N.B. Lavrova of the Sternberg Astronomical Institute. Early issues listed articles and books on the history of astronomy in general and biographical material on personalities eminent in the subject. Later issues are classified in much greater detail. They include a large number of Russian references, with English translations. The last issue to appear was the bibliography for 1979, published in Moscow in 1984. Volume I of a new *Annual Bibliography of the History of Natural History*, covering the literature of 1982 came out in 1985.

Although several of the serial bibliographies have been discontinued, the number of abstracts in the principal serial bibliographies has grown enormously as a result of the growth in publication. The entries in the 'Isis Critical Bibliography' have risen from 1,430 in 1961 to 3,649 in 1988; those in *Bulletin Signalétique* from 1,804 in 1961 to 4,645 in 1988 from nearly 500 journals.

Since the 1950s, several one-volume guides to the literature of the history of science have been published. Similar guides to the sciences would, of course, be out of date now, but guides to the history of science, although they may be incomplete, do not suffer the same fate. Again the pioneer in this field was George Sarton with his *Horus: A Guide to the History of Science*, a one-volume work, published in Waltham in 1952, which is still an indispensable tool for anyone doing research in the subject. Following three essays on the history of science, it is divided into four parts. The first lists books on historical method, encyclo-paedias, and biographical collections, the second general scientific sources, such as titles of periodicals and national scientific societies, and the third, the most important part of the work, secondary literature on the history of science. It includes mainly nineteenth-century books, mostly in English, German, and French, with annotations. They are arranged in a general section, listing chief reference books, treatises, and handbooks, followed by those treating the history of science in different countries, the history of science of special cultural groups, arranged by period and civilization, and finally the history of the special sciences, including medicine. The fourth part deals with the organization and teaching of the history of science.

François Russo, the other outstanding bibliographer of science, published a one-volume work, *Histoire des sciences et des techniques, Bibliographie*, in Paris in 1954 with a second edition which came out in 1969, also in Paris, under the title *Eléments de bibliographie de l'histoire des sciences et des techniques*. This again is a guide to the subject, with sections on methodology, biographies of historians of science, societies, congresses, libraries, and museums. The main body of the work lists articles and books, the latter including not only nineteenth-century works, but major works from earlier periods. General histories of science and works covering more than one period are quoted first, followed by histories of science in particular countries. Next come general histories of technology; then histories of the special sciences, arranged by period and subject. Medicine is included. The index is mostly an author-and-name index, but it includes some subject entries.

Another book that was first published in the fifties, but reprinted in 1965, is Louise N. Malclès, *Les Sources du travail bibliographique*, vol. III. *Bibliographies specialisées (Sciences exactes et techniques)* (Geneva, 1965). It begins with a section on the general history of science, listing works on the different periods and the history of science of different countries, followed by a section on reference works, periodicals, and societies. The remaining ten sections are on the physical and biological sciences, with a short section on the medical sciences. Each section begins with a list of general histories, followed by works on the different periods and finally by subject bibliographies. It lists books only.

A far more recent and very comprehensive book of reference is *A Guide to the Culture of Science, Tehnology and Medicine*, edited by P.T. Durbin (New York, 1980). It covers not only the history of science, technology, and medicine, but includes chapters on the philosophy of science and technology, the sociology of science and technology, medical sociology and technology in medicine, and finally science policy studies. It contains essays on the current state of historiography in the particular fields and extensive bibliographies of the most important recent work.

Two other even more recent guides are Pietro Corsi and Paul Weindling's *Information Sources in the History of Science and Medicine* (1983) and Burghard Weiss's *Wie finde ich Literatur zur Geschichte der Naturwissenschaften und Technik* (Berlin, 1985). The first consists of a number of essays by several authors on different aspects of the history of science and its relation to other fields, and of the history of the separate sciences in the light of published material. The work is very readable, but to each essay is appended a list of secondary literature of fairly recent date, which does not make it easy to consult as a bibliography. One part of the work, which is not very extensive, deals with general bibliographical sources, periodical literature, societies, and research methods, and is similar to the corresponding sections in the handbooks discussed above.

Although part of the second work, which is in German, has special reference to West Germany, dealing mostly with the availability of literature in that country, the remaining three-quarters form a systematic bibliography (not including articles) which is extremely useful to any student of the subject, whatever his or her native language. It is organized in a similar way to the arrangement in the 'Isis Critical Bibliographies', described below.

Another useful guide is S.A. Jayawardene's *Reference Books for the Historian of Science. A Handlist* (Science Museum, London, 1982). It is in three sections: (1) history of science and its sources; (2) history and related subjects; and (3) general reference. It has very good author, subject, and title indexes.

There are three lists of books on the history of science issued by libraries in the United States, one by the John Crerar Library, Chicago, which was first published in 1911, with a supplement in 1916, but reprinted in 1967; the second, a special bibliography compiled by the University of Pennsylvania Library in 1979, which lists literature on the history of science in general, the history of the special sciences, and the history of science in different countries. It omits sources not held by the library, general sources in American and European history, and less important sources in the history of medicine. The third is *The Catalogue of the History of Science Collections of the University of Oklahoma Libraries*, by Duane H.D. Roller and Marcia M. Goodman, published by Mansell in 1976.

John L. Thornton's and R.I.J. Tully's *Scientific Books, Libraries and Collectors* (3rd edn. 1971) is different from the handbooks discussed so far in that a large part of it lists the primary literature of science from the period before printing began up to the present time, including studies on these works. It concludes with an eighty-five page bibliography of general histories of science and the sciences, both books and periodical articles in author order. Another book which should be mentioned as a brief guide to the kind of literature available is Raymond V. Turley's *The Literature of Science and Technology Approached Historically* (Southampton, 1973).

There are a number of short bibliographies and handlists, mainly for use by students and newcomers to the subject. K.J. Rider's *The History of Science and Technology. A Select Bibliography*, first published by the Library Association in 1962, with a second edition in 1970, is a brief but quite useful bibliography of the history of science and the history of technology. Books are arranged as general works, histories by country, by period, and lastly by subject. A brief guide to the literature, principally for students, is R.P. Lorch's *Aids to Research in the History of Science* published in 1977 (Manchester). Treatises on the history of science are not included.

Although some of the handbooks and monographs mentioned above include the history of technology, the outstanding guide to that subject is E.S. Ferguson's *Bibliography of the History of Technology* (Cambridge, MA, 1968), a comprehensive introduction to primary and secondary sources. Many of the references are taken from the 'Current Bibliography in History of Technology' which has appeared annually in *Technology and Culture* since 1962.

A number of reference books must be mentioned here which, although they do not specifically deal with the history of science, nevertheless contain bibliographical references essential to the study of this subject. Besterman's well-known *World Bibliography of Bibliographies*, first published in 1939–40, with a fourth edition in five volumes which came out in 1965–6 (Lausanne), contains references to bibliographies in monograph form, arranged by subject. A supplement covering the years 1964–74, compiled by A.F. Toomey, was published in two volumes in 1977 (Totawa, NJ).

Two biographical dictionaries should not be forgotten. One is J.C. Poggendorff's *Biographisch-literarisches Handwörterbuch zur Geschichte der exacten Wissenschaften*. The first two volumes, covering the years up to 1858, were published in Leipzig in 1863. Volume III, which came out in 1893, covered the years 1858 to 1883; volume IV, published in 1904, 1883 to 1904; volume V, published in 1926, 1904 to 1922; volume VI, published from 1936 to 1940, 1923 to 1931; volume VIIa, published from 1956 to 1962, 1932 to 1953; supplements bring the dictionary up to 1980. This dictionary contains brief biographies of scientists with a list of their publications. The other is the monumental *Dictionary of Scientific Biography*, edited by C.C. Gillespie, published in sixteen volumes from 1970 to 1980. The biographical articles are written by specialists and incorporate bibliographies of primary and secondary sources.

The *Dictionary of the History of Science*, edited by W.F. Bynum, E.J. Browne, and Roy Porter (1981), also includes brief bibliographies at the end of all important entries. J. Mayerhöfer's *Lexicon der Geschichte der Naturwissenschaften*, the first volume of which appeared in 1959 (Vienna), does not seem to have progressed at all. Planned as an encyclopaedia of men and subjects in the history of science, with useful bibliographies, the project has evidently ceased.

All the works so far discussed in this section have been on the history of science in general, not restricted to any particular country or period, nor to any particular science. Some of the serial publications mentioned earlier dealt with the history of science in Russia, Belgium, Sweden, the Netherlands, Poland, Italy, Australia, and Japan. A recently inaugurated series of bibliographies of the history of science and technology, edited by Robert Multhauf and Ellen Wells, includes a monograph on *The History of Science and Technology in the United States: A Critical, Selective Bibliography*, by Marc Rothenberg (New York and London, 1982). It is in classified order, with author and subject index. A work covering the history of science and technology in Spain is J.M. Lopez Pinero, M. Peset Reig, and L. Garcia Bollester, *Bibliografia historica sobre la ciencia y la tecnica en Espana* (Valencia, 1968–73). It is in two volumes. A bibliography of *British Engineering Literature 1640–1840* by A.W. Skempton was published by Mansell Publishing in 1987.

In the field of bibliographies dealing with the history of science in special periods, Sarton's pioneering work, *Introduction to the History of Science*, remains a fount of information on the great men of science from the earliest days to the fourteenth century, with lengthy bibliographies that include books and articles. A recently published bibliography on a particular period, with annotations, is C. Kren's *Medieval Science and Technology*, published in New York and London, 1985, in the special series mentioned above. It is in classified order with a name and author index.

The history of the subject in medieval India (*Science and Technology in Medieval India*, a bibliography of source materials in Sanskrit, Arabic, and Persian) was published in New Delhi by the Indian National Science Academy in 1982. It is in classified order with a name index. *An Annotated Bibliography of Islamic Science* (volume I), by S.H. Nasr came out in Tehran in 1975.

As far as the special sciences are concerned, there are some excellent bibliographies on the history of mathematics. Kenneth O. May's comprehensive *Bibliography and Research Manual of the History of Mathematics* (Toronto, 1973) runs to 818 pages. The research manual is quite short, but there are lengthy bibliographies of mathematicians, sections on mathematical topics, epi-mathematical topics and historical periods. It concludes with short sections on information retrieval and a long list of serials. J.W. Dauben's *The History of Mathematics from Antiquity to the Present* (New York, 1982, no. 6 in the series mentioned above) is a cooperative undertaking by forty prominent historians of mathematics. It contains 2,000 titles on all aspects of the history of mathematics. Although published some time ago, two still useful bibliographical guides are George Sarton's *The Study of the History of Mathematics* (first published in 1936, reprinted New York, 1957), with an appendix on biographies of modern mathematicians, and Gino Loria's *Guido allo studio della storia delle matematiche* (2nd edn, Milan, 1946), which is a bibliographical introduction for students, containing about 1,600 titles.

A bibliography published in the German Democratic Republic (1969) by

D. Wattenberg, *Forschungen und Publikationen zur Geschichte der Astronomie in der DDR, Eine Bibliographie (1949–1969)*, which is no. 2 of the Veröffentlichungen der Archenbold-Sternwarte, clearly refers to German publications only. A Russian bibliography, *Bibliografija astronomiceskich bibliografii* (Moscow, 1962), a bibliography of astronomical bibliographies, by N.B. Lavrova, who compiled the annual bibliography issued by Commission 41 of the International Astronomical Union cited above, includes a summary and contents list in French.

A bibliography of chemistry that ought to be mentioned is published in the Smithsonian miscellaneous collections, 850 and 1253. It is the *Select Bibliography of Chemistry, 1492–1902*, by H.C. Bolton in four volumes from 1893 to 1904 with a supplement that came out in 1967. A more recent work on the subject is Wm.A. Cole, *Chemical Literature, 1700–1860*, a bibliography (published by Mansell Publishing, London and New York, 1988).

The series of bibliographies of special subjects, edited by Multhauf and Wells, already mentioned above, includes bibliographies of classical physics (by W.R. Home), of modern physics (by S. Brush and L. Belloni), of the earth sciences (by R.S. Porter), of meteorology and geophysics (by S.G. Brush and H.E. Landsberg), and of chemical technology (by R.P. Multhauf).

To do justice to bibliographical developments in the history of medicine would require a chapter of some length. Here it is only possible to mention the most important publications in the field. Some of the serials discussed at the beginning of this chapter included the history of medicine. To these must be added those serials that are devoted solely to this subject, the most important being *Current Work in the History of Medicine*, published quarterly by the Wellcome Institute for the History of Medicine since 1954, and *Bibliography of the History of Medicine* published annually since 1965 by the National Library of Medicine (USA). The most important guides to the bibliography of the history of medicine are Garrison and Morton's *Medical Bibliography*, first published in 1943 and now in its fourth edition (1983) and A. Pauly's *Bibliographie des sciences medicales* (Paris, 1874; republished London, 1954). As far as source material is concerned, historians of medicine have the invaluable help of the *Index Catalogue of the Library of the Surgeon-General's Office* (US Army) (first series: 1880–95, second: 1896–1916, third: 1918–32, fourth: 1936–55 and fifth: 1959–61) and *Index Medicus*, first published in 1916 by the American Medical Association and now by the National Library of Medicine.

Both Russo and Sarton were much concerned with the classification of references. The scheme presently adopted in the *Bulletin Signalétique*, which is similar to the one used when the bibliography was first published, divides the field into: generalities, mathematical sciences and techniques, physical sciences and techniques, technology, earth sciences, and life sciences, including medicine. Sarton, on the other hand, continued to make changes in his method of arranging the entries. Not until 1926 did he evolve a classification scheme to which he more or less adhered until he resigned the editorship of *Isis* in 1952. In this he adopted a division into centuries, called the 'fundamental classification'; the 'historical classification' which had three main divisions, antiquity, Middle Ages and oriental sciences and civilizations; and finally a classification by subject. After Sarton resigned, the system was revised by a committee appointed for that task and it has remained in use ever since. The references are arranged in four main divisions: (a) general references and tools; (b) science and its history from special points of view; (c) histories of the special sciences; (d) a chronological classification. As there is no subject index, some of the information is inevitably lost because items in one of the divisions may have relevance to some in others.

Before I embarked on the work of cumulating the entries in the 'Isis Critical Bibliographies' from 1913 to 1965, I made a study of the different classification schemes used. I was particularly struck by Sarton's arrangement, which foreshadowed the use of a facetted technique. This enabled me to construct a scheme based on this without materially changing Sarton's analysis of the subject. The history of science fits naturally into a three-dimensional matrix in which period/civilization is on the first co-ordinate, the subject on the second, and the aspect from which the subject is considered on the third. The notation I chose, which is a mixed one, emphasized the three main facets: numerals denote civilizations and periods, capital letters subject fields, and lower-case letters aspects and forms. I described my scheme in some detail in a paper presented to the XVth International Congress for the History of Science at Edinburgh in 1977 (*Proceedings*, pp. 518–30) and used it in the volumes of the *Isis Cumulative Bibliography, 1913–1965*, which I edited.

Since no subject index to the 'Isis Critical Bibliographies' had ever been published (unfortunately, they are still published without a subject index), it was a matter of urgency that this material be made available to historians of science. With the help of an initial grant, the History of Science Society sponsored the compilation of a cumulative bibliography. The work, begun in 1964, was carried out in premises kindly made available without charge by Imperial College and the Science Museum. The funds, which came from many institutions in the United States and the United Kingdom and also from private benefactors, were limited. Nevertheless, the *Cumulative Bibliography* eventually appeared in six volumes from 1971 to 1984. The first two contain all the entries concerning a personality in the history of science or any aspect of his work, arranged alphabetically, followed by an alphabetical listing of all entries relating to scientific institutions. Volume III (Subjects) comprises references to the history of science, medicine, and technology, unrestricted by period or civilization, arranged in classified order. Volumes IV and V (Civilizations and Periods) contain entries dealing with a particular period or civilization, subdivided by the order of subjects as used in volume III. Volume VI is an author index. Subject indexes are included in volumes III, IV, and V. The work was published by Mansell, who have pioneered the publication of bibliographies in the field. My article in *The Indexer*

(13 (1983): 158–165), gives a full account of the project, which has been described by Ivor Grattan-Guinness in *Annals of Science* (40 (1983): 310), as 'the most remarkable and worthwhile in the history of science of our time'. A cumulation in two volumes covering the years 1966–75, was published by Mansell in 1980 and the two volumes covering 1976–85 in 1990. Both cumulations were edited by John Neu in exemplary fashion. I am very glad that he has been able to continue the project in the way it was planned.

Book catalogues: their varieties and uses

DAVID McKITTERICK

For the first time, the years since the Second World War have seen prolonged and organized attention to catalogues and other book-lists, study that has led in turn to new approaches to the history of collecting, of libraries, and of reading. Historical studies in every field have been affected, and often stimulated, while the existence of a new body of information has provoked debate about critical theory in literature, a debate often conducted between fiercely separate schools of thought.[1] An interest that was once pursued for antiquity's or curiosity's sake has been taken up, shaken, and recreated as one of the central disciplines of bibliographical study.

This change in theoretical approach, and in the range of applications now feasible, has been made possible by the existence, again often for the first time, of two reliable sources of fundamental information: the various short-title catalogues, and vastly increased access to books in public collections described in union catalogues on both sides of the Atlantic.[2] Each has made readily available, on a scale never hitherto approached, information respecting authorship, printing and publication, and the survival of existing copies. The revised editions of the *Short-Title Catalogue* to 1640 and of Wing, the appearance of Nelson and Seccombe's survey of periodicals for the period 1641 to 1700, the rapidly growing files of the *ESTC*, and the foundation of the *Nineteenth-Century Short-Title Catalogue*, have each permitted fuller and more confident extrapolation of early book-lists and other evidence of book ownership.

---

1 For some of the arguments, see D.F. McKenzie, *Bibliography and the Sociology of Texts* (Panizzi Lectures, 1985) (1986), p. 5: 'For any history of the book which excluded study of the social, economic and political motivations of publishing, the reasons why texts were written and read as they were, why they were rewritten and designed, or allowed to die, would degenerate into a feebly degressive book list and never rise to a readable history. But such a phrase also accommodates what in recent critical theory is often called text production, and it therefore opens up the application of the discipline to the service of that field too.' See also Quentin Skinner, 'Hermeneutics and the Role of History', *New Literary History*, 7 (1975): 209–32, and, for another perspective, Jerome J. McGann, 'The Text, the Poem and the Problem of Historical Method', *New Literary History*, 12 (1981): 269–88, repr. in his *The Beauty of Inflections* (Oxford, 1988), pp. 111–32; several other essays in the book are equally pertinent.

2 Some of the background to the creation of the National Union Catalog pre-1956 imprints, and therefore something of its bibliographical limitations, is explored in David A. Smith, 'The National Union Catalog: Pre-1956 Imprints', *BC*, 31 (1982): 445–62.

These 'short-title catalogues', by their full titles limited to the production of the English-speaking world, and by their conception limited to what has survived, present, however, but one part of the experience of reading or other book use in (to take the matter no further) the British Isles. To an exceptional degree, readers in late medieval and early modern Britain were dependent not only on what was printed within these islands, in a printing and publishing trade always dominated by London, but also on what was imported.[3] Latin was, as it had been for centuries, the language of international discourse and of scholarship. Though so far no attempt has been made to establish the overlap between reading literacy and Latinity, the central position of the language in grammar-school and university curricula ensured that, in a library of any size, Latin rather than vernacular often dominated.[4] This much is clear, even if (as is obviously the case) it did not apply to smaller and poorer collections, the assemblages of individuals or families lacking either money to spare or leisure or knowledge to use large or expensive libraries;[5] nor is it as frequently true for libraries, of any size, from the mid seventeenth century onwards, as the English book trade expanded, and first French and then English emerged, with national expansion overseas, as world languages.

But it remains true – as much, if in a different linguistic light, for later periods as for earlier – that these short-title catalogues, fundamental to the interpretation and evaluation of the national printed output (and therefore, to a great degree, the national literature) do not fairly represent either the nature or the extent of the book trade or of what was collected, read, and acted upon. To this end, inventories, catalogues, and surveys of book ownership provide an essential corrective, since they ignore national or linguistic boundaries, and are circumscribed only by their owners' or instigators' cultural dispositions.

3 An obvious point that apparently needs to be repeated. In his review of Elisabeth Leedham-Green's edition of Cambridge book lists (see note 23 below), for example, Patrick Collinson reminded his readers of 'illusions of intellectual insularity, such as can be bred by fixation on the *Short-Title Catalogue* of books printed in England' (*Journal of Ecclesiastical History*, 39 (1988): 278–81). The standard authority on English readers in the early modern period, H.S. Bennett's *English Books & Readers*, 3 vols. (Cambridge, 1952–70) virtually ignores foreign books.

4 For Latin, see J.W. Binns, *Intellectual Culture in Elizabethan and Jacobean England: The Latin Writings of the Age* (Leeds, 1990). For schools, the standard works are T.W. Baldwin, *William Shakspere's Small Latine and Lesse Greeke*, 2 vols. (Urbana, IL, 1944), and H.F. Fletcher, *The Intellectual Development of John Milton*, 2 vols. (Urbana, 1956–61), especially vol.1. For an example of a school library, see G. Woodward and R.A. Christophers, *The Chained Library of the Royal Grammar School, Guildford: Catalogue* (Guildford, 1972). Though now dated, P.J. Wallis's *Histories of Old Schools; A Revised List for England and Wales* (Newcastle upon Tyne, 1966) remains invaluable.

5 Margaret Spufford, *Small Books and Pleasant Histories; Popular Fiction and its Readership in Seventeenth-Century England* (1981). For a survey of probate inventories, in which much of such evidence must be sought, see M. Overton, *A Bibliography of British Probate Inventories* (Newcastle upon Tyne, 1983). For examples, albeit at a rather more exalted economic level, see for example Peter Clark, 'The Ownership of Books in England 1560–1640: The Example of Some Kentish Townsfolk', in L. Stone (ed.), *Schooling and Society* (Baltimore, 1976), pp. 95–111. The most recent study of material wealth in early modern Britain, setting book ownership in the context of other possessions, is Lorna Weatherill, *Consumer Behaviour and Material Culture in Britain, 1660–1760* (1988). A great deal remains to be done in non-scholarly and non-wealthy households.

By their nature, such documents are international: they assume and depend on trade between different countries. Much of the organization of the means whereby books were imported and exported remains scarcely examined, and little is known of the personnel involved, or of the economic bases for their activities; but it is worth remark, as a reminder of the scale of some of these operations, that even the Bible in a modest household had in the seventeenth century often been printed abroad before being surreptitiously imported. Much work that has been done overseas, and especially in the Low Countries, Germany, France, and (for later periods) North America and Australia, has implications for the British book trade and for the British reading public. But in England, the work of two people in particular remains as the inspiration for, and foundation of, the study of catalogues: Graham Pollard and A.N.L. Munby.[6] It may be no chance that both men were originally trained in bookselling, rather than in librarianship. So, also, two of the most influential American figures in this subject, Archer Taylor and Sears Jayne, have come from other disciplines.[7] The standpoint of such scholars, independent of the daily routines of librarianship, perhaps provided them with a necessary independence, though their various approaches have subsequently been widely and constructively taken up by many in that profession.

Ever since the fifteenth century, the book trade has generated its own catalogues, whether from printers, publishers, or booksellers, or from the organizers of auctions. Public and private library catalogues have been printed since the sixteenth century, the earliest extant for a public collection being a brief one for Cambridge University Library in 1574, while the earliest extant for a private one dates from considerably later: that of Sir James Ware in 1648. In a market that has always been to a great extent one strictly defined, and frequently small, the manuscript catalogue is commonplace: although auctions (for which there must have been some stock inventory) are known to have been held in the Low Countries from the fifteenth century, the earliest such printed catalogue to survive dates from 1599. In England, printed auction catalogues date from the Lazarus Seaman sale in 1676, but of many sales no printed catalogue exists. So, too, with printers' and booksellers' stock. In 1566 Plantin issued a catalogue, of

---

6 On Pollard (d. 1976), see *Studies in the Book Trade in Honour of Graham Pollard* (Oxford Bibliographical Society, 1975); Nicolas Barker, 'Graham Pollard', *BC*, 26 (1977): 7–28; and Esther Potter, 'Graham Pollard at work' *Lib*, VI, 11 (1989): 307–27. On Munby, see Patrick Wilkinson, *Alan Noel Latimer Munby 1913–1974; A Memoir* (privately printed, Cambridge, 1975); David McKitterick, 'The Munby Collection at the University Library', *Trans. Cambridge Bibliographical Soc.*, 6 (1975): 205–10; and Munby's own *Essays and Papers*, ed. with an introduction by Nicolas Barker (1977). Most of that part of his library which was not acquired by Cambridge University Library was dispersed at Sotheby's on 22–23 March and 5 April 1976.

7 Sears Jayne, *Library Catalogues of the English Renaissance* (Los Angeles, 1956; reissued with a new preface, Winchester, 1983); Archer Taylor, *Book Catalogues; Their Varieties and Uses* (Chicago, 1957; rev. W.P. Barlow, Winchester, 1986). Both provide an outline of previous work. For some of the applications of earlier catalogues, respecting manuscripts (with which I am not concerned here but see Jenny Stratford, above), the standard work is Albert Derolez, *Les Catalogues de bibliothèques (Typologie des sources du moyen âge occidental)* (Turnhout, 1979).

which no copy is now known, though the printer's and stockholding book-seller's catalogue had been then long known.[8] Not all such catalogues were printed. As in the circulation of poetry, drama, political controversy, and sermons, so in the documents vital to the prosecution of the book trade: manuscript remained as an essential, and often equal, partner. Only when printing became very cheap in the nineteenth century did the habit of organizing extremely short runs to meet very limited demand become commonplace.

Most of these topics were discussed in a book whose appearance in 1965 marked a turning point: Albert Ehrman and Graham Pollard, *The Distribution of Books by Catalogue from the Invention of Printing to A.D.1800*, printed for members of the Roxburghe Club. Though others have supplemented its details, it remains unsurpassed, particularly for the period to 1700, its scope including catalogues from printers, booksellers, and auctioneers, fair catalogues from Frankfurt and Leipzig, prospectuses, publishers' and others' catalogues in books, inventories of private, trade, and institutional collections, and printed cata-logues of private and institutional libraries. Because of their relevance to the subject, English booksellers' daybooks down to 1640 were also surveyed. The attention to manuscript materials relating to the book's theme was not the least valuable part, though the absence of any account of the records of the longer-established institutional libraries – those of universities, colleges, and cathedrals, for example – is one major omission. More importantly, the collection formed by Mr Ehrman that stimulated this book, and one with which Pollard instinctively sympathized, was international in scope, the publications and records from Holland or Germany being as central to this theme as those in the British Isles. And though it is a large book (if also one generous typo-graphically), its scope obliged it at times to be suggestive rather than exhaustive. Few books that have dealt with the history of catalogues have been more influential, and in many respects it remains to be fully exploited.

Pollard and Ehrman set a programme for future work. But, even as they wrote, Munby was not only completing his long study of the formation and dispersal of the vast library of Sir Thomas Phillipps (1792–1872), a task that required exceptional familiarity with the affairs of booksellers and auctioneers; he was also systematically assembling notes on extant British auction cata-logues, paying especial attention to copies that recorded prices and names of buyers.[9] In such catalogues rest not only the richest resource for the history of

---

8 Details are taken from G. Pollard and A. Ehrman, *The Distribution of Books by Catalogue to A.D. 1800* (Roxburghe Club, 1965). But see also, among more recent work, especially that of Bert van Selm, 'The Introduction of the Printed Auction Catalogue', *Quaerendo*, 15 (1985): 16–54, 115–49, and, by the same author, *Een menighte treffelijcke boecken; Nederlandse boekhandelscatalogi in het begin van de zeventiende eeuw* (Utrecht, 1987).

9 A.N.L. Munby, *Phillipps Studies*, 5 vols. (Cambridge, 1951–60); A.W. Pollard, *List of Catalogues of English Book Sales, 1676–1900, Now in the British Museum* (1915). Munby's annotated copy of the latter is now in Cambridge University Library, and a photocopy of it is in the British Library. For the earlier period, see now A.N.L. Munby and L. Coral, *British Book Sale Catalogues, 1676–1800; A Union List* (1977). For Irish sales, see W.G. Wheeler, *Check-List of Auction Sale Catalogues of Irish Libraries*,

private, and often public, collections, but also, if sometimes less clearly, the history of the second-hand book trade. Munby took only a passing interest in the so-called trade-sale catalogues, of copyrights and remainders, that lay at the centre of the new book trade in the eighteenth and nineteenth centuries.[10] He applied his encyclopaedic knowledge of the history of collecting not only to Phillipps, but also to a series of *Sale Catalogues of Libraries of Eminent Persons*, drawing together in twelve volumes the auction catalogues of owners from the seventeenth century to the early twentieth, only some of them describing the properties of men of letters: the series also included sales of the libraries of architects, politicians, historians, actors and seventeenth-century scientists, and was incidentally a demonstration of the strength of such documents in several disciplines.[11] They were readily published in facsimile, and had long been recognized as a means of tracing the wanderings of manuscripts and printed books. Even more ambitiously, Messrs Sotheby made available the complete series of their sales, regardless of content, from the foundation of the firm by Samuel Baker in the 1730s, down to 1970, in a series that is especially valuable for reproducing the annotated set.[12] (Similar series for Christies and for Puttick and Simpson have not so far appeared.) Quite apart from such series, published at a time when microfilm and cheap photo-litho printing made possible for the first time reproduction programmes on a large scale, full-size facsimiles of individual catalogues had been published long previously: examples include that of the books of Laurence Sterne (books sold 1768; facsimile 1930), and Jonathan Swift (books sold at Dublin, 1745–6; type facsimile 1932, edited by Harold Williams).[13] But by themselves (and as Munby well realized), facsimiles of such catalogues, pictures of libraries frozen at a particular moment, often – perhaps usually – offer only an approximation. Several more books are known to have belonged to Swift than appeared in the auction while, conversely, the

1698–1935 (unpublished: photocopy available in Cambridge University Library). All these are supplemented by Jeanne Blogie, *Répertoire des catalogues de ventes de livres imprimés* (Bruxelles, 1982 etc.): vol. III is devoted to catalogues from the British Isles now in the Bibliothèque Albert Iᵉʳ, and includes both auctioneers' and booksellers' lists. But none of these surveys of printed catalogues represents the extent of such sales: see, for example, Elizabeth A. Swaim, 'The Auction as a Means of Book Distribution in Eighteenth-Century Yorkshire', *PH*, 1 (1977): 49–91.

10 On these, see especially Cyprian Blagden, 'Booksellers' Trade Sales 1718–1761', *Lib*, v, 5 (1951): 243–57; Graham Pollard, 'The English Market for Printed Books' (Sandars Lectures 1959), *PH*, 4 (1978): 7–48; Terry Belanger, 'Booksellers' Sales of Copyright: Aspects of the London Book Trade 1718–1768' (PhD thesis, University of Columbia, 1970) and his 'Booksellers' trade sales, 1718–1768', *Lib*, v, 30 (1975) 281–302.

11 A.N.L. Munby (ed.), *Sale Catalogues of Libraries of Eminent Persons*, 12 vols. (1971–5).

12 The Sotheby auction catalogues (recording both prices and names of buyers) were published in 538 reels of microfilm (Ann Arbor, 1973–6). See also Frank Herrmann, *Sotheby's: Portrait of an Auction House* (1980).

13 Recent examples include Jeremiah S. Finch, *A Catalogue of the Libraries of Sir Thomas Browne and Dr Edward Browne, His Son* (Leiden, 1986); Leona Rostenberg, *The Library of Robert Hooke: The Scientific Book Trade of Restoration England* (Santa Monica, 1989); and J.D. Fleeman (ed.), *The Sale Catalogue of Samuel Johnson's Library; A Facsimile* (Melbourne, 1975). See also Fleeman's *A Preliminary Handlist of Copies of Books Associated with Dr. Samuel Johnson* (Oxford Bibliographical Soc., 1984), and David Pearson, 'Unrecorded Books from Samuel Johnson's Library', *Factotum*, 32 (1990): 13–14.

long-standing practice of salting named sales with indistinguishable other stock makes conclusive discussion frequently impossible.[14] Multiple lots, a necessary part of auctioneering, blur the position further still.

If, then, facsimiles of auction catalogues, for all their very considerable use, are rarely all that is needed, it also remains that their value for the study of historic values, and of provenance, is critical. As trade documents they have much greater authority than as personal ones. And yet, booksellers' and other trade catalogues, their retail equivalents, perhaps because they usually lack the obvious reference to individuals, have been re-published much less. In England there have been isolated examples, though in the Netherlands the series of *Catalogi Redevivi* has from the first announced itself as one intended for both auction and stock catalogues.[15] Whereas much effort has been put into identifying and locating book-auction catalogues, the most useful easily available list of those of nineteenth-century booksellers (the terminus for this category in Pollard and Ehrman is set at 1700) is still the brief table in Munby's *The Cult of the Autograph Letter in England* (1962). It lists, in a survey that is very obviously incomplete, but fourteen firms. Other details may be discovered, for example, from the extensive collection of such catalogues in the library of the association of Amsterdam booksellers, which includes examples from many British firms.[16] But, in general, the catalogues of booksellers, and even more those of publishers, have yet to be investigated. For the present, we lack even the most basic finding aids. Collections of catalogues, especially from the second half of the nineteenth century onwards, are to be found in all major libraries, but by no means all of them are clearly catalogued, and few of them contain even nearly complete series for even the major firms. For the eighteenth century, the *ESTC* brings the possibility of a more organized search for, and display of, these central book-trade documents.[17]

---

14 William LeFanu, *A Catalogue of Books Belonging to Dr Jonathan Swift . . . 1715; A Facsimile of Swift's Autograph with an Introduction and Alphabetic Catalogue* (Cambridge Bibliographical Soc., 1988). See also E.J.W. McCann, 'Jonathan Swift's Library', *BC*, 34 (1985): 323–41. Although I am not concerned here with the catalogues of modern book collectors, attention must be drawn also to *The Rothschild Library* (Cambridge, 1954), which is essential to the study of Swift's books. The Rothschild collection is now in Trinity College, Cambridge.

15 *Catalogi Redivivi; A Reprint Series of Dutch Auction and Stock Catalogues from the XVIIth and XVIIIth Centuries*, ed. R. Breugelmans (Utrecht, 1985 etc.)

16 *Catalogus der bibliotheek van de Vereeniging ter Bevordering van de Belangen des Boekhandels te Amsterdam*, vol. VIII: *Supplement-catalogus 1932–1973* (Amsterdam, 1979). The volume includes the pre-1932 collection.

17 For reasons of space, I must omit discussion of many of the categories of catalogue surveyed in Pollard and Ehrman, *The Distribution of Books by Catalogue*. These include, for example, publishers' and booksellers' catalogues inserted at the ends of books. W.W. Greg demonstrated their use in his *Bibliography of the English Printed Drama to the Restoration*, vol. IV (Bibliographical Soc., 1957). In the eighteenth century, many (but emphatically not all) such documents can be retrieved thanks to the search capabilities of *ESTC*. Among trade lists, D.F. Foxon's series of facsimiles of *Catalogues of Books in Circulation* (Farnborough, 1965) is especially valuable for the period from 1595 (the date of Maunsell's *Catalogue of English Printed Books*) to the early eighteenth century. In the nineteenth century, *The Publishers' Circular* has been republished on microfiche by Messrs Chadwyck-Healey. For

Though manuscript catalogues of private and institutional libraries have long been valued, and therefore preserved, it is only since about 1945 that the same kind of attention has been paid to post-Reformation collections as M.R. James and Neil Ker in particular had paid to those of earlier periods.[18]

The publication in 1956 of Sears Jayne's *Library Catalogues of the English Renaissance* drew attention to a body of information that had hitherto been little used, and whose extent was little appreciated.[19] Jayne included both institutional and private libraries, and accepted manuscript and printed catalogues indifferently. His survey commenced in 1500, and was thus intended as to some extent a continuation of and complement to Ker's *Medieval Libraries of Great Britain*.[20] Between then and his terminus in 1640, Jayne identified several hundred catalogues and owners for the first time in print: his survey was especially valuable for its details of probate records, the great majority of them from Cambridge, and of library benefactors' registers whether in London, the universities, or ecclesiastical libraries.

His previous work, in collaboration with Francis Johnson, on the library catalogue of John, Lord Lumley (*c.* 1534–1609) also appeared in 1956. In its way it had marked another turning point, though an example had already been set by W.O. Hassall's study of Sir Edward Coke. By transcribing, identifying individual volumes (the great majority of them in the British Library), and annotating with further bibliographical detail where necessary, the editors provided a guide of a peculiarly specific kind to the library both of Lumley and, no less importantly, to that of Prince Henry into whose household it passed on Lumley's death. The survival in the collection of many of Archbishop Cranmer's books lent the edition a further significance.[21] The editors' example and method have been much followed by others. With suitable modifications (as the collection was very substantially of manuscripts), in the second in the series of catalogues that marked the bicentenary of the British Museum, of which the Lumley catalogue had been the first, Andrew Watson edited the several surviving lists of the books of Sir Simonds D'Ewes (1602–50), a collection of particular interest because an unusual amount of detail survives about the manner in which it was collected. Since then, editions have appeared of the library catalogues of the Norfolk collector Sir Thomas Knyvett (d.1618) and,

---

earlier periods especially, the Frankfurt book fair catalogues are crucial for understanding the place of London-printed books in the international community. The biannual catalogues for 1564–92 have been published in facsimile, ed. Bernhard Fabian, as *Die Messkataloge des sechzehnten Jahrhunderts* (Hildesheim, 1972 etc.).

18 For pre-Reformation collections, see Christopher de Hamel above.

19 See, especially, the review by A.I. Doyle, *Lib*, v, 13 (1958): 64–6.

20 Neil R. Ker, *Medieval Libraries of Great Britain; A List of Surviving Books*, 2nd edn (1964); *Supplement*, ed. A.G. Watson (1987). For non-institutional libraries, see Susan H. Cavanaugh, 'A Study of Books Privately Owned in England, 1300–1450' (PhD thesis, University of Pennsylvania, 1980).

21 Sears Jayne and Francis R. Johnson (ed.), *The Lumley Library; The Catalogue of 1609* (1956); W.O. Hassall (ed.), *A Catalogue of the Library of Sir Edward Coke* (New Haven, 1950). See also D.G. Selwyn, 'The Lumley Library; A Supplementary Checklist', *British Library Journal*, 7 (1981): 136–48. Mr Selwyn is currently preparing a study of Cranmer's library.

especially notable, of John Dee.[22] For their edition of Dee's catalogue, Andrew Watson and R.J. Roberts chose to print the original in facsimile, and thus take advantage of a well-organized and legible original. Facsimile publication also offered the advantage that readers could inspect and evaluate for themselves the various alterations, additions, and marginalia that would otherwise have been impossible to present adequately. As so often, the catalogue was incomplete; but the editors added descriptions of books known from other sources. It is rare, whatever the status of the library under review, for the kinds of catalogue mentioned in this paragraph ever to be complete even in the most skeletal sense.

Among the many libraries and book-lists that have subsequently been investigated thanks to Jayne's work, the largest survey is that by Elisabeth Leedham-Green, of Cambridge probate inventories. Her edition of the lists of some 200 owners between 1535–6 and 1760 (all but four before 1670) added a new dimension to the subject. Apart from a few owners, notably Thomas Lorkyn, John Nidd, and, particularly, Andrew Perne (whose books still dominate the old library at Peterhouse), she did not identify the whereabouts of surviving copies.[23] Instead, by assembling so many lists, all from one location, she had also the opportunity of comparing library with library, and thereby exploring both the range and the comparative frequency of individual authors and titles. The forthcoming volumes in the series issued by the project on the *Private Libraries of Renaissance England* (*PLRE*) will likewise offer comparisons of this kind, as well as accumulated evidence on continental sources of supply. It is expected that one of the early volumes in this series will be devoted to the probate records of the University of Oxford. Although it will be published conventionally, *PLRE* is also designed as a database capable of receiving information from other catalogues, published or unpublished, so that it will be possible to manipulate much greater bodies of bibliographical evidence respecting book ownership than hitherto, and thus perhaps to arrive at more general conclusions.

Apart from extant catalogues and inventories, much effort has been given to identifying and describing books owned by individuals but not previously (so far as is known) listed. There have been many exercises in ascertaining reading on the evidence of content – a long-established critical activity, and perhaps most conveniently exemplified here by J.C. Boswell's work on Milton, or, from another perspective, Felix Raab's account of the absorption of Macchiavellian thought and attitudes in seventeenth-century England, based on extensive reading among a range of contemporary authors.[24] But, like the editions of catalogues

22 Julian Roberts and Andrew G. Watson (eds.), *John Dee's Library Catalogue* (Bibliographical Soc., 1990).
23 E.S. Leedham-Green, *Books in Cambridge Inventories; Book-Lists from Vice-Chancellor's Court Probate Inventories in the Tudor and Stuart Periods*, 2 vols. (Cambridge, 1986).
24 J.C. Boswell, *Milton's Library; A Catalogue of the Remains of John Milton's Library and An Annotated Reconstruction of Milton's Library and Ancillary Readings* (New York, 1975); Felix Raab, *The English Face of Machiavelli; A Changing Interpretation, 1500–1700* (1964). For one example of a rather fuller analysis of an author's books in relation to his reading, see Michael Patrick Gillespie and Erik Bradford Stocker, *James Joyce's Trieste Library; A Catalogue of Materials at the Harry Ransom Research Center, the*

that identify the copies described, and then do not describe or exploit them bibliographically, such exercises often ignore the essentially complementary bibliographical evidence, which can offer much beyond the simple identification of a pertinent text.

This evidence is of different kinds. At its simplest, the pioneer work done in the nineteenth century in identifying Gabriel Harvey's books has been continued in this century by G.C. Moore Smith, and most recently by Virginia F. Stern. Setting aside several books that the latter attributes to Harvey in error, a principal interest in his books is in their annotations, which Lisa Jardine and Anthony Grafton have been studying and interpreting more fully.[25] So, too, Sir Geoffrey Keynes had by the fourth edition of his bibliography of John Donne (1973) identified 213 extant books that could be demonstrated to have been owned by Donne at some stage.[26] Donne's marks of ownership are less dramatic than those of Harvey, who wrote copiously in a bold hand, while Donne (apart from his name and motto on the title-page) restricted himself to pencilled marginal lines. But the principle remained the same: here were not only books that could be shown to have belonged to particular figures, but also books that demonstrated how they had been studied. In this respect, John Harrison's account of Sir Isaac Newton's library offers much more – amply documented, and though not, assuredly, complete, yet providing the guidance that a reader at a distance might reasonably expect or hope for.[27] In later centuries, Coleridge's marginalia, surviving in perhaps 700 volumes, are being edited by a team led by George Whalley.[28] A similar project is in hand for books that once belonged to Charles Darwin, the majority of which are now divided between Cambridge University

University of Texas (Austin, 1986). So far as I am aware, there has been no attempt yet to chart the influence of particular English authors by the kind of detailed census of surviving copies undertaken for works by Copernicus or Galileo: see Robert S. Westman, 'The Reception of Galileo's "Dialogue"; A Partial World Census of Extant Copies', in P. Galluzzi (ed.), *Novità celesti e crisi del sapere; atti del convegno internazionale di studi Galileiani* (Suppl. to *Annali dell'Istituto e Museo di Storia della Scienza*, Florence, 1983), and Owen Gingerich and Robert S. Westman, 'The Wittich Connection; Conflict and Priority in Late Sixteenth-Century Cosmology', *Trans. American Philosophical Soc.*, 78, part 7 (Philadelphia, 1988). The third edition of Sir Geoffrey Keynes, *Bibliography of the Writings of William Harvey*, rev. G. Whitteridge and C. English (Winchester, 1989), laid the foundation for a similar census of Harvey's *De motu cordis* (Frankfurt, 1628), with a list of some sixty-eight copies.

25 Bernard Quaritch, *A Dictionary of Book Collectors*, part 9 (1899); G.C. Moore Smith, *Gabriel Harvey's Marginalia* (Stratford-upon-Avon, 1913); Virginia F. Stern, *Gabriel Harvey; His Life, Marginalia and Library* (Oxford, 1979). See also the reviews of the last by Peter Croft in *RES*, NS, 32 (1981): 442–6, and by David McKitterick, *Lib*, VI, 3 (1981): 348–53. Harvey's reading has been further explored by Lisa Jardine: see A. Grafton and L. Jardine, *From Humanism to the Humanities; Education and the Liberal Arts in Fifteenth- and Sixteenth-Century Europe* (1986).

26 The list has since been further extended: see the various contributions by Sir Geoffrey Keynes, Mary Hobbs, and David Pearson to *BC*, 26 (1977): 29–35; 27 (1978): 570–2; 29 (1980): 590–2; and 35 (1986): 246.

27 John Harrison, *The Library of Isaac Newton* (Cambridge, 1978).

28 On Coleridge, see especially his *Marginalia*, ed. George Whalley (1980 etc.). For further information on his reading, see also his *Notebooks*, ed. Kathleen Coburn and M. Christensen (1957 etc.). See also Ralph J. Coffman, *Coleridge's Library; A Bibliography of Books Owned or Read by Samuel Taylor Coleridge* (Boston, 1987).

Library and his old home at Downe House, Kent.[29] If for a few other collections the identification of copies once in them has seemed to serve as an end in itself, for many more the detective work has contributed in significant ways to intellectual, material, book-trade, and library history. Recent examples of the latter include the work of David McPherson on Ben Jonson, Richard DeMolen on Camden, T.A. Birrell on John Morris, Frans Korsten on Thomas Baker, Fellow of St John's College, Cambridge, and Sir Geoffrey Keynes's return to the library of Gibbon.[30] W.S. Lewis's long commitment to the study of Horace Walpole, manifest in his edition of the correspondence, made Allen T. Hazen's detailed and painstaking account of Walpole's library especially rewarding for reasons quite separate from its own merits. One of the few women to have been studied in this manner is the seventeenth-century Frances Wolfreston.[31]

Some of these studies, recreated catalogues of libraries now dispersed, have been ambitious beyond detective work. But not many books present quite so complex a series of signs of evidence of their owners' use as those of John Locke, who marked his volumes with overlinings, underlinings, code figures and letters, and paraphs, quite apart from signatures and press-marks. These private markings were studied, and ingeniously described, in John Harrison's and Peter Laslett's study of his library.[32] More recently, Nicolas Kiessling's investigation of the books of Robert Burton, now mostly divided between Christ Church and the Bodleian Library, has presented equally full descriptions of his subject, with remarks on annotations, ciphers, and other signs of use. Burton, like Sir Thomas Knyvett, Henry Lucas, and many others, frequently recorded the date of acquisition, and price paid, on his books.[33] Though such notes must be used with circumspection, having respect both to their owners' acquaintance with the

29 M.A. Di Gregario and N.W. Gill (eds.), *Charles Darwin's Marginalia*, 1– (New York, 1990–   ). For the present, the only published list of Darwin's books remains the brief and inadequate list by H.W. Rutherford, *Catalogue of the Library of Charles Darwin now in the Botany School, Cambridge* (Cambridge, 1908).

30 D. McPherson, 'Ben Jonson's Library and Marginalia; An Annotated Catalogue', *Studies in Philology*, 71 (1974), Texts and Studies; R. L. DeMolen, 'The Library of William Camden', *Proc. of the American Philosophical Soc.* 128 (1984): 327–409; Sir Geoffrey Keynes, *The Library of Edward Gibbon; A Catalogue*, 2nd edn (Winchester, 1980); T.A. Birrell, *The Library of John Morris; The Reconstruction of a Seventeenth-Century Collection* (1976) (Birrell's work forms part of a much larger study of the catalogues of the Old Royal Library of the British Museum: see his *The English Monarchs and Their Books from Henry VII to Charles II* (Panizzi Lectures 1986) (1987); Frans Korsten, *A Catalogue of the Library of Thomas Baker* (Cambridge, 1990); Allen T. Hazen, *A Catalogue of Horace Walpole's Library*, with 'Horace Walpole's library', by W.S. Lewis, 3 vols. (Oxford, 1969). For two Scottish examples, see Robert H. MacDonald (ed.), *The Library of Drummond of Hawthornden* (Edinburgh, 1971) and Charles P. Finlayson, *Clement Littill and His Library* (Edinburgh, 1980).

31 Paul Morgan, 'Frances Wolfreston and "Hor Bouks"; A Seventeenth-Century Woman Book-Collector', *Lib*, VI, 11 (1989): 187–219.

32 John Harrison and Peter Laslett, *The Library of John Locke* (Oxford, 1965; 2nd edn Oxford, 1971).

33 Nicolas K. Kiessling, *The Library of Robert Burton* (Oxford Bibliographical Soc., 1988), which should be read in conjunction with Kiessling's Bodleian Library exhibition catalogue, *The Legacy of Democritus Junior* (Oxford, 1990) and his edition of *The Anatomy of Melancholy*; David McKitterick, *The Library of Sir Thomas Knyvett of Ashwellthorpe, c.1538–1618* (Cambridge, 1978); J.C.T. Oates, *Cambridge University Library; A History. From the Beginnings to the Copyright Act of Queen Anne* (Cambridge, 1986), pp. 349–67.

book in question and to whether it was bought new or second-hand, bound or in sheets, they form invaluable complements both to the catalogues of the book trade and to earlier studies of retail book prices by Francis Johnson and H.S. Bennett.[34]

But few thus far have taken the resurrection of old and disbanded libraries a stage further, and sought to discover how all the bibliographical evidence can be brought together to suggest both how and whence collections were assembled, and how they were altered, by rebinding, for example, in their new owners' hands. Such studies are prevented by the repairs found necessary in most major libraries, repairs that too often have discarded the evidence of boards, endpapers, and edges in the belief that only the printed or written text was worthy of preservation. A vivid account of the fate of Garrick's collection of old English plays, first at the hands of Garrick himself, and then at the hands of the British Museum staff, was given by one of the authors of a catalogue of the collection, published in 1982.[35]

Thanks however to the survival at Magdalene College of the library of Samuel Pepys, it has proved possible to demonstrate on a large scale the relevance of the information to be derived from bindings to the information contained more obviously in catalogues, correspondence, and within the books. Pepys left only sporadic comments about his books in his diaries, and not very much more on the subject in his letters. For those interested in the order in which he assembled his collection, and therefore in his relations with the book trade, the manner in which his interests developed, and the shifting change of the market, the principal evidence has lain in the original manuscript catalogues of his library, with their successive additions, interpolations, and alterations. But these catalogues date from a time when the collection was already well established and although a facsimile has now been published, they have never hitherto been studied. The importance of Howard Nixon's book, in the new catalogue of the library now in course of publication, was therefore twofold.[36] First, it set out a mass of information about the finest collection of late seventeenth-century English bindings extant. But second, Nixon demonstrated that most of Pepys's books could be divided not only between a fairly small number of binders, but also into a small number of binding styles, and that those styles altered over the years. Thus, by grouping books by their binding styles and binders, it was possible to demonstrate, very approximately, the probable order in which Pepys acquired his books.

In this light, the dispersal of historical collections is naturally almost always

---

34 F.R. Johnson, 'Notes on English Retail Book-Prices, 1550–1640', *Lib*, v, 5 (1950): 83–112; H.S. Bennett, 'Notes on English Retail Book-Prices, 1480–1560', *Lib*, v, 5 (1950): 172–8.

35 George M. Kahrl and Dorothy Anderson, *The Garrick Collection of Old English Plays; A Catalogue with an Historical Introduction* (1982); Dorothy Anderson, 'Reflections on Librarianship; Observations Arising from Examination of the Garrick Collection of Old Plays in the British Library', *British Library Journal*, 6 (1980): 1–6.

36 H.M. Nixon *Catalogue of the Pepys Library at Magdalene College, Cambridge*, section 6: *Bindings* (Woodbridge, 1984).

controversial, sometimes greatly so. The sale of John Evelyn's books in 1977–8, and with it the destruction of one of the most suggestive private libraries of the late seventeenth century, assembled by a man of wide yet utterly exemplary tastes, in the sciences as in the humanities, was not mitigated either by an unusually detailed sale catalogue or by the strenuous (and largely successful) efforts to acquire the most obviously important books for the British Library.[37] It came within months of a further major auction of books from Sion College.[38] At Ely Cathedral, though many books were given to Cambridge University Library, many more were sold at auction: it is little comfort that the history of the foundation of the cathedral's modern library, in the late seventeenth century, is only now beginning to come to light, too late for the books involved to be properly examined.[39] A similar rescue operation was mounted, this time virtually single-handedly, when the old parish library at Shipdham, in Norfolk, was auctioned in London in 1951, though little could be done about that library's remarkable collection of early Americana – a survival until then of exceptional interest in the remote East Anglian countryside.[40] These are but four examples among dozens of similar sales brought about by the need for money or by the assumption that old books have outlived their usefulness. Among long-standing private libraries thus dispersed or further encroached on may also be mentioned that at Mostyn Hall, a collection dating from the sixteenth century and the object of sale in 1974, and that of Bishop Percy (1729–1811), sold in 1969.[41] Yet among such sales must also be set the close bibliographical interest taken in their historic libraries by some owners, and the greatly increased activities of the National Trust in preserving libraries of all ages, including those of the nineteenth and twentieth centuries, for informed study.[42]

Many of the questions raised by dispersals are very similar to those involving a

37 Sales were held at Christie's on 22–23 June, 12 October and 30 November–1 December 1977, and 15–16 March, 12–13 July, and 8 November 1978. See also Nicolas Barker, 'Sion, Evelyn, and What Next?', BC, 26 (1977): 319–28. For Evelyn as a collector, see especially Sir Geoffrey Keynes, John Evelyn: A Study in Bibliophily with a Bibliography of His Writings, 2nd edn (Oxford, 1968).
38 Books from Sion College were sold at Sotheby's on 13 June 1977. The library's history is discussed in E.H. Pearce, Sion College and Library (Cambridge, 1913) and in Elizabeth Edmondston, 'Sion College', BC, 14 (1965): 165–77.
39 Sale at Sotheby's ('An Ecclesiastical Library'), 9 March 1972. A good deal of further information about the library has come to light since the pamphlet by D.M. Owen, The Library and Muniments of Ely Cathedral (Ely, 1973). Among various other sales from cathedral libraries may be mentioned the group from Ripon Cathedral sold at Sotheby's on 23–24 June 1958 and 31 May 1960.
40 Sale at Hodgson's, 29 March 1951. A residue of the collection is now in Norwich Central Library. See also N.R. Ker, The Parochial Libraries of the Church of England, (1959), p. 97, and M.I. Williams (ed.), A Directory of Rare Book and Special Collections in the United Kingdom and the Republic of Ireland (1985), p.416.
41 Sales from Mostyn Hall took place at Christie's on 9–10, 16–17, and 23–24 October 1974; see also S. de Ricci English Collectors of Books & Manuscripts (1530–1930) and their Marks of Ownership (Cambridge, 1930), pp. 180–1. Bishop Percy's books were sold en bloc at Sotheby's, 23 June 1969, though some had passed to the Bodleian in 1932 and a few had been bought by Rosenbach in 1929.
42 See, for example, S. Pargeter, A Catalogue of the Library at Tatton Park (Chester, 1977), and L.M.J. Delaissé, James Marrow and John de Witt, The S.A. de Rothschild Collection at Waddesdon Manor; Illuminated Manuscripts (Fribourg, 1977).

phrase much used in recent decades, respecting the 'national heritage'. They are questions complicated all the more not only by taxation, but also by the fact that books exist both in isolation (with, for example, individual financial, textual, reading, and historical value) and in the context of collections which may rapidly lose their character by depredations.[43] To disband an historic library is not simply to relocate several artefacts each of which exists as a separate work or volume; it is often also to destroy historical evidence without recognizing wherein that evidence lies.

Although Jayne listed institutional library catalogues down to 1640, and Pollard and Ehrman listed contemporary printed examples on the continent down to 1675 and in America down to 1765, their study continues, perhaps necessarily, to be piecemeal. Those of surviving libraries are noted in the authoritative, but still not quite complete, *Directory of Rare Book and Special Collections*, published by the Rare Books Group of the Library Association in 1985 – an aspect of the Group's activities that reflects its natural links with the Library History Group, part of the same parent body. Catalogues survive alike for cathedral libraries, church libraries, town libraries, school libraries, and society libraries – quite apart from university libraries and the libraries of the colleges of Oxford and Cambridge. While many, particularly of smaller collections, record little more than a single donation, others proffer the opportunity for both chronological and synchronic study. When linked to other surviving financial archives, respecting expenditure on books and on rival needs, they are of still greater interest. But, crucially, they can be linked to specific books still on the shelves – books that in themselves reveal by their bindings, annotations, and other marks, the pattern of use over generations.[44] Neil Ker's report on the parochial libraries of the Church of England (1959) was intended by those who commissioned it as a finding aid to a widely dispersed species; but it also described libraries, many of them in private ownership before becoming the object of bequest, of which successive catalogues survive. Since 1959 modern catalogues of several have been published.[45] More general catalogues, describing specified groups of such libraries, have been published for Shropshire

---

43 A.N.L. Munby, 'The Library', in Roy Strong, Marcus Binney, and John Harris (ed.), *The Destruction of the Country House* (1974). Munby's paper should be read in conjunction with several other contributions to this book, notably that of Peter Thornton.

44 Philip Gaskell, *Trinity College Library: The First 150 years* (Cambridge, 1980); S. Bush and C.J. Rasmussen, *The Library of Emmanuel College, Cambridge, 1584–1637* (Cambridge, 1986); *Catalogue of the Pepys Library at Magdalene College, Cambridge* (Cambridge and Woodbridge, 1978–); Frans Korsten, *A Catalogue of the Library of Thomas Baker* (Cambridge, 1990). Baker's books are now for the most part in St John's College, Cambridge.

45 The standard guides are Neil R. Ker, *The Parochial Libraries of the Church of England* (1959) and M.I. Williams (ed.), *A Directory of Rare Book and Special Collections in the United Kingdom and the Republic of Ireland* (1985). For one recent example of a catalogue of a parochial library, see J. Glenn and D. Walsh, *Catalogue of the Francis Trigge Chained Library, St Wulfram's Church, Grantham* (Woodbridge, 1988); see also the review by J. Goldfinch, *Lib*, VI, 11 (1989): 367–9. Many catalogues of such libraries, compiled in more or less detail, remain unpublished: the Council for the Care of Churches (83 London Wall, London EC2M 5NA) maintains a collection.

(1971) and Suffolk (1977).[46] Among town libraries, the Plume library at Maldon, and the town library at Ipswich, are among several that have attracted catalogues,[47] the latter in the most rewarding detail. For cathedrals, apart from the deliberately summary union catalogue of cathedral libraries, to which the Bibliographical Society has devoted much effort, there now exist modern printed catalogues of the libraries at Peterborough, Lincoln, Lichfield, and Gloucester.[48] Though they might include historical introductions, these catalogues have taken strictly limited notice of information respecting the copies under examination. Most of the books of Michael Honywood, Dean of Lincoln, are identified, for example; but there is no information about the bindings of his books, or evidence noted of where he might have bought them – in England or during his interregnum exile in the Netherlands.

Among all the catalogues of ecclesiastical or municipal institutions, one recent example stands out for its attention to detail beyond what is usually accounted sufficient. Ipswich town library, founded in 1599 with a bequest from a local citizen, and now housed in Ipswich School, depended in its early days partly on gifts of books, and partly on a book fund established in effect by a single benefactor. Its catalogue, published in 1989, drew together the evidence of early library records (principally a benefactors' book), town accounts, successive catalogues, and the evidence of the many marks on and in the books themselves – marks made by booksellers, librarians and readers – to create a remarkably detailed portrait of the intellectual ambitions, assumptions, and achievements of

46 *Catalogue of Books from Parochial Libraries in Shropshire, Prepared by the Shropshire County Library* (1971); A.E. Birkby, *Suffolk Parochial Libraries; A Catalogue* (1977). See also, more generally, the important review of the former by E.G.W. Bill in *Library History*, 2 (1971): 152–7.

47 S.G. Deed, *Catalogue of the Plume Library at Maldon, Essex* (Maldon, 1959); W.J. Petchy, *The Intentions of Thomas Plume* (Maldon, 1985); J. Blatchly and B. Birkby, *The Town Library of Ipswich, Provided for the Use of the Town Preachers in 1599. A History and a Catalogue* (Woodbridge, 1989).

48 M. Hands, 'The Cathedral Libraries Catalogue', *Lib*, v, 2 (1947): 1–13; *The Cathedral Libraries Catalogue; Books Printed Before 1701 in the Libraries of the Anglican Cathedrals of England*, vol. 1, compiled by M.S.G. McLeod, edited and completed by K.I. James and D.J. Shaw. (Bibliographical Soc. 1984). For Peterborough, see J.J. Hall (ed.), *Peterborough Cathedral Library; A Catalogue of Books Printed before 1800 and Now on Deposit in Cambridge University Library* (Cambridge, 1986); for Lincoln, see C. Hurst, *Catalogue of the Wren Library of Lincoln Cathedral; Books Printed before 1801* (Cambridge, 1982), J.H. Srawley, *Michael Honywood, Dean of Lincoln* (Lincoln Minster Pamphlets 5, 1950), D.N. Griffiths, 'Lincoln Cathedral Library', *BC*, 19 (1970): 21–30, Naomi Linnell, 'Michael Honywood and Lincoln Cathedral Library', *Lib*, vi, 5, (1983): 126–39, and her 'The Catalogue of Lincoln Cathedral Library', *Library History* 7 (1985): 1–9; for Lichfield, see E.E.C. Hill etc., *Catalogue of the Printed Books in the Library of Lichfield Cathedral* (Lichfield, 1984); for Gloucester, see S.M. Eward, *A Catalogue of Gloucester Cathedral Library* (Gloucester, 1972). There have been several other studies of such libraries: see, for example, Jean E. Mortimer, 'The Library Catalogue of Anthony Higgin, Dean of Rippon (1608–1624)', *Proc. of the Leeds Philosophical and Literary Soc. Literary and Historical Section*, 10 (1962). References to cathedral libraries have been gathered by E. Anne Read in *A Checklist of Books, Catalogues and Periodical Articles Relating to the Cathedral Libraries of England* (Oxford Bibliographical Soc., 1970); supplement in *Library History*, 4 (1978): 141–63. For Welsh cathedrals, see Maura Tallon, *The Church in Wales Diocesan Libraries* (1962). More general questions respecting the custody and care of cathedral libraries were raised by Neil Ker in 'Cathedral Libraries', *Library History*, 1 (1967): 38–45, repr. in his *Books, Collectors and Libraries*, ed. A.G. Watson (1985), pp. 293–300.

a small body of people in an influential seventeenth-century port and country town.

Where for the future? In a subject in which, thus far, so much has depended on personal enthusiasm and commitment, rather than on team funding or institutional policy or cooperation, it is perhaps especially foolhardy to attempt predictions. But three things are clear. First, there is a great need for further investigation in the history and contents of individual libraries, at every level, both institutional and private. Such study may be pursued for the sake of local or individual interest, and it will always remain valid for that reason. But it has a wider importance. In early catalogues, surviving books, and other relevant archives we can perceive the relationship of different linguistic, cultural, social, and economic parts of the book trade, of books printed in Britain and books printed overseas. This is evidence of a kind that the short-title catalogues do not seek to offer, even though it has often been mistakenly assumed that they do. Second, just as the short-title catalogues correlated the relevant holdings of various libraries, gathering locations of each title and edition, so there remains the challenge of reconciling the information in the many disparate collections or catalogues – a reconciliation that offers the prospect of gauging taste, fashion, the book trade, and other influences, whether on collecting or on other activities. The evidence available may frequently be inadequate and incomplete; but that need not be a deterrent to its properly cautious application. And third, as the visual and tactile implications of reading are perceived increasingly as part of exposure to and absorption of a particular text, in a particular set of circumstances, so the particularities and identification of precise books, editions, and copies assume a critical importance to the historian. Such interpretation requires, certainly, a daunting range of bibliographical and interpretative skills; but such skills offer considerable rewards.

The British provincial book trade

PETER ISAAC AND MICHAEL PERKIN

The very title of this chapter is misleading since it does not deal exclusively either with the provinces or with books. Local pride has resulted in useful bibliographies – an unfortunate use of the word from which we cannot now escape – of books produced in, or about, many counties and towns. These are a valuable source of information for the study of the British provincial book trade, which is now concerned with the spread of the written or printed word both outside London and to and from the metropolis, and also with the trades supporting this – bookselling, printing, bookbinding, papermaking, etc. – and the men and women who practised these trades.

What must be even more particularly noticed at the outset, in the face of W.W. Greg's definition of bibliography as 'the study of books as material objects',[1] is the fact that this chapter appears at all in the Society's centenary volume. *Studies in Retrospect* (1949) takes a very much narrower view of the legitimate concerns of the Society; even Greg's outward-looking statement that 'as the characteristic development of the first half of the Society's career was the study of the technical side of book production, so that of the latter part has been the recognition of the rôle bibliography has to play in the elucidation of textual and literary problems'[2] does not extend the Society's purview to include work on the provincial book trade.[3] Moreover his dictum:

and so the cataloguer, beginning with enumeration and description, is forced by the nature of his work to become the student of everything that affects either the original fashioning or the subsequent fortunes of the books that come within his purview; and if he is philosophically minded he must come in the end to realize that it is this life-history of books that is the true study of the bibliographer, and that actual enumeration and description are only incidental[4]

can cover our concerns only by the extension of 'book trade' in the manner adumbrated at the end of the previous paragraph. However the last half-century may be seen as the heyday of social studies, including, of necessity, economics, and our interests in the book trade in the provinces clearly illuminate social and economic history.

1 W.W. Greg, 'Bibliography – a Retrospect,' in *The Bibliographical Society 1892–1942: Studies in Retrospect* (1949), p. 24.   2 Greg, 'Bibliography', p. 30.
3 Apart from passing references to work published by the Society on the Birchley Hall Press, Wigan, and on printing and bookbinding in Cambridge, Oxford, and York.   4 Greg, 'Bibliography', p. 27.

In his pioneer work *The Provincial Book Trade in Eighteenth-Century England*[5] John Feather demonstrates that the provincial book trade was mainly distributive, rather than productive, and that the distribution networks were closely related to the circulation of local newspapers, following their start at the beginning of the eighteenth century.[6] Provincial production – and this must exclude such important centres as Edinburgh, Glasgow, and Dublin – was at first wholly limited to newspapers, jobbing work (important, but largely unknown), and 'popular literature' (chapbooks, ballad sheets, etc.).

Studies of one or another aspect of the provincial book trade have been published for at least the last two centuries, and it is illuminating to be reminded that one of the earliest was a trade directory.[7] Published later, although much earlier in its origins, is *The Life of Mr. Thomas Gent, Printer, of York, Written by Himself* (London, 1832). During the nineteenth century two kinds of work started, and continue to the present. These are studies of the local press and its books, exemplified by Robert Davies's *A Memoir of the York Press*[8] and Richard Welford's 'Early Newcastle Typography',[9] and lists of early presses, exemplified by W.H. Allnutt's series of articles from 1879 to 1901.[10]

More than thirty years ago Paul Morgan gave one of the earliest reviews of the research into the English provincial book trade.[11] In opening this he quoted H.R. Plomer, 'The history of provincial printing has never yet been written, and the task of tracing out the various printers and their work would be long and arduous',[12] indicating that this was then still true – and it is so yet.

5 John Feather, *The Provincial Book Trade in Eighteenth-Century England* (Cambridge, 1985). A similar survey of the first half of the nineteenth century is clearly a desideratum, but will not be possible until the necessary groundwork has been completed on such matters as the economic and technological framework of the trade from the provincial viewpoint, and on the mechanics and pattern of distribution, mentioned in the final paragraph of this chapter.

6 The great importance of local newspapers to any study of the provincial book trade is now widely recognized. Two books especially have emphasized the central rôle of newspapers and have eased the path for students using them. G.A. Cranfield's *The Development of the Provincial Newspaper, 1700–1760* (Oxford, 1962) deals in particular with methods of news-gathering and distribution; and R.M. Wiles, *Freshest Advices: Early Provincial Newspapers in England* (Ohio State University Press, 1965) is excellent on their content, and thorough on the location of files and individual copies.

7 John Pendred, *The London and Country Printers, Booksellers and Stationers' Vade Mecum* (London, 1785), ed. (as *The Earliest Directory of the Book Trade*) with an introduction and appendix by Graham Pollard, Bibliographical Society (1955).

8 Robert Davies, *A Memoir of the York Press, with Notices of Authors, Printers, and Stationers, in the Sixteenth, Seventeenth and Eighteenth Centuries* (London, 1868). Facsimile reprint, with a new introduction and bibliography by Bernard Barr (York, 1988).

9 Richard Welford, 'Early Newcastle Typography, 1639–1800', *Archaeologia Aeliana*, 3. ser. iii (1907): 1–134; and 4 (1908): 147–53.

10 'Printers and Printing in the Provincial Towns of England and Wales', *Trans. and Proc. of the First Annual Meeting of the Library Association*, 1879, pp. 101–3, and Appendix v, pp. 157–64; 'English Provincial Presses, 1478–1556', *Bibliographica*, 2 (1896): 23–46, 149–80, 276–308; 3 (1897), 481–3 (includes later presses and a concise chronological table 1695–1750); 'Notes on the Introduction of Printing Presses into the Smaller Towns of England and Wales after 1750 to the End of the Eighteenth Century', *Lib*, II, 2 (1901): 242–59.

11 Paul Morgan, *English Provincial Printing*, a lecture delivered to the School of Librarianship, College of Commerce, Birmingham, on 7 May 1958 (Birmingham, 1959).

12 H.R. Plomer, *A Short History of English Printing* (1900), 246.

(Parenthetically, it may be noted that both Paul Morgan and H.R. Plomer refer to printing, although Morgan ends his opening paragraph 'it is especially difficult to keep separate the allied trade of bookselling, so mention of it will inevitably creep in'.) One of the underlying themes of this chapter must be that it is possible to provide a synthesis, even of provincial printing, only if the whole book trade, in its widest sense, is considered; that is to say, if bookselling is seen as a central, not a creeping-in activity. In fact 'book trade', however unsatisfactory, is a very necessary term since, especially in the provinces, the various separate trades were often carried on together and are not easy, sometimes impossible, to distinguish, and hence must be studied together.

Paul Morgan is, perhaps, a little dismissive of those of us who make lists of local members of the book trade, with their productions and brief biographies, but is undoubtedly correct in commenting on the paucity of actual source material, while pointing out that 'one aspect of provincial printing has hardly been touched and rarely mentioned, and that is typography'. This is still a largely untapped body of information on the sources of one important 'raw material' of the book trade, and should attract the attention of the student with a seeing eye. A good example of what can be done is Michael Twyman's *John Soulby, Printer, Ulverston* which focuses on the types the Soulbys used, and the use made of them. This publication and a number other studies clearly stress the importance of facsimiles and illustrations for this and other aspects of book-trade history.[13]

In a review in 1983 Paul Morgan outlines the great changes that have taken place in the study of what he now calls the English provincial book trade since his 1958 lecture.[14]

Then it was largely a matter of serendipity going through local collections and listing titles, names and addresses in imprints and directories. Now a more scholarly approach has become essential – examining archival sources, looking at the actual products more closely, researching biographical details more thoroughly, adopting a less parochial attitude, and appreciating that one place cannot be treated in isolation from the rest of the country or the capital city.

13 Michael Twyman, *John Soulby, Printer, Ulverston: A Study of the Work Printed by John Soulby, Father and Son, between 1796 and 1827* (Reading, 1966). (A collection in the Dept. of Typography and Graphic Communication, University of Reading.) Other examples include Roy and John Lewis, *Politics and Printing in Winchester 1830–1880* (Winchester, 1980. The Stopher Collection, Hyde Historic Resources Centre, Winchester); and *William Davison's New Specimen of Cast-Metal Ornaments and Wood Types*, introduced with an account of his activities as pharmacist and printer in Alnwick, by Peter Isaac, Printing Historical Society (London, 1990). (The 'account' is a revised version of the article published in *Lib*, v, 24 (1969), 1–32.)

14 Paul Morgan, 'Changes in Studies of English Provincial Book Trade History since 1958', in 'Report of the Seminar on the Provincial Book Trade', held at the University of Loughborough, 12 July 1982, Working Paper PH 39/December 1983, History of the Book Trade in the North (and a similar, unpublished, report given to a Seminar on the Provincial Book Trade sponsored by the Rare Books Group of the Library Association at Oxford in 1977). A useful summary listing of work completed, although in need of some revision, is John Feather's *The English Book Trade before 1850: a Checklist of Secondary Sources*, Oxford Bibliographical Society, Occasional Publication No. 16, 1981.

Both this chapter, and a similar review prepared by David Knott in 1973,[15] indicate the sources that are now being quarried: archives, such as the registrations under the Seditious Societies Act of 1799, wills, bankruptcies, etc., newspapers, directories, file copies of printers' work, insurance policies, subscription lists. Ian Maxted adds to these the Inland Revenue registers in the Public Record Office at Kew for the names of masters and apprentices, the stamping of whose indentures are there recorded.[16] Such records are, indeed, of fundamental importance in tracing the movements of individual printers.[17] While some of these sources have been well used in some areas, in many cases not even lists of the names included have been published. For example, William B. Todd in his *A Directory of Printers and Others in Allied Trades, London and Vicinity 1800–1840* (London, 1972) has made extensive use of the registrations under the 1799 Act for London, Middlesex, and Surrey,[18] and Paul Morgan has listed those English counties for which such records survive.[19] Save for Warwickshire, Northumberland, Cumberland, and Hampshire, however, it seems that not even sample lists of the names and dates of registration have been separately published. Here is another relatively easily achieved task calling for action.

Even a cursory survey of the work completed and in progress on the provincial book trade reveals a wide disparity in approach, working methods, the choice and range of sources covered, and the degree of detail provided. This is hardly surprising bearing in mind local circumstances and the various starting points for these projects. It is also evident that there is an uneven coverage in book-trade studies throughout the regions, with, generally, the north and midlands rather better covered than the rest. Much has been achieved since 1958 by Group and Society projects,[20] but as much has been achieved by individuals. Ian Maxted's work on the Inland Revenue registers has already been mentioned; he has been a tireless worker in other directions, notably on the book

15 David Knott, 'Aspects of Research into English Provincial Printing', *JPHS*, 9 (1973/4): 6–21.

16 See for example, Ian Maxted, *The British Book Trades, 1710–1777* (Exeter, 1983). It may be noted here that this publication, like so many dealing with the provincial book trade, was put out by the author in a very limited edition, and is unlikely to be widely available. One desideratum for the future welfare of this facet of the Society's interests is the wider dissemination of the results of local studies in a more permanent form.

17 Ian Maxted in this paper 'Mobility and Innovation in the Book Trades: Some Devon Examples', *Six Centuries of the Provincial Book Trade* (Winchester, 1990), pp. 73–85, discusses the relationship of mobility and innovation on the part of the printer and bookseller.

18 It is not, however, always easy to retrace Professor Todd's footsteps in these registrations.

19 'English Provincial Imprints, 1799–1869', *Lib*, v, 21 (1966): 60–2; 22 (1967): 70. Paul Morgan's editing of *Warwickshire Printers' Notices, 1799–1866*, Dugdale Society, 28 (1970) is a model example of how to present, digest, and assess this source material.

20 For example, publications from the History of the Book Trade in the North project (Newcastle, 1965–   ); the Bibliography of Yorkshire Printing (University of Leeds, Institute of Bibliography and Textual Criticism, 1970s–   ); the West Midlands Book Trade project (Birmingham Bibliographical Society, 1975–   ); and the Book Trade in the North West project (Liverpool Bibliographical Society, 1981–   ).

trade in the southwest.[21] The work of David Knott (Kent) and David Stoker (Norwich) are but two further examples.

A complete index in one sequence of all the names and firms listed in these projects, and in a wide range of other published and unpublished sources, has been a long-felt want. In 1984 a small group launched the British Book Trade Index, a computer-based project, which seeks to list all names and firms in the British Isles up to 1851. The database at the University of Newcastle upon Tyne will eventually be searchable under names, town, occupations, etc. As well as providing valuable statistical information, one obvious advantage of this index will be to reduce the 'parochialism' of our studies, or at least to put them into perspective, by at once suggesting the linkage of names and activities in one part of the country with those in another.[22]

While much work has been completed since the various surveys were published twenty and more years ago, they still serve to point to both original source materials not examined, and to aspects of the subject awaiting investigation. The systematic reading and indexing of files of local newspapers is, indisputably, a long-term task, but one with fruitful results in the form of information from advertisements, announcements of births, marriages, deaths, sales of premises, bankruptcies, etc. The holdings of Record Offices also await detailed listing of their book-trade material, both archival – for example diocesan registers, courts of debtors, property deeds, etc.[23] – and also printed ephemera of all kinds, proformas, bills, posters, auction catalogues, and all kinds of official notices, some with imprints, often found in family papers and usually unrecorded. A national survey might bring to light any last surviving printers' accounts and day books. Local museums, too, house items relating to the book trades, printing presses, etc., and examples of printing such as trade cards. Other classes of records such as port records and Post Office records have not yet been fully explored.

The need for typographical studies has already been mentioned. A special desideratum is the general mapping of the types used in the regions, and their sizes, a listing of typefounders' types, and, especially in the context of the rapid advances in technology after 1800, a knowledge of what printing machines were used, and why and when they were introduced. Rotherham and Steele's work on printing in North Staffordshire (1975) is one of the few book-length studies on this topic.[24] The related and important field of paper studies has yet to find its historian for the provincial trade, although much of the groundwork for the period up to 1800 was covered by A.H. Shorter in his 1957 book *Paper Mills and Paper-Makers in England*.[25] And, especially again for the period after 1800,

21 For example, *Books with Devon Imprints; A Handlist to 1800* (Ian Maxted, 1989).

22 See *PHS Bulletin*, 113 (1984), 141; 21 (1987), 280; 27 (1990), 8–9.

23 See Knott, 'Aspects'.

24 Albert Rotherham and Maurice Steele, *A History of Printing in North Staffordshire* (Stoke on Trent, 1975).

25 A.H. Shorter, *Paper Mills and Paper-Makers in England, 1495–1800* (Hilversum, 1957).

we still do not know enough about what was printed and published in the provinces: how much was produced, in what print-runs, on what subjects, and to what quality standards. Further studies of individual firms such as James Moran's *Clays of Bungay*,[26] and A.N. Daish on the House of Yelf, Newport, Isle of Wight;[27] and of individual places, such as Dr Chilton's on Hull,[28] are also needed to increase our knowledge of the trade in the regions. In particular not enough is known about early nineteenth-century provincial private printers and publishers.

26 James Moran, *Clays of Bungay* (Bungay, 1978).
27 A.N. Daish, *Printers' Pride: The House of Yelf at Newport, Isle of Wight, 1816–1966* (Newport, Isle of Wight, 1967).
28 C.W. Chilton, *Early Hull Printers and Booksellers: An account of the Printing, Bookselling and Allied Trades from their Beginnings to 1840* (Kingston upon Hull, 1982).

Scottish bibliography for the period ending 1801

BRIAN HILLYARD

This chapter reviews the principal contributions of the last fifty years in the main areas of Scottish bibliography for the period up to the end of the eighteenth century, and in so doing suggests some lines of future research. It is divided into five sections. The first two are concerned with printing and publishing 1508–1700 and 1701–1800; the third section is devoted to collecting and reading; the chapter concludes with two short sections, on Gaelic books and on binding.

Ever since the publication in 1904, by the Edinburgh Bibliographical Society, of H.G. Aldis's *A List of Books Printed in Scotland before 1700*, material for the enumerative bibliography of early Scottish books has been accumulating. Some of it had previously been published, but most of it first became available with the publication in 1970, now by the National Library of Scotland, of a revised edition of Aldis's *List*, adding some 1,750 items (138 for the year 1700 were included for the first time) to the original 3,919. Since then more than 400 new items have been noted. A new edition of the checklist (out of print for some years) would be useful to consolidate the record, and thereby facilitate the process of collecting, and it would be particularly appropriate now that *British Newspapers and Periodicals 1641–1700* and the revised editions of *STC* and Wing – against all of which the 1970 edition needs to be collated – are available. Aldis's *List* retains value as isolating, and giving an overview of, the relatively small amount of Scottish material otherwise lost in these larger publications.

Aldis's original compilation – this is a point repeated in the 1970 preface – was intended only as a handlist to help assemble the items for a proper bibliographical catalogue of early Scottish imprints. There is room for discussion as to whether such a catalogue remains a desideratum. The automation of *STC* and Wing to *ESTC* standards (now under way) is relevant here because an expanded Aldis could be seen as a subset of the proposed *STC* and Wing files and could, in theory anyway, be printed out from them as and in what form required. Certainly, duplication of effort cannot be justified, and if Aldis is to be expanded it should be on the basis of starting from the relevant enhanced *STC* and Wing records, or possibly as a contribution to that enhancement.

Eventually consideration could be given to extending Aldis to create a retrospective Scottish bibliography incorporating work published outside Scotland by Scots or about Scotland, rather like J.A. Ferguson's *Bibliography of Australia*. Some of the material for this has been available for some time,[1] while more recently M.A. Shaaber, *Check-List of Works of British Authors Printed Abroad, in Languages other than English, to 1641* (New York, 1975), would be a further source, as also would John Durkan's unpublished full-scale bibliography of George Buchanan. In the light of the amount of activity by Scots on the Continent this is necessary background for writing the history of the book in Scotland in this early period.

To turn now to the more detailed work needed to reconstruct the history of early Scottish printing from the first efforts by Chepman and Myllar in the first decade of the sixteenth century, the standard account remains R. Dickson and J.P. Edmond, *Annals of Scottish Printing . . . to the Beginning of the Seventeenth Century* (Edinburgh, 1890), supplemented, on the typographical side, by F. Isaac's two books, *English & Scottish Printing Types 1501–1535, 1508–1541* (Bibliographical Society, 1930), and *English & Scottish Printing Types 1535–58, 1552–58* (Bibliographical Society, 1932); W. Beattie, *The Scottish Tradition in Printed Books* (Edinburgh, 1949), concentrates on the earlier period, but is only a sketch. Beattie, who later published a collection of notes, 'Some Early Scottish Books', in *The Scottish Tradition: Essays in Honour of Ronald Gordon Cant*, edited by G.W.S. Barrow (Edinburgh, 1974), pp. 107–20, had previously brought out the good Edinburgh Bibliographical Society facsimile *The Chepman and Myllar Prints* (Edinburgh, 1950), the introduction to which includes discussion of several figures important for the close relations in publishing between France and Scotland, namely Jacobus Ledelh, the earliest Scotsman to have his work published – in France – in his lifetime, and two Scotsmen in the French book trade, David Lauxius (i.e. David Lowis) and Denis Roce; on all this see further Beattie, *EBST*, 3 (1948–55): 75–7, and J. Durkan, *EBST*, 3 (1948–55): 78–80, 156–7, and *Bibliotheck*, 4 (1963–6): 200–1. The essential background of early Rouen printing – two books were printed there for Andrew Myllar in 1505 and 1506 – is becoming steadily better known thanks largely to the work by Pierre Aquilon published in *Répertoire bibliographique des livres imprimés en France au seizième siècle*, fascs. 8 (1971), 14 (1973), 22 (1975), 27 (1978), and (out of series) *Bibliographie Normande* (1980); also worth consulting is W.K. Sessions, *The deux Pierres* (York, 1982). The most substantial piece of early Scottish printing is the *Aberdeen Breviary* (1510), of which unfortunately only odd pages are available in facsimile. Wider aspects of this book were studied by J.D. Galbraith, 'The Sources of the Aberdeen Breviary' (unpublished M.Litt. thesis, University of Aberdeen, 1970); see also his article in *Archives* 14 (1980): 140–3, and L.J. Macfarlane, *William Elphinstone* (Aberdeen, 1985), pp. 236–46.

---

1 For example, J.F.K. Johnstone and A.W. Robertson, *Bibliographia Aberdonensis*, 2 vols. (Aberdeen, 1929–30), and J.H. Baxter and C.J. Fordyce, 'Books Published Abroad by Scotsmen before 1700', *Records of the Glasgow Bibliographical Society*, 11 (1933): 1–55, of which only the first part, covering France, was ever published.

Proceeding chronologically, the received view is that after Chepman we come to John Story who appears in the imprint of the eight-page 'Compassio Beate Mariae', dated to *c.* 1520 (facsimile, with introduction, by G.P. Johnston, *Papers of the Edinburgh Bibliographical Society*, 14 (1926–30): 99–118), although W.J. Anderson, in an article remaining unanswered (*EBST*, 4 (1955–71): 137–47), re-assigned it to a date preceding the Aberdeen Breviary. Next comes Thomas Davidson, fragments of whose printing of Gavin Douglas's 'The Palyce of Honour', variously dated 1530–40, were published in facsimile by W. Beattie, *EBST* 3 (1948–55): 31–46. After the middle of the century Scottish books became more numerous, and printing also spread outside Edinburgh. From this later period Beattie published a facsimile, with useful introduction, of *The Taill of Rauf Coilyear*, printed by Lekpreuik at St Andrews in 1572 (Edinburgh, 1966).

It is perhaps not very likely that much hitherto unknown printing will come to light – though for a newly discovered fragment of Holland's *The Buke of the Howlat* see R. Donaldson, *EBST*, 5 (1971–87), part 3: 25–8 – and progress needs to come from research on existing texts. On the typographical side, the only published work we can add to Isaac's *Printing Types* is A.F. Johnson's sketch, 'Type-designs and Type-founding in Scotland', *EBST*, 2 (1938–45): 255–61 (reprinted in *Selected Essays on Books and Printing*, edited by P.H. Muir (Amsterdam, 1970), pp. 317–26), and Beattie, 'Some Early Scottish Books', pp. 115–16. Recently Paul Watry has photographed all the ornaments in known Scottish sixteenth-century books and arranged them in a catalogue which should prove a useful tool (thesis in progress, University of Oxford). Eventually a further general study of the types may clarify the picture. Another promising way forward is through archive material: for example, J. Durkan, *Bibliotheck*, 11 (1982–3): 1–2 (on an unknown Davidson imprint), and 129–35 (on an important contract of Lekpreuik's), and C. Clair, *Lib*, v, 14 (1959): 43–5 (Plantin archive).

Seventeenth-century printers were once much studied: for example, J.P. Edmond, *Aberdeen Printers 1620–1736* (Aberdeen, 1886), W. Cowan, 'Andro Hart and His Press', *Papers of the Edinburgh Bibliographical Society*, 1 (1896): no. 12, and G.H. Bushnell, *The Life and Work of Edward Raban* (St Andrews and Cupar, 1928). But the last thorough treatment of an individual printer of this period was W. Beattie's 'A Handlist of Works from the Press of John Wreittoun at Edinburgh 1624–*c.* 1639', *EBST*, 2 (1938–45): 89–104. More recent work has concentrated on individual books or other limited topics.[2] D. Stevenson, 'A Revolutionary Regime and the Press: the Scottish Covenanters and their Printers, 1638–51', *Lib*, VI, 7 (1985): 315–37, stands alone in giving a broad view of Scottish printing in the seventeenth century, seeing it in relation to

---

2 For example, W.R. MacDonald, 'Scottish Seventeenth-Century Almanacs', *Bibliotheck*, 4 (1963–6): 257–322; R.G. Cant, 'The St Andrews University Theses 1579–1747', *EBST*, 2 (1938–45): 105–50, 263–72; P. Morgan, 'Some Bibliographical Aspects of the Scottish Prayer Book of 1637', *Bibliotheck*, 5 (1967–70): 1–23; C.B.L. Barr, 'Early Scottish Editions of "The Seven Sages of Rome"', *Bibliotheck*, 5 (1967–70): 62–72, and B. Hillyard, 'Some Seventeenth-Century Scottish Editions of Virgil', *EBST*, 5 (1971–87), part 4: 25–35.

political events, and considering why Scottish printers printed what they did. More research of this kind is needed.

For the sixteenth and seventeenth centuries, the basic facts known about the members of the book trade are recorded in the indexes to Aldis, but the 1970 edition did not include much revision of the existing indexes (see introduction, p. xi) and no doubt more can be unearthed, for example from the lists and correspondence of Archibald Hislop, 1668–78 (Scottish Record Office). Though long known and used, the George Chalmers collections (National Library of Scotland Adv. MSS.16.2.21–2, 17.1.16, 81.9.6–7; Edinburgh University Library MSS.La.II.448, 452) need to be fully exploited (see the strictures by Beattie, 'John Wreittoun', p. 99). Research could usefully be directed towards, in the first place, a directory, and, second, a history of the book trade, both extending beyond this period, into the nineteenth century.

Earlier work at the National Library of Scotland to produce an eighteenth-century sequel to Aldis was made redundant by *ESTC*, whose file incorporates the National Library's holdings. But this should in fact make the study of eighteenth-century Scottish printing and publishing that much easier by giving ready access to a larger amount of detailed information and enabling the output of individual Scottish printers to be better established and analysed as well as showing the publishing history of particular titles; for example, some Aberdeen imprints which are apparently page-for-page reprints of Foulis reprints of London publications would bear investigation. The number of occasions on which *ESTC* records a London imprint as false and probably printed in Scotland shows the importance of a thorough knowledge of piracies. When David Foxon was compiling *English Verse 1701–1750* he built up a file of ornaments (since presented to the National Library of Scotland) on the basis of which he attributed many of these Scottish printings to Ruddiman, Fleming, or Cheyne. There is a good basis here for further work. The rôle of reprints in the growth of the Scottish book trade has been explored by Warren McDougall (see below).

If a pre-1701 retrospective Scottish bibliography were ever realized, its extension to cover the eighteenth century would be a vast undertaking. Inroads have in fact been made with some author or topical bibliography (for example, David Hume, Robert Burns, James Boswell, and Anglo-Scottish pamphlets 1701–14), but the matter cannot be pursued here.

More so than in the earlier period, study of the output of individual printers has made significant progress, though all the work previously done now needs to be checked in the light of the *ESTC* file. The fame of the Foulis press has meant that the descriptive side of its study has received a head start. P. Gaskell's paper 'The Early Work of the Foulis Press and the Wilson Foundry', *Lib*, v, 7 (1952): 77–110, 149–77, and his subsequent full bibliography, *The Foulis Press* (London, 1964; revised edition, Winchester, 1986) are extremely useful, and his contribution to the study of Wilson typefaces is important, as also is his work – which should be copied for other printers – on distinguishing issues by quality of paper as part of a book's publication history. In his review of *The Foulis Press*

Foxon hoped for 'a general history of the Foulis family, their work and their associates' (*Lib*, V, 20 (1965): 251-2), and there is indeed much room for further research into the business and editorial aspects of their publishing, with perhaps an edition of their correspondence, as has been suggested by Carnie.[3] Gaskell himself illustrated ('Early Work', p. 87, with plate opposite p. 110) a binding style – crossed spine panels – that *might* have come from the Foulis bindery, but more recently, especially after the Colquhoun of Luss sale (Christies, Glasgow, 9 and 16 November 1983), there has arisen a dangerous habit of positively identifying 'Foulis' bindings. This requires proper investigation.

The output of Hamilton, Balfour, and Neill was listed and studied in Warren McDougall's unpublished PhD thesis, 'Gavin Hamilton, John Balfour and Patrick Neill: A Study of Publishing in Edinburgh in the 18th century' (University of Edinburgh, 1974). McDougall is continuing his work, and has recently published a checklist of their publications in *Spreading the Word*, edited by R. Myers and M. Harris (Winchester, 1990), pp. 187-232, and used some of the other material in 'Copyright Litigation in the Court of Session, 1738-1749, and the Rise of the Scottish Book Trade', *EBST*, 5 (1971-87), part 5: 2-31, and 'Scottish Books for America in the mid 18th Century', *Spreading the Word*, pp. 21-46.

A bibliography of works from the press of James Watson of Edinburgh, 1695-1722, with a lengthy introduction, compiled by D. Wyn Evans, appeared as *EBST*, 5 (1971-87), part 2; supplementary material was published in *EBST*, 5 (1971-87), part 5: 41-8. *Rules and Directions to be Observed in Printing-Houses*, 1721 (*EBST* 5: Evans 464), is an important document for the history of the printing trade in Edinburgh, and recent acquisition of the only known copy by the National Library of Scotland was closely followed by the publication, with an introduction by Evans, of a type facsimile (Tom Rae, Greenock, 1988).

Similar work could be done for some other Scottish firms, for example, Urie of Glasgow and Chalmers of Aberdeen, which are considered alongside Foulis and Hamilton by R.H. Carnie in an article, 'Scholar-printers of the Scottish Enlightenment 1740-1880', in *Aberdeen and the Enlightenment*, edited by J.J. Carter and J.H. Pittock (Aberdeen, 1987), pp. 298-308. R.A. Gillespie is continuing the work he began with 'A List of Books Printed in Glasgow 1701-1775 with Notes on the Printers and Booksellers' (unpublished FLA thesis, Glasgow, 1967). He is particularly interested in Urie, on whose parentage he published a note in *Bibliotheck*, 5 (1967-70): 38-40.

In a paper given to the Bibliographical Society in London in January 1961, and printed as 'Scottish Printers and Booksellers: A Study of Source Material' in *Bibliotheck*, 4 (1963-6): 218-27, Carnie called for a revision of the Scottish

---

3 See R.H. Carnie, 'The Letters of Robert Foulis to James Beattie', *Bibliotheck*, 9 (1978-9): 33-46, and 'Andrew Foulis the Younger: Some Illustrative Letters', *Bibliotheck*, 6 (1971-3): 93-4; B. McMullin, 'An Anatomy of the Foulis Press Duodecimo Ciceros of 1748 and 1749', *PBSA*, 74 (1980): 177-200; J. Burnett, 'Robert Simson's Euclid and the Foulis Press', *Bibliotheck*, 11 (1982-3): 136-48, and 'A Note on the Foulis Homer of 1756-1758', *Bibliotheck*, 12 (1984-5): 33-5; and B. Hillyard, 'The Edinburgh Society's Silver Medals for Printing', *PBSA*, 78 (1984): 295-319.

entries in H.R. Plomer's *A Dictionary of the Printers and Booksellers Who Were at Work in England, Scotland and Ireland from 1668 to 1725* (Bibliographical Society, 1922) and of Bushnell's Scottish section in H.R. Plomer, G.H. Bushnell, and E.R.McC. Dix, *A Dictionary of the Printers and Booksellers Who Were at Work in England, Scotland and Ireland from 1726 to 1775* (Bibliographical Society, 1932). He himself did some of the necessary work, and, partly in collaboration with R.P. Doig, published it, as supplements to Plomer and Bushnell, in *SB*, 12 (1959): 131–59, 14 (1961): 81–96, and 15 (1962): 105–20; see also *Bibliotheck* 1, no. 4 (1958): 24–39 (Perth), and 3, no. 2 (1960): 53–60 (St Andrews). Since then the National Library of Scotland has compiled an index – from which contributions are being made to the British Book Trade Index – of its eighteenth-century Scottish imprints; relevant information has been incorporated from the major Scottish newspapers. Much miscellaneous information is still to be extracted from manuscript collections, ranging from the papers of institutions or individuals acquiring books to the records of printers, publishers, and booksellers.[4] More finding-aids, such as *Scottish Record Office Court of Session Productions c. 1760–1840*, List & Index Society Special Series 23 (Richmond, 1987), are needed. An important document requiring study that has recently come into public ownership (NLS MS.Acc.9800) is a daybook in which an unidentified Edinburgh bookseller records, with the names of his clients, books both bought and sold, 1715–17. This is a rare surviving record of a Scottish bookseller's business in the first half of the eighteenth century; the only comparable sources – not exploited in D. Duncan's otherwise useful *Thomas Ruddiman* (Edinburgh, 1965) – are Ruddiman's printing-shop ledger 1710–15 and the records of the distribution of his publications (NLS MSS.762–3). There are many later sources still to be fully exploited: for example, the Neill printing-house ledgers 1764–73 (NLS MS.Dep.196), use of which was well demonstrated by R.H. Carnie, 'Boswell's *Account of Corsica* 1768: An Edinburgh Cancel in a Glasgow Book', *BC*, 26 (1977): 186–94; the papers of William Creech in the Signet Library and Edinburgh Public Library, used by I.R. Grant, 'William Creech' in *Books and the Man: Antiquarian Booksellers' Association Annual* (London, 1953), pp. 70–6; and the records (1776–   ) of the Edinburgh Booksellers' Society (NLS MS. Dep. 303).

On the typographical side not much can be added to Johnson's sketch and Gaskell's important work on the Wilson Foundry. D.J. Bryden has brought together information on types used by John Reid, in *Bibliotheck*, 6 (1971–3): 17–21. The 'strong face' type of the Edinburgh typefounder John Baine has been called a pioneering design by Berthold Wolpe (unpublished Edinburgh Bibliographical Society lecture); cf. J. Alden, 'Scotch Type in Eighteenth-century America', *SB*, 3 (1950–1): 270–4. There have been passing references to Baine (for example, W.B. Todd, *SB*, 6 (1954): 34), but this is clearly somebody who needs comprehensive treatment. On the invention of stereotyping by William

---

4 See, for example, on the Ogstoun family, R.H. Carnie and B. Hillyard, *Bibliographical Society of Australia and New Zealand Bulletin*, 6 (1982): 141–8, and 10 (1986): 82–8, respectively.

Ged, earlier work has now been replaced by John Carter, *Lib*, v, 15 (1960): 161–92, and 16 (1961): 143–5.[5] As Carter himself indicated, the last word on this has not been said.

Complementing the study of the output of books is the analysis of their consumption. This has barely begun: we need more data on the contents and use of both institutional and private collections, not to mention the contribution that can be made by subscription lists (cf. R.H. Carnie, 'Working-Class Readers in Eighteenth Century Scotland: The Evidence from Subscription Lists', *Scottish Tradition* 7/8 (1977–8): 77–94, which deserves to be better known) and the study of bookselling.

Of the major libraries, the history of the collections of the Advocates' Library is still to be fully researched; in the meantime see the book of essays *For the Encouragement of Learning: Scotland's National Library 1689–1989*, edited by A. Matheson and P. Cadell (Edinburgh, 1989), supplemented by B. Hillyard, 'Thomas Ruddiman and the Advocates' Library, 1728–52', *Library History* 8 (1988–90): 157–70. For Edinburgh University Library the foundation collection has been studied by C.P. Finlayson, *Clement Litill and his Library* (Edinburgh, 1980), and further studies have been published in *Edinburgh University Library 1580–1980*, edited by J.R. Guild and A. Law (Edinburgh, 1982). The history of St Andrews University Library has been sketched by Bushnell in *Henderson's Benefaction*, edited by J.B. Salmond and G.H. Bushnell (St Andrews, 1942), pp. 25–48, and *BC*, 7 (1958): 128–38; on the role of copyright deposit see also P. Ardagh, *EBST*, 3 (1948–55): 179–211, and E.A. Frame, *EBST*, 5 (1971–87), part 4: 1–9. There is an account of Glasgow University Library's early history by J. Durkan, *Bibliotheck*, 8 (1976–7): 102–26. Aberdeen University Library is partly covered by J.R. Pickard, *A History of King's College Library, Aberdeen, until 1860*, 3 vols. (privately published, Aberdeen, 1987), in which, however, the outline and salient details are lost in over 1,000 unindexed pages. Some other institutional libraries have fared better: see G.H. Ballantyne, *The Signet Library Edinburgh and its Librarians 1722–1972* (Glasgow, 1972), and M.V. Mathew, *The Royal Botanic Garden Library* (Edinburgh, 1987).

Smaller libraries of a different type have been relatively more studied. Drawing on J. and M. Lough, 'Aberdeen Circulating Libraries in the Eighteenth Century', *Aberdeen University Review*, 31 (1945): 17–24, and on some of his own earlier published work, Paul Kaufman's 'The Rise of Community Libraries in Scotland', *PBSA*, 59 (1965): 233–94, containing a valuable listing of circulating, non-profit-making, and public libraries of eighteenth-century Scotland, was a major piece of research. Even more systematic work, which needs to be repeated for the rest of Scotland, is W.R. MacDonald's 'Circulating Libraries in the North-East of Scotland in the Eighteenth Century', *Bibliotheck*, 5 (1968): 119–37. Of the miners' libraries he listed, Kaufman has himself written on the

5 See also R. Donaldson, *Lib*, v, 22 (1967): 352–4, P. Gaskell, *Bibliotheck*, 4 (1963–6): 76, John Morris, *Journal of the Printing Historical Society*, 1 (1965): 97–8, and B. Hillyard, *Lib*, VI, 13 (1991): 156–7.

Leadhills Library (*Libri*, 17 (1967): 13–20), which has now been restored (the books previously in Edinburgh on deposit have been returned), and Wanlockhead Library has been studied by John Crawford and Stuart James: see most recently their joint work, *The Society for Purchasing Books in Wanlockhead 1756–1979*, Scottish Library Essays 1 (Glasgow, 1981). The library at Laurencekirk, founded by Lord Gardenstone and visited by Johnson and Boswell in 1773, has now been described by J.R. Barker, *Bibliotheck*, 6 (1971–3): 41–51.

The study of private libraries is useful as part of a general examination of the movement of books and of reading habits – and here subscription and other lists (such as inventories) provide useful evidence – but at the 'upper' end includes the study of book collecting; and the libraries of great thinkers or writers are important in an understanding of their owners. This is an area in which scholars are very active at present, and where there is perhaps scope for beginning a work of synthesis; see B. Hillyard, 'Working towards a History of Scottish Book Collecting', in *Six Centuries of the Provincial Book Trade in Britain*, edited by P. Isaac (Winchester, 1990), pp. 181–6.

The early period, ending in 1560, is covered by J. Durkan and A. Ross, *Early Scottish Libraries* (Glasgow, 1961), supplemented by Durkan himself and others, *Bibliotheck*, 12 (1984–5): 85–90 (with references to earlier supplements); a new consolidated edition is needed. Durkan has also tackled in detail the problem of books owned by Mary Queen of Scots, in *Mary Stewart, Queen in Three Kingdoms*, edited by Michael Lynch (Oxford, 1988), pp. 71–104, and I.D. McFarlane's *Buchanan* (1981), pp. 527–31, summarizes what is known of Buchanan's library. Finlayson's work on Clement Litill has already been mentioned. An early-seventeenth-century library has been reconstructed by R.H. MacDonald, *The Library of Drummond of Hawthornden* (Edinburgh, 1971). Moving into the later seventeenth and early eighteenth centuries, M.C.T. Simpson's unpublished PhD thesis, 'The Library of the Reverend James Nairn (1629–1678): Scholarly Book Collecting in Restoration Scotland' (University of Edinburgh, 1988), lists and analyses an individual library; see now *A Catalogue of the Library of the Revd James Nairn (1629–1678) Bequeathed by him to Edinburgh University Library* (Edinburgh: Edinburgh University Library, 1990). The unpublished part of the thesis contains much discussion of collectors contemporary with Nairn, including Robert Leighton, whose library, now housed and properly catalogued at Dunblane (a recently compiled card catalogue is available in both Stirling University Library and the National Library of Scotland), has been discussed by G. Willis, *Bibliotheck*, 10 (1980–1): 139–57, and *The Leighton Library, Dunblane: Catalogue of Manuscripts* (Stirling, 1981); compare M.C.T. Simpson, *Bibliotheck*, 12 (1984–5): 91–2. Andrew Fletcher (1653–1716) assembled a large library which remained more or less intact, apparently, until unfortunately dispersed in the 1960s: working from a manuscript catalogue, Mary Norton and John Robertson have begun an attempt to reconstruct this library. Smaller but remaining essentially intact was the library belonging to Lord George Douglas, son of the Duke of Queensberry, and presented to the Advocates' Library by the Duke in 1695, after his son's early death: it has been listed and analysed by

W.A. Kelly, 'The Library of Lord George Douglas (*c.* 1667/8–1693?)' (unpublished MA thesis, Dept. of Librarianship, University of Strathclyde, 1975). A bibliophile who advised both Fletcher and Lord George Douglas and also provides links with the noted English collector the Earl of Sunderland, was Alexander Cunningham: a study by Katherine Swift is in preparation. Another collector whose library was acquired by the Advocates' Library was James Sutherland (1638(?)–1719): see M.V. Mathew, *Bibliotheck*, 14 (1987): 1–29, and, for a catalogue, W.A. Kelly, *Bibliotheck*, 14 (1987): 30–106. The libraries of Archibald Pitcairne (1652–1713) and Robert Erskine (1677–1718), both now in Russia, have been studied by J.H. Appleby and A. Cunningham, *Bibliotheck*, 11 (1982–3): 3–16, J.H. Appleby and J.V. Howard, *Bibliotheck*, 11(1982–3): 101–7, and J.H. Appleby, *Bibliotheck*, 12 (1984–5): 137–9. Pitcairne's letters contain many interesting references to his book collecting: see *The Best of Our Owne: Letters of Archibald Pitcairne, 1652–1713*, collected and annotated by W.T. Johnston (Edinburgh, 1979).

To come to the 'enlightenment' period proper, the reconstruction of Adam Smith's library has been under way for many years now, and progress continues to be made: see H. Mizuta, *Adam Smith's Library: A Supplement to Bonar's Catalogue with a Checklist of the Whole Library* (Cambridge, 1967), and M.C.T. Simpson, *Bibliotheck*, 9 (1978–9): 187–99; a new complete catalogue, by Mizuta, is forthcoming. The fate of David Hume's library has long been a mystery, but now David and Mary Norton have argued, in largely unpublished research, that his books became the property of his nephew, Baron David Hume, and are therefore included in an extant catalogue of the Baron's library. Analysis of this catalogue continues, and related publications may be expected in the next few years. The only other detailed published information about a Scottish library of the second half of the eighteenth century – leaving aside William Hunter's (formed in London, though bequeathed to Glasgow University; Helen Brock is editing his correspondence)as not truly Scottish – is the facsimile of the 1801 sale catalogue of Hugh Blair's library, with an introduction by Hugh Amory, in *Sale Catalogues of Libraries of Eminent Persons*, edited by A.N.L. Munby, vol. VII (1973). Blair's library is described by Amory as very fine, but a much finer library, including the first copy of the 42-line Bible known for certain to have been in Scotland, was that collected by David Steuart (1747–1824), Lord Provost of Edinburgh in 1780–2; see B. Hillyard, *Bibliotheck*, 12 (1984–5): 105–25, and 15 (1988): 21–4.

On the bookselling side, Scottish auction and booksellers' catalogues are included in A.N.L. Munby and Lenore Coral, *British Book Sale Catalogues 1676–1800: A Union List* (1977), but that is based on extant catalogues (imperfectly, as *ESTC* now shows), and, besides, a proper study of the trade requires the use of newspapers and other sources. The late W.R. MacDonald's 'Book-Auctions and Book-Sales in the Aberdeen Area, 1749–1800', *Aberdeen University Review*, 42 (1967): 114–32, is a model piece of work which needs to be repeated for the rest of Scotland. As many of the catalogues are very rare, and some available only in the United States, research would benefit from the building up of an archive of microform copies.

Books printed in Scottish Gaelic – the first dates from 1567 – form an important and integral part of the Scottish book trade, but early Gaelic books have been little studied since D. Maclean's *Typographia Scoto-Gadelica* (Edinburgh, 1915; facsimile reprint 1971; a typescript supplement by D. MacKinnon is held by NLS); for a sketch of Gaelic bibliography see Ann Matheson, *State Librarian*, 30 (1982): 8–9 and 14, reprinted in *Library Association Rare Books Group Newsletter*, 20 (November 1982). In the 1970s work began at the National Library of Scotland to produce a new bibliography, but this was soon put aside in favour of the union catalogue of Gaelic books, eventually published as Mary Ferguson and Ann Matheson, *Scottish Gaelic Union Catalogue: A List of Books Printed in the Scottish Gaelic from 1567 to 1973* (Edinburgh, 1984), of which a second volume, recording new items and further locations from private United Kingdom collections and overseas libraries, is in preparation. In their preface the editors express the hope that this listing with locations 'will encourage the compilation of a full bibliography of Gaelic books'. That such a new bibliography, with attendant study of the Gaelic book trade, is a major desideratum appears all the more clearly in the light of the publication of *Libri Walliae*. Unfortunately no plans are known to exist at present, although, by contrast, interest in modern Gaelic bibliography is very strong.

One particular aspect of the Scottish book trade that has always attracted attention is decorative binding. For the early period W.S. Mitchell, *A History of Scottish Bookbinding 1432 to 1650* (Aberdeen, 1955), was the first detailed overview ever published; little has appeared since. Later – beginning with the first bindings to which a name can be attached, those of Alexander Ogstoun (see M.M. Foot, *BC*, 29 (1980): 255–7) – more has been done. This is the period dominated at first by the two main styles, as outlined by John Morris, 'Wheels and Herringbones: Some Scottish Bindings 1678–1773', *Bookbinder*, 1 (1987): 39–50. An illustrated handlist of some examples was published by M.J. Sommerlad, *Scottish 'Wheel' and 'Herring-bone' Bindings in the Bodleian Library*, Oxford Bibliographical Society Occasional Publications 1 (Oxford, 1967), and examples in other collections are regularly noted, for example by M.M. Foot, *The Henry Davis Gift II* (1983), nos. 271–7. A work of synthesis would be welcome.

As these styles declined, others came to the fore. The one that stands out, both from its visual impact and because the craftsmen can be clearly identified, is that associated with James Scott, and his son William (see B. Hillyard, *Lib*, VI, 8 (1986): 269), whose joint careers ran from 1773 to 1787. Their work was carefully documented in J.H. Loudon's *James Scott and William Scott, Bookbinders* (1980), completed before the appearance of M.M. Foot's independent treatment in *The Henry Davis Gift*, vol. I (1978), pp. 115–25. Many other examples have since come to light (e.g. *The Henry Davis Gift*, vol. II, nos. 281–2 with notes), and it will soon be possible to compile a sizeable supplement and perhaps to advance the study of the Scotts' binding as a business. Another identifiable maker of later eighteenth-century Scottish bindings is also emerging, Charles Cleland, whose label occurs on Edinburgh theses bound in a Scott style; see J. Collins, *BC*, 36 (1987): 372–4, and John Morris, *BC*, 38 (1989): 544–6.

The continued publication of good-quality photographs of hitherto unpublished decorative bindings is essential for further research. The investigation of archive sources – including the study of the history of institutional and private libraries – needs to be pursued in order to find fresh evidence relating to the identity of binders and their businesses.

But decorative binding can have been only a small part of the trade. Opportunities exist, and should be taken while they can (before rebinding destroys the evidence), for the study of more ordinary bindings. To take only one example – which probably applies to other libraries – most of the bindings done for the Advocates' Library in the period 1702–54, including those on the copyright intake, can be related to binders' accounts, though very few of them have survived completely intact to the present day.

From autograph to automation: Welsh bibliography

EILUNED REES

The Welsh language is believed to have evolved in a recognizable form by the second half of the sixth century. The earliest extant manuscripts date from the thirteenth century, though there are brief Welsh texts and glosses, together with inscriptions, of much earlier date. The Welsh literary tradition in modern times has been complemented by another tradition, a corpus of Anglo-Welsh literature. Welsh bibliography, therefore, covers an interesting variety of topics. The following subject areas are discussed here: printed books, periodicals and newspapers, ballads, music, almanacs and chap-books, manuscripts, Anglo-Welsh literature, and Welsh Americana.

The first Welsh bibliographer was Moses Williams, cleric and antiquary. He compiled *Cofrestr o'r holl lyfrau printjedig gan mwyaf a gyfansoddwyd yn y iaith Gymraeg neu a gyfieithwyd iddi hyd y flwyddyn 1717* (A Register of All Printed Books Mainly Written in the Welsh Language or Translated into it up to the Year 1717.) The book was printed in London by the King's Printers in 1717. Like all good bibliographers, Williams had no illusions about the compilation and his own copy, duly annotated in preparation for a second edition, may be seen in the Bodleian Library. No second edition materialized and the next major bibliography of Welsh printed books was published in 1869. The Welsh title is *Llyfryddiaeth y Cymry . . .* and the English title is *Cambrian Bibliography: Containing an Account of the Books Printed in the Welsh Language, or Relating to Wales, from . . . 1546 to the End of the Eighteenth Century; with Bibliographical Notices.* The author, William Rowlands, a circuit minister for the Wesleyan Church, did not live to see his catalogue in print; the work was edited after his death by Daniel Silvan Evans and printed and published by John Pryse in Llanidloes. Moses Williams and William Rowlands travelled extensively in Wales, the former in connection with his work for the Society for Promoting Christian Knowledge and the latter on his preaching tours; they were well placed to trace copies of Welsh books. Even so, they faced a difficult task because early Welsh books had been printed in small editions and the quality of printing was not such as would encourage their survival as collectors' treasures. Rowlands had to rely to some degree on the information sent to him from book owners, information which was often misleading as the science of bibliography was hardly a feature of rural life.

Moses Williams's catalogue had been arranged alphabetically; William Rowlands chose a chronological sequence, an unfortunate decision in view of the fact that so many Welsh books bear no date. Inspired by his example, Charles Ashton decided to compile a catalogue of Welsh books, from 1800 to the year in which he submitted the manuscript to a National Eisteddfod literary competition, 1892. Ashton was a self-educated man, an eccentric, whose 'manuscript' is made up of scraps of paper of all shapes and sizes. Nevertheless, he was a reliable bibliographer and his descriptions of books are accurate in everything save format. The founder of the National Library of Wales, Sir John Williams, intended to sponsor the publication of the manuscript in seven or eight volumes and Ashton set out to edit it and add entries for books up to 1900. Unfortunately, he committed suicide in 1899. In 1908, the Eisteddfod Committee published the first part of the manuscript, unedited, under the title *Llyfryddiaeth Gymreig o 1801 i 1810*, the printers being Woodall, Minshall, Thomas and Co., Oswestry. Its value is diminished as it has no index; even an index as variable in quality as that in the *Cambrian Bibliography* would have helped.

The National Library of Wales was founded by Royal Charter in 1907. Prior to its foundation, the most comprehensive collection of Welsh material in the country was that belonging to Cardiff City Library, now the headquarters of South Glamorgan County Library. In 1898, the following work appeared: *Cardiff Free Libraries. Catalogue of Printed Literature in the Welsh Department. By John Ballinger and James Ifano Jones* (Cardiff, 1898.) It is a dictionary catalogue, which cannot be too highly praised. John Ballinger was City Librarian of Cardiff and he became the first Librarian of the newly founded National Library, which, naturally, gave due attention to bibliographical projects. A 'Short-title List of Welsh Books 1546–1700', later extended to 1710, was compiled and printed in the *Journal of the Welsh Bibliographical Society* (1916–23, 1932–6). A copy of the *Cambrian Bibliography* was interleaved and annotated with corrections and additions; it proved useful as a checklist during the nineteen forties, when early Welsh books were stored in a tunnel for fear of enemy bombing.

In 1987, the National Library published *Libri Walliae: A Catalogue of Welsh Books and Books Printed in Wales 1546–1820: catalog o lyfrau Cymraeg a llyfrau a argraffwyd yng Nghymru 1546–1820*, compiled by a member of staff specifically appointed for the task, Eiluned Rees. Although the catalogue was based on the Library's extensive holdings, every effort was made to trace relevant items in other public repositories and in private collections. Catalogues, advertisements, private correspondence, etc., were scrutinized in order to trace references to works of which no copies survive. *Libri Walliae* is arranged alphabetically by author. There are five indexes: title, general, chronological, the book trade (Wales), the book trade (outside Wales).

Libri Walliae contains over 5,500 entires. Few people would stake their reputation on estimating the number of entries which will be included in the sequel. Even with the advantages of automation, the task of cataloguing the output of the nineteenth century is a formidable one. It is, however, already being tackled in the National Library. The period covered is 1821 to 1908.

Material from 1909 onwards has been listed in the Library's annual current bibliography, *Bibliothece Celtica. A Register of Publications Relating to Wales and the Celtic Peoples and Languages*, the first issue of which appeared in 1910. *Bibliotheca Celtica* ceased after the volume for 1984 appeared and its place is taken by *Llyfryddiaeth Cymru: Bibliography of Wales*. This new current publication also assumes part of the function of *The Subject Index to Welsh Periodicals*, which originally started in 1931 under the auspices of the Wales and Monmouthshire Branch of the Library Association and which was taken over by the National Library in 1968. The first issue of *Llyfryddiaeth Cymru*, for 1985–6, is due to appear in 1991. It is arranged in two sections, a subject sequence following the pattern of *The British Humanities Index* and an author sequence. There will be indexes to periodicals, titles, publishers, and editors. Included will be books and articles in the Welsh language and those relating to Wales.

The Board of Celtic Studies of the University of Wales has been responsible for a number of relevant bibliographies. Its History and Law Committee invited Philip Henry Jones, lecturer in the Department of Information and Library Studies, to edit a third edition of *A Bibliography of the History of Wales*. The previous editions were published in 1931 and 1962, with supplements issued in the *Bulletin of the Board of Celtic Studies*. Although pre-history and Roman Wales have been excluded in the third edition, the growth in Welsh history studies swelled the number of entries to about 22,000. The main database is on computer and publication (by Gwasg Prifysgol Cymru, the University of Wales Press) in 1989 was on microfiche. There are three sets of 48x microfiche: a classified sequence, an author/title index and a KWIC (Key-word in context) index. The classified sequence is thus: generalia, Welsh history to *c.*1536, 1536–1780, 1780 to the present. Full bibliographical entries are provided, with evaluative annotations. The whole or part of the *Bibliography* may appear in more conventional form at a later date.

The Board of Celtic Studies published in conventional form bibliographies of Welsh literature and the Welsh language: *Llyfryddiaeth Llenyddiaeth Cymraeg*, edited by Thomas Parry and Merfyn Morgan (Cardiff, 1976) and *Llyfryddiaeth yr Iaith Gymraeg*, arranged by Marian Beech Hughes and edited by J.E. Caerwyn Williams (Caerdydd, 1988). A supplement to the former was compiled by Gareth O. Watts, an Assistant Keeper in the National Library of Wales, and published in *The Bulletin of the Board of Celtic Studies* in 1982. It will be superseded by a supplement, 1976–86, also compiled by Gareth Watts, which is to be published in 1991 under the joint imprint of Gwasg Prifysgol Cymru and the National Library of Wales.

Certain categories of publications are not included in *Libri Walliae* or its sequel: periodicals, newspapers, ballads, music, and almanacs. Two retrospective catalogues of Welsh periodicals are being prepared by Dr Huw Walters, Assistant Librarian in the National Library of Wales, for publication by the National Library. The first volume, for 1735–1850, is scheduled for publication in 1991, while the second volume, for 1850–1900, is in course of preparation. The periodicals are listed alphabetically by title, with entries containing as much information about the publication as is available. Indexes are provided to printers, publishers, editors, etc.

What is in effect a union list of Welsh newspapers (papers published in Wales and by Welsh communities elsewhere) from 1804 onwards will appear in 1992 as part of the NEWSPLAN project co-ordinated by the British Library.

Welsh poetry from early times was composed in intricate metrical forms. There was, however, another kind of poetry in wide circulation from the beginning of the eighteenth century, the popular ballad. In 1911, the Honourable Society of Cymmrodorion, London, published J.H. Davies's *A Bibliography of Welsh Ballads Printed in the 18th century*. The arrangement, by place of publication and printer, is not very satisfactory, especially as the indexes (to ballad-writers and printers) are inadequate. A more systematic survey of Welsh ballads has been undertaken as a private venture by Mr Tegwyn Jones, an editor of *Geiriadur Prifysgol Cymru*. Mr Jones's bibliography covers the nineteenth century and the early years of the twentieth century, up to the outbreak of the First World War. It is also arranged by place of publication and publisher, but there are indexes to titles, first lines, tunes, authors, names, and the book trade. No firm date of publication has yet been announced.

Another private venture is a University of Wales PhD thesis submitted in 1991 in the Welsh language by Dr Rhidian Griffiths, Senior Assistant Librarian in the National Library of Wales: 'Welsh Music Publishing, with Particular Reference to the Period 1860–1914'. A definitive catalogue of Welsh music is the definition of the impossible. Music was printed locally in the tradition of jobbing printing. With the growth of the choral tradition in Wales, the demand for music for specific occasions was prodigious, and the fact that tonic sol-fa was so popular meant that printing could be done without the expense of engraved plates. Sheet music tended to receive the same cavalier treatment as ephemera. Griffiths concentrated on recording the output of music publishers who did not aspire to issuing catalogues. He also recorded items published as supplements to music journals. As at present there is no bibliography of Welsh music in print, publication of parts of his thesis will receive a ready audience.

The story of Welsh almanacs provides a fascinating insight into social life and publishing intrigue. No one, however, has attempted a bibliography of Welsh almanacs. It would not be quite as daunting a task as compiling a catalogue of Welsh music and would provide much entertainment. Sadly, too few chap-books have survived to justify a bibliography. Although doubtless many have disappeared, the paucity of extant copies indicates that chap-books were never as popular as ballads in Wales.

Wales has produced many antiquaries of note but the greatest of them is undoubtedly Edward Lhuyd, who succeeded Dr Robert Plot as Keeper of the Ashmolean Museum, Oxford. The first and only volume of Lhuyd's *Archaeologia Britannica* was published in Oxford in 1707. On pp. 254–65 may be found

Antiqua Britanniae lingua scriptorum quae non impressa sunt, catalogus; additis quantum licuit authorum temporibus & designatis in quibus hodie extant, bibliothecis. His pioneer attempt to produce a catalogue of Welsh manuscripts inspired his disciple, Moses Williams, to seek support for a more ambitious project, 'A Collection of Writings in the Welsh Tongue, to the Beginning of the Sixteenth Century'. Proposals were issued in 1719, but the number of subscribers proved insufficient to meet the cost of publication. Williams did at least succeed in publishing an index to early Welsh poetry: *Mosis Gulielmii . . . Repertorium poeticum, sive poematum Wallicorum, quotquot hactenus videre contigit, index alphabeticus, primam singulorum lineam, & loca ubi inveniantur, exhibens . . .* (London, W. Roberts, 1726).

Welsh manuscripts continued to be treasured in the gentry libraries, even after the owners had become anglicized. Welsh scholars were allowed access to some of the libraries during the eighteenth century and transcriptions of early texts were published. Not all the owners of collections opened their library portals, however, and it was not until the beginning of the nineteenth century that comprehensive catalogues of manuscripts materialized. Angharad Llwyd and Aneurin Owen were prize-winners in a competition set at the Welshpool Eisteddfod of 1824; they both compiled catalogues of Welsh manuscripts in North Wales, which were published in the *Transactions of the Cymmrodorion Society* in 1828. Useful though these lists undoubtedly were, they pale into insignificance in comparison with the Historical Manuscripts Commission's *Report on Manuscripts in the Welsh Language*, which was published between 1898 and 1910. Its compiler was J. Gwenogvryn Evans, a remarkable man, whose transcripts of texts, if not his interpretations, are still valued by Welsh scholars. The small hand-press on which he printed facsimile editions of old Welsh texts is housed in the National Library of Wales. When he compiled the *Report*, Welsh country-house libraries were still *in situ*; it is a remarkable fact that despite the dispersal of libraries, none of the collections he described has been lost to the nation and those formerly in private hands are now in the National Library of Wales. Tribute must be paid to Sir John Williams, whose foundation gift included the manuscripts which had once belonged to Moses Williams (called the Llanstephan Collection after Sir John's country seat of Plas Llanstephan) and the Hengwrt-Peniarth Welsh manuscripts, which remain the cream of the National Library's collection. Over the years, many fine collections and individual items have further enriched the Department of Manuscripts and Records.

In 1921, the National Library published a *Catalogue of Manuscripts*, vol. I: *Additional Manuscripts in the Collections of Sir John Williams*, compiled, apparently as a labour of love, by the bibliophile, J.H. Davies. The term 'additional' is used to denote manuscripts other than the Llanstephan Manuscripts described in Gwenogvryn Evans's *Report*. No further volumes in this series were published. However, since 1941 (twenty years too late, in the opinion of a former Librarian, Dr E.D. Jones) a *Handlist of Manuscripts in the National Library of Wales* has appeared in parts as supplements to the *National Library of Wales Journal*. The parts have subsequently been gathered into four volumes, issued in 1943, 1951,

1961 and 1982 respectively, an index to the fourth volume appearing in 1986. The four volumes described accessions up to the 1940s. The form of description in the later volumes extends far beyond that of a handlist while falling short of that of a full catalogue. The next volume to be published (no longer as a supplement to the *Journal*) will describe accessions for the period 1981 onwards; its form will be that of a summary catalogue.

The Department of Manuscripts and Records holds substantial collections of public records and family archives, there being no Public Record Office in Wales. Calendars of some of the collections have been published, but for the most part information about the archives is available in the form of typewritten schedules. The schedules, over 700 in number, which list manuscripts and books amongst the archives, are as vital to the needs of researchers as the *Handlist*.

The resources of the Department have been extensively used for the compilation of an index to Welsh poetry before 1830, *Mynegai i Farddoniaeth Gymraeg*, under the auspices of the University of Wales Board of Celtic Studies. The index, at present available in typescript, is being computerized and will provide access by first line, poet, subject, person addressed, place, kind of poem, metre, and references to printed versions.

Ideally, in the light of modern scholarship, Gwenogvryn Evans's catalogue of manuscripts in the Welsh language should be revised, but financial backing for such an ambitious project is not easily obtainable. However, Mr Daniel Huws, Keeper of Manuscripts and Records, is preparing for publication a catalogue of medieval manuscripts in the National Library of Wales.

The National Library is not the only public institution in possession of Welsh manuscripts; Cardiff City Library was the main Welsh repository before the creation of the National Library and there is also a substantial collection in the British Library, deposited by the Honourable Society of Cymmrodorion in 1855 in what was then the British Museum. The Society published a *Catalogue of the Manuscripts Relating to Wales in the British Museum*, compiled by Edward Owen of Gray's Inn, in 1900–22. Of the constituent colleges of the University of Wales, Bangor has the largest collections of Welsh manuscripts and archives. Schedules have been compiled but not printed.

Anglo-Welsh literature, like Anglo-Irish literature, is difficult to define, and yet most people would immediately recognize its distinctive qualities. Nowadays, it is often referred to as 'the English-language literature of Wales'. The archives of many Anglo-Welsh writers have been acquired by the National Library of Wales; they are listed in the *Location Register of Twentieth-Century English Literary Manuscripts and Letters*, published by the British Library in 1988. The register is, by its nature, already out of date and the National Library of Wales will be producing its own supplementary list to the Anglo-Welsh archives.

Meanwhile, printed works are being recorded in 'A Bibliography of the Twentieth-Century English Language Literature of Wales'. The project is being directed by Dr John Harris in the Department of Information and Library Studies at the University College of Wales, Aberystwyth, and the bibliography is being compiled on computer. It will up-date and extend the work published in 1970 by the Wales and Monmouthshire Branch of the Library Association: *A Biblio-graphy of Anglo-Welsh Literature, 1900–1965*, compiled by Brynmor Jones, Assistant Keeper, National Library of Wales. It has been suggested that a useful addition to Anglo-Welsh studies would be an index to Anglo-Welsh poetry on the lines of the afore-mentioned *Mynegai i Farddoniaeth Gymraeg*.

The first Welsh book to be printed in the United States of America appeared in 1721, only three years after the first commercially printed book appeared in Wales. It was not until the nineteenth century, however, that Welsh publishing got into its stride amongst the Welsh exiles. Henry Blackwell, bookbinder and bookseller in New York, himself of Welsh origin, compiled *A Bibliography of Welsh Americana*, two editions of which were posthumously published by the National Library of Wales in 1942 and 1977. The arrangement is by author.

Wales is a comparatively small country. It is remarkable that a distinctive Welsh culture has survived the immigrations of the centuries; Romans, Saxons, Normans, Flemings, Irish, and Scandinavians had settled amongst the Iberians and Celts long before the industrial revolution attracted our English neighbours. The bibliographical activities of three centuries testify to its strength.

The silken purse: bibliography in Ireland

CHARLES BENSON AND MARY POLLARD

Bibliographical studies have made slow and erratic progress in Ireland over the past century. Bibliographical societies have come and gone; so have journals. As we face into the 1990s the prospects look better: impressive research is being carried on – and the results are being published. Ireland has experienced enormous social and political changes during the last hundred years. In 1920 and 1922 new political establishments began to govern separate jurisdictions in the partitioned island. There have been wholesale changes in the ownership of land, and these have resulted in the break up of the vast majority of country-house libraries at a time when the Irish institutional libraries were too poor to take real advantage of the sales. The opportunity to build up the resources which could be the basis for future research was largely lost. In the newly established Irish Free State after 1922 there was little enthusiasm at official level for any aspects of the Anglo-Irish heritage, among which most of the earlier productions of the printing press could certainly be counted.

The most substantial bibliographical achievement of the nineteenth century was the publication of Trinity College's *Catalogus librorum impressorum*, 9 vols. (Dublin, 1864–87). Near the end of that project the Library Association held its annual meeting in Dublin in 1884, and besides being entertained by Henry Dix Hutton on the intricacies of making the catalogue, was also addressed by the great Irish bibliographer Henry Bradshaw. Though Bradshaw's working life belongs to the history of English bibliography, his influence on Ireland, and on E.R. McClintock Dix, in particular, was great. The catalogue of the Irish collection he gave to Cambridge University Library arranged in its natural-history order provided a substantial guide to Irish printers. His speech to the Library Association meeting in Dublin, reported in the *Freeman's Journal* on 3 October 1884 'suggested that in every chief library of the provinces, a collection or museum should be formed in order to show everything that had been printed or published in the locality . . . The collection would perhaps include rubbish, but, for their purpose, rubbish ceased to be such, when put in order. Every newspaper or scrap of information illustrative of their object should be included.' This clearly influenced Dix, for he reprinted it with an appreciative introduction in *Irish Book Lover*.[1]

We would like to thank Dónall Ó Luanaigh of the National Library for many facts and helpful suggestions.
1 *Irish Book Lover*, 1 (1909): 13–16.

Dix, by profession a solicitor in Dublin, was the outstanding figure in Irish bibliography for the first three decades of the century. By 1898 he was already engaged on his life's work, in the strain recommended by Bradshaw, recording the early imprints in Dublin to 1700 and in provincial towns to 1800. He collected widely and wrote extensively. His gifts of Irish printed books to Dublin libraries were lavish, particularly in the case of the National Library of Ireland to which he gave about 10,000 volumes, now arranged in chronological order under each town. Though the bulk of his output lay in the field of enumerative bibliography, he was well aware of the complexity of book-trade history. His articles on such matters as copyright, piracy, and legal restraints on printing are still worth reading. He was a co-founder and first chairman of the Irish Bibliographical Society in 1918. His address echoed Bradshaw: 'We also hope, if the Society increases in membership, to bring its work before the Librarians of Ireland *generally*, enlisting them as members and also their staffs, and, particularly, securing their co-operation in making their Libraries centres for the collection of all books, pamphlets, etc., relating to their locality, or printed locally, or written by persons born in, or connected with the locality.' He went on to outline the tasks of the society listing the study of the material parts of the book, author and subject bibliography, 'another great task which must be faced sometime is to catalogue all the 18th century Dublin printing', the bibliography of music, childrens' books, school-books. His vision even extended to hoping for a listing of Irish manuscripts, a dream partially realized in *Sources for the History of Irish Civilisation* (Boston, 1965).

The Bibliographical Society of Ireland continued to meet until 1954 and published papers as late as 1958. In fact it retains a shadowy existence to the present day, having at least three members and a small bank balance. The papers it published, though invariably slight, are of considerable interest and use. They were in the main the productions of the old guard who had first been associated with Dix in the 1920s. By the mid 1950s most of these had followed Dix, who died in 1936, to the grave. The most prolific of them was T.P.C. Kirkpatrick, a doctor by trade, who collected and published a useful amount on medical bibliography. The least familiar was Francis O'Kelley, d. 1950, who suffered in an extreme measure from the chronic disease of Irish bibliographers, a reluctance to publish. His papers, full of accurate notes from a wide variety of sources, were bequeathed to the Bibliographical Society and deposited in the library of the Royal Irish Academy; they have provided a valuable quarry for scholars since then. After his death, his notes on book sale catalogues were issued in the Bibliographical Society of Ireland's *Papers*, volume VI, the sole published result of a lifetime's bibliographical research. The demise of the Society as an independent publisher was followed by its association in 1959 with a new periodical *The Irish Book* edited by Liam Miller of the Dolmen Press. The association was short lived: *The Irish Book* lasted only until 1964.

Another periodical, *The Irish Book Lover*, died in 1957. It had been chattily bibliographical since 1909. The valedictory note by its owner and editor Colm Ó Lochlainn summed up the loneliness of Irish scholars:

I have only succeeded in printing sixteen volumes in 30 years. There were many difficulties. Lack of material: lack of money, as the Book Lover never paid, and never took advertisements. Many a time I had to fill a number almost unaided; but I do not regret having carried it on; it gave me a certain joy in the making. After all, 1909 to 1957 is a good spell for any Irish journal.

The third periodical to die was the annual *Bulletin of the Friends of the Library of Trinity College*. Although, understandably, largely of domestic concern there were articles of wider interest. Ironically this journal disappeared just as Trinity College Dublin was gathering funds for a new library building.

Younger scholars were doing work of a more exacting standard in the 1950s. Brian Inglis completed a doctoral thesis at Trinity College Dublin in 1950 which appeared in book form as *The Freedom of the Press in Ireland 1785–1841* (1954). His work has not been superseded. An American student in Trinity, James Phillips, produced in 1952 a PhD thesis 'A Bibliographical Inquiry into Printing and Bookselling in Ireland from 1670 to 1800'. It has been a considerable loss to the wider bibliographical community that this fine work was never published. It has remained the standard reference source on many aspects of its subject. John Alden examined Irish seventeenth-century imprints and listed over 200 additions and corrections to Wing in his *Bibliographica Hibernica* (Charlottesville, 1955). Another American, Robert Munter, turned his attention to the press producing *A Handlist of Irish Newspapers 1685–1750* (1960), and his narrative *The History of the Irish Newspaper 1685–1760* (Cambridge, 1967). His handlist has proved to be sadly inaccurate though it formed the basis for a useful microfilm edition of the papers.

The National Library of Ireland, inspired by its director, Richard J. Hayes, embarked on a major project, no less than an 'Irish national bibliography'. As originally planned by Hayes, this was breathtaking in scope and was to include manuscripts, and printed books, prints and drawings, maps and music, in order to provide for all material relating to Ireland one index bringing together sources usually physically separated on library shelves.[2] In the event the plan for printed matter has never been fully developed, but the publication in 1965 of *Manuscript Sources for the History of Irish Civilisation*, edited by Richard J. Hayes, 11 vols. (Boston, 1965), was itself an immense achievement. Owing to the nature of the history of Ireland and its people, the chief problem was the wide dispersal of the manuscripts outside Ireland. For the early period to 1200, Dr Ludwig Bieler searched the medieval collections of Europe and identified some 4,000 Irish manuscripts; of these 'less than 100 are to be found in Ireland' (R. Hayes, Introduction to *Manuscript Sources*). For the later period (1200 to 1900), though major sources are located in Great Britain in the State Papers, continental archives were also examined, the most important being in France, the Vatican Library, and the Sacra Congregazione di Propaganda Fide. Of the utmost use to Irish readers was a programme of selective microfilming that accompanied the

2 R.J. Hayes, 'Irish National Bibliography, *An Leabharlann*, 18 (1960): 5–13.

search. This was funded by the government and the films are held in the National Library.

The arrangement of this catalogue was ambitious and, at the time, innovative. The entry for each manuscript can appear under any or all of the following sections: persons (vols. I–IV), subjects (vols. V–VI), places (vols. VII–VIII), date (vols. IX–X). Manuscripts in the Irish language received special treatment and, as well as full entry in the main sections, are listed separately in volume XI. This list complements the work of R.I. Best, *Bibliography of Irish Philology and Manuscript Literature* (Dublin, 1942) and R.J. Hayes, *Clár litridheacht na Nua-Ghaedhilge* (3 vols. Dublin, 1938–40).

A supplement to *Manuscript Sources* appeared in 1979 in three volumes. In the meantime, the staff of the National Library and others had been kept busy with the index to articles in selected learned and literary periodicals, all published in Ireland. This was published in nine volumes in 1970 as *Sources for the History of Irish Civilisation: Articles in Irish Periodicals* and followed the pattern of arrangement already established.

In that most optimistic of decades, the 1960s, the focus of bibliographical developments moved away from individual endeavour. Institutional libraries were able to employ more than the barest minimum of staff needed for maintenance. Most of the improvements in the last thirty years have been in the universities. Specialist departments to care for early printed books were established in Queen's University Belfast in 1967, in Trinity College Dublin in 1968, in St Patrick's College Maynooth in 1985, in University College Cork in 1986. The librarians in these departments formed the nucleus for the formation of a Rare Books Group in 1984. This has now developed to fill the rôle of a bibliographical society. Conservation laboratories were established in Trinity College Dublin in 1972 and in Marsh's Library in 1988: that in the National Library of Ireland was built and equipped in 1988, but, in July 1991, was still without staff. Outside the universities, some important collections and library buildings have been restored and refurbished by generous donations from industry and various foundations, in particular the Linenhall Library in Belfast, the Diocesan (now the GPA–Bolton) Library in Cashel, and Marsh's Library in Dublin.

While the library in University College Dublin had been running a library school since the 1930s this did not become a fully fledged department until 1977. The new professor, John Dean, was soon able to appoint a full-time lecturer in historical bibliography, though this subject was regrettably not a compulsory part of the syllabus. The story in the other Irish library school in Queen's University is less happy. The school from its institution in 1964 had Gordon Wheeler as part-time lecturer in historical and analytical bibliography, a position he only vacated in 1988 upon the transmogrification of what had become the School of Library and Information Studies into a Department of Finance and Information Studies. Where once historical bibliography could be studied they now offer television studies (1 Samuel 4:21).

Long Room, a new periodical devoted to bibliography, appeared in 1970.

Published by the Friends of the Library, it is an enlarged and improved successor to the *Annual Bulletin* published from 1946 to 1958. Initially published bi-annually, since 1975 it has been an annual. Its scope goes far wider than matters relating to Trinity College Dublin Library. A rival journal, *Irish Booklore*, was published in Belfast from 1971 to 1980 and this title in an attenuated form continues as a section of *Linenhall Review* from volume 3 (1986) on. Experience suggests that the market for Irish bibliographical journals is so limited that they cannot survive without institutional underpinning. The current national bibliography was started by the School of Librarianship in University College Dublin Library in 1968, covering publications of 1967, and was continued there by the Library from 1977 to 1988 when responsibility was taken over by the National Library.

A considerable body of work has been done by scholars abroad, particularly in the field of author bibliography such as the Teerink–Scouten *Bibliography of Swift* (Philadelphia, 1963), W.B. Todd's *A Bibliography of Edmund Burke*, 2nd edn (Godalming, 1982), and G. Keynes's *Bibliography of George Berkeley* (Oxford, 1976). In the case of more modern authors (whose publishing history lies largely outside Ireland anyway) there are, for instance, Slocum and Cahoon's *A Bibliography of James Joyce* (1953), Allan Wade's *W.B. Yeats*, and Dan Laurence's *Bernard Shaw: A Bibliography* (Oxford, 1983).

On more historical topics R.C. Cole extended articles written for the *Papers of the Bibliographical Society of America* into a study of *Irish Booksellers and English Writers 1740–1800* (1986). His thesis was 'that Irish booksellers through cheap reprints disseminated the works of the major British writers of their time and augmented the audience for these writers not only in Ireland but in Britain and the United States of America'. After a bibliographical silence of twenty years, Robert Munter returned to the Irish scene with *A Dictionary of the Print Trade in Ireland 1550–1775* (New York, 1988). This beautifully produced book, while adding considerably to the information in the Bibliographical Society's dictionaries of printers and booksellers, is flawed in that it does not carry the list to the logical stopping point of 1800 and takes no account of scholarship published since the early 1970s. A great boost to studies in the nineteenth century was given by *The Waterloo Directory of Irish Newspapers and Periodicals 1800–1900* (Waterloo, Ont., 1986). This has huge merits as a trail-blazing work, notwithstanding the inaccuracies inevitable in covering such a wide field.

Periodicals were particularly important for Irish writers after the press became subject to British copyright law in 1801 but the eighteenth century, when the fledgling printing and bookselling business grew to full and independent maturity, remains the book trade's most interesting period. It was encouraging therefore that it should have been considered a suitable subject for the Lyell lectures given by M. Pollard in 1986/7. These were recently published as *Dublin's Trade in Books 1550–1800* (Oxford, 1989, i.e. 1990) and as a first full length study this forms a base for further exploration.

Maurice Craig's important work on bookbindings, *Irish Bookbindings 1600–*

1800 (1954), has been continued in a limited area by J. McDonnell and P. Healy in their *Gold-Tooled Bookbindings Commissioned by Trinity College Dublin in the Eighteenth Century* (Leixlip, Irish Georgian Society, 1987), and further detailed studies are promised. A very difficult field was tackled with some success by J.R.R. Adams, *The Printed Word and the Common Man: Popular Culture in Ulster 1700–1900* (Belfast, 1987), a revamping of an MA thesis for Queen's University. Other recent theses being recast for publication include D. McGuinne's definitive study of Irish typefaces, 'Printing Types in the Irish Character' (PhD, University of Dublin, 1989)[3] and V. Kinane's 'The Dublin University Press in the 18th Century' (Library Association of Ireland, Fellowship, 1982) which forms the basis for a book on that press scheduled for publication in 1992. Two other Library Association of Ireland theses continue R. Munter's *Handlist 1685–1750* for Dublin-printed periodicals, and a third amplifies the *Waterloo Directory* (C. Bennett, 'A Short-title Catalogue of Dublin-printed Periodicals 1751–1775' (1976); B. McLoughlin, a continuation from 1775 to 1800 (1985); and K. O'Neill, a continuation from 1801 to 1825 (1985)).

Two recently discovered printers' ledgers, of Daniel Graisberry 1777–85, and Graisberry and Campbell 1797–1805, are now being edited for publication by V. Kinane and C. Benson. The latter is also engaged in listing the members of the Dublin book trade from 1801 to 1850, and Pollard is working on more detailed accounts of the seventeenth- and eighteenth-century members than yet exist. A large concern of many librarians is to ensure a comprehensive Irish representation in the *ESTC*. Surveys suggest that there may be 130,000 eighteenth-century books in Ireland, many in libraries that are run on a shoestring. A company, Irish Short Title Records, has been formed to collect entries for the project; 77,000 records have now been sent to the *ESTC* editorial offices. Trinity College Dublin had been one of the core locations for *STC* and Wing, and is again a core library for the nineteenth-century *STC* being produced by Avero.

It will be obvious from the foregoing that what is yet to be done is almost everything, from studies of paper making and individual printers and booksellers to the economics of the book trade in the nineteenth and twentieth centuries. In particular the neglected area of textual studies demands attention; little has been done here within the country, some major texts remaining unexamined as well as reprints of texts and the work of many minor Irish writers. We have a long way to go when we consider that the American editors of Swift's poems have currently collated twenty-seven copies of Faulkner's 1735 edition.

Lots of money would be lovely, but what we need first is a good supply of committed bibliographers.

---

3 Now published as *Irish Type Design: a History of Printing Types in the Irish Character* (Blackrock, Co. Dublin, 1992).

La bibliologie in France

DAVID SHAW

The 1945 *Studies in Retrospect* contained a chapter by Henry Thomas on 'The Society's Contribution to Foreign Bibliography'. Written almost entirely from the perspective of the Society's own work in this field, it gave no account of the traditions of bibliographical work in each of the several European countries treated. In the case of France there is an honourable history of bibliographical work stretching back into the sixteenth century. The beginnings of a French national bibliography are traced back to the works of François de la Croix du Maine (1584) and Antoine Du Verdier (1585).[1] The French seventeenth and eighteenth centuries saw a succession of historical and textual scholars and librarians whose work is still of relevance today. Rigoley de Juvigny produced an augmented edition of La Croix du Maine and Du Verdier.[2] As in England, the nineteenth century saw the laying of foundations on which more recent work is based. The centralization and the dispersals which occurred as a result of the confiscation of royal, aristocratic, and religious libraries at the time of the French Revolution provided both stimulus and discouragement of a sort which did not arise in England with its smaller number of scholarly libraries.

A succession of bookseller–bibliographers from before the Revolution (de Bure, Osmont) had their successors: in particular, Brunet, whose bibliographical dictionary has served many generations of collectors and is still of scholarly use today.[3] Many towns produced catalogues of their new *bibliothèque municipale*, formed from revolutionary confiscations and consisting overwhelmingly of pre-1800 imprints. This work helped to maintain some of the scholarly traditions of the *ancien régime* and a knowledge of the literatures of medieval and Renaissance Europe and the physical forms of the books in which they survived. Working in the same spirit as writers and historians of the Romantic movement,

1 Louise-Noëlle Malclès, *La Bibliographie* (Que sais-je? no. 708, Paris, 1967), p. 32; *la bibliographie* here is purely documentary and does not include descriptive or analytical bibliography of the sort undertaken by members of the Society.

2 François La Croix du Maine and Antoine Du Verdier, *Les Bibliothèques françoises*, 2nd edn. revised by Rigoley de Juvigny, 6 vols. (Paris, 1772–3).

3 Guillaume François de Bure, *Bibliographie instructive: ou traité de la connoissance des livres rares et singuliers* (Paris, 1763–8); J.B.L. Osmont, *Dictionnaire typographique, historique et critique des livres rares* (Paris, 1768); Jacques-Charles Brunet, *Manuel du libraire et de l'amateur de livres*, 5th edn. 5 vols. (Paris, 1860–4); *Supplément*, 2 vols. (1878–80).

nineteenth-century bibliographers not surprisingly concentrated on the great, heroic names of the past. Another bookseller, A.-A. Renouard, produced important bibliographical studies of the presses of the Aldus and Estienne families.[4]

Printer bibliographies were also produced by his great-grandson, Philippe Renouard, one of the great figures of French historical bibliography, himself a printer by profession.[5] Renouard's status is equivalent to that of Duff, Greg, or McKerrow among the heroic figures of English bibliographical studies in the early twentieth century. He produced a dictionary of Parisian printers and publishers to 1600 and an excellent repertory of Parisian printers' devices.[6] But Renouard's greatest achievement, though still incomplete nearly sixty years after his death, was his work on a projected bio-bibliography of sixteenth-century Parisian printing. In his desire to record the work of all the printers of the century, great and small, Renouard anticipated some of his more recent compatriots' interests in social aspects of bibliography. His practice in descriptive and enumerative bibliography paralleled developments in the 'Anglo-Saxon' world in national retrospective bibliography. The manuscript notes of his epic work are preserved in the Réserve at the Bibliothèque Nationale and from them have come two sets of publications: one a chronological listing of the surviving Parisian production under the care of Brigitte Moreau,[7] the other a complete bio-bibliographical study of all the Parisian printers and publishers of the sixteenth century under the initial direction of Jeanne Veyrin-Forrer.[8] These two series have given French sixteenth-century printing studies a different orientation from comparable work on England in the same period. The emphasis has been particularly on studies of printers and publishers, and on chronology and geography, rather than on the establishment of a national corpus focused on authors and titles, as in the Society's equally epic venture, the *Short-Title Catalogue*.

The same is true of the work of Renouard's near-contemporary, Henri Baudrier, known as *le président* Baudrier, whose *Bibliographie lyonnaise*[9] is also

---

4 Antoine-Augustin Renouard, *Annales de l'imprimerie des Estienne*, 2nd edn (Paris, 1843); *Annales de l'imprimerie des Alde*, 3rd edn (Paris, 1834).

5 Philippe Renouard, *Bibliographie des éditions de Simon de Colines, 1520–1546* (Paris, 1894); *Bibliographie des impressions et des oeuvres de Josse Badius, imprimeur et humaniste, 1462–1535, avec une notice biographique*, 3 vols. (Paris, 1909).

6 Philippe Renouard, *Les Marques typographiques parisiennes des XVe et XVIe siècles* (Paris, 1926); Philippe Renouard, *Répertoire des imprimeurs parisiens, libraires, fondeurs de caractères et correcteurs d'imprimerie depuis l'introduction de l'imprimerie à Paris (1470) jusqu'à la fin du XVIe siècle*, reprinted with supplements by Jeanne Veyrin-Forrer and Brigitte Moreau (Paris, 1965).

7 *Inventaire chronologique des éditions parisiennes du XVIe siècle*, par Brigitte Moreau d'après les manuscrits de Philippe Renouard (Paris, 1972 (1501–10), 1977 (1511–20), 1985 (1521–30), in progress).

8 *Imprimeurs et libraires parisiens du XVIe siècle* (Paris, 1964– ; vols. I–III: Abada-Blumenstock; and separate vols. for: Breyer, Brumen, Cavellat).

9 Henri Baudrier, *Bibliographie lyonnaise. Recherches sur les imprimeurs, libraires, relieurs et fondeurs de lettres de Lyon au XVIe siècle*, publiées et continuées par J. Baudrier. 12 vols. (Lyon, 1895–1925); Georges Tricou, *Tables*, Geneva, 1950.

organized by presses or publishing houses. Intellectually, this places work on the French sixteenth century firmly in the tradition of Robert Proctor and the modern incunabulists who developed his ideas of classification, though it is not clear to what extent Proctor influenced this work in France.

There is no French equivalent to the Society's *STC*, which is a great drawback for those working in the field of sixteenth-century literature or history, but the sheer quantity of sixteenth-century French printing makes a national catalogue a daunting task (though not unachievable with the resources of modern computer technology). The British Library's two catalogues of French books to 1700 have been a very useful stand-by.[10] There exists a large-scale bibliographical series for books published in French printing towns other than Paris and Lyon.[11] This too organizes its material for each town by printer or publisher and has been extended to the seventeenth and eighteenth centuries for some printing centres. This is a large-scale collaborative project and, inevitably, there is a considerable variety in the completeness and methodological soundness of the work done. Some of the recording of copies can be very summary and uncritical, but an attempt is generally made to refer to relevant bibliographical reference sources and to list locations of copies (a feature frequently neglected in less-inspired French work). Of particular interest to English scholars is the section on Normandy in the very capable hands of Pierre Aquilon. There seems to be no plan at present to produce a bibliography for seventeenth- or eighteenth-century Paris, the major printing centre in France and a major European intellectual centre. Nothing comparable to *ESTC* in scope or methodology has been attempted for France.

On the other hand, there has been a respectable tradition of incunable studies in France. Claudin's work is still important, as is the mammoth catalogue of incunables in French libraries undertaken by Mlle Pellechet and completed by Louis Polain.[12] More recently, the Bibliothèque Nationale, Paris, has embarked on the production of a very serviceable catalogue of its own incunables under the direction of Dominique Coq and Ursula Bauermeister.[13] The Société des Bibliophiles de Guyenne, our sister society in France, has been responsible for the publication of a series of regional catalogues listing the incunables held by municipal and other libraries.[14] The individual volumes are of variable quality

10 *Short-Title Catalogue of Books printed in France . . . from 1470 to 1600* (British Museum, 1924); Supplement (British Library, 1989); V.F. Goldsmith, *Short-Title Catalogue of French Books 1601–1700 in the Library of the British Museum* (1969–73). One could also mention more specialized reference books such as R. Arbour, *L'Ere baroque en France, répertoire chronologique, 1585–1643* (Geneva, 1977–85).

11 *Répertoire bibliographique des livres imprimés en France au XVIe siècle*, Bibliotheca bibliographica Aureliana (Baden-Baden, 1968–).

12 A. Claudin, *Histoire de l'imprimerie en France*, 4 vols. (fifteenth-century Paris and Lyons) (Paris, 1900–5); M. Pellechet and L. Polain, *Catalogue général des incunables des bibliothèques publiques de France* (Paris, 1897; reprinted Liechtenstein, 1970).

13 Bibliothèque Nationale, *Catalogue des incunables* (Paris, 1981–).

14 *Catalogues régionaux des incunables des bibliothèques publiques de France*, vols. I–VII (Bordeaux, 1979–90).

and have not all been the work of specialist incunabulists but they are collectively useful in making available a record of surviving production of the fifteenth century which may well stimulate further work in France on this still buoyant area of research. The British Library's catalogue of incunables (vol. VIII for France) is indispensable in this field.[15]

It would be true to say, however, that there has been no scholar in France who could be compared with Proctor in achievement in the field of the methodology of description and classification of incunabula, nor even any really strong commitment to follow up Proctor's methods (though this is not the case in the sixteenth century, where as we have seen, both Renouard and Baudrier had a method which was essentially that of an enumeration, press by press, of individual printing towns, but without the same typographical focus).

In part, differences in bibliographical emphasis between France and *le monde anglosaxon* can be attributed to the continuing fashion for *bibliophilie* as opposed to antiquarianism in France. It is said that where a French collector would immediately send off a decrepit sixteenth-century binding to be replaced by a smart new confection, an English collector would be delighted at the survival of an example, even if tatty, of the binder's historic skills. There are, of course, excellent collections of historic bindings in France, with the Réserve of the Bibliothèque Nationale prominent among the centres which have taken up their study. Modern English scholars have been particularly important in this field of the history of bindings, and the Society itself has provided a home for many of them.

Is there a specifically French contribution to bibliographical studies? A distinctive strand of scholarship in the past thirty years has been the 'history of the book', better known by its French name of *histoire du livre*. This has been the bibliographical branch of the *Annales* school of history, which rejected the *histoire événementielle* of kings, wars, prime ministers, and revolutions and emphasized the study of economic, social, and socio-psychological phenomena instead. One of the founders of this school was the great French historian Lucien Febvre and, for the history of the book, the founding text is *L'Apparition du livre* written by Henri-Jean Martin under Febvre's direction.[16] This was the first in an impressive series of monographs by Henri-Jean Martin, during a very distinguished career in library administration and university teaching. As an introduction to bibliography, this book gives quite a different emphasis from either McKerrow or Gaskell and is not at all the same sort of history as, for example, Colin Clair's two works on English and European printing.[17]

The difference in methodology between English bibliography and French *bibliologie*, as it is sometimes called, is that the English method has emphasized

15 *Catalogue of Books printed in the XVth Century Now in the British Museum*, part VIII: France, French-speaking Switzerland (British Museum, 1949).

16 Lucien Febvre et Henri-Jean Martin, *L'Apparition du livre* (Paris, 1958); English translation: *The Coming of the Book: The Impact of Printing, 1450–1800* (1976).

17 Colin Clair, *A History of European Printing* (1976); *A History of Printing in Britain* (1965).

the internal or archaeological examination of the book as evidence for the book and the book trade, whereas the French have concentrated on work with archival material to provide a social and economic background to the history of the book. This is not to say that there are no traces of the other's methodologies in each country's work. The Bibliographical Society's biographical dictionaries were based in part on archival work, especially for the earliest periods, and French descriptive bibliographers working on the Renouard project at the Bibliothèque Nationale have clearly learned much from the Greg–Bowers methods of analysis and description. Nevertheless, the emphases have been different. A sample of articles in the *Revue française d'histoire du livre* presenting statistical findings on readership, or on book distribution in the provinces, or on censorship and clandestine literatures, has a particular flavour. There is nothing in the French tradition which can be compared with technical articles in *The Library* on compositorial analyses, running-title evidence, typographical analysis, or the like. Nor do the French journals carry articles with the textual-critical stance of the English and American bibliographical journals. In essence, French historians of the book usually are historians, whereas English bibliographers are very often trained as literary specialists, even when their work is historical. The English concentration on the book as artefact or as text, as opposed to the book as a fragment of a social context, might account in part for the amount of energy which has been channelled into creating reference works like *STC*, Wing and *ESTC*, whose prime intention is to make copies locatable for further scholarly investigation.

Archival work in England has certainly gone on: the history of the Stationers' Company, for example, and work on the Ackers and Cambridge University Press ledgers. More recently the growth in interest in book-trade history in the eighteenth and nineteenth centuries has pushed English work in a French direction, arguably as a direct result of the influence of *l'histoire du livre*. However, there is still no English equivalent to Annie Charron-Parent's study of the structure of the Parisian book trade in the mid sixteenth century,[18] the result again of differences in theoretical and methodological approaches. Where English-speaking historians themselves have tackled this new bibliographical territory, the results have been mixed. Elizabeth Eisenstein criticized her fellow historians for their neglect of printing in the history of early modern Europe, but her own work, in spite of exciting and important insights into the cultural and intellectual interactions involving the book trade, has not been without critics of its imperfect grasp of bibliographical concepts.[19] Another well-known historian writing on French bibliographical topics is the American, Robert Darnton, who has made frequent contributions on the eighteenth century, including articles in the *Revue française d'histoire du livre*.

One of the main achievements of French bibliographical scholarship (with

18 Annie Parent, *Les Métiers du livre à Paris au XVIe siècle (1535–1560)* (Geneva, 1974).
19 Elizabeth L. Eisenstein, *The Printing Press as an Agent of Change: Communications and Cultural Transformations in Early Modern Europe*, 2 vols. (Cambridge, 1979).

international collaboration) in the 1980s has been the publication of the four-volume *Histoire de l'édition française*.[20] This presents a history of the book trade in France from the Middle Ages to the mid twentieth century and uses modern printing technology and design techniques to great effect. The methodological standpoint of this history is an interesting amalgam of the economic historical and quantitative approach of the French *histoire du livre* and the technical investigations of the archaeology of the book more typical of the Bibliographical Society up to the point when the influence of the new French methodology became felt.

The emphasis on the social dimension of producers and consumers of books has led to a considerable body of work on the history of printing, bookselling, and reading in the French provinces. Given the greater size of the book trade in France in the early modern period, it is not surprising that there were many more centres of production than in England. These have been catalogued in the *Répertoire bibliographique* discussed above. A number of studies has been devoted to readership, an interesting topic which seems to be less thoroughly covered in British work. The topic of course grows out of a traditional interest in rates of literacy on the part of social historians, but for bibliographers it is an important area situated at the opposite end of the spectrum of production and consumption from that traditionally investigated by printing historians.[21] Other work on the French provinces has included the study of individual businesses, usually by means of analyses of their archives, rather than by enumeration of their surviving production. English bibliographical work is of course increasingly adopting this methodology, especially for the eighteenth and nineteenth centuries where it is especially associated with *Publishing History*.

It is not surprising that the modern French *bibliologie* with its methodologies drawn from economic and social history has not developed the field of textual bibliography to the same extent as have English and American scholars from a background in English literature. There have been eminent French textual scholars in the palaeographical field but work on the textual study of printed books has either been inadequate or has been derivative of English methods. Any self-respecting editor of a French literary text with a complex textual history has of course realized the need to choose a base text to reproduce, and the need to present an *apparatus criticus* of variant readings. What has been lacking has been a desire to elaborate a theory of textual transmission to support this process of textual editing. There has been no McKerrow or Greg or Bowers in French textual studies. The theoretical interests of French literary scholars have notoriously tended to structuralist criticism and its various offshoots, many of which have stressed the reader's rôle in re-creating the identity of a text as he reads it. There has been a bias against the notion of texts having an author who possesses some sort of textual right of ownership and there has been a

20 *Histoire de l'édition française*, sous la direction de Henri-Jean Martin et Roger Chartier, 4 vols. (Paris, 1982–6).
21 Roger Chartier, *Lectures et lecteurs dans la France d'Ancien Régime* (Paris, 1987).

consequent lack of interest in the concept of a 'correct' text restored through the study of the historical process of transmission.

Among the Anglo-American ideas which have not found a ready audience in France has been the question of variation within an edition, particularly the need to account for cancels and press-variants. The practice of French textual critics has been caricatured as taking the earliest Bibliothèque Nationale copy of a book as the authoritative text and simply failing to understand the need to explore the latent complexity of potential copy-texts. Equally, there has been a strong bias in favour of reproducing the earliest state of an author's work as the base text and showing all later variants in chronological order in the *apparatus*. Or alternatively, the last state corrected by the author (or simply the last published in his lifetime) is reproduced with the earlier variants. Needless to say this is not always a successful strategy, but a theory of copy text is needed before any other is possible. The ideas of substantive and accidental variants and the concept of a composite text formed from manipulation of these has not taken root in France. The attempt to identify authorial spelling systems through the analysis of compositorial practices has not been widely pursued.[22] Critical editions have tended to be diplomatic. Up to about 1600, old-spelling texts are the rule; after 1600, there is a tendency to prefer modernized or normalized spellings even for critical editions, though English practice does seem to have had some influence here in the post-war period.

In the case of an author with an extremely complex textual history such as the great Renaissance poet Pierre de Ronsard, who was a notorious amender and rewriter of his poems, a sonnet first published in 1552 and tinkered with many times until the end of Ronsard's life will, in its final form, be a totally different poem from the original. This problem has been solved, not on theoretical grounds, but by the practical expedient of having three collected works, one based on the earliest versions of all texts, another on the last edition in Ronsard's lifetime (1584), and the third on the first posthumous edition incorporating Ronsard's last thoughts as collected by his literary executors (1586).[23] The pragmatism of this solution is ironic in the field of literary studies, where the French are typically considered the theoreticians and many English scholars have preferred more commonsensical approaches.

An unusual source of textual work on French problems has been associated with the *Australian Journal of French Studies* and the postgraduate teaching of Professor Wallace Kirsop. Kirsop's *Bibliographie matérielle et critique textuelle*[24] attacked the prevailing French textual methodologies and attempted to introduce the principles associated with Greg and Bowers. A subsequent French

---

22 Work has been done on the development of spelling systems in the Renaissance period, e.g. N. Catach, *L'Orthographe* (Paris, 1973), but I am not aware that this has been of much use in the area of textual editing.

23 Pierre de Ronsard, *Oeuvres complètes*, ed. P. Laumonier, 20 vols. (Paris, 1937–75); *Oeuvres complètes*, ed. G. Cohen (Paris (1950), text of 1584); *Oeuvres, texte de 1587*, ed. I. Silver (Washington, 1966–70).

24 Wallace Kirsop, *Bibliographie matérielle et critique textuelle: vers une collaboration* (Paris, 1970).

Introduction à la textologie by Roger Laufer[25] had a dedication to McKerrow and tried to combine Anglo-American textual methods with some structuralist insights and use of mathematical techniques for analysis of variants, in part influenced by Greg's little-known *Calculus of Variants*.[26] One has to say that these and other ventures have not had the influence which one would have hoped.

Some textual work by British scholars can be cited. For the sixteenth century, there have been editions of Rabelais, of Du Bellay, and of Scève, which have been influenced to a greater or lesser extent by Greg–Bowers methodology.[27] Although it does not come specifically under the umbrella of the Bibliographical Society, mention should also be made here of the work of an annual one-day seminar on textual bibliography, founded by Conor Fahy (formerly Professor of Italian at Birkbeck College, London) and now organized by John Flood from the Institute of Germanic Studies at the University of London. A number of the regular members of the seminar are from French departments in British Universities or are French specialists from academic and national libraries.

Henry Thomas's chapter in the *Studies in Retrospect* was compiled from the list of lectures given to the Society and from the articles published in *The Transactions* and in *The Library* and so gave a rather partial picture of the work which had been done by foreign scholars working on continental bibliography. In the section on France (pp. 169–70), no contributions by foreign scholars are recorded at all. During the past fifty years, the Society has enjoyed the cooperation of several French scholars. The Bibliothèque Nationale in Paris has been particularly prominent in this respect: Mme Jeanne Veyrin-Forrer, for many years the distinguished *conservateur en chef* of the rare-books reading room, has spoken to the Society twice and has published in *The Library*.[28] Among her colleagues, one could mention Mme Basanoff who for many years meticulously undertook the compilation of Recent Books and Periodicals for France. A prominent Belgian member is Jean-François Gilmont who has published in *The Library* and who is very active in stimulating publishing activities in Belgium in which his knowledge of and enthusiasm for the methodologies of the Bibliographical Society have won him many admirers.[29]

Among British members of the Society who have worked on French topics in the past quarter-century, pride of place should perhaps be given to Richard

25 Roger Laufer, *Introduction à la textologie: vérification, établissement, édition des textes* (Paris, 1972).

26 Sir W.W. Greg, *The Calculus of Variants, An Essay on Textual Criticism* (Oxford, 1927).

27 François Rabelais, *Gargantua*, ed. M.A. Screech and R. Calder (Geneva, 1970); Joachim Du Bellay, *Les Regrets, Les Antiquités de Rome*, ed. M.A. Screech and J. Jolliffe (Geneva, 1966); Maurice Scève, *Délie*, ed. I.D. Macfarlane (Cambridge, 1966); work has also been done on the text of *Délie* by D.B. Wilson, introduction to the facsimile of *Délie* (Menston, Yorks, 1972).

28 Jeanne Veyrin-Forrer, 'Aperçu sur la fonderie typographique parisienne au XVIIIe siècle', *Lib*, v, 24 (1969); 199–218; (with Annie Parent), 'Claude Garamont: New Documents', *Lib*, v, 29 (1974): 80–92. Both of these articles are reprinted in the recent volume of her collected articles which marked her retirement as *conservateur en chef* of the Réserve des Imprimés at the Bibliothèque nationale: *La Lettre et le texte: trente années de recherches sur l'histoire du livre* (Paris, 1987). She has more recently still (1990) spoken to the Society on new printing technology used to produce banknotes during the French Revolution.   29 J.-F. Gilmont, 'Printers by the rules', *Lib*, VI, 2 (1980): 129–55.

Sayce who was editor of *The Library* for a number of years and who worked particularly on Montaigne and on techniques of compositorial practice.[30] Other teachers of French literature who have been members of the Society and, although not primarily bibliographers, have made contributions to the subject include Dudley Wilson and Ian MacFarlane in the sixteenth century and Vivienne Mylne in the eighteenth; among professional librarians, one can include Giles Barber, Stephen Rawles, and the late John Jolliffe and Robert Shackleton.

No one would want to claim that French studies have had a particularly central rôle to play in the Society since *Studies in Retrospect*, but where there has been scope for cross-fertilization between two different national traditions of bibliographical work, it is to the Society's credit that it has been able to provide an occasional forum for both foreign scholars and for British workers in the French field.

30 R.A. Sayce and D. Maskell, *A Descriptive Bibliography of Montaigne's Essais, 1580–1700* (Bibliographical Society and Modern Humanities Research Association, 1983); 'Compositorial Practices and the Localisation of Printed Books, 1530–1800', *Lib*, v, 21, (1966): 1–45, reprinted Oxford Bibliographical Society, Occasional Publications no. 13 (1979). Richard Sayce was Editor of *The Library* from 1965 to 1970.

Bibliography and oriental literature

B.C. BLOOMFIELD

If this chapter has a predecessor in *Studies in Retrospect* it must be the contribution by Henry Thomas entitled 'The Bibliographical Society's Contribution to Foreign Bibliography' but that did not range beyond Europe and virtually ignored the Society's rather small contribution to the bibliography of the Orient. Since, as Edward Saîd has forcefully reminded us, the whole concept of orientalism is ill-defined and perhaps demeaning, it should be made clear that this chapter deals with bibliography in relation to the peoples and literature of Asia even though the boundaries of the continent may be rather fluidly defined. Yet all the world's great religions, the majority of its population, and many of its most influential cultural traditions spring from Asia and they retain their importance for the future. However, it is first prudent to note certain major factors that have dominated Asia since 1945 when the Society celebrated its jubilee. The end of the Second World War enabled those countries affected, and most were, to begin to recover and rebuild, but it also presaged the collapse of the former European colonial and imperial governments and the independence of many new states. Almost as a consequence of this new division of political power, over the last fifty years Asia has been the scene of major conflicts in the sub-continent – in Korea and Vietnam – and there have been civil wars in Afghanistan, Malaysia, China, the Philippines, and other countries. None of this is conducive to the development of scholarship and bibliography, or to the survival of libraries, manuscripts, and rare printed material. In addition, compared with scholarship and bibliography as applied to Western texts, oriental bibliography was and remains underdeveloped; the first International Congress of Orientalists met in Paris in 1873 and it was not until the Congress in Ann Arbor, Michigan, in 1968 that a separate section was devoted to bibliography. But within the countries of Asia, higher education expanded rapidly after 1945 and more scholars were trained and in post to undertake bibliographical studies of their own literature and cultures, and libraries were founded and expanded to serve them. However, many of the most important manuscript and printed book collections remain preserved in the former colonial and imperial countries. This has led to claims for the restitution of cultural

I am grateful to my colleagues in the British Library (especially Mr G.W. Shaw), the School of Oriental and African Studies library, and other institutions, for help in writing this chapter.

property and to accusations of 'cultural imperialism'; it has necessitated scholars from Asia continuing to visit European institutions for research and bibliographical work. It also meant that European scholars with these unparalleled resources at their disposal have undertaken much of the significant and new bibliographical work, applying techniques and methods developed for dealing with Western literatures. One other factor needs to be mentioned in this initial examination, and that is the increasing specialization and professionalization of academic work in oriental studies. This had often been left to amateur or part-time scholars, but as more scholars came into the field, they grouped together in societies, and they inevitably published more and stimulated research and enquiry in previously neglected topics. So much for the preliminaries; in the small space allotted I propose to treat bibliography under the two main heads of 'enumerative' and 'descriptive' and to attempt to deal with some of the major initiatives over the past fifty years, giving selected examples.

More scholars, more publications, and more students led inexorably to more enumerative bibliographies and guides to the literature. The most recent and useful guide being J.D. Pearson, *A World Bibliography of Oriental Bibliographies* (Oxford, 1975) founded on Besterman's original work but enhanced by some 4,471 additional titles. More discursive, and including vernacular titles, is G. Raymond Nunn, *Asia Reference Works: A Select Annotated Guide* (1980). An even more select, short, helpful booklet is the *Library Guide* issued by the School of Oriental and African Studies of the University of London (1969; 4th rev. edn, 1980). J.D. Pearson's *Oriental and Asian Bibliography* (1966) gives a general descriptive view of the field and is supplemented by his article 'Orientalist Libraries Today' (*International Library Review*, 2 (1970); 3–18) while *Area Studies and the Library*, ed. T.-S. Tsien and Howard Winger (Chicago, 1966) is mainly devoted to North America. A parallel study of the United Kingdom is Anne Benewick, *Asian and African Collections in British Libraries – Problems and Prospects* (Stevenage, 1974).

For the Soviet Union's contribution to oriental studies, Patricia Polansky's paper, 'The Russians and Soviets in Asia' (*International Library Review*, 14 (1982); 217–62) presented to the International Association of Orientalist Librarians, 1980, is exceptionally useful for those who have no Russian and Harry Halen, *Handbook of Oriental Collections in Finland . . . and Russian Minority Literature* (1978) fulfils the same function for that country. Stephen Roman, *The Development of Islamic Library Collections in Western Europe and North America* (1990) covers the more important library collections for that part of Asia. There are numerous other similar guides to individual country or national collections.

Most of the new countries of Asia started national bibliographies to record their printed national output and guides to these can most easily be found in *Commonwealth National Bibliographies: An Annotated Directory* (2nd edn Commonwealth Secretariat, 1983), the *Guide to Current National Bibliographies in the Third World*, by G.E. Gorman and M.M. Mahoney (Oxford, 1983), and the *Inventaire général des bibliographies nationales retrospectives*, edited by Marcelle Beaudiquez (Munich, 1986). These national enumerative bibliographies were supplemented by the facsimile reproduction of many of the world's major library catalogues for oriental studies issued by G.K. Hall (Boston, MA). The catalogue of the Library of the School of Oriental and African studies appeared in 1963; first supplement, 1967; second supplement, 1973; third supplement, 1979; and the fourth supplement in microfiche form by Inter Documentation Company (1985?); the library catalogue of the South-East Asian collection at Cornell University in 1976; first supplement, 1985; the Singapore – Malaysia collection of the University of Singapore library, 1968; Garland issued the catalogue of the Harvard–Yenching Library in 1985–6; and the Bibliothèque Nationale in Paris published its *Inventaire des livres imprimés arabes, 1515–1959*, ed. Josée Balagna, in 1986. All these catalogues shared the same method of reproduction by arranging and photographing in page format the original library-catalogue cards; they were expensive to buy and their large size made them cumbersome to use, but they opened up for scholars and bibliographers huge library resources hitherto less than well known.

The bibliography of periodical and serial titles is often neglected and the last fifty years have seen the publication of several important union catalogues and location lists, such as G.R. Nunn's *Southeast Asian Periodicals: An International Union List* (1977) which is arranged by country and then title and covers titles found in Southeast Asia and the United States, while the South-East Asia Library Group sponsored *Periodicals for South-East Asian Studies: A Union Catalogue of Holdings in British and Selected European Libraries*, ed. Brenda Moon (1979) which is simply arranged by title. These were supplemented by D.C. Johnson, *Index to Southeast Asian Journals, 1960–1974* . . . (Boston, MA, 1977) with its supplement for 1975–9 (1982). W.R. Roff, *Bibliography of Malay and Arabic Periodicals Published in the Straits Settlements and the Peninusular Malay States, 1876–1941* (1972) is a similar list with locations, so that South-East Asia is well covered.

The bibliography of the periodical literature of other Asian countries is less comprehensive but modern China is fairly well served with the Contemporary China Institute's *A Bibliography of Chinese Newspapers and Periodicals in European Libraries*, ed. W. Brugger (Cambridge, 1975) and John Lust's *Index Sinicus, 1920–1955* (Cambridge, 1964) indexes Western periodical literature on China following Henri Cordier's work and is supplemented by T.L. Yuan, *China in Western Literature* (New Haven, 1958) which mainly lists books and mono-graphs. Japan is more comprehensively covered by similar listings of which the most important is perhaps the *Gakujutsu zasshi sogo mokuroku* (4 vols., 1966–73) sponsored by the Japanese Ministry of Education (Mombusho) and serves as a union list by categories of the holdings of academic journals in major Japanese libraries. There is an index to Japanese periodical literature from 1948, compiled by the National Diet Library, *Zasshi kiji sakuin* (Tokyo, 1948–). There are occasional studies still unpublished but of importance in the field of periodical bibliography and Wishar Kareem Muhammad, 'A History and Union Catalogue of Kurdish Periodical Literature, 1898–1958' (unpublished MPhil thesis, University of London, 1977) is a good example, founded to some extent on the collection of Kurdish language books and periodicals collected by the late C.J. Edmonds and deposited in the SOAS Library. Most Asian countries have made some attempt at such systematic bibliographic coverage but it would be tedious to attempt to list or describe them all in detail.

However, there is another source of enumerative bibliography which, given the flourishing of academic scholarship, deserves mention. These are bibliographies of higher-degree theses. Frank Shulman's *Doctoral Dissertations on Asia: An Annotated Bibliographical Journal of Current International Research* (Ann Arbor: Xerox University Microfilms for the Association of Asian Studies, vol. 1– , no. 1– , Winter 1975) is essential for assessing the current state of scholarly activity and includes theses from universities world-wide, in all languages, and has abstracts. Peter Sluglett, *Theses on Islam, the Middle East and North-West Africa, 1880–1978 Accepted by Universities in the United Kingdom and Ireland* (1983) is an example of a finite regional listing and there are numerous other regional and topical lists of university dissertations.

As well as the general and more topical kinds of enumerative bibliography dealing with Asia there are general regional bibliographical guides that deserve mention. For the Near and Middle East there is the Middle East Library Committee's *Arab Islamic Bibliography . . . Based on Giuseppe Gabriele's Manuale di bibliografia musulmana*, edited by Diana Grimwood-Jones, Derek Hopwood, and J.D. Pearson (Brighton, 1977) and the same Committee's *Middle East and Islam: A Bibliographical Introduction*, also edited by Diana Grimwood-Jones (Zug, 1979). These guides are supplemented by J.D. Pearson's invaluable *Index Islamicus, 1906–1955: A Catalogue of Articles on Islamic Subjects in Periodicals and other Collective Publications* (Cambridge, 1958) with six supplements, first published by Heffer, now by Mansell, and continuing the work to the end of 1985. An assistant editor, Wolfgang Behn, carried the work back in time with his *Index Islamicus, 1665–1905* (Millersville, PA, 1989).

The countries of South Asia have two general bibliographical guides in the South Asia Library Group's *South Asian Bibliography: A Handbook and Guide*, edited by J.D. Pearson (Brighton, 1979) and Maureen Patterson's *South Asian Civilisations: A Bibliographical Synthesis* (Chicago, 1981), while Robert J. Kerner's *Northeastern Asia: A Selected Bibliography* (Berkeley, 1939), although now dated, is still a major source of reference. The South-East Asia Library Group has also produced *South East Asia Languages and Literature: A Select Guide*, edited by Patricia Herbert and Anthony Milner (Arran, 1989) which although less extensive than the preceding works is extremely clear and useful. Turning to China, G.W. Skinner, *Modern Chinese Society: An Analytical Bibliography* (Stanford, 1973) covers the period from 1644 to 1972 and includes references in Western languages, Chinese, and Japanese and is perhaps the one essential bibliographical tool; for Japan the Kokusai Bunka Shinkokai *K.B.S. Bibliography of Standard Reference Books for Japanese Studies with Descriptive Notes* (Tokyo, 1959–) is still in progress with at least ten volumes published so far. This is supplemented retrospectively by the *Bibliographischer Alt-Japan-Katalog, 1542–*

1853, compiled by the Japaninstitut in Berlin and the Deutsches Forschungs-
institut in Kyoto (Kyoto, 1940) itself supplementing Cordier's *Bibliotheca japonica*
(Paris, 1912) and Friedrich von Wenckstern's *A Bibliography of the Japanese
Empire* (Leiden and Tokyo, 1895–1907). Akira Yuyama's unpublished paper, 'A
brief survey of Japanese bibliographies on South Asia studies', presented to the
Colloquium on South Asian Studies, 24–26 April 1985, is mainly devoted to
philological, religious, and textual studies but is a revelation of important
bibliographical activity in those fields concentrating on Buddhist studies.

As Pearson's bibliography of Asian bibliographies indicates, there are now
thousands of enumerative lists covering the languages, religions, customs,
history, and almost every aspect of Oriental' bibliography. Many are collaborative works and this is becoming more common as the range of materials
published increases and the coverage and scholarship become more demanding.
But one-man enterprises still continue and a notable example in this category
which should not escape mention is H.A.I. Goonetileke, *A Bibliography of Ceylon*
(Zug, 1970–83) which endeavours to list in five volumes the retrospective
bibliography of this island in all fields of knowledge.

From this partial survey of oriental enumerative bibliography, let me turn to
the even more difficult task of attempting a cursory estimate of the progress of
descriptive and historical bibliography in oriental studies.

A major effort has been devoted to listing and describing collections of
manuscripts in oriental languages; almost no Asian country has adequate
bibliographical control of the surviving manuscripts in its libraries and
repositories and, indeed, most are preserved outside these institutions. In
addition the manuscript tradition and the production of fine manuscripts is still a
living force in the majority of Asian countries for, although printing was
invented in Asia, it was not quickly or universally adopted in lithographic,
xylographic, or moveable type formats. Significant discoveries of manuscripts
with hitherto unknown texts are still made, and the definitive versions of
religious and historical works are still, as a consequence, to be sought. Such
early texts are of especial importance in Asia where the traditional method of
editing a text was eclectic, the previous texts used for comparison often being
destroyed once the new authorized text was issued.

Thus, much scholarly time has been devoted to identifying and describing
manuscripts in accurate detail so as to provide a basis for textual scholarship,
and a good deal of this work of description has been carried out in Western
institutions which hold the most significant manuscripts recorded so far. For
general surveys of the material J.D. Pearson's *Oriental Manuscripts in Europe and
North America: A Survey* (Zug, 1971) is the most useful starting point and this
can be supplemented by G.R. Nunn's *Asia and Oceania: A guide to Archival and
Manuscript Sources in the United States* (1985). The series of guides to the national
archives of Asia sponsored by the International Council on Archives and
published under the cumbersome title of 'Guides to the Sources of Asian History'
is still in progress and provides much helpful information – the guide to the

Chinese historical archives, for example. M.I. Moir's *A General Guide to the India Office Records* (1988) supersedes Foster's previous guide and describes what is perhaps the most important single archival source for the history of Asia.

Turning from archival listings to more extensive descriptions of manuscripts the major initiative in this field is the 'Verzeichnis der orientalischen Handschriften in Deutschland' (VOHD) which has provided a model for almost all succeeding catalogues. The first volume was published by Franz Steiner Verlag in Wiesbaden in 1961 and the preface by Wolfgang Voigt sets out the ambitious intention to catalogue and describe fully all the 60,000 Oriental manuscripts in Germany. By 1990, 110 volumes had been published in twenty-two groups and the project is briefly described by Voigt in 'die Katalogisierung der orientalischen Handschriften und das Verzeichnis' (*Jahrbuch preussischer Kulturbesitz*, XII (1976): 157–67). Scholars are recruited internationally to undertake the work and deal with some fairly intractable material, e.g. T.G.T. Pigeaud and P. Voorhoeve, *Handschriften aus Indonesien* (*Bali, Java, Sumatra*) (Stuttgart, 1985; VOHD, vol. XXVIII, 2) which attempts the systematic description of Batak birchbark books!

In the field of Arabic manuscripts C. Brockelmann, *Geschichte der arabischen litteratur* (2nd edn, Leiden, 1943–9; 3 supplementary volumes, 1937–42) is the standard source of manuscript reference, but is now supplemented by Fuat Sezgin, *Geschichte des arabischen schrifttums* (Leiden, 1967–) with nine volumes published by 1990. Other catalogues providing descriptive models such as Rudolf Mach's *Catalogue of Arabic Manuscripts (Yahuda Section) in the Garrett Collection, Princeton University Library* (Princeton, 1977) and the revised edition by Derek Hopwood of H.L. Gottschalk's *Catalogue of the Mingana Collection of Manuscripts . . . preserved at Selly Oak Colleges' Library*, volume IV: *Islamic Arabic Manuscripts* (Zug, 1985) are also of interest. Ismail K. Poonawala, *Bibliography of Ismaili Literature* (Malibu, 1977) is an example of a catalogue of manuscripts compiled by cumulating material from a variety of other sources.

But the most prolific descriptive catalogues of manuscripts have been produced in the South Asian area. One significant initiative has been Iravatham Mahadevan's *The Indus Script. Texts, Concordances and Tables* (New Delhi, Director General, Archaeological Survey of India, 1977, Memoirs, no. 77) which provides a computerized concordance, indexes, and texts for this script from Harappa and Mohenjodaro. The computing programs were developed at the Indian National Centre for Software Development and Computing Techniques and the Tata Institute for Fundamental Research in Bombay. For Sanskrit the major development has been V. Raghavan's *New catalogus catalogorum* (Madras, University of Madras, 1949–) with eleven volumes published so far from the projected thirty, including, already, a revised version of volume I. This work, supplementary to Aufrecht's, does not break new ground descriptively although it lists many newly discovered manuscripts; innovation in this field is to be found principally in Janert's work for the VOHD volumes dealing with Sanskrit. D.N. Marshall, *Mughals in India: A Bibliographical Survey of Manuscripts* (1985), should also be mentioned as an example of a special, careful, and detailed bibliography of historical source material.

Although perhaps of more strictly aesthetic than bibliographical interest, Persian, Mughal, and Indian paintings in manuscripts have attracted much study and detailed description. J.P. Losty's *The Art of the Book in India* (British Library, [1982]) was designed to accompany an exhibition for the Festival of India but is the best recent survey, with an extensive bibliography, while Norah Titley's *Persian Miniature Painting* (1983) is a monograph dealing with the history of the genre. B.W. Robinson's catalogues of the collections in the India Office Library (1976) and the John Rylands Library (1980) describe the paintings rather than the physical manuscripts but are fundamental listings, while the catalogue of *The Keir Collection: Islamic Painting and the Arts of the Book* (1976) edited by Robinson and others is of major interest. Toby Falk and Mildred Archer's *Indian Miniatures in the India Office Library* (1981) is an important catalogue of a single collection. The various festivals of India and consequent museum displays resulted in many valuable and well-illustrated catalogues which provide useful descriptive information. *The Arts of the Book in Central Asia, 14th–16th Centuries,* edited by Basil Gray (1979) should also be noted.

For South-East Asia there is *Indonesian Manuscripts in Great Britain,* by Merle Ricklefs and P. Voorhoeve (1977), which is a short-title guide, and the more extensive *Literature of Java: Catalogue Raisonné of the Javanese Manuscripts in the Library of the University of Leiden . . .* (The Hague, 1967–80) provides in four volumes an example of extended treatment. There are not many examples of the detailed analysis of manuscripts but P. Voorhoeve, 'A Malay scriptorium' (*Malay and Indonesian Studies: Essays Presented to Sir Richard Winstedt on his 85th Birthday,* ed. J.S. Bastin and R. Roolvink (Oxford, 1964, pp. 256–66)) and 'An Essay at Dating and a Description of a Malay Manuscript', by Russell Jones and Clare Rowntree (*Kajian Malaysia,* I, 2, December 1983: 1–13) provide two models which may attract successors. One further example of detailed treatment following the VOHD exemplar is Walther Heissig's *Catalogue of Mongol Books, Manuscripts and Xylographs* [in the Royal Library] (Copenhagen, 1971) which deals with a mixed category of physical materials.

Turning to printed books, it is not possible to do more than indicate a few studies of various types which break new ground or show the direction bibliographical research may take in the future. For South Asia, J.B. Primrose's article 'The First Press in India and its Printers', (*Lib,* IV, 20, 3 (1924): 241–65) and V. Rosenkilde's 'Printing in Tranquebar, 1712–1845' (*Lib,* V, 4 (1949): 179–95) both owe their appearance to the Bibliographical Society. Katharine Smith Diehl's *Early Indian Imprints* (New York, 1964) was an early attempt at precise description continued by the author in a series of periodical articles mostly published in out-of-the-way journals. To a considerable extent this work has been superseded by Graham Shaw's *The South Asia and Burma Retrospective Bibliography (SABREB). Stage 1: 1556–1800* (British Library, 1987) which lists some 1770 titles with about 900 locations in a number of libraries. Entries are based on actual examination of copies and follow the style and principles of the *ESTC* project. All the languages of the sub-continent are covered in romanized form. Stage 2 of the project awaits further funding and is planned to cover the period 1801–67. All the major national libraries and archives in Europe, North America, and the sub-continent are involved in this important undertaking. A more exotic piece of bibliographical work is *Publications Proscribed by the Government of India: A Catalogue . . .* (1985) also by Graham Shaw and the late Mary Lloyd. Similar studies of subversive or banned literature are needed for many Asian countries.

A Descriptive Catalogue of the Pre-1868 Japanese Books, Manuscripts and Prints in the Library of the School of Oriental and African Studies, by D.G. Chibbett, B.F. Hickman, and S. Matsudaira (1975) recorded a small collection, but the descriptions provided a model for a number of other catalogues like J.S. Edgren's *Catalogue of the Nordenskiöld Collection of Japanese Books in the Royal Library, Stockholm* (Stockholm, 1980) and Eva Kraft's *Japanische Handschriften und traditionelle Drucke aus der Zeit vor 1868 . . .* (Wiesbaden, 1982–8; VOHD, vol. XXVII, 1–3).

Lesley Forbes, *Catalogue of Books Printed between 1500 and 1599 in the Library of SOAS* (preliminary edition, 1968) attempted a more detailed description of books in a number of European languages mainly drawn from the Marsden and Auboyneau collections, but giving additional locations in the British Library. A model for Tibetan can be found in Zuiho Yamaguchi, *Catalogue of the Toyo Bunko Collection of Tibetan Works on History* (Tokyo, 1970) which carefully describes non-canonical works in this field. Rolf du Rietz, *Bibliotheca Polynesiana. A Catalogue of Some of the Books in the Polynesian Collection formed by the late Bjorne Kroepelien and now in Oslo University Library* (Oslo, 1969) has no innovative description but deals with an area which is otherwise sparsely covered.

The study of printing and publishing history has produced more examples of bibliographical activity in more Asian countries. Since most printing with moveable types originated with Christian missions the *Bibliotheca missionum* edited by Robert Streit and Johannes Dindinger (Freiburg, 1917–) is very valuable and volumes IV – XIV and XXVIII – XXX are entirely devoted to regions of Asia. Jean Muller and Ernst Roth, *Ausser-europäische Druckereien im. 16 Jahr-hundert* (Baden-Baden, 1969) is complementary to Deschamps and other similar typographical gazetteers, and the catalogue of the Lilly Library exhibition *Exotic Printing and the Expansion of Europe, 1492–1840: An Exhibit* (Bloomington, 1972) provides interesting illustrations from the Boxer collection. South Asia has probably produced more such studies of varying quality than any other region. Anant K. Priolkar, *The Printing Press in India, its Beginnings and Early Development* (Bombay, 1958) is still perhaps the best, short, readable introduction, and Margarita Barns, *The Indian Press* (1940) covers the newspaper and periodical press. Dennis Rhodes's slender *The Spread of Printing. Eastern Hemisphere, India, Pakistan, Ceylon, Burma and Thailand* (Amsterdam, 1969) is a work of synthesis based on the British Library collections. C.R. Boxer's work is rightly well known and his 'A tentative checklist of Indo-Portuguese imprints' appears in the *Arquivos do Centro Cultural Portugues* (9 (1975): 567–99). The Bibliographical Society's contribution, and a major one, to this area was the publication in 1981 of Graham Shaw's *Printing in Calcutta to 1800* which listed, analysed, and described the pattern of printing and publishing in the East India Company's main presidency. B.S. Kesavan's *History of Printing and Publishing in India: A Story of Cultural Awakening* (New Delhi, 1985–) has so far produced two large volumes and is extensively and firmly based on previous work, dealing with India by regions. There are a number of special studies that may simply be listed: G. Schurhammer and G.W. Cottrell, 'The First Printing in Indic Characters' (*Harvard Library Bulletin*, 6, 2 (Spring 1952); 147–60); M.H. Khan, 'History of Printing in Bengali Characters up to 1866' (PhD thesis, University of London 1976); J. Mangamma, *Book Printing in India with Special Reference to the Contribution of European Scholars to Telegu, 1746–1857* (Nellore, 1975); K.S. Diehl, 'Lucknow Printers, 1820–1850' (*Comparative Librarianship: Essays in Honour of Professor D.N. Marshall*, ed. N.N. Gidwani, Delhi, [n.d.]; 115–28); A.R. Butt, 'The Origin and Development of Printing Press in Sind' (*Pakistan Library Bulletin*, 12, 3/4 (September – December 1981): 1–10); Graham Shaw, 'Printing in Devanagari' (*Monotype Recorder*, N.S. 2 (September 1980): 28–32); Chumar Choondal, *The Missionaries and Malayalam Journalism* (Trichur, 1975); and Nasir Ahmad, 'Development of Printing in Urdu, 1743–1857' (MPhil, University of London, 1976). These are simply examples of activity in an area which has been better tilled than most.

For Sri Lanka there is K.S. Diehl, 'The Dutch Press in Ceylon, 1734–96' (*Library Quarterly*, 42 (1972): 329–42) and G.P.S.H. de Silva, *Printing and Publishing in Ceylon* (Colombo, 1972), and for Nepal, G.B. Devoktā, *Nepālako chāpākhānā ra patra-patrikāko itihāsa* (Kathmandu, 1967). Finally no survey, however incomplete, of this area should omit at least some mention of Auguste Toussaint who single-handedly created the bibliography of Mauritius; his *Early Printing in Mauritius, Réunion, Madagascar and the Seychelles* (Amsterdam, 1969) is the most conveniently available summary.

For the Near and Middle East the most convenient and up-to-date summary may be found in the new edition of the *Encyclopedia of Islam* under the heading 'Maṭbaʻa' (vol. VI, fasc. 111–12, pp. 794–807) which covers Persia, Turkey, the Arab countries, Muslim India, and Afghanistan. Geoffrey Roper's article 'Arabic Printing in England before 1820' (*British Society for Middle Eastern Studies Bulletin*, 12, 1 (1985): 13–32) can be supplemented by Robert Jones, *The Medici Oriental Press (Rome 1584–1614) and Renaissance Arabic Studies* (1983) and entries in *Index Islamicus*. Jale Baysal's *Muteferrika 'dan bitinci meşrutiyete kadar. Osmanli Turkerinin bastiklari kitaplar* (Istanbul, 1968) deals with a famous press and publisher.

In South-East Asia the colonial presence of the British and the Dutch stimulated a number of studies. Professor B.R. Pearn's 'Burmese Printed Books before Judson' (Burma Research Society. *50th Anniversary Publications*, vol. II (1960), 475–6) is interesting. Cecil K. Byrd's *Early Printing in the Straits Settlements, 1806–1858* (Singapore, 1970) is a brief sketch and was followed by four more detailed studies: B.C. Bloomfield, 'A.B. Bone and the Beginning of Printing in Malaysia' (*India Office Library and Records. Report for the year 1979* (1980), pp. 7–33) was originally read as a paper to the Society; Ibrahim bin Ismail, 'Missionary Printing in Malacca, 1815–1843' (*Libri*, 32, 3 (1982): 177–206); Leona O'Sullivan, 'The London Missionary Society: A Written Record of Missionaries and Printing Presses in the Straits Settlements, 1815–1847' (*Journal of the Malay[si]an Branch of the Royal Asiatic Society [JMBRAS]*, 57, 2 (1984): 61–104); and Annabel Teh Gallop, 'Early Malay Printing: An Introduction to the British Library Collection' (*JMBRAS*), 63, 1 (1990): 85–124). Nik Ahmad bin Haji Nik Hassan, 'The Malay press' (*JMBRAS*, 36, 1 (1963): 37–78) deals with the periodical and newspaper press. H.J. De Graaf, *The Spread of Printing, Eastern Hemisphere. Indonesia* (Amsterdam, 1969) is a useful survey, and so is C. Hooykaas, 'Books Made in Bali' (*Bijdragen tot de Taal-, Land- en Volkenkunde*, 119 (1963): 371–86). Chun Prabhavi Vadhana, 'Special Publications for Free Distribution' (*Journal of the Siam Society*, 61, 1 (1973): 227–60) deals with the Thai custom of distributing freely at cremation ceremonies authoritative editions of Buddhist literature. John Lent has supplemented the bibliography of the Philippines with three articles in this area: 'Philippine Provincial Press' (*Silliman Journal*, 16 (1969): 273–90); 'The Press of the Philippines, its History and Problems' (*Silliman Journal*, 14 (1967): 67–90); and 'Guerilla Presses of the Philippines, 1941–45' (*Asian Studies*, 8 (1970): 270–4).

For Japan, D.G. Chibbett, *the History of Japanese Printing and Book Illustration* (Tokyo, 1977) is the best and most convenient summary in English, while Kazuo Inoue, *Keicho irai shoka shūran: shosekishō meikan* (*Directory of Publishers since the Keicho Period, 1596–1614*) revised and enlarged by Muneko Sakamoto (Osaka, 1970) contains more than 3,000 entries in directory form. Small-scale studies of Japanese printing and publishing abound and many are included in the proceedings of the colloquium organized by the British Library and the School of Oriental and African Studies in 1988 and published as *Japanese Studies*, ed. Yu-Ying Brown and Hamish Todd (British Library, 1991) – for example, 'Provincial Publishing in the Tokungawa Period', by P.F. Cornicki; 'The Origins of Newspapers and Magazines in the Bakumatsu and Meiji Periods', by Haruhiko Asakura; and 'Centres of Printing in Mediaeval Japan', by K.B. Gardner. (Bibliography in Japan is discussed below by Akihiro Yamada.)

For China it is sufficient simply to record Tsien Tsuen-Hsuin's *Science and Civilisation in China*, vol. v, part 1: *Paper and Printing* (Cambridge, 1985) which was long in gestation but covers all aspects of printing, publishing, and book production and deals with both Chinese and foreign scholarship and sources.

E. McKillop, 'A History of Korean Printing' (*Monotype Recorder*, n.s. 7 (1988): 2–12) is a brief convenient summary. But the preeminent study is Sohn Pow-Key's *Early Korean Typography* (new edn, Seoul, 1982) which describes and analyses the earliest printing by moveable types so far dated and provides a model for others to follow, even to the extent of reproducing specimen pages of the works described. The examples range from the twelfth century to 1895; this magnificent work is beautifully produced. The author ascribes the invention of the process to Korea and asserts that printing spread through China to the West, an assertion naturally controverted by Tsien in his survey.

But there are not many special studies of typography in the oriental field comparable to Sohn Pow-Key's authoritative work. Vivian Ba, 'The Odyssey of the First Burmese Types' (*Journal of the Burma Research Society*, 45 (1962): 209–13) is interesting, as is Mary Lloyd's piece on the pioneer of Indian printing, the Indian 'Caxton' as he was once known, 'Sir Charles Wilkins, 1749–1836' (*India Office Library and Records. Report for the year 1978* (1979), pp. 9–39); but the discovery of some of Wilkins's original matrices for the Bengali and Modi types even including the original pattern drawings by Wilkins was reported and described in 'An Unexpected Legacy and its Contribution to Indian Typography' by Fiona Ross and Graham Shaw (*Matrix*, 7 (Winter 1987): 69–79). B.S. Naik's *Typography of Devanagari* (3 vols., Bombay, 1971) should be noted.

Paper has always attracted considerable attention and has been prized in Asian countries. Dard Hunter was responsible for many studies which are listed in his *Papermaking* (2nd edn. New York, 1947) the most extensive being *Papermaking by Hand in India* (New York, 1939). This is complemented by Jesper Trier's *Ancient Paper of Nepal* (Copenhagen, Jutland Archaeological Society, 1972. Publications, vol. x, sponsored by the Royal Library). Tsien's work in Joseph Needham's *Science and Civilisation in China* (7 vols., 20 parts, Cambridge, 1954–) deals more exhaustively with papermaking in China and Sukey Hughes, *Washi: the World of Japanese Paper* (Tokyo, [1978]) is perhaps the best and most thorough study of Japanese paper among a number of recently published books. It also has the advantage – as do a few others – of presenting a range of paper samples. O.P. Agrawal, *Conservation of Manuscripts and Paintings of South-East Asia* (London, 1984) is misleadingly titled since it deals mainly with South Asian materials, but many of those discussed are paper based and the book has interest from that point of view.

The recent collaboration between the British Library, which holds much of the material recovered by Sir Aurel Stein from the Caves of the Thousand Buddhas, and the Institute for Dunhuang Studies of the Academy of Social Sciences in China may prove of significant interest for paper studies in China. *The Diamond Sutra*, AD 868, the world's oldest dated printed document, is to be studied and restored as part of a collaborative programme of research in association with the School of Oriental and African Studies, the British Academy and other funding bodies. Chemists at the University of Sussex have so far tentatively identified the yellow dye in the paper as berberine; more detailed analysis will be necessary before any preservation work proceeds and it will be possible to study not only the paper but the ink and the other physical characteristics of the document (*New Scientist*, 127, 1729 (11 August 1990): 22).

Bookbinding has always attracted attention in Islamic countries and there are a number of early studies. *Islamic Bindings and Bookmaking*, by Gulnar Bosch, John Carswell, and Guy Petherbridge (Chicago, 1981) is nominally the catalogue of an exhibition, but actually much more than that and represents the best modern survey and analysis of techniques and methods. David Jacobs and Barbara Rodgers, 'Developments in the Conservation of Oriental (Islamic) Manuscripts at the India Office Library, London' (*Restaurator*, 11 (1990): 110–38) is a recent technical analysis of problems involving the binding structures. Duncan Haldane's *Islamic Bookbindings in the Victoria and Albert Museum* (London, 1983) is a well-illustrated and conveniently available guide, while *Some Oriental Bindings in the Chester Beatty Library*, by B. van Regemorter (Dublin, 1961) covers a wider range of countries and styles.

Coming to a pause after this hectic gallop through half the world's area and most of its population and cultural activities, it is time to try to forecast the future of bibliographical work in oriental studies. First, any progress depends on peace, stable economic conditions, control of population growth, and the development of educational institutions. These basic factors assume a greater importance in Asia than in many other continents and countries and to these must be allied stability and growth in libraries, archives, and institutions of deposit for cultural records. Given these, and at the time of writing they appear most unlikely, then bibliographic work in oriental literature will increasingly centre more in Asia itself than in the West. Bibliographers will absorb more rapidly the lessons of descriptive and analytical scholarship pioneered in Europe and will work to establish the canon of their religious, historical, and literary texts with more certainty than now exists. This is likely to take the next fifty years at least and if the Bibliographical Society chooses then to review progress and its activities again, another member will undertake this task almost certainly in a spirit of wonder at what we had not foreseen and what really needed to be done.

However, one avatar perhaps worth mentioning to encourage imitation is the recent formation of The Bibliographical Society of India which, in emulation of our Society, has already produced *The National Union Catalogue of Incunabula and Early Printed Books*, ed. R.D. Singh (Calcutta, 1986) listing some 5,000 editions of mainly European imprints in some hundred libraries.

Finally one must note that the ideas of the *Annales* school and the *histoire du livre* have made little impact so far on Oriental bibliography, but two works should be mentioned that set the contact between Europe and Asia in a wider context and provide essential background to our studies: they are Donald F. Lach, *Asia in the Making of Europe* (5 vols., Chicago, 1965–77) and Raymond Schwab, *The Oriental Renaissance: Europe's Rediscovery of India and the East, 1680–1880* (New York, 1984).

Tradition and innovation: bibliography in Australia and New Zealand

WALLACE KIRSOP

Although specialists working in the two countries came together in 1969 to launch the Bibliographical Society of Australia and New Zealand, it would be rash to assume that there must be a common Antipodean stance in this branch of scholarship. The facts that New Zealand did not join the Australian Federation at the beginning of this century and that old intercolonial rivalries still influence relationships between the different parts of the continent should be a caution against supposing that uniformity ought to characterize the intellectual life of two nations derived from the British model. Things are more complex than this, and any study of the way bibliography has developed in Australia and New Zealand needs to take account of the diversity of the traditions at work. At the same time a shared experience of distance from the great libraries of the northern hemisphere and of comparative isolation of individuals and small groups across a vast territory helps to explain a certain detachment from orthodoxy and a readiness to improvise and even to innovate that mark contributions to the discipline made from Auckland, Wellington, Dunedin, Sydney, and Melbourne. It is in the tension between the heritage of Old World erudition and the inventiveness dictated by residence in the New World that one can perhaps best grasp the nature of bibliographical research in the Antipodes.

Observers of countries of relatively recent European settlement and even their inhabitants are often confused about questions of cultural identity. Too much importance is attached to the accident of location, and far too little heed is paid to the determining factor of language, reinforced in some cases by the demands of an exclusive creed. That movement beyond the seas does not dissolve the ties of art, literature, and music is frequently not understood. Yet it is necessary to bear constantly in mind the dictum of Thérèse Radic, a student of the various traditions enriching Australian musical life in the nineteenth and twentieth centuries: 'What was theirs is ours, because we were once them.' New developments and adaptations are not excluded, but the weight and shaping power of a transported past cannot be denied or suppressed. It is obvious that the collecting of books and the study of them as physical objects do not escape this underlying condition.

When M.W. MacCallum acknowledged in the preface to his *Shakespeare's Roman Plays and their Background* (1910, p. x) his 'obligations to the book-loving colonists of an earlier generation, to whose irrepressible zeal for learning their successors owe access to many volumes that one would hardly expect to see under the Southern Cross', he was recording the debt that the new modern-literature professionals installed in Australian universities in the 1880s owed to the amateurs who from the beginning of the century had imported private libraries that enshrined the European cultural heritage. More important, the pioneers had laboured to secure for the various colonial cities those institutions, including universities, public libraries, and learned societies, that would guarantee general access to the fruits of scholarship. The calendars, catalogues, and proceedings of the bodies concerned provide an ample printed record of the values and aspirations of immigrants who were less narrowly materialistic than is often claimed. Similarly one finds reflected in the numerous book-auction catalogues and advertisements of all the major centres in the nineteenth century the priorities and fashions of collecting in the northern hemisphere. In other words a climate for bibliographical curiosity and enquiry was being created and sustained by the trade itself, something that matches what was happening at the same period in Europe and in the United States of America. Collectors, public men, and 'cultural evangelists' like Charles Nicholson, Redmond Barry, and George Grey operated in Australia and New Zealand according to the same canons and with the same presuppositions as their contemporaries elsewhere, and they were served by antiquarian booksellers like H.T. Dwight in Melbourne and Angus & Robertson in Sydney working within the same tradition.

Despite the fact that Antipodean fortunes in the nineteenth and early twentieth centuries were notably less substantial than those amassed on the other side of the Equator, as W.D. Rubenstein has shown ('Men of Wealth', *Australian Cultural History*, 3 (1984): 24–37), this did not prevent considerable benefactions going to public institutions. The contributions of Grey, Alexander Turnbull, T.M. Hocken, Nicholson, and D.S. Mitchell furnished Auckland, Wellington, Dunedin, and Sydney not only with manuscripts and early printed books representative of their European inheritance but also with the primary sources essential for the exploration of the old indigenous and new immigrant civilizations of Britain's South Sea colonies. The push towards collecting the materials for a national bibliographical history is visible soon after 1850, but it gathers pace and has in many ways its supreme flowering in the decades before the First World War. Nonetheless it would be quite misleading to suggest that the role of bibliophiles, of amateurs in all senses, has ceased to be crucial in the preservation and proper appreciation of local resources and hence of their scholarly exploitation.

The preoccupations of the basically non-professional administrators of nineteenth-century libraries in Australia and New Zealand mirrored those of their counterparts elsewhere in the English-speaking world. Trustees were often noted collectors and their employees men of wide reading or literary inclinations. It is not surprising then to find older types of connoisseurship alongside concern with matters of classification and practical management at the meetings held between 1896 and 1902 of the transient Library Association of Australasia. The extensive exhibitions that normally accompanied these intercolonial gatherings demonstrated amply that local history and the European heritage were equally in favour.

At the beginning of this century and for a long time thereafter scholarship in the humanities was often better supported outside universities that had to concentrate on training candidates for first degrees. Research was promoted by learned societies or was very much a matter of individual effort. The resources in books and journals needed for these pursuits were more likely to be found in public libraries, with that in Melbourne clearly preeminent amongst them until the 1950s. It is no accident then that of the seven institutional memberships of the Bibliographical Society taken out before 1939 in Australia and New Zealand only one (the University of Sydney Library in 1907) was not in the dominant group of national and public libraries.

The relative weakness of the universities in research and research training till recent decades explains in part the rather haphazard dissemination of northern hemisphere traditions of bibliographical investigation and of textual editing. The fact that Badham was, in Housman's phrase, 'finally transported to the antipodes' in 1867 did not mean that he had an enduring impact on what was done in classical studies, the central discipline in the Sydney and Melbourne Faculties of Arts in the nineteenth century. Significantly it was the poet Christopher Brennan, himself the author of a precociously revisionist article 'On the Manuscripts of Aeschylus' (*Journal of Philology*, 22 (1894): 49–71), who contributed the entry on Badham to the *Australian Encyclopaedia* in 1925 (I, 119) and who best understood – not least through practice on French Symbolist verse – the nature of work 'along the arduous and subtle lines of textual criticism'. Australian and New Zealand classicists have occasionally since been editors, but those who, like James Willis in his *Latin Textual Criticism* of 1972, have indulged in explicit reflection on and instruction in their art are few. Although the phenomenon is by no means confined to the southern hemisphere, it is noteworthy that there is little dialogue or interaction with scholars concerned with establishing texts of the medieval and modern periods.

In modern languages too, the modest size of the humanities departments until after 1945 helped to determine attachment to some networks, schools, or ideologies rather than others. It was not just by chance that Sydney graduates chose to pursue a variety of research fields at German universities before 1914 or that Australians found their way fairly regularly to Balliol College, Oxford and Pembroke College, Cambridge to take higher degrees. Since places and people tended to be paramount in these intellectual chain migrations, exposure to bibliographical scholarship was not guaranteed at all and was often incidental for persons who went abroad seeking other sorts of sustenance. It is not easy to trace in this field the sort of scientific lineage that chemists are in the habit of claiming.

Apart from the regular movement of Australians and New Zealanders to Europe and North America and back again, one has to reckon with the continuing recruitment of librarians and university teaching staff from overseas as part of the process of transfer of modes of research. Tertiary education has not ceased to be hospitable to people trained elsewhere and their backgrounds and prejudices are reflected in curricula and in programmes of investigation. Bibliography and textual studies have been as much affected by this as other pursuits.

Keith Maslen has told us ('The State of Bibliography in New Zealand', *BSANZB*, 8 (1984): 141–6) how formal instruction in bibliography and textual criticism began in the constituent institutions of the former University of New Zealand after the introduction in 1949 of a final-year option on 'Methods and techniques of scholarship'. Most of the now-separate universities have taken advantage of this possibility. The names of Maslen himself, the late W.J. Cameron, D.F. McKenzie, J.C. Ross, and MacD.P. Jackson amongst the teachers indicate clearly enough how close these courses have been to contemporary research trends. The creation of a Department of Librarianship under Roderick Cave at the Victoria University of Wellington in 1979 has given a place to the history of books. In short, with the benevolent backing of heads of department like Ian Gordon, New Zealanders have long had opportunities to embark on bibliographical studies of a structured kind.

In Australia arrangements have been generally less satisfactory. Before training in librarianship moved exclusively into tertiary-education institutions, the Registration Examination of the Library Association of Australia (now the Australian Library and Information Association) included an optional paper on historical and descriptive bibliography. Although the syllabus had become more wide-ranging by the time the procedure was discontinued in 1980, there was an unrealistic emphasis on incunabula given the extreme modesty of local collections of fifteenth-century books. The opportunity to promote interest in eighteenth- and nineteenth-century printing and publishing – periods of obvious relevance to Australian research libraries – was largely missed through this conservatism. Despite concern in Sydney and Adelaide in particular, English teaching in the universities attached less importance to systematic instruction in bibliography and editing. Even in more recent decades the number of serious courses available has remained proportionally lower than in New Zealand. The competing attractions of Leavisism and, latterly, of critical theory, have tended in some places to isolate and marginalize bibliographers, who have had little to do in most of the new library schools.

Too sharp a contrast betwen Australia and New Zealand would also be misleading. Bibliographical presses began to appear in the former country also in the early 1960s, as B.J. McMullin's survey demonstrates ('Bibliographical Presses in Australia and New Zealand', *BSANZB*, 3 (1977): 55–64). Mostly they were linked to teaching, an activity in which native scholars like Harrison Bryan, Harold Love, and Alan Brissenden were joined by recruits from the northern hemisphere. Peter Davison in Sydney in the 1960s and Arthur Brown and Brian McMullin at Monash University helped to widen the circle of literary students and librarians familiar with the 'bibliographical way'. Other influences also came into play. A group of French specialists associated with Monash University participated in the attempts being made in Oxford and in Paris itself to foster *la bibliographie matérielle* (the translation successfully proposed from Melbourne for 'physical bibliography'). At the same time, that is, in the mid 1960s, therefore appreciably earlier than in Britain and in the United States, explicit lessons were being drawn for Australian circumstances from the work of H.-J. Martin. Later, at the University of New South Wales, Martyn Lyons was to reinforce the link with younger members of the French school of *historiens du livre*.

Research and publication, as opposed to teaching, have had a much longer history in Australasian bibliographical endeavours. Well before the emergence of the Bibliographical Society of Australia and New Zealand or the creation of Monash University's Centre for Bibliographical and Textual Studies, there were bodies and individuals devoted to investigations in this field. The name alone can be deceptive. The Bibliographical Society of Queensland that was active in the 1930s seems to have concentrated on reprinting historical and literary works of local interest. On the other hand the Book Collectors' Society of Australia, first in Sydney and later in Melbourne, has for nearly half a century provided a regular meeting place for people interested in the world of books. Walter Stone (1910–81), long-time editor and printer of its small journal *Biblionews and Australian Notes & Queries* (founded in 1947), also established the series 'Studies in Australian Bibliography', which now numbers more than thirty titles, including author bibliographies and catalogues of special collections of books and manuscripts. Under the direction of John Fletcher this coalition of academic and bibliophilic industry has continued its vigorous life throughout the 1980s.

Predictably Fletcher's *Index 1947–1979 Numbers 1–245* (Sydney, 1982) to *Biblionews* includes the names of the three crucial figures in the compilation of a retrospective Australian national bibliography. Edmund Morris Miller, J.A. Ferguson, and Edward Ford in their major contributions, respectively *Australian Literature from its Beginnings to 1935*, 2 vols. (Melbourne, 1940), *Bibliography of Australia*, 7 vols. (Sydney, 1941–69), and *Bibliography of Australian Medicine 1790–1900* (Sydney, 1976), laid a solid foundation for future research. Details have been corrected, notably in the catalogues of a growing band of antiquarian booksellers across the country, and younger bibliographers occasionally criticize what they see as outdated conventions of enumeration and description. However, it should be remembered that the works were planned and begun decades before their publication dates and that they had to fit into the leisure time and retirement years of busy careers devoted to other academic and professional fields. Whatever scope there is for improvement and refinement, the productive power of utter dedication unaided by government grants and the advantage of building bibliographies on purposeful personal collecting can be commended to newer generations.

The lesson was not lost on Ian F. McLaren, who, since his retirement as a parliamentarian, has produced a remarkable succession of bibliographies and documentary studies of nineteenth- and twentieth-century Australian and New Zealand publishing houses and literary figures. His own very large collection, rich in variant issues and all the publication forms of the texts and editions he has recorded, is now available in the Baillieu Library of the University of Melbourne for other scholars. The necessary rôle of the imaginative bibliophile in complementing the unavoidable deficiencies of institutional acquisitions could not be better illustrated.

Professional librarians, with or without the support of their employers, have also played a part in a cooperative enterprise where enumerative, descriptive, and reference bibliography are not always easily distinguishable. The encouragement of periodicals like *New Zealand Libraries*, *The Australian Library Journal*, and *Australian Academic and Research Libraries* has also been important in sustaining bibliographical work, especially on local topics. The founding editor of the last-named journal, Dietrich Borchardt, has defended by example and precept over four decades the view that librarians should engage in scholarly activities, in particular in bibliography and the history of books. Apart from his own substantial contributions he launched the valuable series of 'La Trobe University Library Publications' and remains the editor of *Reference Australia* and of the 'Historical Bibliography Monographs' that grew out of the Australian Bicentenary ferment of the 1980s. Many gaps in Ferguson's nineteenth-century record have been filled in this way, and the links betwen bibliography and social history have been effectively highlighted.

Institutions themselves have not neglected their responsibilities in this area. The National Library of Australia has not only reprinted Ferguson and issued a not-altogether-satisfactory supplement (*Bibliography of Australia: Addenda 1784–1850 Volumes I to IV*, Canberra, 1986) but also compiled the massive *Australian National Bibliography 1901–1950*, 4 vols. (Canberra, 1988). Somewhat earlier its counterpart on the other side of the Tasman published A.G. Bagnall's *New Zealand National Bibliography to the Year 1960* (5 vols. in 6, Wellington, 1969–84).

The solicitude for making resources known continues to extend to non-Australasian materials. A.B. Foxcroft's catalogues in the 1930s of the fifteenth-century books and fragments in the State Library of Victoria can be matched by two initiatives of the State Library of New South Wales: H.G. Kaplan's *A First Census of Incunabula in Australia and New Zealand* (Sydney, 1966) and John Fletcher and Rose Smith, *A Short-Title Catalogue of Sixteenth Century Printed Books Held in Libraries and Private Collections in New South Wales with a List of Provenances* (Sydney, 1979). *The Short Title Catalogue of Books Printed in the British Isles, the British Colonies and the United States of America and of English Books Printed Elsewhere 1701–1800 Held in the Libraries of the Australian Capital Territory*, 2 vols. (Canberra, 1966), ed. W.J. Cameron and Diana J. Carroll and its 1970 and 1980 supplements represent the commitment the National Library of Australia made in happier times to bibliographical and other investigations into eighteenth-century civilization. The interest of the Alexander Turnbull Library in an earlier period found clear expression in Kathleen Coleridge's *A Descriptive Catalogue of the Milton Collection in the Alexander Turnbull Library* (Wellington, 1980).

The impression could easily be given that all the energies of bibliographers in both countries have gone into tasks of an essentially enumerative character. That a special priority has been given to this side of the subject is undeniable. It springs in part from the sense of isolation and deprivation felt by specialists in European studies cut off from the great libraries of the northern hemisphere. Exact inventories of holdings became necessary if only to assess what scholarly work could continue to be done. It is not by chance that private attempts to provide union catalogues of such material were begun in the late 1950s and early 1960s precisely when universities were beginning to expand and bibliography was assuming a new place in the curriculum. W.J. Cameron had already participated in New Zealand efforts to list local Wing and *STC* items when he published *A Short-Title Catalogue of Books Printed in Britain and British Books Printed Abroad 1641–1700 held in Australian Libraries* (Sydney, 1962). Later in the same decade came John Fletcher's *Short-Title Catalogue of German Imprints in Australia from 1501–1800* (Melbourne, 1970) and K.V. Sinclair's *Descriptive Catalogue of Medieval and Renaissance Western Manuscripts in Australia* (Sydney, 1969). Given the extent of interest in these undertakings it was natural that, when Australians and New Zealanders decided to contribute to *ESTC* at the end of 1977, they would do so in the framework of the Australian and New Zealand Early Imprints Project (ANZEIP) and try to catalogue all their pre-1801 imprints. Although an impressive corpus has already been assembled and partly published, access to research funding has become much more difficult and the project is now moving very slowly. In so far as the bibliographical community is vitally concerned to see a successful outcome, this is a matter for considerable disquiet.

Until quite recently critical editing in both countries – on a range of authors from the sixteenth century to D.H. Lawrence – proceeded in an individual and unconcerted way. Recognition by literary students that many standard texts by local authors are available only in hopelessly corrupt commercial reprints (see H.H.R. Love, 'Report of the BSANZ Subcommittee on Standards for the Editing of Australian and New Zealand Literature', *BSANZB*, 8 (1984): 1–21) has hastened cooperation and stimulated discussion of editorial theory. The 'Colonial Texts Series' launched by the English Department, University College, Australian Defence Forces Academy, with Elizabeth Morrison's edition of Ada Cambridge's *A Woman's Friendship* appearing in 1988, and the same Department's conference in 1989 (see Paul Eggert, ed., *Editing in Australia*, Canberra, 1990) have focused attention on practical and methodological questions. Active support from the Australian Academy of the Humanities promises new editions of canonical texts over the next few years. Quite suddenly lively debate and active research have emerged from silence and sloth.

The editorial imperative has strengthened interest in the ways texts have been printed and distributed in Australia and New Zealand. Local bibliographers and historians did not wait for the launching of Anglo-American projects in the 1980s, but, taking their cue directly from the French school, embarked much earlier on enquiries that are slowly coming to fruition. Publishing history is being studied from the archives left by Angus & Robertson in Sydney and Lothian in Melbourne. Conferences on library history have moved from a sterile administrative approach to wider social and cultural problems. Mechanics' institutes, commercial lending libraries, the auction market in the nineteenth century, retail customer records of the 1830s and 1840s, colonial editions, speculative consignments, the serialization of fiction in Australian newspapers, advertising practices, oral-history interviews of early-twentieth-century readers, advances in literacy, these are some of the topics now being explored. General historians, long inclined to dismiss the whole area rather cavalierly, have begun to take note. A forthcoming number of *Australian Cultural History* on 'The Australian Reader' is the promise of a secure place for *l'histoire du livre* in the study of the Antipodean past since European settlement.

When one moves from investigation of local phenomena to bibliography applied exclusively to the European experience, where then is the Australian or New Zealand accent? Some research has been able to exploit material held in the two countries, for example the work of Margaret Manion and Vera Vines on illuminated manuscripts and even the studies made by Brian McMullin and his pupils on compositorial practices. Special collections of eighteenth-century French prospectuses and booksellers' discount catalogues at Monash University have been an invitation to look at rather neglected aspects of the Paris trade and to ignore some current fashions. Similarly the concentration of several travel accounts and imaginary voyages in libraries in Canberra, Sydney, Melbourne, and Wellington offers an almost unique opportunity for exhaustive analyses. This is a certain pragmatism in action: the topics are undoubtedly significant and they can be followed up on the spot. The fact that C.J. Mitchell is also based in Melbourne and can draw on his work on the *ESTC* corpus is an accidental bonus for his colleagues looking at the habits of compositors. An effect of critical mass thus created is an obvious stimulus to perceptive research. On the margin one has to strive harder and one learns to be opportunistic.

How does one explain other preoccupations? Some sort of chance that determined that Antipodean graduate students in Britain would be put to work on subjects or archives that led to recognition of the rôle of scribal publication in the seventeenth century or to radical scepticism about 'printers of the mind'? Can the achievements of W.J. Cameron, H.H.R. Love, D.F. McKenzie, and K.I.D. Maslen be linked as examples of a preparedness to doubt and to innovate that flourishes far from London and New York? Is this the sturdy resourcefulness of the bush, the talent for improvisation that could even show itself in the Cavendish Laboratory? Discounting national myth-making, one can still point to openness to the concerns and methods of historical scholarship at large. It is, of course, the direction that the discipline in general is learning to take.

Despite difficulties, for example, the slow and tentative emergence of printing historical societies in Sydney and Melbourne, bibliography in Australia and New

Zealand is not in an antiquarian backwater. Broad issues can be discussed in the *La Trobe Library Journal* and *The Turnbull Library Record*. Conferences and visits strengthen contacts with the northern hemisphere. Dialogue and participation are not impeded. Above all, essays like D.F. McKenzie's *Oral Culture, Literacy & Print in early New Zealand: The Treaty of Waitangi* (Wellington, 1985 – a reworking of the 1984 paper in *The Library*) demonstrate bibliographers challenging the assumptions of mainstream historians. One cannot ask more of a living science.

Further reading

Borchardt, Dietrich and Wallace Kirsop (eds). *The Book in Australia: Essays towards a Cultural & Social History*. Melbourne, 1988

Eggert, Paul (ed.). *Editing in Australia*. English Department, University College, ADFA, Canberra, 1990

Elliott, V.G. 'Early Printed Books in New Zealand: Some Thoughts on the Origins of Institutional Collections', *BSANZB*, 6 (1982): 175–84

Kirsop, Wallace, *Towards a History of the Australian Book Trade*. Sydney, 1969

'The Book Trade: Conservative Force or Agent of Change?', *Australian Cultural History*, 2 (1982/3): 90–103

Love, H.H.R. 'Report of the BSANZ Subcommittee on Standards for the Editing of Australian and New Zealand Literature', *BSANZB*, 8 (1984): 1–21

McLaren-Turner, Patricia (ed.). *Australian and New Zealand Studies. Papers Presented at a Colloquium at the British Library 7–9 February 1984*. British Library, 1985

McMullin, B.J. 'The Australia and New Zealand Early Imprints Project: The Background', *BSANZB*, 6 (1982): 163–73

McMullin, B.J. 'The Eighteenth-Century *STC* in the Australian Context', *Library Association of Australia: Proceedings of the 19th Biennial Conference held in Tasmania, August 1977: Libraries in Society*. Hobart, 1977, 231–43

Maslen, K.I.D. 'The State of Bibliography in New Zealand', *BSANZB*, 8 (1984): 141–6

Mills, Trevor. *Rare Books Collections in Australian Libraries: An Annotated Bibliography*. BSANZ, Melbourne, 1985

Developments in editing biblical texts

SEBASTIAN P. BROCK

At the conclusion of his masterly little volume *Textkritik* (Leipzig, 1927), where he provided the guiding rules for dealing with classical texts possessing purely 'vertical' or 'closed' textual traditions, Paul Maas made the laconic final remark 'Gegen die Kontamination ist noch kein Kraut gewachsen' ('no specific has yet been discovered against contamination'). In a review, whose second edition was to end up in a book of 525 pages in 1952, Giorgio Pasquali took up this Parthian shot and demonstrated the unfortunate fact that closed traditions are extremely rare, and that in reality matters are normally far more untidy – and complicated.[1] In his ample illustrations Pasquali barely touches on biblical texts, though it is here, above all, that 'contamination' (or cross-fertilization, to give it a less pejorative term) is endemic. Karl Lachmann, whose 'method' (set out with such admirable concision by Maas) was developed in connection with Lucretius, was in fact well aware that a different approach was needed when dealing with open traditions, demonstrating this with his own edition of the Greek New Testament (1831), which has the distinction of being the first edition to make a radical break with the sixteenth-century textus receptus, based on late manuscripts.

A sixteenth-century textus receptus, usually based on late and sometimes corrupt manuscripts, has been the parent against which editors of biblical texts, of the Old as well as of the New Testament, and in a variety of different languages, have needed to react. It so happens that the standard academic editions of the Hebrew Old Testament (*Biblia Hebraica Stuttgartensia*, 1977) and the Greek New Testament (Nestle–Aland edn 26, 1979), end up by using radically different procedures, the former printing the text of a single early complete manuscript (Leningrad B 19A of AD 1008), whereas the latter provides an eclectic text based largely on the early uncials Vaticanus and Sinaiticus. Just as no serious editor of the Greek New Testament is today likely to print the text of a single early Greek manuscript for general use, so no editor or the Hebrew Bible is likely to produce an eclectic text. Why should these two quite different editorial practices be found side by side, especially as they are both the end result of a

---

1 G. Pasquali, *Storia della tradizione e critica del testo* (Florence, 1952). See further, E.J. Kenney, *The Classical Text. Aspects of Editing in the Age of the Printed Book* (Berkeley, 1974), ch. 6.

reaction against a sixteenth-century textus receptus with very similar characteristics? Furthermore, is this state of affairs to be welcomed?

A response to the second question will be delayed until later, but the answer to the first lies largely in the different natures of the two textual traditions: though both are open traditions, where 'contamination' has taken place on a large scale, each in fact has to be handled in a different way. The same also applies to other ancient biblical textual traditions such as the Greek Septuagint, the Syriac Peshitta, the Old Latin, and the Aramaic Targum, all with their own subsequent histories of revision. The determining factor for the way in which an editor of a biblical text proceeds will be the nature of the textual evidence available to him; in what follows we shall see something of the variety of different problems that arise, and the varying ways in which modern editors have tried to handle them.

For the Greek New Testament one could almost speak of an *embarras de richesses.* Here we have over 3,000 manuscripts, mostly ranging in date from the fifth to the sixteenth century and consisting of some 90-odd papyri (all fragmentary, but some belonging to the fourth, third, and even, in at least one case, second century), over 270 uncials and 2,700 minuscules. Besides all this there are important early versions and citations in Church Fathers. Clearly no edition can take account of all of this material, and even the most comprehensive can only cite a selection.[2]

At the middle of this century the standard academic editions fell into two groups on confessional lines: among the Reformation churches the influence of Westcott and Hort's text of 1881, based primarily on the so-called 'Neutral' text of Vaticanus and Sinaiticus, lived on above all in the editions by E. Nestle (based, since the third edition of 1901, on the majority agreement of the trio of earlier editors, Westcott and Hort, Tischendorf, and Weiss), while on the Catholic side, in part reaction, were the editions of Vogels, Merx, and Bover, all of which make their eclectic choice of readings from a wider range of witnesses, including the 'Western' and 'Antiochene' (or 'Byzantine') witnesses. The twenty-sixth edition of Nestle–Aland (1979) abandoned Nestle's convenient but timid rule of thumb, but retained a heavy reliance on the two great uncials, claiming not only that this text could now be shown to represent the text of *c.* AD 200 (thanks to the discovery of Bodmer XIV (P 75), dated to *c.* 175/225, with a text very similar to that of Vaticanus), but that this text, the oldest attainable, is furthermore likely to be virtually identical with that of the authors' autographs. Both claims, as will be seen, are open to challenge, and so it is unfortunate that the ecumenical edition produced by the United Bible Societies (ed. 1, 1966) has, over the years, become virtually identical in text with the self-proclaimed 'Standard Text' of Nestle–Aland 26 (above all from UBS edn 3, 1975, onwards).

---

2 Much effort has been expended on ways of classifying and selecting manuscripts; see F. Wisse, *The Profile Method for the Classification and Evaluation of Manuscript Evidence as Applied to the Continuous Greek Text of the Gospel of Luke* (Studies and Documents 44, Grand Rapids, MI, 1982).

By no means all NT textual critics agree with the editorial approach of K. Aland and the Münster Institut für neutestamentliche Textforschung, with its cursory dismissal or 'Western' and 'Antiochene' witnesses where they go against the Alexandrine text. In Britain, G.D. Kilpatrick, J.N. Birdsall, and J.K. Elliott, in particular, have argued cogently for a much wider basis for making editorial choices, recognizing that it is in fact most unlikely that all original readings should be confined to one particular textual grouping: each variant reading needs to be examined on its own intrinsic merits, and not prejudged by the colour of the witness which contains it. An excellent model for this sort of carefully reasoned approach was significantly provided by a classical scholar, G. Zuntz, in his Schweich Lectures, *The Text of the Epistles* (1953). As with archaic forms in languages, so with texts an archaic reading can end up preserved in some witness that is marginal to the mainstream of tradition. It is a matter of sadness that Kilpatrick did not live to produce his promised edition of the New Testament, based on the eclectic principles he had consistently advocated.

What is basically at stake here is a different weighting given to the various criteria by which an editor makes a judgement: do external factors (such as the age or perceived quality of a witness) or internal ones (such as intrinsic probability, conformity with the author's language and style) predominate in the editor's mind? An editor who neglects one set of criteria at the expense of another is courting trouble, and the two need always to be held in delicate balance. Thus the editor's reasoning needs to follow a spiral process, with each set of criteria illuminating the other: a reading which commends itself on internal grounds as original will lead to a judgement about the witness(es) that contain it, and then this judgement will in turn be helpful in assessing between variants where no clear guidance is given by the various internal criteria available.

The panel of New Testament scholars who produced the New English Bible (1961) commendably did not restrict their vision to the text presented in Nestle–Aland, and their underlying eclectic text was subsequently reconstructed for publication by R.V.G. Tasker (1964); the fact that this edition has not perhaps received the attention it merits is probably due to the absence of any apparatus.

A particularly interesting example of a more open approach is found in M-E. Boismard and A. Lamouille's *Le Texte occidental des Actes des Apôtres: réconstruction et réhabilitation* (Paris, 1984). As is well known, the Western text of Acts is often very different from that of the rest of the tradition; Boismard and Lamouille elucidate this state of affairs (to which a variety of explanations has been given) by claiming that both texts are authentically Lukan (in this they follow Blass's theory of two editions); consequently they edit the text in two columns, one with the form preserved in Western witnesses, the other with that in Alexandrine ones (once again, the possibility that original readings may on occasion be preserved only in Antiochene witnesses is evidently excluded).

An edition may sometimes deliberately print a text which has no claims (or likelihood) to be the original: such is the case with the two-volume edition of

Luke produced by the British and American Committees of the International Greek New Testament Project (1984, 1987), where the focus of attention is the very extensive apparatus. Here, in order to let the earlier witnesses, and especially the earlier versions, stand out in the apparatus, the printed text against which collations were made is the textus receptus. Such an edition aims primarily at providing a wide range of materials upon which future editors of critical editions can base themselves.

Two further recent editions deserve mention, since they illustrate the variety of editorial practice. K. Junack, W. Grünewald, E. Güting, U. Nimtz, and K. Witte, *Das Neue Testament auf Papyrus* (vol I, 1986; vol. II.1, 1989) is a product of the Münster Institut, and it usefully prints in synoptic fashion the extant text of witnesses to the New Testament on papyrus (it needs of course to be remembered that, though many papyri are old, papyri *per se* are by no means more important witnesses than fragments on vellum, often contemporary in date). The Greek New Testament according to the Majority Text edited by Hodges and Farstad (1982), by contrast prints the text to be found in the bulk of Byzantine manuscripts (of which the Textus Receptus was a later and more developed form); although it would be easy to dismiss this edition, whose text is constructed on over-simple principles, merely as an attempt to lend respectability to the Greek text underlying the King James Version, it nevertheless can serve some useful purpose in that it conveniently provides the type of text with which Byzantine writers would have been familiar: with a text regarded as sacred, its state at different stages in its history can be of considerable significance, and so worthy of academic attention.

Nowhere is this last statement more true than in the case of the Hebrew Bible, where the 'Masoretic Text' (MT), as edited by Jewish scholars of the ninth and tenth centuries AD, has dominated virtually all editions of books of the Hebrew Bible. Partly this situation is due to the nature of the surviving materials: until the beginning of this century all surviving Hebrew biblical manuscripts (with the possible exception of the fragment of Deuteronomy known as the Nash papyrus) were of the ninth century or later; although the subsequent discovery of the Cairo Geniza provided some slightly earlier fragmentary manuscripts, there still remained a vast gap in time between the original texts and their earliest witnesses. Several nineteenth- and early twentieth-century scholars had laudably tried to overcome this problem by reconstructing the Hebrew texts underlying the earliest of the versions, the Greek Septuagint (the earliest books of which were translated in the third century BC), but misuse of this tool had led to a reaction in favour of the MT, heralded by Nyberg's commentary on Hosea (1935). With the discovery, in the Judaean Desert during the decade or so from 1948, of biblical and other manuscripts dating from roughly the second century BC to the second century AD, the situation became radically altered: it now became possible to see at first hand the kinds of Hebrew biblical texts which were circulating at the turn of the Christian era. What has emerged from the study of this material (not all of which, alas, has yet been published) is of supreme importance for our understanding of the transmission of the Hebrew Bible. Certain salient facts emerge: the earliest manuscripts exhibit a great variety of textual types; some of these are at considerable variance with the MT, often being instead closely related to the Hebrew text which can be presumed to underlie some of the books of the Septuagint (thus justifying the careful textual use of the Septuagint by nineteenth-century scholars like Wellhausen and Cornill); other manuscripts provide the form of the Pentateuch, slightly expanded in places, which happened also to be adopted by the Samaritan community (whose manuscripts are all medieval or later); yet others witness to a consonantal text very similar to that found in MT, thus providing clear evidence of the antiquity of that particular textual tradition. When one turns to the early second-century manuscripts the situation has changed: only one text type is represented, that behind the MT. Clearly, with the reconstruction of Judaism after the fall of Jerusalem in AD 70 and the destruction of the Second Temple, a single normative text tradition was propagated. How this text (whose quality differs in different books) was chosen is unclear: one tradition actually states that a criterion analogous to that adopted by Nestle in his third edition onwards was adopted!

Unfortunately none of these biblical manuscripts from the Judaean Desert is anything like complete, even for a single book, and so, despite the newly gained realization (some would say, confirmation) that the Masoretic textual tradition is but one among several that were once in existence, for practical purposes editions of the Hebrew Bible can hardly avoid continuing to be based on early medieval Masoretic manuscripts. Owing primarily to the nature of the work of the Masoretes (concerned with vocalization, reading accents, and marginalia), the standard academic edition of the Hebrew Bible, the *Biblia Hebraica Stuttgartensia* (BHS), is based on a single Masoretic manuscript, even to the extent of reproducing its idiosyncrasies. In this respect *BHS* carries to a logical conclusion the principles already adopted by R. Kittel in the third edition of the *Biblia Hebraica* (*BH*3; 1937), where he had initiated the policy of basing his text on that of a single manuscript.

Another modern academic edition, by N.H. Snaith (1958) is likewise based on a single manuscript considered authoritative. (Photographic editions of the Cairo and Aleppo codices have also been produced.)

In view of this policy of printing the text of a single manuscript, the role of the apparatus takes on all the greater importance. BH3 offered its readers a double apparatus, the first with the more significant variants of Geniza and other medieval manuscripts and of the ancient versions, the second with the less significant; the first apparatus not only includes directives to the reader '*l(ege) c(um)*', but also a selection of modern conjectures. *BHS* distinguishes itself from its predecessor by having only a single (and shorter) apparatus, and by being less adventurous in its directives to the reader. Both editions are open to serious criticism in their selection of material in the apparatus, and far more satisfactory (as well as far more ambitious) is the Hebrew University Bible Project's edition of Isaiah, edited by M.H. Goshen-Gottstein, still in progress (Sample edition, 1965; ch. 1–22, 1975; ch.22–44, 1981; ch.45–66, in preparation). The text (with its

Masora) is based solely on the Aleppo codex (thought to be the very manuscript whose text was approved by Maimonides). The apparatus, which usually takes up about half the page, is divided into five sections: (1) the evidence for any variants presupposed by the ancient versions, given consistently in full (and not in the highly selective fashion of *BH*3 and *BHS*); succinct interpretative comments are provided in the fifth section; (2) variants in the fragmentary manuscripts from the Judaean Desert (there are two important scrolls from Isaiah), and quotations in Rabbinic literature; (3) variants in medieval Hebrew biblical manuscripts; (4) Masoretic minutiae; and (5) notes.

The Hebrew University Bible Project's edition provides the scholar with virtually all the information he needs if he wishes to reconstruct an earlier form of the biblical text than the Aleppo codex, which it reproduces. Though no scholar has yet tried to produce such an edition of the Hebrew Bible, it is worth asking what is possible and practicable. (An interesting edition with a reconstructed Hebrew text of a single book, Hosea, has recently been published by P. Borbone (1990).) One obvious possibility is to follow the model of *Das Neue Testament auf Papyrus*, and provide an edition of a biblical book in the form of a synoptic presentation of the available fragments from the Judaean Desert. More interesting, but more difficult, would be to provide an eclectic edition which aimed at recovering a particular stage in the history of the transmission of the text. The possibilities here were set out (with the translator, rather than editor, in mind) by Dominique Barthélemy in vol. 1 of his *Critique textuelle de l'Ancien Testament* (Fribourg/Göttingen 1982): what might be thought the most obvious choice, possessing what Barthélemy calls 'literary authenticity', that is, a form of text as close as possible to that of the original authors, is rejected as being a desideratum whose attainment would be far too hypothetical to make it a practicable choice (some valuable attempts with archaic poems have, however, been made, using methods pioneered by W.F. Albright and his followers). A goal more attainable, given skill and good judgement, would be a form of text current shortly before the time of our earliest witness to the Hebrew biblical text, namely the Greek translation. This would clearly be a very worthwhile undertaking in the case of, for example, Jeremiah, where the Hebrew text underlying the Septuagint had a shorter text than MT and a different order of chapters (a text form also attested in a small Hebrew fragment from Qumran); some experiments along these lines have already been attempted. A much easier task, also worthwhile, would be to provide an edition of an early form of what was to become, after the process of standardization, the normative consonantal text; such an edition would provide an approximation of the Hebrew text current at the time when Judaism and Christianity parted ways; as such, the text would have the status of what Barthélemy terms 'scriptural authenticity', being a text regarded as authentic by a religious community at a particular time.

The textual tradition of each of the early versions offers its own individual set of problems. Here there is only space to consider the most important of these, the Septuagint (LXX). As with the Greek New Testament, the manuscript material is abundant, with more or less complete texts already in the great fourth and fifth century uncials, and a good number of fragmentary papyri, a few of which date from before the Christian era, and so must be of Jewish provenance; early translations into Latin, Coptic, Armenian, and other languages also serve as important witnesses. Variation between different witnesses can be very marked, especially in certain books. The textual tradition has been made all the more complex by the fact that revisions, based on the developing Hebrew text, have left their mark, none more pervasively than Origen's, incorporated (probably) into his monumental synoptic edition known as the Hexapla. The discovery in the Judaean Desert of some Greek fragments of the Twelve Prophets, and the brilliant interpretation of their significance by Barthélemy in his *Les Devanciers d'Aquila* (Leiden, 1963), has radically altered our understanding of the early history of the Greek Old Testament text, for it now becomes clear that revision of the LXX, on the basis of the proto-Masoretic text, goes back to pre-Christian times, and that the work of Aquila in the early second century AD represents, not a new translation, but the culmination of this process of 'correction'. Sorting out the 'sea' of variants (as it has been described) now becomes both more urgent and more complex.[3]

The two major editions of the Septuagint produced this century proceed on diametrically opposite editorial principles. The Cambridge edition, by A.E. Brooke and N. McLean (never completed: nine parts appeared from 1906–40), followed the example of H.B. Swete's hand-edition of 1887–1904 in printing the text of a single manuscript, Vaticanus. It so happens that the textual character of this manuscript differs considerably from book to book, and this inconvenient fact has landed several unwary users in trouble. The value of the Cambridge edition lies elsewhere, in its rich apparatus. So far the Cambridge edition has only been duplicated in a few books by its German counterpart, edited from Göttingen. This edition, too, follows the principles of an earlier hand-edition, by A. Rahlfs (1935); unlike Swete, Rahlfs aimed to reconstruct, as far as possible, the text as it left the various translators' hands. Rahlfs' edition, and the Göttingen *editio maior* (1931– ; twenty-one volumes to date [1992]),[4] are based on sound eclectic principles, and the extensive apparatus in the *editio maior* is a model of concision and clarity. In books where there are two distinct textual traditions, such as Daniel and Tobit, both text forms are given; Rahlfs in his hand-edition of 1935 did the same thing for Judges, a book not yet covered by the *editio maior*: here, however, with our greater knowledge today of the early development of the Septuagint text, it may eventually prove possible to attain to a single original text. Yet even in this generally admirable *editio maior* there are places where the editor has been swayed unduly by the external criteria of number and nature of the witnesses, when reason and internal criteria dictate a different solution: thus in his edition of Job, Ziegler anomalously prints the

---

3 A valuable survey of some of the theoretical problems of classifying open traditions of manuscripts is provided by M. Weitzman (a Hebraist who has done pioneering work in mapping relationships between manuscripts of the Syriac Psalter), 'The Analysis of Open Traditions', *SB*, 38 (1985): 84–120.
4 Edited by A. Rahlfs, J. Ziegler, R. Hanhart, J. Wevers, and W. Kappler.

original LXX interspersed with the supplements later inserted from Theodotion (the only witnesses to preserve what must have been the original state of affairs are the Coptic Sa'idic and the fragmentary Old Latin).

Since the Septuagint became, and remains, the official Old Testament text of the Greek Church, editions of particular stages in its history are of interest. Two excellent undertakings of this nature have appeared within the last few decades, the first covering the *Prophetologion*, or OT lectionary text (by C. Hoeg and G. Zuntz in the series *Lectionaria* of the *Monumenta Musicae Byzantinae*, Copenhagen, 1939–81), and the second (by N. Fernandez Marcos, Madrid, 1980– , in progress) editing the distinctive Antiochene (or Lucianic) text of the historical books, whose antiquity and value in certain parts of this corpus has been reevaluated in the light of Barthélemy's *Les Devanciers d'Aquila*.

With the Greek New Testament it is possible to reach back to *a* text (rather than '*the* text') current about AD 200; in the case of the Hebrew Bible the proto-Masoretic text can be taken back to the first century of the Christian era, with the added knowledge that before that date there was great textual variation and fluidity. It is generally recognized that in all textual traditions the greatest range of variation is likely to occur at the earliest period in the history of a text, and this is above all likely to be the case with a text which soon came to be regarded as sacred. This consideration, and the evidence of second-century witnesses like Justin Martyr, consequently make it improbable that the current 'standard text' of Nestle–Aland 26/UBS 3 is as close to the autographs as is often claimed. Here, as elsewhere in all other areas of biblical text editions, there is ample work still to be done.

Further reading

Aland, K. and B. Aland. *The Text of the New Testament* (tr. E.F. Rhodes). Grand Rapids, 1987

Elliott, J.K. *Essays and Studies in New Testament Textual Criticism* (*Estudios de Filologia Neotestamentaria*). Cordoba, 1990

Harl, M., G. Dorival, and O. Munnich. *La Bible grecque des Septante*. Paris, 1988

Kilpatrick, G.D. (ed. J.K. Elliott). *The Principles and Practice of New Testament Textual Criticism: Collected Essays* Leuven, 1990

Metzger, B.M. *The Text of the New Testament*, 3rd edn, Oxford, 1992

Tov, E. *The Textual Criticism of the Bible: An Introduction*. Jerusalem, 1989. (In Hebrew; English translation forthcoming, 1992)

Vaganay, L. and C.B. Amphoux, *An Introduction to New Testament Textual Criticism* (tr. J. Heimerdinger). Cambridge, 1991

Würthwein, E. *The Text of the Old Testament* (tr. E.F. Rhodes). London, 1979

Notes on theory and practice in editing texts

FREDSON BOWERS

The term 'definitive text' has been roundly criticized – and justly in many cases – as a concept impossible to formulate in practice. For my purposes there is no point in splitting hairs. Depending upon the document to be edited and the method adopted, the ideal is not always impossible to achieve; but we may agree that especially when multiple authority is involved, or a single text is faulty in some respects, two editors may legitimately differ about the treatment of details and possibly even of fundamentals. Hence to label each as a definitive text of a given work,[1] in any precise sense of the word, would certainly be an anomaly. The term 'definitive edition' is another matter, however. A definitive scholarly edition is created from various interlocking parts in which the text composes only one element even though it is the central one.[2] As a consequence, some consideration must be given to the kind of text proper to take its rightful place in a definitive edition.

An editor may choose from among several kinds of texts according to their purposes, mainly governed by the audience at which the editions are aimed. This paper must ignore such specialized forms as diplomatic transcripts, parallel texts, editions of medieval manuscripts, editions of letters, just as it must ignore modernized texts and popular reprints. Instead, it concentrates on what at the present day seems to be the general standard for presenting literature (in its

---

Fredson Bowers was ill when he submitted a very long version of this contribution. He asked the editor to produce a much shortened version. He approved a detailed description of the article as it now stands but he did not wish to see this revised and shortened version. He died before proofs could be sent to him. In undertaking this small service for Fredson, the editor has endeavoured to adhere strictly to what he took to be its author's wishes.

1 For a useful distinction of 'work' from 'text', see G. Thomas Tanselle, *A Rationale of Textual Criticism* (Philadelphia, 1989), pp. 14 ff. This constitutes a legitimate differentiation of two often carelessly used words. However, in all but the most formal writing, it may prove difficult to observe rigorously, and hence the present paper may be looser in its usage than is strictly desirable.

2 When economics present too great a problem for a full-fig edition complete with appendices, experiments have been made in publishing separately an apparatus and notes keyed to some available text. For an example, see M.J. Bruccoli, *Apparatus for F. Scott Fitzgerald's The Great Gatsby* (Columbia, SC, 1974). Such a shell may have its uses even though it is less than an ideal solution and it necessarily differs in form and content from the apparatus in learned editions, see Don L. Cook, 'Some Considerations in the Concept of Pre-Copy-Text', *TEXT* 4 (1988), 84–91.

broadest sense) in a form designed to gain more than transitory acceptance. At present this customarily takes the shape of a scholarly reading edition the format and characteristics of which are relatively well established. Perhaps the central criterion for such a reading edition is that its text is intended to serve two audiences – the scholarly and the generally informed non-professional public, in each case without essential compromise.

This service takes two forms. It is a fact of life not to be escaped by retreat to the scholarly cloister that the every-increasing cost of producing books requires the distribution of more copies than are ordinarily purchased by libraries and a few specialist scholars. Thus the central criterion for such a reading edition is that it must appeal to an expanded audience consisting not only of the scholarly (both general and specialist) but also the intelligent non-professional public. What constitutes a reading text, then, needs some description.

By definition the text must be constructed for easy and agreeable reading. With earlier literature, from the Renaissance well into the eighteenth century, purely formal elements in the printing, or inscription, offer problems to the untrained eye. The old long f takes experience before the reader becomes indifferent whether he is reading 'f' or 's'. The u–v and i–j conventions are also orthographic, not meaningful, and in turn they create problems for a reader not specifically trained in automatically assimilating these transpositions. At the least, the transfer of such conventions to present-day usage involves no loss of meaning in anything but an antiquarian sense and serves to remove a major roadblock to conventional apprehension. If necessary, a specialist can readily reconstruct the original forms.

Such orthographic adjustment is only the leading edge to the consideration of other non-meaningful or at least peripheral conventions of presentation. The general reader is comforted by an external uniformity that removes the need for constant shifting of gears that slows the reading. For instance, in the presentation of the Renaissance drama the expansion of speech-prefixes to a standard full form materially aids the rapid apprehension whereas the variable abbreviations of the originals, often dependent only on the compositor's justification of a line, cause some stumbling. The virtue of instant recognition furnished by typographical uniformity suggests that various early conventions be regularized, such as the use of italic for stage-directions with characters' names in roman, consistent italic for personal and place names within the roman text, uniform placement of stage-directions, agreed-on standards for speech-prefixes. Spacing to indicate linked part-lines forming a pentameter, generally attributed to Capell, is of important service to any reader, professional or general. Such externals or appendages of the dialogue text proper make more palatable the presentation and remove at least one barrier to apprehension of old-spelling dramatic texts.

Thoroughly modernized texts of older literature are a necessity for many purposes of instruction or of simplified enjoyment. They can scarcely be called unscholarly in content when, for example, their wording is identical with the most painstakingly reconstructed and authenticated scholarly text of the same work.[3] Nevertheless in various important respects they do wrench the presentation of a work out of its period and they introduce a different sensibility replacing something of independent value that goes well beyond simple nostalgia for the past. Without argument, therefore, I assume that the text contained in a definitive edition will be reproduced in what may be called its unmodernized 'accidentals', thus preserving the work's contemporary form in an important manner. Only one comment is needed in support of this position. By necessity, complete modernization of a text carries well beyond its spelling, which is only one of a complex of signs by which forms convey meaning. It is as impossible to conceive the practicality – let alone the utility – of an old-spelling text with fully modernized pointing, for example, as of a modernized-spelling text retaining the early rhetorical and sometimes sketchy system of punctuation. This contrast may readily be applied to the body of the other accidentals such as capitalization, word-division, italic emphasis, paragraphing, and the like.

Because of imperfections in the practices of printing-houses (and of authors and scribes), early literature edited for the present-day reader requires more emendation than works nearer to our own times. (For the moment I am thinking in terms of texts of single authority. The special problems of emendation in texts of multiple authority, whether early or late, will be described later.) Emendation is of two kinds. The first and least troublesome is that of the accidentals necessitated by the use of an unmodernized base-text: in early documents accidentals' changes are likely to be far more numerous than those necessitated by faults in the substantives – the words themselves. Emendation of accidentals is also less subject to the logic of rules governing substantive emendation. Editorial taste and a response to the assumed needs of the reader play a larger rôle in deciding what to retain and what to change.

Early syntax and its rhetorical pointing offer occasional ambiguities, but ordinarily no especial difficulties to the experienced scholar, although some thought may be required. On the other hand, the more general reader may feel syntactically at sea on occasion, puzzled by the various breaches in the conventions of modern sentence structure and its pointing to which he is accustomed. There is no getting around the fact that reading unmodernized early texts requires an act of adjustment until familiarity breeds content, but the difficulty may be eased by judicious editorial assistance. Less-experienced editors of Renaissance plays, however, are likely to over-react in favour of an innocent reader and to interfere more than is strictly necessary in strengthening punctuation and creating fresh sentences as when the original has a string of independent clauses not in series and separated only by commas or by a not always consistent gradation of commas, semicolons, and colons. Once a reader becomes accustomed to the running-together of clauses or phrases without signpost punctuation, an editor can preserve most of the original light comma pointing without sprinkling in too many intrusive though helpful semicolons or

---

3 For a useful analysis of 'authenticated' as applied to edited texts, see Peter L. Shillingsburg, *Scholarly Editing in the Computer Age: Theory and Practice* (Athens, GA, 1986), pp. 40 ff.

the stronger colon stop. Controlled strengthening of erratic punctuation (or none at all) is sometimes required, but less often than editors are inclined to assume.

More troublesome are the editorial compromises necessary in some texts which offer arbitrary conventions of pointing, such as an almost automatic caesural or line-ending comma in blank verse. Editors of unmodernized texts must of necessity aim at an audience equipped or prepared to venture on the necessary adjustments. But a cautious helping hand will straighten out occasional ambiguities caused by carelessness or early conventions without the sophistication of too many compromises in the direction of modernization. It is an essential rule, for example, that editorial emendation of pointing be made in terms of the original system, and as much as possible in terms of the compositor setting the passage. The Elizabethan systems found in the average dramatic quarto are usually viable in their own terms, even by early standards, with but minor editorial assistance of a kind for which even the original reader might have been grateful.

With the passage of years the nature of editorial treatment of accidentals alters. As we approach modern times, in the eighteenth century and certainly in the nineteenth, the unknotting of tangles is likely to dissolve into the repair of slips. Once general uniformity of styling becomes the norm, emendatory emphasis may shift towards promotion of this uniformity. We enter here an area where conservative and more radical opinions clash as to the propriety of interfering with the general accidentals of a chosen later text. It is true that no uniformity of spelling could have been expected of an Elizabethan author or printing-house nor should it be editorially imposed except on the most convincing evidence of positive error. It is also true that modern authors are not always uniform in their generally adopted spelling system, but it must be emphasized that such variation is usually not by choice and therefore meaningfully to be preserved. More by instinct than by volition, perhaps, some modern authors violate standard rules of syntax, pointing, and other non-verbal transmitters of meaning. That an editor has every justification to correct misspelling, and possibly egregious faulty grammar (this last with record) but little to reorganize authorial syntax should go without saying. What I have in mind is the occasional lack of uniformity in externals that is partly authorial but, as often, may result from compositor or copyreader, or the imposition of house-style not always in a consistent manner and especially when by accident a compositor lets slip through his net some idiosyncratic authorial characteristic that he was intent to iron out. For example, William James spelled with the *-our* ending only 'colour' and ordinarily 'honour'; otherwise he used the American *-or* that was taking over in his day. As to be expected in what was a time of transition, some old-fashioned compositors not only passed his *colour* and *honour* but grafted onto him an assortment – not always consistent – of other *-our* spellings that would never have been present in his manuscript. Some compositors regularly spelled *-or* but would occasionally let slip in an *honour* or *colour* from the manuscript. As a result it is unusual to find an extensive text of

William James that is thoroughly consistent either in his own practices or in the styling of the compositor. Interestingly, James had a special idiosyncracy of spelling national adjectives with minuscules like *french, greek, latin*. Once in a while a compositor would let such a form through his vigilance, showing clearly what the custom had been in the manuscript printer's copy.

Conservative editors may feel that there is no harm in reproducing an inconsistent mixture of modern compositorial and authorial spellings when house-style has faltered. But in an age that strives for consistency (and expects it as an aid to rapid reading) variation in styling is a blemish not necessarily the fault of the author; and the results can be distracting as when the five compositors who set Nathaniel Hawthorne's *Fanshawe* imposed five different styles or degrees of permissiveness on his spelling and punctuation, ranging even to the variant styling of the epigraphs heading each chapter. No argument for authority – except of the limited documentary authority – can apply to such diversity within an individual text. As a consequence it is possible to recommend the higher authority of the author's own style that in at least some specific respects can be reconstructed over that of whatever compositor happened to be setting some portion of his text. Thus it is possible within certain definite and rigid laws of evidence to regularize to the established authorial system such internal diversity of accidentals as the two distinct spelling systems found in remnants within William James's texts, this as a normal part of the attention to accidentals that an emending editor of a modern text may apply.[4]

However, the main emphasis on emendation must fall on the editorial treatment of substantives, the words themselves, and not merely their texture. When only a single authoritative text has been preserved, the normal truisms about emendation still hold good. Error should be close to demonstrable before alterations can be accepted. Emendation should be governed by a scrupulous reconstruction of the intended meaning within context assisted by whatever technical suggestions can be hazarded from assumed palaeographical evidence, or the study of compositorial characteristics centred when possible on the identified workman setting the passage in question.[5] Evangelistic enthusiasm should be avoided but over-conservatism may be an equally serious, and more common, fault. In a single-authority text, all an editor can do with substantives is to correct what he regards as errors. He must not revise, a process reserved for authors. Of course, just what constitutes revision as distinct from corrections

4 For the distinction between regularization and normalization, and the suggested rules of evidence in present-day texts, see Bowers, 'Regularization and Normalization in Modern Critical Texts', *SB*, 42 (1989): 79–102. Suggestions for regularization in earlier texts may be found in Bowers, 'Readability and Regularization in Old-Spelling Texts of Shakespeare', *Huntington Library Quarterly*, 50 (1987): 199–227.

5 In Hawthorne's *House of the Seven Gables* (centenary edition, Ohio State University Press, 1965, p. 90), the first-edition commonplace 'barnyard fowl' was the more easily assigned as a sophistication of the idiomatic MS. 'barndoor fowl' because the phrase was set by Compositor Jackman, who statistically in this document was four times more likely to err in his setting than the best of the five compositors who worked on the book.

may be arguable. For example, editors of F. Scott Fitzgerald's *Great Gatsby* customarily alter Gatsby's sitting on the *dashboard* of his auto to *running-board* but their interference is revision not correction, since in an open car it is quite possible to turn around and sit on the dashboard. More troublesome is his description of a clam-digger and a salmon-fisher in Lake Superior, since the Lake has neither clams nor salmon, although locally mussels are known as clams and steelhead trout as salmon. That Fitzgerald knew these niceties is moot since elsewhere he shows his ignorance of Lake Superior by giving it tides when it is, in fact, tideless. Moreover it is not a fictive name but evidently a factual error to place a *Little Girl Bay* in Lake Superior instead of the actual *Little Girls Point*. Chicago's Union Station is not *Union Street station* as in the novel. To go to Central Park from West 158th Street in New York City one heads southward and not *eastward*. A problem comes in Fitzgerald's ignorant error *transept* altered in proof by his editor to *transit*, which Fitzgerald accepted although confessing that he had meant *compass*. My own view is that Fitzgerald's numerous mistakes should be corrected (although there is nothing one can do about the clam-digger and salmon-fisher), despite the conservative argument that such errors should be retained and the text not tinkered with. To some extent we come here to a clash of documentary authority against what may be denoted, not very precisely, as authorial intention. Fitzgerald's various errors of fact such as names, places, and even the chronology of events in his narrative (this latter usually owing to not thoroughly worked-over revision) were not deliberate but partly careless and partly ignorant. When damning lists of factual errors appeared in the reviews of his first novel, *This Side of Paradise*, he was appalled and did everything he could to see that they were corrected in later printings, even though some escaped his instructions and others went undetected. The kinds of errors he made, and his firm intention to correct them when they were pointed out to him may well encourage an editor to assist. Such editorial cleaning-up should not be confused with the revision of what was already correct and suitable in the manner of the more imaginative of the eighteenth-century editors of Shakespeare. Correction can be applied as the proper term for the alteration of any unwilled error. William James corrected himself in the second printing of *Principles of Psychology* when he recognized that in 'Goltz concluded from this that the hemispheres are the seat of intellectual power in frogs' (1.23.4), a vital 'not' had been inadvertently omitted after 'are', thus precisely reversing the intended meaning. If James failed to notice the error, an alert editor should have caught it on the evidence of context (and reference), without being accused of revision.

It would be easy to assert that only an author can revise himself, but such a sweeping statement causes more difficulties than not when applied to an editor creating an eclectic text. Narrowly focused, any editorial interference with the documentary evidence of the base- or control- or copy-text – even an easy correction – starts the process of eclecticism in that it intermingles two authorities. In elementary cases of single texts the authority of the editorial rational analysis of error is grafted onto the documentary authority holding the assumed error. Each authority, one may assert, has its special validity, although that of the editorial analysis is the more shifting. The aesthetic[6] or bibliographical considerations are of another kind from the monolithic evidence of the document; hence the editorial interpretation of evidence may not be equally weighed by all editors and uniform results may not be expected except in the simplest of cases. No two editors (arrant copying aside) are likely to construct an identical text for any single-text Shakespearian play.

Except for such corrupt texts as are often found in the Elizabethan drama, serious problems in the texts of single authority do not ordinarily arise that match those in texts of multiple authority; nevertheless, degrees of what can be legitimately called editorial correction can still reflect various editorial opinions. If we take as an example William James's short essay, 'Human Immortality', an editor could be content with an exact diplomatic reprint since it contains no substantive errors needing correction. But an eclectically minded editor intent on removing not authorial error but (in so far as evidence permits) printer's unauthorized styling, could determine that an anomaly exists in the variant spelling of 'pre-exist' (James's own form) and 'preëxist' (the printer's) and in a modest way he could regularize this to what he knew would have been the authorial spelling in the holograph printer's copy, thus restoring even in small part some documentary authority from the lost manuscript to replace the printer's known departure from copy as evidenced by the variants. If he chose, a bolder editor could observe that, in Hawthorne's *Scarlet Letter*, the compositor(s) had styled the text according to a house system that arbitrarily spelled some words with the *-our* ending and others with *-or*. A conservative editor, and even a regularizing eclectic, would not touch these since they are completely consistent and thus offer no documentary evidence as to the system that prevailed in the lost holograph printer's copy. Nonetheless, a student of Hawthorne would recognize that at this period Hawthorne spelled with the American *-or* ending all but two words. With this information a devotedly eclectic editor – though sure to meet with critical opposition – might find it in his heart to normalize all but two *-our* forms in the copy-text first edition, the only authority, thus creating a text based not exclusively on the documentary authority of the first edition of *The Scarlet Letter* but in narrow application to these specific forms, on the documentary evidence of Hawthorne's manuscripts of the period with their invariable spelling characteristic.

Only with multiple authority can an editor attempt anything like a significant reconstruction of the lost underlying copy to a print. But the theory behind the examples for single authority suggest that an eclectically edited text can take some few steps to restore, as limited by the evidence, various of the accidental as well as substantive readings of the lost printer's copy. For single texts the

---

6 I use 'aesthetic' in Peter Shillingsburg's sense that 'an editorial concern for the "best" text is always an appeal to an aesthetic orientation toward forms' and that aesthetic editors rely on taste. For an interesting discussion of aesthetic, historical, and sociological orientation in editing, see his *Scholarly Editing in the Computer Age*, pp. 19 ff.

amount of emendation of this nature is limited and it grows increasingly limited as present-day documents are edited and the irregularities fade that need attention in older texts, especially if the editor has a strong documentary sense and is unwilling to regularize on what evidence is present or, more venture-somely, to normalize the few accidental features of a text that can be treated with confidence.

As a result, an editor cannot penetrate very far in back of a single-authority copy-text. Substantive emendation is at best limited and is 'aesthetic' in method even though guided when possible by linguistic, paleographical, and bibliographical suggestions. Correction is the desideratum. Manuscripts of single authority may offer more opportunity than prints, chiefly because they are more authoritative and are likely to exhibit traces of the history of textual transmission to their latest form. A special example – albeit an unusual one – comes in the John Fletcher play, *Sir John Van Olden Barnavelt*, known only in a scribal manuscript that may or may not have been used as a rough-and-ready prompt-book. Whatever its ultimate function, the manuscript reveals preparation for acting. In considerable detail, Ralph Crane's transcript of Fletcher's working papers was adjusted to the capacities of the company by the merging of various characters in order to concentrate the interest and reduce the number of actors required. Since the play was a political hot potato, the company ordered some self-censorship, principally of the satire on the clergy. However, some now lost state of the political dramatization must also have been altered, on the evidence of *cancellans* leaves of a different paper and ink. Here and there the company cut the text slightly. Then Sir George Buc censored the play vigorously, demanding a number of omissions and revisions. The company observed these instructions and, when necessary, had bridge passages written to fill in the gaps. Finally two large cuts in static scenes were made for purely theatrical reasons and the play was produced.

A scholar of the work's transmission will need to consult the Malone Society Reprint of this manuscript, but except for specialist use this can scarcely be called a reading edition. The editor of a reading text of this manuscript must make up his mind what are the needs of the audience he is addressing. If he reproduced the manuscript in its original entirety, restoring all theatrical trimming as well as censorship cuts and modifications, he will come as close as the evidence permits to the authorial working papers submitted to the company before preparation for the stage was begun. This would represent the maximum literary text. At the opposite pole would be a strict reproduction of the final form of the text as it was probably acted on the stage, this being a pure theatrical version that ignores the authorial originals altered by censorship and by the exigencies of staging.

Either choice is defensible but an eclectic approach might seem to offer a compromise adjusted for the general scholar of the drama as well as any interested reader. In this compromise an editor would restore all censored passages of any kind but at the same time he would observe such preparation for the stage as was purely theatrical, such as the reduction in the number of characters and the cutting of tedious speeches. The aim would be a reading text of the play as it would have been performed by the company had it had its own way without the external pressures of the censorship, Buc's or the company's own in anticipation of Buc. That is, as it had been originally planned in purely theatrical terms for acting. Omitted text would be provided in an appendix so that nothing would be lost of the fullest version in the authorial working-papers before theatrical shaping.

The possibilities for multiple authority vary so greatly that they are scarcely subject to rule or even to the generalization attempted above, let alone categorization. Multiple authority exists when more than one text of a work has been preserved that contains some authority not present in the other. An eclectic editor believes that the judicious merging of the two authorities will create a new text that represents the fullest extent of authorial intention better than that of either document. One is immediately cast loose from documentary editing as it is generally understood in that the editor is usually attempting, not to present the best form of a single text, but instead to reconstruct a lost document of generally superior authority to either of the preserved. There are exceptions, but this is the frequent situation. Critics who are uneasy about eclectic texts usually assert that the edited result is a form of the work's text that never existed. Some relatively scarce situations of this order may develop but ordinarily this is a misapprehension and one finds that an eclectic editor is in fact attempting to reconstruct some lost specific document.

A simple case will illustrate. The holograph printer's-copy manuscript of Hawthorne's *House of the Seven Gables* has been preserved. No copyreader or other publisher's functionary was involved in the production of the book: Hawthorne prepared the copy for the printer, read the proofs alone, and in all respects dealt directly with the Riverside Press without outside intervention of any sort from the publisher. Following the Gregian rationale of copy-text, we may agree that in respect to its accidentals of spelling, pointing, word-division, and the like, the manuscript has a generally superior authority over the first-edition print which was styled in the typesetting by five different compositors in several thousand respects. On the other hand, whenever Hawthorne made one of his comparatively scarce substantive proof-revisions in the copy, the revised reading – once identified – has a superior authority that an editor would wish to accept. If an editor were to adopt a single-text technique and reproduce an edition of the manuscript text he would omit the revised authorial readings to be found in the book. If he edited the book as his documentary text, he would be adopting a system of accidentals that in many respects is more compositorial than authorial, and in addition he would be reprinting as authoritative not only Hawthorne's proof-revised substantives but also some non-authorial verbal corruptions introduced by compositor(s). The Gregian eclectic theory, however, permits him to sift the book's substantive variants for authorial or non-authorial origin and to adopt what he regards as Hawthorne's revised wording in place of the manuscript's readings but set within the texture of the authorial accidentals of the manuscript. In effect, an editor is endeavouring to reconstruct what would have been the document had Hawthorne made a fair copy, revising slightly along the way, instead of having a few second thoughts when reading the proof.

The House of the Seven Gables exhibits a relatively common case of pre-publication authoritative documentation. Post-publication revision is also common, a classic case being Henry Fielding's *Tom Jones*. Here a second edition was set from the first but without authorial intervention. A third edition was also set from the first without Fielding's attention. However, for the fourth edition he annotated in some detail a copy of the third. The application of textual logic narrows the number of variant readings in the fourth edition for which an editor must decide the authority. (The second edition is a dead end and can be left out of all consideration.) The third edition being without authority, any reading in which the fourth follows the third as against the first is automatically to be rejected unless it marks a clear case of the correction of error. An editor is left only with the variants between the fourth and the first as those requiring his scrutiny to decide whether they represent transmissional mistakes or else Fielding's marginal annotations in the third edition. The first edition which alone has authority in its accidentals becomes the copy-text, and into its texture are inserted the variant substantives of the fourth edition deemed to be Fielding's alterations. Rejected are first-edition errors perpetuated in the third and fourth. It is true only in a limited sense that the resulting text represents a form that never existed. The recovery of authority is made in two steps. In the first, the substantively annotated copy of the third edition is reconstructed by the rejection of all readings not judged to be Fielding's annotations. It is assumed that Fielding did not materially, if at all, revise the accidentals of the third edition, and if he did they would be indistinguishable from ordinary compositorial smoothing.[7] That is, the ideal for the substantives would be to reconstruct the actual document that Fielding produced by annotation to serve as printer's copy for a third edition. But no one wants this edition's derived accidentals at a remove from the nearest authority of the first edition. Hence the second and necessary step is quite simple: an editor merely substitutes the first for the third edition, reproducing what the document would have been like if Fielding had annotated it instead of the third. Similarly, with *The House of the Seven Gables*, an editor attempts to retrieve for the substantives the revisions (as distinct from the corrections) that Hawthorne made in the proofs so that substantively a reconstruction as close as possible is made of what the actual corrected proof-sheets would have been like. Then, for the texture of the first edition, is simply substituted the purer accidentals of the manuscript with whatever

7 For the difficulty of distinguishing authorial revision of accidentals from compositorial variation and the consequent rejection of the texture of a revised edition as suitable for copy-text in early literature, see Bowers, 'Greg's Rationale of Copy-Text Revisited', *SB*, 31 (1978): 90–161, but also, and especially, the narrow case in 'Current Theories of Copy-Text, with an Illustration from Dryden', *MP*, 48 (1950): 12–20. On the other hand, unusual circumstances can cause an editor to give special authority to the accidentals of a revised edition. See, for example, the textual introduction to William James, *Pragmatism*, gen. ed. Frederick Burkhardt, textual ed. F. Bowers (Cambridge, MA, 1975).

correction is necessary. In either case a reconstruction of a physical document in the transmission is attempted and then this document is treated editorially as if it actually had been preserved in relation to the authoritative extant document selected as copy-text.

When syndicated publication results from the distribution of a set of lost proofs to serve as copy for the prints in different organs, statistical analysis of the variants in the multiple authorities can establish with high probability not only the exact substantive readings of the master proof (the closest one can get to the lost preceding manuscript) but also with relative exactness its actual accidentals, as can be observed in a number of Stephen Crane's syndicated pieces.[8] This reconstruction of a physical document can be applied not only to the usual syndication. The newspaper publication in serial form of Crane's novel, *The Third Violet*, enabled the editor to reconstruct in an earlier form, closer to the manuscript, a typescript that had not been drastically house-styled as was its mate used to set the book, thus providing information that could be used in bringing the book closer to Crane's original. Works simultaneously published in two countries can also offer evidence to reconstruct their common copy, as can be done for the typescript and its carbon used to set Crane's 'Price of the Harness' both in England and in the United States. In his 'Scotch Express', English proof-sheets were sent to the United States for magazine publication before they had been subjected to drastic editing. That earlier state assists in recovering some features of the lost manuscript, obscured by the English styling. In fact, this includes the original ending, omitted in England in favour of a large illustration.

Post-publication revision does not always require resetting and the production of a new edition. In later printings an author can correct and revise his text in minor ways by means of plate-alterations. William James actively corrected and revised his *Principles of Psychology* in as many as 164 readings between the second and the eleventh printings. Scribner attempted to correct in later printings the numerous gaffes that reviewers had noticed in Fitzgerald's *This Side of Paradise*. An interesting anomaly occurs in the printing history of Sinclair Lewis's *Babbitt* whereby the publisher corrected the plates of the first four printings but did not keep up to date so carefully a duplicate set of plates, so that, when these were sold to another house which continued publication of the novel, the text actually regressed. By bad luck, in wartime chaos, Knopf published in the collected authorized edition of Willa Cather's works the volume containing *Death Comes to the Archbishop* using as copy, not an edition she had revised, but instead the first and unrevised edition. These represent only the potential for eclectic editing of the usual first-printing first-edition text, since in each case the base-text can be moved up to the best-corrected printing. The edition (the typesetting) remains the same for the plates, except in the example of Cather's novel where the reset authorized text must be rejected in favour of a superior earlier revised edition.

A number of chronologically authoritative documents may intervene be-

---

8 A typical example is a despatch from Greece in 1897 entitled, 'An Impression of the "Concert"', with nine examples (*Reports of War*, Charlottesville, VA, 1971), pp. 411–20.

tween a preserved authorial manuscript and the final printed result without greatly complicating the eclectic editing of a text. For example, from F. Scott Fitzgerald's holograph of *Tender Is the Night*, itself considerably revised, was made a typescript which in turn was so heavily revised that a second typescript had to be made from it, this was then revised in such detail that a now lost typescript had to be prepared from which were set the proofs for the serial publication. Fitzgerald then took these galley proofs and prepared copy for the book by such a massive rewriting that pages of fresh typescript replaced some galleys. From this much-altered copy a fresh typescript would need to have been made to provide setting copy for the book, and on this copy the publisher imposed a final house-styling. The book proofs were not read by the author.

Since each stage in Fitzgerald's revision directly replaced its predecessor in a linear manner with fresh authority, an eclectic editor finds few substantive gleanings from the various stages of this transmission with which to alter the book text, which he is forced to make his base-text. The book is in so many respects removed from the manuscript that the Gregian theory of copy-text could not apply, it being quite impracticable to insert the finally worked-over readings in the marked-up serial galleys into the texture of the manuscript without an apparatus of emendation that might well dwarf the text itself. A conservative documentary-minded editor would thus be content to reprint the first-edition book text, corrected from the plates of later printings, and with necessary editorial alterations of Fitzgerald's mistakes in names and other details to produce a standard of correctness that would have resulted from better copyreading approved by the author. A more eclectically minded editor would be aware that the successive stylings of the type-scripts, the serial printer, and finally the publisher of the book (all passed by Fitzgerald, who was intent only on revising the substantives) had materially altered Fitzgerald's mostly acceptable light pointing system in his manuscript to a heavier, uncharacteristic, one and in the process had in some part suppressed certain idiosyncratic marks that Fitzgerald certainly associated with his shaping of meaning, such as his special use of the dash. Still using the book (or better, the final galley proofs) as base-text, this editor would abstract the documentary evidence of the transmission from the manuscript system in order to restore as much as possible the viable pointing of the manuscript as originally intended by Fitzgerald but altered beyond his control in the transmission. Such a text would combine the superior substantive authority of the last document that he revised with the superior authority of so much of the manuscript accidentals as could be utilized, the result being a text that on documentary evidence represents authorial intention in both respects in a manner superior to any given document in the chain. Actually, this is Greg in reverse but with substantially the same results.

The categories, and examples, of mixed authority making possible eclectic treatment to secure the highest authenticity are so varied as to defy fuller illustration here. Only two special situations may be briefly mentioned. The first involves censorship, whether self or externally imposed: this is as varied in its problems as are the occasions. Rightly or wrongly, the editor of Hawthorne's *Blithedale Romance* restored one passage referring to sexuality and two approving the drinking of liquor that had been deleted in the manuscript, it taking no active imagination to identify here the influence of Hawthorne's teetotal wife Sophia Peabody. More clearly, the editor of Fletcher's *Barnavelt* may be thought justified in restoring the company's own censorship of religious satire (and one highly charged sexual phrase) in anticipation of the official censor's disapproval, as well as restoring the passages of political and religious tenderness and one vividly sexual passage subsequently deleted by the censor. The censorship of D.H. Lawrence's novels that was imposed without his prior knowledge may readily require different treatment from the more difficult cases where he approved the alterations that would enable the book to gain the publisher's acceptance and even on occasion rewrote passages according to suggestions or demands. The respect given to, and indeed the true authority of a writer's approval of, external pressures ranging from such censorship to stylistic and structural recommendations from friends or publishers, even to the imposition of house-styling on copy, involves a question so variable and delicate in its manifestations as to receive no more than a mention here.[9]

Less common but still posing a problem to an eclectic (and to a document-arian) editor are the occasions when drafts or even relatively finished states are preserved in two or more authorial versions that are of essentially equal authority. In William James's *Some Problems of Philosophy* (interrupted by his death) a typescript and its carbon exist, each autograph revised in part by reference to the other but also in part quite independently and never cross-annotated. A documentary text would be absurd and an editor is surely justified in accepting the maximum number of revisions drawn from both copies, a problem arising only when the same word or sentence is revised in each of different ways.

A second example is more subject to temporality. D.H. Lawrence prepared setting copy for the English and American editions of his *Boy in the Bush* by revising by hand, simultaneously, a ribbon and a carbon copy of the typescript, at intervals transferring to the other document what he had altered in the first. However, he took as his master copy either ribbon or carbon typescript at random, so that each in part has his original layer of revision and in part what had been transferred. When he transferred these alterations he sometimes inadvertently overlooked some of the revised material; more complicating, he might in the process of transfer think of something different which he then inscribed without going back to alter the original. It takes some doing to sort out the exact order of revision and to identify the later readings as they occur now in one and now in the other typescript.

This example is highly interesting as editorial detective work that on physical evidence would select the later and more authoritative text from the two

---

9 The pressure to ensure publication may certainly be thought of as a form of self-censorship that would otherwise not have been imposed. Examples abound in Lawrence, who had good reason to feel the struggle to get his works into print. Fitzgerald accepted suspect moral advice in *This Side of Paradise*, which contains passages in the manuscript that should be restored.

documents without resorting to unsubstantiated critical opinion. Nevertheless, an eclectic editor finds that such opinion may be the only way to resolve some ultimate problems, but it should be the fairy wand and not the walking stick of eclectic editing. For instance, common experience shows that few if any authors can make a fair copy of their text without alteration. Some of the changes will be conscious improvements, for each act of transcription triggers fresh creative juices. On the other hand, certain changes will definitely be inadvertent. An editor may be faced with working to rule – that is, say, choosing the later reading as a matter of principle (or convenience). But he may choose on occasion to evaluate the causes or reasons behind the variants and to select one or other reading aesthetically, by critical analysis. Chronology need not be decisive in such a situation and not all unconscious changes need be for the better, one may suggest: it could be an open question which one an author would consciously choose if the discrepancy were pointed out to him. This problem is, of course, residual in many a Lawrence work.

No edition should be called 'definitive' on text alone. What distinguishes the edition is, of course, the apparatus that illuminates the text and provides the reader with every essential piece of evidence on which the text was founded, and – as a bonus – something of its subsequent history from the earliest documents to current editions. Customarily a scholarly edition of the kind sought contains a textual introduction (a critical one also, if desired), a list of the emendations made to the text (which may be divided between substantives and accidentals), an historical collation of substantive variants from the earliest to the latest of the original documents, carried forward if desired to show the subsequent history of the text in editions before the current one, a list of ambiguous word-divisions at line-endings both in the original and in the edited text, and – most important – when a manuscript is one of the authorities, a complete descriptive account of every change made in it during inscription or on revision. These being complete, the reader should have to hand as much information as that possessed by the editor as to the readings of the documents on which the edited text has been based.[10]

10 For apparatus suitable for early literature, particularly the dramatic, see *The Dramatic Works in the Beaumont and Fletcher Canon* published by CUP. The edition of Fielding's *Tom Jones*, ed. M.C. Battestin, published jointly by Wesleyan University Press and Clarendon (1975) could be useful for somewhat later non-dramatic works; and *The Works of William James*, Harvard University Press, for early-twentieth-century writing. F. Bowers, 'Notes on Editorial Apparatus', *Historical and Editorial Studies in Medieval and Early Modern English for Johan Gerritsen*, ed. Mary-Jo Arn and H. Wirtjes (Groningen, 1985): 147–62 may be consulted for an overall descriptive view of apparatus and its rationale; and his 'Transcription of Manuscripts: The Record of Variants', *SB*, 29 (1976): 212–64 offers a descriptive system for the recording of manuscript variants either within the text itself or in the form of notes. G. Thomas Tanselle, 'Some Principles for Editorial Apparatus', *SB*, 25 (1972): 41–88, and his 'Editorial Apparatus for Radiating Texts', *Lib*, v, 29 (1974): 330–7, should also be consulted; the first has been reprinted in his *Textual Criticism and Scholarly Editing* (Charlottesville, VA, 1990), 403–50. The Fletcher–Massinger play, *The Elder Brother*, may be taken as something of a paradigm of the problems and virtues of eclectic textual editing. For a full account, see *The Dramatic Works of Beaumont and Fletcher*, vol. VIII, 1991.

Analytical and textual bibliography in Germany and Italy

❖

JOHN L. FLOOD AND CONOR FAHY

The creators of 'analytical' or 'critical' bibliography were A.W. Pollard, R.B. McKerrow, and W.W. Greg, all of them leading lights in the Bibliographical Society. All three emphasized the importance of 'critical bibliography' for literary research, with Greg, in his seminal paper 'What is Bibliography?', read before the Society in 1912, going almost as far as to equate critical bibliography with textual criticism: 'Critical bibliography is the science of material transmission of literary texts, the investigation of the textual tradition as it is called, in so far as that investigation is possible without extraneous aids. It aims at the construction of a calculus for the determination of textual problems.' McKerrow too underlined the value of critical bibliography for literary research, first in 'Notes on Bibliographical Evidence for Literary Students and Editors of English Works of the Sixteenth and Seventeenth Centuries', in *Transactions of the Bibliographical Society*, 12 (1911–13), 211–318, and later in *An Introduction to Bibliography for Literary Students*, Oxford 1927. Greg later restated the case, in his classic formulation:

Bibliography is the study of books as tangible objects. It examines the materials of which they are made and the manner in which those materials are put together. It traces their place and mode of origin, and the subsequent adventures that have befallen them. It is not concerned with their contents in a literary sense, but it certainly is concerned with the signs and symbols they contain (apart from their significance) for the manner in which these marks are written or impressed is a very relevant bibliographical fact. And, starting from this fact, it is concerned with the relation of one book to another: the question which manuscript was copied from which, which individual copies of printed books are to be grouped together as forming an edition, and what is the relation of edition to edition. Bibliography, in short, deals with books as more or less organic assemblages of sheets of paper, or vellum, or whatever material they consist of, covered with certain conventional but not arbitrary signs, and with the relation of the signs in one book to those in another.[1]

Fredson Bowers took the matter further by distinguishing the 'pure' science of 'analytical bibliography' and its application to specific texts, 'textual bibliography': analytical bibliography he defines, in his article 'Bibliography' in the

---

1 'The Function of Bibliography', in W.W. Greg, *Collected Papers*, ed. J.C. Maxwell, (Oxford, 1966), p. 271. See also Greg's 'Bibliography – An Apologia', *Lib*, IV, 13 (1933): 113–43.

1961 edition of *Encyclopaedia Britannica*, as 'the technique of investigating books as tangible objects without regard for their contents', while 'textual bibliography is the backbone of textual criticism'.

It is a curious fact that while analytical bibliography has flourished in Britain and the United States, its methods have been slow to be adopted in continental Europe. This is especially strange in the case of Germany where there has long been a strong tradition of bibliographical research. Indeed, as early as 1823 Friedrich Adolf Ebert had drawn a distinction between 'pure' bibliography (by which he meant what we would call enumerative bibliography) and 'applied' bibliography, defining the latter in terms that anticipate the approach of the 'critical' bibliographers:

This applied bibliography is not merely a pleasant, admittedly occasionally even an idle pastime, it sometimes proves very useful. It leads to bibliographical criticism such as has been totally lacking hitherto, at least in Germany, and which is so urgently needed when one is faced with false dates or a lack of any date, false title pages, false imprints, editions falsely claiming to be new, and with errors in other bibliographical works which can only be detected and corrected in this way.[2]

Though there have been individual German scholars who may be seen to have made early contributions to analytical bibliography – one thinks of Gustav Milchsack, Otto Deneke, Gustav Bogeng, Karl Schorbach, and the incunabulists Georg Wolfgang Panzer, Ludwig Hain, Gottfried Zedler (whose work on the Mainz *Catholicon* has recently attracted renewed interest), and above all Konrad Haebler, as well as more recent scholars, among them Josef Benzing and Irmgard Bezzel, who have made major contributions to charting German printing in the sixteenth century – Martin Boghardt is probably right in believing that what impeded the healthy development of analytical bibliography in Germany was the lack of a unifying force such as the Bibliographical Society has represented in Britain.[3] As Boghardt puts it, 'the bibliophiles were too esoteric, the incunabulists were not disposed to go beyond the year 1500, and the textual critics confined themselves to particular major editions' (such as Karl Goedeke's Schiller edition, the Lessing edition by Lachmann and Muncker, and the Weimar edition of Goethe). The real strengths of German bibliographical scholarship have on the whole lain in other areas of study, notably the history of printing and the reception of literature.

A major stimulus for the development of analytical bibliography in the English-speaking world has of course been the problematic transmission of the works of the major dramatist, Shakespeare. The transmission of the writings of the German classics – who lived two centuries after Shakespeare – is generally

2 Translated from the article 'Bibliographie', in *Allgemeine Encyklopädie der Wissenschaften und Künste*, ed. J.S. Ersch and J.G. Gruber, part 10 (Leipzig, 1823), p. 48.
3 Martin Boghardt, *Analytische Druckforschung*, (Hamburg, 1977), p. 16. The influential role of the Society has also been recognized by Friedrich Adolf Schmidt-Künsemüller, 'Frühdruckforschung und Shakespeare-Philologie', in *Ars impressoria. Entstehung und Entwicklung des Buchdrucks*, ed. H. Limburg, H. Lohse, and W. Schmitz, (Munich, 1986), pp. 72–87.

perceived to be relatively unproblematic. Only comparatively recently have German editors begun to examine systematically the phenomenon of variants in different copies of the same edition, of crucial concern to analytical bibliographers. Nevertheless such variants were already observed decades ago. Thus Konrad Haebler remarked that, particularly in the study of the older incunabula, there were almost always passages to be found in which the setting did not correspond in all copies.[4] In some cases it was simply a matter of press corrections, in others there were significant alterations to the text. Even before Haebler, Gustav Milchsack, a former librarian at the Herzog August Bibliothek at Wolfenbüttel, an institution which today is very much at the centre of the study of the history of the book in Germany, had noticed that there were many so-called *Doppeldrucke* to be found amongst early editions of the German classics. By *Doppeldrucke* are meant editions in which, in whole or in part, a resetting of the original text can be identified.[5] This discovery was fruitfully pursued by Wilhelm Kurrelmeyer who published a number of studies concerned predominantly with Wieland, Goethe, and Schiller, examining the bibliographical features of particular works from the point of view of the *Doppeldruck* phenomenon.[6] Kurrelmeyer's findings proved productive later for Waltraud Hagen's comprehensive manual on the bibliography of the works of Goethe.[7] By the end of the 1920s this pioneering work of Milchsack and Kurrelmeyer had made such strides that G.A.E. Bogeng (he too was a librarian at Wolfenbüttel) was able to outline the nature of the phenomenon and to establish appropriate terminology.[8] It is worth noting that Bogeng also recognized the value of stereoscopy, the technique which underlies the Hinman Collator, for bibliographical studies.[9]

Yet, interestingly, all this important work seems to have gone virtually unnoticed by the broad stream of those involved in the editing of German texts, though Kurrelmeyer's work was rediscovered by American Germanists such as Edith Muriel Harn and Taylor Starck.[10] More recently, however, and – encouragingly – in Germany itself, much excellent work has been done on the bibliography of another major German writer of the eighteenth century, Friedrich Gottfried Klopstock. In 1960 Ludwig Sickmann published a first major study of Klopstock and his publishers Hemmerde and Bode,[11] and since then

4 Konrad Haebler, *Handbuch der Inkunabelkunde*, 2nd edn (Stuttgart, 1966), p. 132.
5 Gustav Milchsack, 'Doppeldrucke' in, G.M. *Gesammelte Aufsätze über Buchkunst und Buchdruck, Doppeldrucke, Faustbuch und Faustsage sowie über neue Handschriften von Tischreden Luthers und Dicta Melanchthonis* (Wolfenbüttel, 1922), cols. 281–302.
6 These are listed in the bibliography of Kurrelmeyer's writings, in, *Modern Language Notes*, 68 (1953): 291–9.   7 Waltraud Hagen, *Die Drucke von Goethes Werken* (Berlin, 1971).
8 G.A.E. Bogeng, *Einführung in die Bibliophilie* (Leipzig 1931), pp. 126ff. Reprinted in G.A.E. Bogeng, *Buchkundliche Arbeiten*, ed. Bernhard and Ursula Fabian, vol. III (Hildesheim, 1968).
9 Bogeng, in B. and U. Fabian *Buchkundliche Arbeiten*, pp. 138–40.
10 Edith Muriel Harn, 'Wieland Studies', *Modern Language Notes*, 68 (1953): 303–8; Taylor Starck, 'Goethean Doppeldrucke', *Modern Language Notes*, 68: 309–11.
11 Ludwig Sickmann, 'Klopstock und seine Verleger Hemmerde und Bode,' *Archiv für Geschichte des Buchwesens*, 3 (1960): 1,473–610.

Martin Boghardt in particular has done further important work on him, one major outcome of this work being the publication of an authoritative descriptive bibliography of contemporary editions of Klopstock's works as part of the new historical-critical edition of the author.[12] It is interesting and significant that the authors specifically acknowledge the assistance of Bernhard Fabian, Professor of English at Münster, who drew their attention to Anglo-American analytical bibliography. They add 'Let us not fail to mention that our work on Klopstock was begun in ignorance of this long-established direction in research and that Professor Fabian and some of his pupils were the first to bring about a change here [in Germany]' (vol. I, p. xix). Bernhard Fabian continues to play an important rôle as an apostle of analytical bibliography in Germany.[13]

The lessons that Boghardt learned and the insights he gained from his work on Klopstock were set down in his book *Analytische Druckforschung* (Hamburg, 1977), a truly invaluable guide to analytical bibliography with exemplification drawn from German material and demonstrating to the German scholarly community the very real advances in understanding which can be achieved through the application of such methods. Alas, the impact of this book seems as yet to have been slight and progress continues to be slow in the German-speaking countries. Even Ferdinand Geldner's invaluable handbook *Inkunabelkunde. Eine Einführung in die Welt des frühesten Buchdrucks* (Wiesbaden, 1978) unaccountably fails to mention analytical bibliography. A loose organization of persons concerned with the editing of German texts, the Arbeitsgemeinschaft für germanistische Edition, established at the University of Osnabrück in 1985, has so far published four issues of its important year-book *editio*, yet in none of these does analytical bibliography figure at all prominently.[14] This discouraging impression is reinforced by a glance at Horst Meyer's *Bibliographie der Buch- und Bibliotheksgeschichte (BBB)*. Meyer's bibliography is remarkable for its comprehensiveness and one must expect it to be especially complete in its coverage of German publications. Yet out of 205 entries under the heading 'Analytische und deskriptive Bibliographie' in vols. I (1981) to VIII (1988) only ten are German contributions. Boghardt's view that one reason for this is the lack in

12 *Die zeitgenössischen Drucke von Klopstocks Werken. Eine deskriptive Bibliographie*, by Christiane Boghardt, Martin Boghardt, and Rainer Schmidt. 2 vols. (Berlin and New York, 1981). See the review by John L. Flood, *Lib*, VI, 4 (1982): 450–3.
13 See for instance his paper, written jointly with Dieter Kranz, 'Interne Kollation. Eine Einführung in die maschinelle Textvergleichung', in Gunter Martens and Hans Zeller (eds.), *Texte und Varianten. Probleme ihrer Edition und Interpretation*, (Munich, 1971), pp. 385–400.
14 *editio. Internationales Jahrbuch für Editionswissenschaft*. Herausgegeben von Winfried Woesler. Tübingen: Niemeyer. vol. I– , 1987– . On some shortcomings of German editorial approaches and with some examples of the value of analytical bibliography as applied to German texts see John L. Flood, 'Schwarze Kunst – graue Theorie? Some Reflections on Textual Bibliography and German Literature', *London German Studies II*, ed. by J.P. Stern, (1983), pp. 18–30. One welcome sign of improvement has been the recognition by Stephen Füssel and Hans Joachim Kreutzer in their edition of the 1587 *Historia von D. Johann Fausten* (Stuttgart, 1988), the first literary manifestation of the Faust story, that the transcription of black letter texts into roman is not as straightforward a matter as has generally been assumed (see their 'Editorischer Bericht', pp. 169f.).

German-speaking countries of the guiding influence of an organization of the eminence of the Bibliographical Society has already been cited. Another is without doubt the fact that, until very recently, German bibliography has not had the benefit of such comprehensive handbooks as exist for English (such as *STC*). The reasons for this lie in the large number of libraries in Germany and above all perhaps in the fact that (until 1990) only from 1870 until 1945 was there a united Germany. Only now is a concerted attempt being made, under the direction of Bernhard Fabian to survey comprehensively the antiquarian holdings of some 800 to 1,000 libraries in the Federal Republic of Germany whose collections are of importance to scholarship, the aim being to produce a *Handbuch der historischen Buchbestände*; meanwhile Erdmute Lapp's *Katalogsituation der Altbestände (1501–1850) in Bibliotheken der Bundersrepublik Deutschland einschießlich Berlin (West)* (Berlin, 1989) makes interesting reading. Nevertheless, the eighties have seen remarkable advances in the provision of major bibliographical aids. While the *Gesamtkatalog der Wiegendrucke* remains a sad torso, even though publication resumed, fitfully, in 1972, other projects are proceeding apace. The long-awaited catalogue of the incunable collection of the Bavarian State Library at Munich (with 16,785 items, the largest collection after that of the British Library) started appearing in 1988. The same library's alphabetical catalogue of books published between 1501 and 1840 also commenced publication in 1987. The *Verzeichnis der im deutschen Sprachbereich erschienenen Drucke des 16. Jahrhunderts (VD 16)*, based principally on the holdings of Munich and Wolfenbüttel, commenced publication in 1983. For the seventeenth century Martin Bircher's *Deutsche Drucke des Barock 1600–1720 in der Herzog August Bibliothek Wolfenbüttel* (Nendeln, 1977ff.) and Gerhardt Dünnhaupt's *Bibliographisches Handbuch der Barockliteratur* (Stuttgart, 1980–1) are invaluable, but one looks forward to completion of David Paisey's short-title catalogue of the British Library's substantial holdings of German books of this period. German plans for a comprehensive catalogue similar to *VD 16* for the seventeenth century cannot yet be implemented for financial reasons. As for the eighteenth and subsequent centuries, apart from bibliographies of particular authors, the best tools currently available are the two series of the retrospective national bibliography, *Gesamtverzeichnis des deutschsprachigen Schrifttums (GV)*, covering 1700–1910 in 160 volumes (Munich 1979–87) and 1911–65 in 150 volumes (Munich 1976–81), though their usefulness is limited because locations are not given. There are, in general, grounds for optimism, but until all the holdings of major collections are accessible through published catalogues or databases, one perhaps cannot expect more than a sporadic application of the techniques of analytical bibliography.

Nevertheless, there are some signs of increasing awareness and interest. To some extent these may be said to have been encouraged by Allan Stevenson's more refined approach to the problems presented by paper and watermarks.[15] A

15 See Allan Stevenson, 'Paper as Bibliographical Evidence', *Lib*, v, 17 (1962): 197–212, and especially his *The Problem of the Missale Speciale* (1967).

more critical analysis of watermark evidence was applied in Germany by Theo Gerardy who really sparked off the current debate about the Mainz *Catholicon* (GW 3182), a work originally compiled by Johannes Balbus of Genoa in the 1280s, by revealing the conflict between the date in the colophon, 1460, and watermark evidence which showed that some – but not all – of the paper stocks used were not available much before 1469.[16] Gerardy, who believed that all the copies were printed at the same time, resolved the problem for himself by assuming that the date in the colophon was wrong and that the whole edition left the press in about 1468, the earliest possible date at which all the paper stocks involved were available. This in turn stimulated Eva Ziesche and Dierk Schnitger to apply beta-radiographic techniques to this and other early printed books. They dated the *Catholicon* copies with the bull's head watermark 1460 (thus restoring faith in the colophon) but put those with the Galliziani mark at 1468–9 and those with the tower-and-crown mark at 1472 (which would mean that the last at least could not have been produced by Gutenberg himself).[17] Since then Ziesche and Schnitger and others have redated a number of other important books; for instance the Bamberg *Ackermann aus Böhmen* (GW 193), long thought to have been printed by Albrecht Pfister in about 1460, is now put at 1470–5 (which precludes the possibility of its having been printed by Pfister who died in 1466), and the *Heldenbuch*, a major survival of medieval German heroic poetry, printed by Johann Prüss the Elder at Strasbourg, has been dated 1479.

If Elizabethan drama provided the stimulus for the development of the techniques of analytical bibliography in the English-speaking world, in Germany it may well turn out that general awareness of their importance will eventually grow, appropriately enough, from current work on some of the earliest Mainz printing, particularly the problem of the *Catholicon* and typographically related books, Matthias de Cracovia's *Dialogus rationis et conscientiae* and the *Summa de articulis fidei* of Thomas Aquinas. Gerardy's questioning of the colophon of the *Catholicon* has already been mentioned, and the problems this gave rise to encouraged renewed study of the typography itself, resulting in Paul Needham's controversial claim that the book was printed from two-line slugs of text, that is from some kind of secondary castings from moveable types.[18] Notwithstanding

---

16 Theo Gerardy, 'Gallizianimarke, Krone und Turm als Wasserzeichen in großformatigen Frühdrucken', *Gutenberg-Jahrbuch* 1973, pp. 105–25.

17 Eva Ziesche and Dierk Schnitger, 'Elektronenradiographische Untersuchungen der Wasserzeichen des Mainzer Catholicon von 1460', *Archiv für Geschichte des Buchwesens*, 21 (1980), cols. 1,303–60, and also issued separately under the same title in 1981.

18 The arguments are too complex and the literature too extensive for a summary to be attempted here. Building on the seminal work of Gottfried Zedler, *Das Mainzer Catholicon* (Mainz, 1905), some of the most important contributions to the current debate are: Paul Needham, 'Johann Gutenberg and the Catholicon Press', *PBSA*, 76 (1982): 395–456; Walter J. Partridge, 'The Type-setting and Printing of the Mainz Catholicon', *BC*, 35 (1986): 21–52; Paul Needham, 'The Type-setting of the Mainz Catholicon', *BC*, 35: 293–304; Martin Boghardt, 'Die bibliographische Erforschung der ersten "Catholicon"-Ausgabe(n)', *Wolfenbütteler Notizen zur Buchgeschichte*, 13 (1988): 138–76; Paul Needham, 'The Catholicon Press of Johann Gutenberg: A Hidden Chapter in the Invention of

its description by Albert Kapr, the distinguished Leipzig typographical designer, as a 'bizarre hypothesis'[19] and whatever the final outcome of the debate, there can be no doubt that it has encouraged important research in Germany itself, prominent among which is Martin Boghardt's work, in part involving the use of composite-imaging, on cancels in the *Catholicon* and also his demonstration, with the help of the Hinman Collator, that Matthias de Cracovia's *Dialogus rationis et conscientiae* was printed using the same technique as the *Catholicon*.

As in Germany, so also in Italy. Here too the basic situation is that, until very recently, the techniques of analytical and textual bibliography have at best been utilized sporadically. But many of the detailed factors are different. In Italy there has long been a strong interest in the history of printing, which over the years has resulted in the publication of many useful, well-documented contributions on the economic, cultural, and artistic aspects of printing history from the fifteenth to the nineteenth centuries. Interest in descriptive bibliography has been largely confined to the compilation of annals of individual printing houses. Though bereft, until very recently, of the sort of terminology which the English-language reader takes for granted in bibliographical studies, these annals, when in the hands of good scholars, do sometimes allow the reader access to the world of bibliographical analysis, permitting the identification of variant states and issues, and of other interesting features.[20]

Even when not conducted with full rigour, they also form a contribution to the overcoming of what has been one of the main obstacles to the development of analytical bibliography in Italy, as in Germany, namely the lack of adequate catalogues of library holdings. In Italy, the root causes of this unsatisfactory situation are historical and political: historical, in that Italy's vast bookstock is dispersed among scores of libraries in the numerous urban centres of importance which rose and fell during the many centuries of Italy's fragmented pre-unification history; political, in that since unification Italy has failed to adopt sound policies either for the organization of the libraries or for their training of the librarians.[21] At the beginning of this century, when analytical bibliography was developing in England and Germany, no major Italian library had an adequate catalogue of its printed books, even for internal use, and few librarians were sufficiently well trained to supply the deficiency at any level beyond the

Printing', *Wolfenbütteler Notizen*, 13: 199–230; and Lotte Hellinga, 'Analytical Bibliography and the Study of Early Printed Books. With a Case-Study of the Mainz Catholicon', *Gutenberg-Jahrbuch 1989*, pp. 47–96. Hellinga and Needham continued to debate the issue in the 1990 and 1991 volumes of the *Gutenberg-Jahrbuch*.

19 Albert Kapr, *Johannes Gutenberg. Persönlichkeit und Leistung*, 2nd edn (Munich, 1988), p. 231.

20 For some post-war examples see Valentino Romani, 'Gli studi sull'editoria romana del Cinque e Seicento', in *Per Francesco Barberi: Atti della giornata di studio 16 febbraio 1989*, Miscellanea della Società Romana di Storia Patria, 30 (Rome, 1989), 41–60. A new dimension has recently been added to Italian descriptive bibliography by the publication of Neil Harris's *Bibliografia dell'"Orlando innamorato"* (Modena-Ferrara, 1988), compiled in strict accordance with Bowers's *Principles*.

21 For an overview see Enzo Bottasso, *Storia della biblioteca in Italia* (Milan, 1984).

most elementary. It is significant, too, that only briefly, and that many years ago, from 1896 to 1915, has Italy had a prestigious bibliographical society (the 'Società bibliografica italiana') where librarians could meet with other scholars interested in the printed book under various aspects, and which could serve as a forum, as the Bibliographical Society has done, for the discussion and publication of new ideas. In this context, publications in the field of analytical bibliography have understandably been extremely sparse. Apart from a precocious and isolated nineteenth-century precursor, Giacomo Manzoni's *Studii di bibliografia analitica* (Bologna, 1881–2), which comprises three separate studies, preceded by a *Proemio* with some interesting methodological consider-ations,[22] the only one which comes to mind is, significantly, not the work of a librarian, but of a literary scholar interested in the printed book, Roberto Ridolfi's *Le filigrane dei paleotipi* (Florence, 1957), a pioneering study of paper, written in complete ignorance of the work of Allan Stevenson, which duplicates some of his results (watermarks are twins, for example).

Since the Second World War, however, a start has been made on tackling the problem of uncatalogued collections. Both from an inherent love of generaliz-ation, and from a more practical realization that the crying need of Italian scholarship is for general bibliographical aids, even if, because of the imperfec-tions of the catalogues of individual libraries, these aids would contain many errors and omissions, the problem has been approached on a national level. What is in effect the *STC* of incunables in Italian libraries is now complete: *Indice generale degli incunaboli delle biblioteche d'Italia* (Rome, 1943–81). A start has been made on an ambitious, computer-based short-title catalogue of sixteenth-century Italian editions in Italian libraries, much influenced by the British *ESTC*, except that it finds room in its descriptions of each item for a fingerprint, a British invention which has found more honour abroad than in its own country.[23] Something akin to, and inspired by, the *English Nineteenth Century Short Title Catalogue* is also planned. The work on the sixteenth-century catalogue, in addition to its obvious value to bibliographers and scholars in numerous disciplines as a record of the activities of one of the major areas of European book production, is also serving as an invaluable educational experience for the librarians involved, providing a schooling in elementary bibliographical analysis and introducing them to basic operations like the determination of format and to fundamental concepts like those of issue and state. Italian librarians are indeed now largely aware of the importance of descriptive and analytical bibliography, and current problems in this area are frequently aired in periodicals such as *La Bibliofilia*, *Biblioteche Oggi*, and *Il Bibliotecario*. Meanwhile, some sophisticated

22 Valentino Romani, 'Della "bibliografia analitica" e dei suoi primi sviluppi nell'Ottocento italiano', *Accademie e Biblioteche d'Italia*, 57, n.2 (1989): 44–54. Romani notes that 'after Manzoni's work and after this first sign of interest in the subject, Italians seem to have completely forgotten about "analytical bibliography"' (54). The copy of Manzoni's *Studii* in the British Library lack the *Proemio*.
23 On the Italian sixteenth-century catalogue see Conor Fahy, 'The *Censimento delle edizioni italiane del XVI secolo*', *Bulletin of the Society for Italian Studies*, 16 (1983): 24–8, and the review of volume I by Neil Harris, *Lib*, VI, 9 (1987): 181–4.

work is being done on fifteenth- and sixteenth-century printing by a handful of librarians and scholars based on Rome, which houses two centres of library and archive studies, one at the Vatican and the other at the university.[24] Two lines of enquiry are of particular interest. One concerns the study of manuscripts which have served as printer's copy. These are numerous for the fifteenth and sixteenth century – for major Renaissance authors, for example, there are complete or fragmentary manuscripts of works by Castiglione, Ariosto, and Tasso – and their systematic exploration should provide interesting material for a deeper understanding of the methods of early printing. There is also a growing interest in the description and analysis of what Roger Laufer has called *l'espace visuel* of the early printed book. The influence here is as much French as Anglo-American – not only Laufer but also French codicology – and is likely to provide a fruitful extension of the items and concepts of bibliographical analysis to include those aesthetic elements which have always interested the Mediterranean mind, but have till now been generally subjected only to impressionistic appreciation and description.[25]

The history of Italian textual criticism differs widely from that of German textual criticism, but is equally far from its English counterpart, which determined the rise of textual bibliography. Modern Italian textual criticism reflects the history of Italian literature and the predominant place occupied by Dante studies in modern Italian literary historiography and criticism, just as English textual criticism reflects the predominance of Shakespeare. Two hundred years of sophisticated vernacular literature, including the works of the *tre corone*, Dante, Petrarch, and Boccaccio, antedate the invention of printing. Italian textual criticism, encouraged by the classical bias of Italian education, has concentrated on the problems of the manuscript transmission of vernacular texts, in which area it has developed a methodology of great sophistication, and achieved many notable results.[26] Until recently, the general view, encouraged by the widespread ignorance of analytical bibliography already referred to, was that printed transmission was a much simpler affair since, in the words of a highly reputed manual of textual criticism first published in 1975, 'in general all the copies of an edition have the value of a single witness'.[27] This was despite the

24 Important samples of the work being done at or in the orbit of Rome are to be found in the two volumes of seminar contributions published in Vatican City in 1980 and 1983 under the title *Scrittura, biblioteche e stampa a Roma nel Quattrocento: aspetti e problemi*, edited respectively by Carla Bianca and Massimo Miglio.
25 See, for example, Giorgio Montecchi, 'I progetti grafici di Domenico Rococciola', in his volume *Aziende tipografiche, stampatori e librai a Modena dal Quattrocento al Settecento* (Modena, 1988), and the Oxford DPhil thesis *The Printed Transmission of Lyrics in Italy from 1470 to 1530: The Book of Verse*, (1991), by Nadia Cannata, a graduate of Rome University who came to England to perfect her bibliographical knowledge.
26 For an up-to-date and well-balanced general survey see Alfredo Stussi, *Nuovo avviamento agli studi di filologia italiana* (Bologna, 1988).
27 Franca Brambilla Ageno, *L'edizione critica dei testi volgari* (Padua, 1975), p. 18, n. 7. The comment was repeated in the second edition, published in 1984.

fact that two great modern Italian textual critics, Santorre Debenedetti and Michele Barbi, working respectively on Ariosto's *Orlando furioso* (1532) and Manzoni's *I promessi sposi* (1840–2), had, independently of each other and in complete ignorance of English-language work on textual bibliography, recorded the presence and understood the significance of press-variants, many of them authorial, present in substantial numbers in the editions they were considering.[28] Barbi and his helpers even arrived at the concept of ideal copy, at least in so far as it is relevant to textual criticism. Their achievements are a remarkable tribute to their integrity and perspicacity as textual critics. Debenedetti did not understand the structure of the edition he was working on (a quarto in eights), and consistently identified gathering with sheet; furthermore, though he made no attempt to place each variant in its bibliographical context, a failure which illustrates an inability to grasp even the most obvious way in which an understanding of bibliography can ease the work of the textual critic, yet on linguistic and stylistic evidence alone he accurately identified the variant of the corrected state in all but one of the thirty-seven cases he considered – a striking illustration of his sensitivity as a critic. His edition has been much admired – rightly so, as it is one of the masterpieces of modern Italian textual criticism, and the critical text he established is still wholly valid – but the exemplary nature of the 1532 *Furioso* was not appreciated by Debenedetti (in the critical note at the end of his edition he characterized the 1532 *Furioso*, with its frequent authorial intervention in the form of press-variants, as constituting 'one of the strangest cases offered by the history of printing'), and it has thus had no impact on the development of bibliographical awareness among Italian textual critics.[29]

The same is true, for different reasons, of Barbi's work on *I promessi sposi*. The definitive edition of this famous novel was published over two years in fifty-four instalments, each comprising two *dispense*, and a well-nigh complete series of proofs with authorial corrections has survived. Each instalment constitutes a discrete publishing unit, comprising two sheets of eight pages each, and thus invites the conclusion that the critical text of the whole work should be compiled from the corrected state of each of these sheets, in a combination not necessarily found in any of the surviving copies. Here again, the special circumstances (publication by instalment, survival of multiple proofs) have militated against the generalization of Barbi's experiences and methods by other Italian textual critics. It has to be said, too, that, like Barbi, Debenedetti was not interested in the technical aspects of the printing of the books, which was carried out on a

---

28 See Ludovico Ariosto, *Orlando furioso*, edited by Santorre Debenedetti, 3 vols. (Bari, 1928), especially *Nota*, 3, pp. 397–447; Michele Barbi, 'Il testo dei *Promessi Sposi*', in Michele Barbi, *La nuova filologia e l'edizione dei nostri scrittori da Dante al Manzoni*, 2nd edn (Florence, 1973), pp. 195–227, and the critical edition of Manzoni's novel published in Milan in 1954, edited by Alberto Chiari and Fausto Ghisalberti, incorporating Barbi's work.

29 For further information on the merits and limits of Debenedetti's work on the *Furioso* see Conor Fahy, 'Some observations on the 1532 edition of Ludovico Ariosto's *Orlando Furioso*', and 'More on the 1532 edition of Ariosto's *Orlando Furioso*', in *SB*, 40 (1987), 72–85; 41 (1988): 225–32.

Stanhope press of large dimensions, each sheet of eight pages being imposed as if for the printing of an octavo by half-sheet imposition.[30]

A first attempt to take up, on behalf of Italian textual criticism, the invitation implicit in the critical work of Debenedetti and Barbi was made in 1955 by Giovanni Aquilecchia, who produced an edition of the first of Giordano Bruno's 'London' dialogues, *La cena de le ceneri*, which not only showed the importance of internal collation but was also in effect the first Italian example of an 'old-spelling' critical edition of a Renaissance text. This latter feature provoked some adverse criticism in Italy, and the fact that Aquilecchia's subsequent academic career has been passed entirely in Britain (after a spell at University College London he was Professor of Italian first at Manchester and then at Bedford College, London) has allowed the lessons of this and of his subsequent critical editions (the *Sei giornate* of Pietro Aretino (1969) and Bruno's second 'London' dialogue, *De la causa, principio et uno* (1973)) to be largely ignored in Italy.

In general, Italian textual criticism remains understandably orientated towards the problems of manuscript transmission, but in the last ten years has come an increasing awareness that the methodology developed to deal with these problems will not necessarily suffice for printed transmission. Perhaps because of the richness of Renaissance literature and the importance of Renaissance printing, it is mainly among Renaissance scholars that this awareness is to be found. A recent edition of some of the macaronic poems of Teofilo Folengo, emanating from the school of Gianfranco Contini, the most eminent and influential Italian textual critic of the second half of this century, acknowledges in its critical note the importance now being assumed in Italian editorial work by the methodology of 'la critica del testo a stampa' (this periphrasis is characteristic: Italians are not enamoured of the expression 'bibliografia testuale').[31] Another straw in the wind was the publication in 1987 of an anthology of articles and extracts comprising, in Italian translation, some fundamental contributions of Anglo-American textual bibliography, Greg's 'The Rationale of Copy-Text', Tanselle's 'The Concept of Ideal Copy', Bowers's 'Multiple Authority: New Problems and Concepts of Copy-Text', for example.[32] These contributions suffer, in Italian eyes, from the disadvantage of containing an exemplification drawn entirely from English and American literature. It was partly in order to offset this disadvantage that Conor Fahy recently published a

---

30 These aspects are explored in Conor Fahy, 'Per la stampa dell' edizione definitiva dei *Promessi sposi*', *Aevum*, 56 (1982): 377–94, reprinted in Conor Fahy, *Saggi di bibliografia testuale* (Padua, 1988), pp. 213–44.

31 Teofilo Folengo, *Macaronee minori: Zanitonella, Moscheide, Epigrammi* (Turin, 1987), p. 558. It is characteristic of the as yet imperfect assimilation of bibliographical techniques by Italian textual scholars that the bibliographical descriptions provided in this otherwise excellent edition do not include the format of the volumes concerned, while the identification of the bibliographical context of the press variants listed does not go beyond the gathering in which they occur.

32 *Filologia dei testi a stampa*, edited by Pasquale Stoppelli (Bologna, 1987). The editor, who is Professor of Italian in the University of Salerno, is one of the keenest advocates of textual bibliography in Italy.

collection of his own articles, all in Italian, containing contributions on individual problems of textual bibliography in Italian literature, as well as general discussions of some methodological aspects of the discipline.[33]

Italian textual criticism – like German – is flourishing and self-confident, even if, at times, somewhat inward-looking. It is prepared to recognize that it has given insufficient attention to the problems of transmission by the printed word, and to learn from those who have made this their specialism. It would probably be reluctant, however, otherwise to modify its practices. While willing to accord a place to analytical bibliography among the tools of the trade, on a par with palaeography, which it has for long acknowledged as an essential ancillary science for those working on manuscript transmission, it is less likely to accept unconditionally those aspects of textual bibliography which are more strictly concerned with textual criticism. In particular, normal Italian editorial practice permits discreet modernization of graphic phenomena, particularly in cases where there is no evidence of authorial influence. In this, of course, it runs counter to one of the corner-stones of current Anglo-American editorial practice. Greg's theory of copy-text, however, if known, is usually viewed with suspicion not only in Italy, but elsewhere in continental Europe. It is not just a matter of old-spelling versus modernization: at issue are more fundamental questions concerning the validity of eclectic texts, and the desirability of an editorial practice not rigidly bound, as is the theory of copy-text, to a wholly writer-oriented theory of literature.

There is no doubt that analytical and textual bibliography will be growth points in continental bibliographical and critical scholarship in the remaining years of the twentieth century, and beyond. Though there is much, in terms of experience and method, which has simply to be learnt, it will not be a passive assimilation, if only because, at least until the nineteenth century, continental printing was a much more complex phenomenon than the corresponding English industry. It will be fascinating to see the ways in which the Anglo-American scion, grafted on to the already flourishing tree of continental bibliographical and critical studies, will produce new fruit.

33 See Fahy, *Saggi.*

Bibliographical studies in Japan

AKIHIRO YAMADA

Japan cherished the scholarly study of its own literature, particularly as represented by its manuscript tradition, well before the end of the nineteenth century, by which time German and British influences began to affect the study of literature in Japan. English literature was taught for the first time at the University of Tokyo in 1873 by the English scholar, James Summers. (He had formerly taught Chinese at King's College London.) Apart from a short break, it has since been a regular part of the curriculum in Japanese colleges. Among the outstanding scholars who taught English literature in Tokyo were Edmund Blunden (1924–7 and 1947–50), William Empson (1931–4), and, perhaps surprisingly, R.B. McKerrow (1897–1900). McKerrow's interest in bibliography left no trace in Tokyo; his capacity for systematic analysis and lucid presentation was, however, demonstrated in a book on the pronunciation of English of which he was joint author.[1] This was published two years after he had left Japan and its three hundred pages are full of tables, illustrations, and 'new' phonetic signs, the better to exemplify the argument.

It is not surprising that the teaching of English literature did not for some time concern itself with bibliography. Such study in Japan can be traced back to a chance meeting in the Library of the British Museum in 1930. The Japanese scholar, Rintaro Fukuhara, whilst working there on the manuscripts of Gray's *Elegy*, chanced to meet Henry Bergen, then working on his edition of Lydgate's *Troy Book* for the Early English Text Society (1906–35). Bergen took an interest in Fukuhara's comparative study of the Eton, Wharton, and Pembroke manuscripts of the *Elegy*, and he suggested that they join forces. Their edition was published in 1933 as *An Elegy Written in a Country Churchyard by Thomas Gray: Three Manuscripts*.

Some years after his return to Tokyo, Fukuhara described this experience to two friends, Kikan Ikeda and Takanobu Otsuka. Although there had been a tradition of bibliographical study in Japan since the latter half of the seventeenth

In preparing this chapter I have been given valuable assistance by a number of colleagues. I should particularly like to acknowledge the kindness of two medievalists, Professor Tadao Kubouchi and Professor Yuji Nakao. I am also indebted to my old friend, Professor Toshiro Yui.

1 R.B. McKerrow and Hiroshi Katayama, *Eigo Hatsuongaku* ('English Phonetics'), Tokyo, 1902; 2nd rev. edn, 1902.

century,[2] it was from this moment in 1938 that the influence of modern British bibliography on the study in Japan of both vernacular and English literatures can be traced. Ikeda prepared his seven-volume edition of *The Tale of Genji* (Tokyo, 1946–55), establishing him as a leading scholar of Japanese literature. Otsuka worked on English works of the Elizabethan period. He produced an edition of *The First Voyage of the English to Japan by John Saris* (Tokyo, 1941) – a transcript of Saris's journal of his voyage of 1611–13, dedicated to Francis Bacon. Owing to the outbreak of war, Otsuka had to restrict his textual studies to a collation of Saris's manuscript held in the Oriental Library, Tokyo (PB-30) with variant manuscripts reported in an edition printed in London in 1900 and in *Hakluytus Posthumus or Purchas His Pilgrimes* (Glasgow, 1905). Otsuka also took issue with Dover Wilson's 'Bibliographical Links between the Three Pages and the Good Quartos' in *Shakespeare's Hand in 'The Play of Sir Thomas More'* (ed. A.W. Pollard, Cambridge, 1923). After the Second World War, he published an article refuting Dover Wilson's thesis. This, being written in Japanese, had only local influence but, as with his other articles, stimulated the interest of a new generation of Japanese scholars of English literature in bibliographical studies. Otsuka also proposed a large-scale programme of facsimiles of editions of Shakespeare in order to facilitate English studies in Japan. His project came to fruition with the publication of *A Facsimile Series of Shakespeare Quartos*, 70 vols. (Tokyo, 1975).

Studies in the Humanities were discouraged during the Second World War, but soon after its conclusion they developed rapidly. Bunsho Jugaku, who had written a dozen books on Blake and had published a 750-page *Bibliography of William Blake* (Tokyo, Kyoto, and Kobe, 1929), published *A Bibliographical Study of William Blake's Note-Book* (Tokyo, 1953), with a foreword by Edmund Blunden.[3] The tradition of studying national manuscripts attracted many Japanese scholars of English literature to focus attention on English manuscripts. These studies, usually done in isolation, led to a growing interest in English medieval manuscripts, work associated especially with the name of Fumio Kuriyagawa of Keio University. A second line of interest was, perhaps unsurprisingly, the study of Shakespeare and Elizabethan and Jacobean writers. Here, the pre-eminent name from the mid fifties was Jiro Ozu of Tokyo University.

It is not too much to claim that Fumio Kuriyagawa opened the way to medieval manuscript studies in Japan. A specialist in Old and Middle English Literature, he took full advantage of a short visit to the Bibliothèque Nationale in 1953, where he discovered an unpublished medieval prose manuscript, without title, bound with several other untitled works (MS. anglais 41). He identified

---

2 This tradition developed markedly at the beginning of the nineteenth century and Japanese scholars were influenced by *Altertumswissenschaft* at the very time that McKerrow was teaching in Tokyo. Kikan Ikeda's training was almost certainly influenced by this German tradition and that affected his early work on *The Tale of Genji*.

3 Jugaku was ironically amused, rather than offended, when he discovered that his 1953 *Bibliographical Study* had been pirated in an edition published in New York in 1971.

these in the British Library and continued his research in Tokyo, collating the Paris manuscript with those in the British Library, Lambeth Palace, and at Oxford and Cambridge. His interim results were published in 1958 and the complete edition appeared in Tokyo in 1967, as *Walter Hilton's Eight Chapters on Perfection*. Four years later he published a critical edition of the *Eight Chapters* based on the Inner Temple manuscript, Petyt 524 (*Studies in English Literature*, English Number 1971). In the same journal, in 1977, Kuriyagawa's pupil, Toshiyuki Takamiya, published a critical edition of Hilton's *Of Angels' Song*. A few years later he worked on the *Eight Chapters of Perfection* in British Library MS. Add. 60577, collating it with other known manuscripts. He published his edition in the Japanese journal, *Poetica*, 12 (1981 for Autumn, 1979). Among his other publications is an edition of a hitherto unedited manuscript of Trevisa's *De Proprietatibus Rerum* held by Keio University Library. This appeared in a Festschrift for Professor Yoshio Terasawa on his sixtieth birthday, *Philologia Anglica* (Tokyo, 1988). This Festschrift also included a note by another of Kuriyagawa's pupils, Tadahiro Ikegami, on the printer Robert Copland, who contributed an envoi to Wynkyn de Worde's edition of *The Life of Ipomydon* (*STC* 5733). Ikegami, assisted by his wife (yet another of Kuriyagawa's pupils), prepared a two-volume edition of this work, published in Tokyo from 1983 to 1985. The first volume gives a text based on the manuscript and the second, one based on the two printed editions.

Kuriyagawa realized that there was a need for a centre where Japanese medievalists could have ready access to the vast corpus of research material held by libraries throughout the world. With two friends, Michio Masui and Kikuo Miyabe, a research programme was set up and, funded by a Ministry of Education grant, the Centre for Mediaeval English Studies was established at the University of Tokyo in 1969. Miyabe, the youngest of the three, initially took the lead in directing its programme; he worked on the *Ancrene Riwle* and *The Form of Living* in the Vernon MS. in the Bodleian Library. Unfortunately, his untimely death in 1981 cut short his work but publication of what he had completed appeared in *Poetica* 11 and 13 (1979 and 1982 for Spring 1980) and in his own Festschrift, *Eigo no Rekishi to Kozo* ('History and Structure of English'), Tokyo, 1981. In that same Festschrift there also appeared a textual study of a neglected manuscript of the Wycliffite Bible in the Herzog August Bibliothek, Wolfenbüttel, which Yoshio Terasawa (who had succeeded Miyabe as Head of the Centre) collated with ten other important manuscripts. On Terasawa's retirement recently, the management of the Centre was taken over by Tadao Kubouchi. His interests are philological but he is completing the work Miyabe left unfinished.

Another major work left unfinished owing to its editor's unexpected death is a parallel text of *Ancrene Riwle* and *Ancrene Wisse*. Kiyoshi Awaka published the first section he had completed in 1974 in the *Bulletin of the Faculty of Education of Mie University*, 25; later sections appeared in the *Bulletin*, 26–8, 1975–77. Awaka also prepared a transcript of *The Pains of Sin*, published in the *Bulletin*, 33, 1982, complete with a 'tentative modernization'. Caxton's part in Malory's *Le Morte Darthur* has been analysed by two scholars: Shunichi Noguchi (*Poetica*, 8

and 20, 1977 and 1984), and Yuji Nakao (*Poetica*, 25–6, 1987). Nakao
concluded (on the basis of philological rather than bibliographical argument)
that Caxton, not Malory, was the author of the Roman War story in *Le Morte
Darthur*, Book v.

Japanese medievalists have not confined their attention to English manuscripts. Yorio Otaka and Hideka Fukui have produced fine facsimile editions in
colour of *Apocalypse Anglo-Normande* (Osaka, 1977) and *Apocalypse* (Osaka,
1981). Both have transcripts and the latter has an introduction by Felix Lecoy.

Although bibliographic studies of the work of Shakespeare and his contemporaries have been less prolific in Japan than of medieval manuscripts, they are
now beginning to gather pace. They were stimulated by Jiro Ozu following his
year studying under C.J. Sisson at the Shakespeare Institute, Stratford-
upon-Avon, 1954–5. One of his early publications on Shakespeare was 'Textual
Problems' in *Sogokenkyu Shakespeare* ('Comprehensive Studies in Shakespeare',
Tokyo, 1960), pp. 197–227, which he co-edited with Yoshio Nakano. This was
an educational essay, written in Japanese, which challenged 'the general
indifference' to the text by 'presenting as many facts and problems as possible
before the younger students of English literature' (p. 225). Ozu successfully
focused attention on the importance of textual problems despite the fact that the
primary interest of Japanese scholars was in literary criticism. First as
Secretary-General and then as President of the Shakespeare Society, Ozu proved
an influential advocate of textual scholarship. However, such studies developed
slowly owing to the lack of research materials – originals and facsimiles – in
Japan, and because textual studies were deemed to be more rigorous and less
immediately rewarding than was literary criticism. Ozu wrote no more on
textual matters but concentrated on arousing awareness of Shakespearian
textual scholarship by inviting aspiring scholars to contribute papers to
publications he edited.

An early example of this policy was a paper, 'Shakespeare's Text' by Kazuo
Chujo in *A Shakespeare Handbook* (Tokyo, 1969), 578–99, which Ozu edited.
Chujo had studied bibliography with Takanobu Otsuka, and as early as 1956
had published a paper on the bibliographical links between Q2 and F1 of *Hamlet*,
attempting to refute Alice Walker's theory (*Eigogaku* ('English Philology'), 1
(1956), 98–117). From 1962, Ozu edited the annual *Shakespeare Studies*, and
among those invited to contribute was Akihiro Yamada. His bibliographical
study of Chapman's *The Gentleman Usher* (1606) appeared in volume II, 1963,
and he contributed to each annual until VII, 1969. His finding of a proof-sheet
for *An Humorous Day's Mirth* (1599) was reported in *Lib*, v, 21 (1966), the first of
three articles to be published in *The Library*. His edition of *The Widow's Tears* was
published in London, 1975, and the following year his doctorate was awarded
for a bibliographical study of Chapman's plays, undertaken at the Shakespeare
Institute. Throughout the 1980s, Yamada has worked chiefly on Marston, first
for a Festschrift for Ozu (*Poetry and Drama in the English Renaissance*, Tokyo,
1980, 107–32). Next came his study of an Elizabethan printing house, *Thomas
Creede: Printer to Shakespeare and His Contemporaries* (Matsumoto, 1981). Then,

following a series of studies on press variants in Marston's plays, he published an analysis of the transitional stages of the printing of three editions of *The Malcontent* (*Studies in Humanities*, 22 (1988): 53–60). Yamada has continued Kuriyagawa's lead in building up research materials; a collection of forty-eight books and eighty-seven articles on 419 fiche was published as *Bibliotheca Shakespeariana, Unit 7: Printing and the Book Trade* (Oxford, 1988).

Among other scholars working on bibliographical subjects in English literature of the period are Yasumasa Okamoto, who published an article on *The Merchant of Venice* in *Shakespeare Studies* (Japan), 15 (1976–7), 57–75; Yuji Kaneko, whose article on the drawing of a scene associated with *Titus Andronicus*, defending the date 1595, appeared in *Eigo Eibei Bungaku* ('English Language and Literature'), 26 (1987): 1–14; and Hiroshi Yamashita, who, like Kaneko, studied at the Shakespeare Institute, and who has worked intensively on *The Faerie Queene*, culminating in the publication of a concordance thereof, in association with colleagues (1991). Okamoto is now making a study of stage directions in Elizabethan plays; Kaneko, intrigued by the increase in collected works in the seventeenth century, is preparing a socio-cultural history of printing to 1700; and Yamashita has turned to Japanese literature. Whereas Japanese literature before 1868, which exists mainly in manuscript or woodcut form, has been studied by Japanese scholars for generations, little attention has been paid to works published since then using moveable type. Contemporary editions are often seriously deficient and Yamashita has been attempting to draw attention to their failings and apply Greg's 'Rationale of Copy-Text' to their editing.

Earlier Japanese literature has always received the attention of scholars; commercial publishers, rather than university presses, have been most willing to publish editions. Two major post-war series deserve mention; the Nihon Koten Zensho ('The Japanese Classics'), 108 vols., 1946–74, published by the book section of the leading newspaper, *Asahi Shimbun*; and the Nihon Koten Bungaku Taikei ('The Iwanami Japanese Classic Literature Series'), 100 vols. plus two index volumes, published by Iwanami Shoten, 1957–67. Early in 1989, Iwanami started a new, similarly named, series. This will again be of 100 volumes but will draw on a wider range of literature. Many of the editors of these series are scholars disciplined in bibliography, such as Kikan Ikeda, who had been much intrigued by Fukuhara's account of what he had learned when working with Henry Bergen at the British Museum Library.

In 1963, the first volume of the Japanese equivalent of the Bibliographical Society's *STC* was published. The commercial publisher, Iwanami Shoten, celebrated its golden jubilee by publishing the first of nine volumes of *Kokusho So-Mokuroku* ('A Complete Catalogue of Japanese Books', Tokyo, 1963–76). This lists some half-million titles by about 60,000 authors. A revised edition began to appear in 1989. In 1980, the National Institute of Japanese Literature launched a computer-aided catalogue with, as its database, new information gathered after 1960. This amassed some 10,000 new titles and much additional information to that already listed in the *Complete Catalogue* and led to the compilation of *Kotenseki Sogo-Mokuroku* ('A Comprehensive Catalogue of Ancient Books'), 3 vols., 1990, also published by Iwanami Shoten. These three volumes, and the revised edition of the *Complete Catalogue*, can together be regarded as the Japanese equivalent of the *Revised STC*.

It is apparent, therefore, that, since the end of the Second World War, Japanese bibliographers have been increasingly active in the fields of Japanese and English literature, and, in the former especially, their labours have been very fruitful.

Bibliography in the computer age

ROBIN ALSTON

That we are living at a time of great changes in the ways in which knowledge is produced, disseminated, and acquired no one can doubt.[1] Whether they are wholly beneficial for the commonwealth of learning is not quite so clear. The computer age has commonly been called a second industrial revolution; or as Alvin Toffler has called it the 'third wave'[2] – the first being the agricultural revolution, the second the industrial revolution. Its effects upon everything from the management of our money to the ways in which we are increasingly required to buy groceries are probably clear enough, and some of these developments are undoubtedly an improvement; but I have serious doubts about the seemingly inexorable drift towards colossal marketing organizations that effectively turn us from individuals with choices into obedient servants of a gigantic planned society invisibly controlled by market forces. What, one is tempted to wonder, lies beyond the hypermarket? The model of the supermarket is now pervasive in Western societies, and it will not be long before libraries are encouraged to offer their resources in a comparable manner. A slogan for the new age might be something close to: 'If you can find it, you can buy it.'

When did this all begin? Like other developments in science and technology that have affected social behaviour – indeed, like the weather in Northern Europe – the computer age has been evolving for at least forty-five years: since 1946 when Eckett and Maunchly invented the ENIAC (Electronic Numerical Integrator and Calculator), a primitive calculator used to compute missile trajectories which contained over 18,000 vacuum-filled thermionic valves – the sort used in radios and early hi-fi sets. It is not my purpose here to trace the history of computers but 1964 is a convenient point of departure for developments which are changing the ways in which bibliography as a discipline is conducted – bibliography in its widest connotation, which includes the compilation of bibliographies; how they are used; and the study of the transmission of texts.

1 The text of this essay is substantially that of the Presidential Address delivered to the Bibliographical Society in 1990. Some developments in microcomputer technology since then are referred to in the notes, but it has not been possible to incorporate all such developments.

2 Alvin Toffler, *The Third Wave* (1980). His optimistic view of the rôle which computers will play in our lives is summed up in the statement: 'The Third Wave is for those who think the human story, far from ending, has only just begun.'

Why 1964? Well, for a personal reason it was the year in which I abandoned a collaborative project based at the universities of Leeds, Edinburgh, Michigan, and Oxford to produce a *Dictionary of Tudor English* (to continue up to 1600 the work of *The Middle English Dictionary*) and started Scolar Press – a radical change in direction which brought me into close contact with developments in the printing industry for nearly ten years. In that year the National Graphical Association (NGA) was formed, and for many years attempted to resist the introduction of automated procedures into all aspects of printing.[3] IBM released the Magnetic Tape Selectric Typewriter, which used 16mm. magnetic tape and which could hold 8,400 characters on 35 feet of tape, and referred, in its publicity for the machine, to its remarkable capabilities as a 'word-processor'. The first Photon ZIP phototypesetter, developed by Higonnet and Moyroud and capable of running at 2 million ems per hour, was installed at the National Library of Medicine in Bethesda.[4] Computaprint in London was created in the same year to provide the first high-speed electronic typesetting service for electronic databases. Richard Clay became the first British company to install a computer typesetter – the Linasec, developed by Compugraphic, a company with a long tradition of introducing new technology to the printing industry.[5] The newly formed English subsidiary of Rocappi Inc., a company formed in 1963 to provide an electronic typesetting service bureau using an RCA 301 computer started work at Otford in Kent on typesetting for Dent the *Collected Poems* of Dylan Thomas, a work which was not published until 1966. John Duncan contributed a much-quoted article in the *Penrose Annual* on computerized composition entitled 'Look! No Hands!'[6] The Bickmore–Boyle system for

3 Although the NGA was involved in numerous major confrontations with printing firms between 1970 and 1980, including Times Newspapers, and large firms printing for commercial publishers, the *Graphical Journal* did print a number of very important articles in 1964 including: 'Computers in the Printing Industry' by C.T. Ross of the National Cash Register Company (May); 'The Craftsman and New Techniques' by Robert Willis (June); 'Automation and the Printing Industry' by Democrates (October). 'In Defence of Automation' by Ron Clements of the National Coal Board appeared in the January 1965 issue. For a period all outwork which formed part of the production process had to have an approved label certifying that it had been executed in conformity with NGA rules.

4 The National Library of Medicine was one of the first libraries in America to perceive the advantages of automation, and in 1958 embarked upon the Index Mechanization Project, which bore fruit in 1964 as the computerized *Index Medicus* produced on what was then the fastest phototypesetting system known as GRACE (Graphic Arts Composing System) which was built by Photon and used a Honeywell 800 computer. The software used for information retrieval for its on-line system (ELHILL) was the software adopted by the British Library in 1976, and is still in use.

5 For an account of the early history of this innovative company, founded by W.W. Garth and E.P. Hanson, see Computer Typesetting Conference, Institute of Printing, University of Sussex, July, 1966. The most significant typesetters introduced by Compugraphic were the Linasec (1963), the CG2961 (1968), the CompuWriter (1972), and the MCS 6000 (1986). The company also pioneered Optical Character Recognition (OCR), and introduced the Uniscanner (1975) which could read courier and OCR-B fonts at 1,000 characters per second.

6 In that article C.J. Duncan pleaded for 'a new vision of printing, one in which the old well-tried and honoured aesthetic traditions are retained and reinforced within a framework of advanced technology'. After surveying recent developments he went on to say: 'For the future it can be expected that authors and editors will prepare mss., layouts, typescripts, and tapes, up to the finally corrected production tape stage, at locations which may be relatively remote.'

automated cartography was launched in prototype form by the Cartographic Department of Oxford University Press in collaboration with Dobbie McInnes Electronics of Glasgow. The Canadian Government Printing Bureau decided to install computer typesetting equipment to produce the proceedings of the Canadian Parliament. HMSO successfully produced the *Astronomical Ephemeris* from punched cards produced at the Nautical Almanac Office using a Monophoto filmsetter. And in 1964 an internal committee was formed at the Library of Congress to investigate the possibility of producing bibliographical records on a computer.[7] The birth of Machine Readable Cataloguing (MARC) took place quietly, and with little fuss; but the driving forces behind what became known as the MARC Pilot Project, to have its first meeting in January 1965, were Henriette Avram and Fred Kilgour, then at Harvard, but later to become the dynamic President of the Ohio Cooperative Library Center (OCLC).[8] To an astute observer of what was happening in 1964 it should have been clear that bibliography, and the handling of the description of books in libraries, would never be the same again. Few of those involved in bibliographical enterprises of various sorts noticed. One exception was John Jolliffe, who began work at about the same time on developing a strategy for converting the British Museum's *General Catalogue*, a task which has taken nearly twenty-five years to be completed.[9] For the most part, bibliography was content to continue in much the same way as it had done for a hundred years.

The quarrels between the print and photographic unions and publishers over the introduction of computer technology in the period between 1964 and 1974 are well known.[10] That is why during this period it is so difficult to discover how typesetting was actually done. Chronicling the technological developments is quite a simple matter: the introduction of the IBM model 1130 in 1965; the Photon 713–20 which would accept unjustified tapes in 1966; the Linotron

7 Library of Congress, *Proceedings of the Third Conferene on Machine-Readable Catalog Copy* (Washington, 1966). This report provides a useful synopsis of events up to February, 1966. It contains the following statement of principles: 'Decisions to convert current or retrospective catalog records to machine-readable form may eventually involve the library community in multimillion dollar expenditures. Perhaps even more important, decisions involving the information content of the machine-readable record in a very real way determine the nature of the library of the future with respect to file searching capabilities. These problems are multiplied if each library pursues automation independently and these decisions are not coordinated.'

8 Now called the Online Computer Library Center and based at Dublin, Ohio. The OCLC database contains over 22 million records (August 1990) and is now an international bibliographical utility serving libraries in over twenty countries. With the newly developed EPIC software it is now the largest information database in the world.

9 Jolliffe's report on the conversion of the *General Catalogue* was produced as an internal document in 1967, though work on it with A. Cain had begun in 1964. After three unsuccessful attempts the conversion was finally completed in December, 1990. A CD-ROM version is available.

10 Robert Willis saw technology somewhat differently from many of his colleagues in the NGA, and in 1964 wrote: 'unless we are prepared to recognize that film taking the place of type falls within the category of a compositor's work then other people will be recruited to do that work with consequent redundancy of our own members. It is folly in the extreme to attempt to fight the new innovations which are taking place' (*Graphical Journal*, June, 1964).

505 which used Cathode Ray Tube technology and was marketed by Linotype-Paul; the Intertype Fototronic 1200 which incorporated integrated electronic circuitry in 1968; the Monophoto 600, the first electronic machine produced by Monotype, unveiled at GEC Milan in 1969; Compugraphic's CompuWriter, the first inexpensive direct-entry phototypesetter in 1971; Monotype's Lasercomp in 1976; the Mergenthaler Linotype CRTronic desk-top phototypesetter with video editing screen and floppy-disc drives in 1979; and so on, to the present day where microcomputers have the power and the software to produce books in the home.[11] But you will look in vain on the versos of title-pages for information stating how and by whom a book was actually typeset.

Since 1964 we have witnessed startling developments in the production of newspapers, magazines, and books; developments which bibliography will have to take account of if we are ever to make any sense of the transmission of texts in the future. It is clear why Philip Gaskell decided to maintain a dignified silence on developments since 1950 in his *New Introduction to Bibliography*: because coming to terms with the new technology demands a complete re-thinking of some fundamental principles. Even so, his chapter on 'Printing Practice in the Machine Press Period' is a negative treatment of a complex history.[12] It is quite reasonable to articulate principles for the analysis of texts up to 1950 predicated on what the eye perceives, but it was in that year than an experimental model of the Monophoto filmsetter was first demonstrated. In 1957 Allen and Richard Lane produced a Christmas gift by phototypesetting Erik Linklater's *Private Angelo* – possibly the first book to be produced by this method in England.[13] It was set on an Intertype Fotosetter in Garamond, and printed by offset lithography by McCorquodale. A commercial re-issue, published by Penguin, followed in 1958.

For texts produced in increasing numbers since 1964 the eye can be an unreliable aid, and one of the traditional descriptors, format, is becoming increasingly difficult to determine, due to the movement of the signature to the fold, and the practice (in some libraries) of re-binding paperbacks using over-stitching and even drastic cropping – thereby making a nonsense of the American alternative cataloguing convention of measuring centimetre height. For long runs produced on multi-station offset and rotogravure presses the 'section' becomes meaningless, since gathering and stitching are now entirely automated processes, and reel-fed presses do not normally use watermarked paper, so watermarks are of no help in determining how a book was produced. Further, while publishers are careful (on the whole) about which company prints their books they seldom divulge details about the origination of the copy.

11 For an account of technological developments in the printing industry see: Richard E. Huss, *The Development of Printers' Mechanical Typesetting Methods 1822–1925* (Charlottesville, 1973); L.W. Wallis, *A Concise Chronology of Typesetting Developments 1886–1986* (Wynkyn de Worde Society, 1988); A. Holmes, *Electronic Composition: a Practical Guide to Modern Developments* (Northwood, 1984).   12 Philip Gaskell, *New Introduction to Bibliography*, (Oxford, 1972).

13 Eric Linklater, *Private Angelo* (privately printed 1957).

The first edition of Peter Porter's *The Cost of Seriousness*[14] was printed by the Bowering Press in Plymouth in 1978. The 1987 reprint, printed by J.W. Arrowsmith in Bristol is, on the evidence of the eye, an offset replica, though on better paper than the first edition. But how was the 1978 edition produced? Both editions are perfect-bound on unwatermarked paper. I suspect film-setting, for no other reason than the placement of the punctuation and the inflexible letter-spacing.

It is difficult to be certain which was the first computer-set book. One reason for that difficulty is that, until the 1980s, many publishers were reluctant to declare how their books were set. Until a few years ago it was uncommon to find colophons in which the manner of setting was stated. In Britain, publishers were fearful of becoming involved in disputes with the National Graphical Association which had, and was willing to exercise, the power to 'black' work from companies too eager to embrace the evolving technology of electronic type-setting. That explains why Dent made so little fuss about the fact that the Everyman edition of Dylan Thomas's *Collected Poems* was computer typeset by Rocappi at Otford in Kent. Whether or not the setting of the Thomas volume preceded Margaret Drabble's *The Millstone*,[15] also set by Rocappi, is uncertain, but it is clear that Rocappi's equipment was better at setting prose than poetry.

The American parent company, Rocappi Inc., must have been involved in computer typesetting for commercial publishers at least as early as 1964, yet I have still to find evidence which confirms this. The OCLC record for Andrew Garve's (i.e. Paul Winterton's) thriller, *The Long Short Cut*, published by Harper and Row in 1968, includes the statement that 'This is the first book for which the complete text was set by electronic composition.' The text was set in 10 point Videocomp Janson on an RCA machine at a speed of 600 characters per second, and was printed from film positives by The Haddon Craftsmen. The pages were screen-assembled, and careful examination of the book reveals errors which could only have occurred on such equipment.[16]

Since about 1980 publishing has capitalized on the technology to reduce costs – but without reducing prices – by delegating to the author the responsibility for producing Camera Ready Copy [CRC]. An early example of this is the second edition of a highly technical book entitled *Principles of Interactive Computer Graphics* by William Newman and Robert Sproull, published by McGraw-Hill in 1979. As the authors explain in their Preface:

The Xerox Palo Alto Research Center very generously made its facilities available for what turned into a somewhat ambitious project to produce camera-ready copy directly from the edited manuscript. [Note the use of 'manuscript'.] The line illustrations were created with the aid of an interactive graphics system, and the text was edited on-line, formatted, combined with the line illustrations and printed on a xerographic matrix printer.

14 Peter Porter, *The Cost of Seriousness* (Oxford, 1978; reprinted 1987).
15 Margaret Drabble, *The Millstone* (1965); computer set by Rocappi, Otford, Kent; printed by C. Tinling & Co., Prescot, Lancashire.
16 For example, the page number on page 21 has slipped to the position which would have been occupied by the running-title.

Newman and Sproull's book contained, amongst other novelties, the first manifestation in print of what has now become for users of the Apple Macintosh the familiar Windows.[17] The book also incorporated numerous features for handling both text and screen images – features which were to be incorporated into desktop publishing programs like Ventura, which bring typesetting into the home.

In 1983 computer typesetting from a floppy disc supplied by the author was certainly uncommon. John Walsh, Production Manager at the Harvard University Press, assures me that the first book produced from an author's floppy discs is Ithiel de Sola Pool's *Technologies of Freedom*,[18] published in 1983, the same year in which the Introduction to the first version of *ESTC* (The British Library Collections[19]) was set from a Sirius disc supplied by me. It was, according to Walsh, produced by Pool at the Massachusetts Institute of Technology on a Honeywell 6800 word processor. The book was designed in September 1982, and editorial work was completed by December. The edition was delivered in March 1983. It is interesting to learn from Pool's acknowledgements that:

The manuscript has greatly benefited from the good ideas and meticulous attention of Michael Aronson and Virginia LaPlante of Harvard University Press. The greatest burden has been borne by Nancy Wilson and, above all, by Suzanne Planchon, who tirelessly managed the manuscript on every step of the way.

The book reveals nothing of the way in which it was produced, an unimportant omission perhaps since it is unlikely that anyone is ever going to subject Pool's book to bibliographical scrutiny. But what of the Cambridge edition of Lawrence?[20] It is an interesting story, and one that will illustrate the new challenges which face bibliography in the computer age.

Cambridge struck a deal with Granada to publish the definitive text of Lawrence's works in cheap format without the notes. Cambridge agreed to supply Granada with the tapes which they could format as they wished. The first book in the series was *Apocalypse* – Lawrence's last work. Fortified with this knowledge, there can be no reason for a bibliographer to compare the two texts: they *must* be identical, except for typographic conventions such as double or single quotes. Unless, that is, Granada received a tape which belonged to a different generation from that which produced the Cambridge text. And that is exactly what happened. Last-minute corrections never reached Granada – an understandable human error – and so we cannot assume that the Cambridge and Granada texts are identical. Careful comparison of the two texts does, in fact, reveal minor differences, which can only be accounted for by the circumstances of the manner in which the two editions were produced.

One last example of how the eye can be deceived. The English edition of

---

17 The full implementation of Windows on IBM and compatible machines was released in 1990.
18 Ithiel de Sola Pool, *The Technologies of Freedom* (Cambridge, MA, 1983).
19 The *Eighteenth-Century Short Title Catalogue*, the British Library Collections (microfiche, 1983).
20 D.H. Lawrence, *Apocalypse and the Writings on Revelation*, Mara Kalnins (The Works of D.H. Lawrence, Cambridge, 1980).

Salman Rushdie's *The Satanic Verses*[21] is stated as having been 'printed in Great Britain and filmset in Monophot Bembo'. The American edition declares itself to have been 'printed in the United States of America in Bembo'. Except for preliminaries and divisional titles, they are identical. No equipment currently available can, from a magnetic source, in different countries, produce pages which will pass the test of photographic super-imposition. Yet sample pages put to this test reveal not the slightest difference. It must be assumed that production of both editions took place in one production unit. Penguin/Viking are, understandably, reluctant to discuss the matter, but it is certain that a tape exists which could, if circumstances allowed, produce the copy for paperback editions in a matter of weeks.

Bibliography must take account of the fact that before long most writers will be composing their work on personal computers, and it will soon be common-place to find poets taking charge of the entire page layout of their work. The latest generation of desktop publishing (DTP) packages and their companion laser printers provide a wide variety of fonts (in electronic form), and complete control over the disposition of type on the page: the necessity to use expensive typesetting equipment capable of very high resolution (1,200 lines per inch) for origination is no longer necessary, since laser printers can now produce positive printing masters, thereby obviating the need for the camera stage.

The development of printing technology and that of the personal computer have come together notably in the Apple Macintosh. The Mac can drive a Linotronic 300, provided that it is equipped with a Raster Image Processor (RIP). It is hardly surprising that in America and Europe it is the preferred machine among authors and academics. The WIMP environment (Windows, Incons, Mouse, Pull-down Menus), developed by Xerox at the Palo Alto Research Center (PARC) led to a generation of Macs in which all software is controlled in a familiar manner, obviating the necessity for carrying in one's head a variety of command languages and instruction protocols. Once one has learned how to handle a Mac there is very little difficulty in mastering new software written for it. This is not the case with MSDOS applications running on the ubiquitous IBM and its clones. The original IBM PC was not an innovative machine: on all counts it was inferior to the Sirius/Victor 9000. Had IBM invented the Apple Mac, then it would no doubt be the world standard. Recognizing that to ignore a world increasingly dominated by Microsoft and IBM, it was not long before Apple accepted the inevitable and provided the facilities to handle both MSDOS and UNIX applications. The rapidity with which the market responded to desktop publishing is evident in the growing number of word-processing programmes (like Word, Wordperfect, Wordstar) which come very close to what could only be achieved on a Mac three years ago.[22] At the time of writing it is

---

21 Salman Rushdie, *The Satanic Verses* (London, Viking, 1989; New York, Viking, 1989).
22 See K. Wilson-Davies, *Desktop Publishing* (1989); *Desktop Publishing Today* (Tonbridge, 1986–); Richard Stutely, *Advanced Desktop Publishing* (Chichester, 1989); James Carson, *Desktop Publishing and Libraries* (1988); Richard J. Jantz, *Ventura Publisher for the IBM PC* (New York, 1987).

probably fair to say that desktop publishing is dominated by two packages: Aldus Pagemaker and Xerox Ventura. The former is page-based, and highly effective for short documents; the latter is document-based, and can handle documents of up to 9,999 pages, and is ideal for the production of full-length books. A recent book on desktop publishing[23] includes a directory of Postscript bureaux in the British Isles equipped with Linotronic imagesetters (series 100/300/500) that can output a Postscript file at high resolution (e.g. 1,200 dots per inch) on to bromide paper, film, or plate material. All the bureaux listed accept files created with either Pagemaker or Ventura.

An example of a substantial book produced using a Mac SE and Pagemaker output to a Linotronic 100 is *The Age of William III & Mary II*,[24] intended as a reference encyclopaedia and exhibition catalogue to accompany the exhibition held at the Grolier Club in New York and the Folger Shakespeare Library in Washington in 1988–9. It is a complex book, with several hundred illustrations, and only occasionally betrays its manner of composition – which is fully documented in the colophon.

Before leaving the subject of text origination in order to suggest some of the wider implications for bibliography of the computer revolution, it is worth noting a novel technology which might well appeal one day to an adventurous publisher. It is a process whereby a typeface – any typeface – or a script is captured in digital form, subjected to editing in order to tidy its appearance, and then loaded electronically into a laser printer. In other words, it makes possible a genuine type/script-facsimile of any book whenever printed or written. I am indebted to Michael Lesk for granting permission to reproduce pages from his remarkable facsimile of the first edition of *Tristram Shandy* (illustration 1), and his computer version of Jaggard's type as used in the 1623 edition of Shakespeare (illustration 2). It is obvious that the better the original printing, the more convincing can be the electronic replica, and the possibilities yielded by well-printed type-specimen books are endless. Now that the Oxford Shakespeare is available in electronic form for microcomputers,[25] there is no reason why students should not be provided with legible texts printed in a typeface which would have been familiar to Shakespeare's readers.

Computers are changing rapidly the ways in which bibliography can be carried out in research libraries, and while it is obvious that *ESTC* can serve the community of eighteenth-century literary and historical research far better than the printed volumes of *STC* and Wing, it has proved to be an extremely expensive enterprise. It was intended as a model for machine-readable enumerative bibliography, but has inevitably succumbed to international library politics. It must be borne in mind that the standards still upheld by some national libraries evolved in the 1970s – a decade of relative affluence compared with what we face now and are likely to have to face in the next ten or more years. The

---

23 K. Wilson-Davies, *Desk Top Publishing* (1989), pp. 175–90.
24 *The Age of William III & Mary II. Power, Politics, and Patronage 1688–1702* (Williamsburg, 1989).
25 *The Works of Shakespeare* (electronic edition, Oxford, 1990).

progressive automation of libraries in Europe and North America is based upon the belief that somehow computers will make the administration of libraries easier, widen the horizons of knowledge, assist scholarship, and benevolently lead us from darkness to light. It is, of course, as fatuous a dream as ever entered the head of a Laputian professor. The evangelical tone of the prophets of the New Jerusalem makes curious reading today.

In 1964 the *New Scientist* started publishing a series of articles on computers and their likely impact on civilization. In the following year it solicited the views of a number of eminent scientists and men in public affairs, and published these in a curious pamphlet entitled *The Gentle Computer*. Lord Bowden contributed the introduction which has the title: 'The Second Industrial Revolution'. Having enumerated all the benefits which would flow from their widespread adoption he concludes:

[24]

ſes,—their coins and their cockle-ſhells, their drums and their trumpets, their fiddles, their pallets,——their maggots and their butterflies? —and ſo long as a man rides his HOBBY-HORSE peaceably and quietly along the King's highway, and neither compels you or me to get up behind him,——pray, Sir, what have either you or I to do with it?

C H A P. VIII.

—*De guſtibus non eſt diſputandum*;—that is, there is no diſputing againſt HOBBY-HORSES; and, for my part, I ſeldom do; nor could I with any ſort of grace, had I been an enemy to them at the bottom; for happening, at certain intervals and changes of the Moon, to be both fiddler and painter, according as the fly ſtings: --- Be it known to you, that I keep

(25)

keep a couple of pads myſelf, upon which, in their turns, (nor do I care who knows it) I frequently ride out and take the air; — tho' ſometimes, to my ſhame be it ſpoken, I take ſomewhat longer journies than what a wiſe man would think altogether right.——But the truth is,— I am not a wiſe man; ——and beſides am a mortal of ſo little conſequence in the world, it is not much matter what I do; ſo I ſeldom fret or fume at all about it: Nor does it much diſturb my reſt when I ſee ſuch great Lords and tall Perſonages as hereafter follow; — ſuch, for inſtance, as my Lord A, B, C, D, E, F, G, H, I, K, L, M, N, O, P, Q, and ſo on, all of a row, mounted upon their ſeveral horſes;--ſome with large ſtirrups, getting on in a more grave and ſober pace; ---- others on the contrary, tuck'd up to their very chins, with whips acroſs their

1a A computer-generated Caslon fount created by Michael Lesk used to set an edition of *Tristram Shandy* using a microcomputer and Postscript printer. Reproduced by courtesy of Michael Lesk. (Reduced size.)

I could go on for a long time detailing such examples, but enough has been said to show the way in which computers, properly used, can increase both our wealth and, indirectly, our culture. It is clear that the 'growth' of computers is desirable. In any case, the economic facts of life will force them upon us, just as cottage industries were forced out of existence by the first industrial revolution.[26]

Nigel Calder said that:

American experience has shown that the business espousing computers and taking them seriously makes money with them; those who merely toy with them find that, with computers, as with women, the mistress is costlier than the wife.'[27]

26 'The Second Industrial Revolution', *The Gentle Computer*, p. 5.
27 'The Hottest Invention', *The Gentle Computer*, p. 5.

[24]

fes,—their coins and their cockle-fhells, their drums and their trumpets, their fiddles, their pallets,——their maggots and their butterflies? —and fo long as a man rides his HOBBY-HORSE peaceably and quietly along the King's highway, and neither compels you or me to get up behind him,——pray, Sir, what have either you or I to do with it ?

CHAP. VIII.

—*De guſtibus non eſt diſputandum* ;—that is, there is no difputing againſt HOBBY-HORSES; and, for my part, I feldom do; nor could I with any fort of grace, had I been an enemy to them at the bottom; for happening, at certain intervals and changes of the Moon, to be both fiddler and painter, according as the fly ſtings : --- Be it known to you, that I keep

(25)

keep a couple of pads myfelf, upon which, in their turns, (nor do I care who knows it) I frequently ride out and take the air ; — tho' fometimes, to my fhame be it fpoken, I take fomewhat longer journies than what a wife man would think altogether right.----But the truth is,--- I am not a wife man ; ——and befides am a mortal of fo little confequence in the world, it is not much matter what I do ; fo I feldom fret or fume at all about it : Nor does it much difturb my reft when I fee fuch great Lords and tall Perfonages as hereafter follow ; --- fuch, for inftance, as my Lord A, B, C, D, E, F, G, H, I, K, L, M, N, O, P, Q, and fo on, all of a row, mounted upon their feveral horfes ;--fome with large ſtirrups, getting on in a more grave and fober pace ; ---- others on the contrary, tuck'd up to their very chins, with whips acrofs their

1b A facsimile of an opening from *Tristram Shandy* (1750–1). Reproduced by permission of the British Library Board. (Same size.)

Patrick Ryan sounded a warning note that has particular relevance for some large institutions today:

Besides kindly proliferating its own acolytes, the computer allays fears of unemployment in the clerical market by making Nirvana for that familiar work-waster who lurks in all centralised administrations, the Statistical Maniac . . . Previously confined to harassing operational staff with such interminable analyses of past figures as were obtainable with quill pen or comptometer, he now finds that the computer provides facilities for fiddling with figures beyond even his wildest, maniacal dreams. More clerks are soon needed in the field to deal with replies to his questions about meaningless variations in statistical patterns.[28]

Since 1964 we have witnessed an enormous investment by commerce and industry in the creation and distribution of machine-readable data. Libraries, and those who use them for research, have predictably lagged behind; doubtless because the necessity for instantaneous information about the whereabouts of

28 'The computer, You and I', *The Gentle Computer*, p. 8.

Oh that this too too solid Flesh, would melt,
Thaw, and resolue it selfe into a Dew:
Or that the Euerlasting had not fixt
His Cannon gainst Selfe slaughter. O God, O God
How weary, stale, flat, and vnprofitable
Seemes to me all the vses of this world?
Fie on t? Oh fie, fie, tis an vnweeded Garden
That growes to Seed: Things rank, and grosse in Nature
Possesse it meerely.

Oh that this too too solid Flesh, would melt,
Thaw, and resolue it selfe into a Dew:
Or that the Euerlasting had not fixt
His Cannon gainst Selfe slaughter. O God, O God
How weary, stale, flat, and vnprofitable
Seemes to me all the vses of this world?
Fie on t? Oh fie, fie, tis an vnweeded Garden
That growes to Seed: Things rank, and grosse in Nature
Possesse it meerely.

2 A computer-generated fount created from a page of the First Folio, 1623. This fount was then used to set this passage using a microcomputer and a Postscript printer. It is not intended to be a type-facsimile of the original setting. Reproduced by courtesy of Michael Lesk.

an eighteenth-century political tract is less than for the latest article concerned with tissue-rejection in transplant surgery. Technologies which service the profit motive thrive because industry will always pay the market price for information. Research in the humanities and social sciences, by contrast, tends to rely upon numerous and disparate sources, is less focused, commands a very much smaller market value, and cannot expect its means to be financially well endowed. Another factor which differentiates scientific and technical information from that required by the humanist and social scientist is the relatively short half-life of the former, which is why retrieval of computer-held data is generally 'last in first out'.[29] An article on interferon quickly becomes obsolete, whereas most historical research would benefit greatly if the enquirer could specify that the results of a key-word or subject search were displayed in chronological sequence. There seems at present no on-line system in any library which provides this simple facility.[30]

Warren Haas spelt out the changes affecting research libraries in 1980:

The lives of those charged with managing large, general research libraries are no longer as simple as they once seemed. The sheer size of these collections, which have tended to double every fifteen or twenty years during much of this century, has made all operations more difficult. That growth, coupled with rising costs of labour and materials, has been accompanied in the past two decades by the application to library operations of the new technology of computers and communications, resulting in new intellectual, financial, and organizational demands. Add new and higher levels of expectation held by a growing body of users: a situation emerges that is forcing an intense and comprehensive review of the way research libraries work, both individually and together.[31]

That statement is as true in 1991 as it was a decade ago; yet we are no nearer a solution to the dilemma of balancing the needs and expectations of advanced research.

Designing an On-line Public Access Catalogue (OPAC) for a library concerned for the most part with servicing pre-determined and well-understood needs is not very difficult: such systems are successfully operating throughout North America and Europe, but their success depends, generally speaking, on a clear perception by the host of the needs of the user. For a large encyclopaedic library that perception is crucially important, and more often than not conspicuously absent. For one thing, a complex research collection demands a collegial perception, resident not in any one mind, but shared amongst a skilled and scholarly staff who understand the collections for which they are responsible, but who are conscious of the defects of the various tools at their disposal. Richard de Gennaro predicted in 1979:

---

29 On most on-line databases records retrieved are displayed in reverse order of input, regardless of date of publication.

30 The special on-line EPIC retrieval system permits off-line prints of records sorted in chronological order, a facility not available on other large databases.

31 Warren J. Haas, 'Research Libraries and the Dynamics of Change', *Scholarly Publishing*, 11 (April 1980): 195–202.

What is needed, and what is being developed and implemented, is a new library technology based on electronics as well as fundamental restructuring of traditional library goals, relationships, and dependencies; this restructuring will force all libraries to undergo a major transformation in the coming decade . . . The economic benefits of automation seem likely to be marginal at best if library managers aspire simply to substitute the computer for manual procedures rather than use it to transform the nature of library operations.[32]

The transformation is what should interest us. If it means making research libraries more like supermarkets, then the horizons for bibliographical research will shrink rather than widen, and discovery – which is one of the strongest motivations for research – will diminish. It need not be so, but I am not confident that it will be otherwise. The forces of economic determinism seem insuperable, and there is too ready a willingness to pin our faith on electronic solutions to problems which have not been clearly grasped. Using a computer to try and solve a problem not clearly understood invariably results in muddle. The full-scale transformation predicted by de Gennaro will demand valid solutions to problems many orders of magnitude greater than libraries have had to face in converting manual catalogues to machine-readable form.

The model proposed for this transformation is that of the network, in which all libraries are interconnected, and it becomes theoretically possible to discover from any networked node what is available everywhere else. It is technically feasible, of course, but there are important details which must be resolved first. One is the need to develop transparent software which can translate a search formulated according to a familiar protocol into one understood by a remote computer using an incompatible protocol, and containing data differently structured. Another will be the development of local systems capable of handling hundreds of simultaneous interrogations, many of which require connection to remote hosts. Then there is the logistical problem of providing the hardware and storage space, because the possibilities provided by automation typically yield results which take much longer to assimilate than consulting a linear catalogue, in whatever medium: printed, card, or microfiche. Observation of readers consulting an on-line terminal confirms the view that more time is needed to retrieve the required information than consulting manual catalogues. Access to a diversity of sources will necessarily increase the time needed. Experience has shown that the architects of on-line systems invariably underestimate both the volume of transactions and the number of terminals needed to satisfy the local community. When the system begins to show signs of collapse two remedies are possible: (1) restrict the volume of data accessible; (2) restrict the kinds of search allowed. For all but the simplest of searches the user is then required to pay a premium. However it is put, it adds up to another tax on knowledge. An alternative, made possible by the development of optical disc technology and the CD-ROM, is to package data in marketable collections and force the user (i.e. the

---

32 Richard de Gennaro, 'Research Libraries Enter the Information Age' (Richard Rogers Bowker Memorial Lecture, 1979), *Library Journal*, no. 20 (15 November 1979): 2,405–10.

other library) to provide the hardware. Either way, someone has to pay for the service.

What is clear is that information technology will force libraries to be different from what we have known. What is not clear, however, is the impact that the difference will have on the way research is conducted, and the relationship which will develop between those who preserve and administer research collections and those who use them. The administrators may, indeed, have a better idea of where they are going now than they did in 1964: but do they know how to get there?

Long-term aspirations of universities and the needs of scholarship must be kept firmly in mind. The public-interest case, to extend access to recorded information world-wide, at acceptable costs, and without constraint, must be pressed with skill and conviction by all who feel concern.[33]

The sincerity with which that plea was made almost suggests that its author was aware of a struggle all but lost.

So, were the prophets wrong when, twenty years ago, they promised us a bright future in which information about everything would be available everywhere? Joseph Raben encouraged such hopes in 1979:

Whatever the historians of the future make of our period, they will undoubtedly record that it corresponded in its potential to the Renaissance, to the opening of men's minds to all kinds of new and old knowledge as that knowledge was made accessible through the technology of the printing press. If we can recognize the revolutionary nature of the latest technological advance, we may also contribute to another birth of learning.[34]

I must say, I am not at all sure that I am living in a second Renaissance, though I am sure it is a revolution. If bibliographers lose their enthusiasm for determining the transmission of knowledge, and librarians their enthusiasm for ensuring that the texts which record that transmission are acquired, preserved, and made available, then we are far from living in a Renaissance.

33 Warren J. Hass, 'Research Libraries and the Dynamics of Change', *Scholarly Publishing*, 11 (April 1980): 202.
34 Joseph Raben, 'The Electronic Revolution and the World Just Around the Corner', *Scholarly Publishing*, 10 (April 1979): 195–209.

History of the book

D. F. McKENZIE

The history of books, if not 'history of the book', has been implicit in the work of the Bibliographical Society since it began. For the writing, replication, distribution, and reception of texts were always legitimate objects of enquiry and report. Their description, collection, and classification, whether as manuscripts or printed books, have drawn upon studies of the labour, materials, technologies, and processes used to make, sell, and house them.

Almost a quarter-century before the Society was founded, Edward Arber's *A Transcript of the Registers of the Company of Stationers of London, 1554–1640* (1875–94) had already begun to open up a treasury of evidence for contextual studies. Arber's work laid the foundations for the Society's *Century of the English Book Trade* (1905) by E. Gordon Duff, the handlists of printers which Duff also originated, H.R. Plomer's and others' dictionaries of printers, the lists of printers' and booksellers' wills and of alien members of the book trade, and the editions of further Stationers' Company and other records by W.W. Greg, Eleanor Boswell, and William A. Jackson. The work instrumental in making the physical book and its production fundamental to literary studies, McKerrow's *Introduction to Bibliography for Literary Students* (Oxford, 1927), began life in *The Library* in 1912–13.

Two concerns dominated the Society's first half-century – to create a systematic record of the extant printed books to the end of 1640, and to establish precisely how Britain's most important literary texts from the same period were transmitted from manuscript to print. Each of those concerns implied a history of the documents in their sequential relationships.[1] Indeed, without such a basis, no comprehensive history of books and their making, and no adequate account of the forms of texts and their influence, is possible.

If one defines bibliography by what is done in its name, as distinct from theoretical formulations of its function, it is incontestable that the Society's understanding of the discipline was generously hospitable to a wide range of historical enquiries. Yet it remains true to say that such a concern for history was no more than implicit in the Society's aims. For the distinguished

---

1 For an excellent account of 'The Bibliographical Society as a Band of Pioneers', see the contribution by Julian Roberts to *Pioneers in Bibliography*, ed. Robin Myers and Michael Harris (Winchester, 1988), pp. 86–99.

triumvirate who set its priorities in the earlier twentieth century – A.W. Pollard, R.B. McKerrow, and W.W. Greg – the rationale of bibliography and its application lay rather in tracing the relations between the extant witnesses to the texts of a limited corpus of English classics and the even earlier versions, now lost, that their readings might be argued to imply. That enterprise and the specific bibliographical skills it calls for remain highly significant functions of the discipline. They contribute to and are informed by our understanding of the crucial historical rôles of the book as such. But in the Society's earlier years, those rôles, let alone the relevance to them of the production of all texts in their great diversity of forms and functions, were not thought to be, strictly, a bibliographical matter.

For that extended and explicit interest in the book trade, we need to look instead to a distinct group of bibliographers brought into being in the early 1930s by John Johnson, Printer to the University of Oxford. These were principally Johnson himself, Strickland Gibson, Stanley Morison, Theodore Besterman, and Graham Pollard, three at least of whom earned their living from the making or selling of books. Their story is admirably told by Esther Potter.[2] Johnson had long been collecting materials towards a history of printing and bookselling and by 1932 had begun to plan a collection of articles illustrative of trade practices. Within a month these had become, in prospect, a series of monographs. Percy Simpson was approached to write on proof-correction, Morison on the Fell types, Pollard on binding prices; Gibson, Besterman, Laurence Hanson, A.F. Johnson, and Turner Berry were also recruited; and Johnson laid plans for Pollard to edit 'a modest chrestomathy of the principal documents' for the history of the book trade down to 1830. In the event, seven major works appeared.[3]

Yet much of the interest aroused by Johnson and so actively developed by Pollard in the 1930s was to bear fruit only much later, as in Pollard's 1959 Sandars Lectures, 'The English Market for Printed Books' (*Publishing History*, 4 (1978): 9–48), Pollard's and Ehrman's *The Distribution of Books by Catalogue from the Invention of Printing to 1800* (Cambridge, 1965), and Morison's *John Fell, the University Press and the 'Fell' Types* (Oxford, 1967).

Throughout those same years, however, from the early 1930s to the mid 1960s, and long before *histoire du livre* became a fashionable focus of enquiry, many other works contributed significantly to an understanding of the history of books and the role of the book in history. One thinks of Morison's *History of The Times* (1935–52), Marjorie Plant's *The English Book Trade: An Economic History of*

---

2 'Oxford Books on Bibliography', *Pioneers in Bibliography*, ed. Myers and Harris, pp. 101–16.
3 *Proof-Reading in the Sixteenth, Seventeenth and Eighteenth Centuries* (Oxford, 1935), by Percy Simpson; *Catalogue of Printing Types by English and Scottish Printers, 1665–1830* (Oxford, 1935), by W. Turner Berry and A.F. Johnson; *The Beginnings of Systematic Bibliography* (1936), by Theodore Besterman; *English Printers' Types of the Sixteenth Century* (1936), by Frank Isaac; *Government and the Press, 1695–1763* (Oxford, 1936), by Laurence Hanson; *The Publishing Firm of Cadell and Davies. Select Correspondence and Accounts, 1793–1836* (Oxford, 1938), edited by Theodore Besterman; and *Print and Privilege at Oxford to the Year 1700* (Oxford, 1946), by Strickland Gibson and John Johnson.

the Making and Sale of Books (1939), Ellic Howe's *The London Compositor: Documents Relating to Wages, Working Conditions and Customs of the London Printing Trade, 1785–1900* (1947), H.S. Bennett's *English Books and Readers* (Cambridge, 1952–70), Cyprian Blagden's rich and intelligent forays into the history of the Stationers' Company, Allan Stevenson's *The Problem of the Missale Speciale* (1967), Richard D. Altick's *The English Common Reader: A Social History of the Mass Reading Public, 1800–1900* (Chicago, 1957). There were also many studies of publishers and their relations with authors, house histories of printing firms, and accounts of the more peripheral products of the press like ballads and chapbooks, children's books, maps, prints, and music.

The relevance of contextual evidence was always tacitly accepted and at times even openly avowed.[4] There was no lack of commitment to the principle of a national retrospective short-title catalogue and its value in collection building, no lack of theory in textual criticism, and no lack of major historical studies. The Society itself, as a distinctive and mutually supportive community of librarians, academics, collectors, and working members of the book trades, was ideally placed to demonstrate the unity of all bibliographical enterprise and the means by which it entered into the fabric of all historical enquiry, whether literary, religious, political, social, economic, or more broadly cultural.

The record is one of a remarkably diverse and sustained scholarship devoted to the historical study of the book trade in Britain, from at least Caxton to the mid-twentieth-century newspaper press. And for the years up to 1700 it had unrivalled bibliographical control of the objects themselves – books as the products of trade – and of the record, by printer and publisher, of the contexts of their production. While the full extension of that control into and beyond the eighteenth century had to await a new technology, not to mention the experience and energies of a Robin Alston,[5] there were no conceptual doubts about the need. D.F. Foxon's magisterial *English Verse 1701–50: A Catalogue of Separately Printed Poems* (Cambridge, 1975) advanced the frontier with every assurance that in the detail of such a *catalogue* there also lay the evidence for a *history* of text production in the first half of the eighteenth century. Such is the

---

4 Julian Roberts, for example, in 'The Bibliographical Society as a Band of Pioneers', p. 96, notes Michael Sadleir's wider awareness and cites the following passage from Sadleir's article in *Studies in Retrospect*: 'The bibliographer may, therefore, be called upon to show knowledge or understanding of the relationship between author and publisher; the type of contract usual at any period . . . the fashion for part issue merging into that for magazine serial; the processes of book manufacture – paper, typography, illustration, binding and end-papers – in vogue at different times; the machinery of sale by publisher to wholesaler, retailer and circulating library, involving trade terms and other technicalities; the sequence of "secondary" and cheaper editions and their physical qualities; the publisher–jobber who sold other firms' sheets over his own imprint; the gradual development of the remainder as we understand it to-day' (p. 154).

5 As director of the Scolar Press, Alston had made facsimile editions of hundreds of early books cheaply available for study on the premise that, when texts were reproduced in forms as close as possible to those in which they originally appeared, they recovered important historical evidence lost to modern editions. His perception of the historical significance of enumerative bibliography was influential in shaping the editorial principles applied in *ESTC*, of which he was the initial editor.

testimony of its second volume of indexes, especially the still under-exploited appendix of notabilia, and such the application in his 1976 Lyell Lectures, now published as *Pope and the Early Eighteenth-Century Book-Trade* (ed. James McLaverty, Oxford, 1991). Short-title catalogues, though not themselves arranged chronologically, serve both diachronic and synchronic forms of historical enquiry: a chronological index (or computer sort by date) may in fact be less significant in tracing the life-work of one author, printer, or bookseller than in opening up study *across* the full range and inter-relationship of (printed) texts produced in any one year.

What then was missing? Why should that larger enterprise seem to have been initiated, not in Britain but in France, with the publication in Paris in 1958 of *L'Apparition du livre* by Lucien Febvre and H.J. Martin? The fact is that if one were to seek, in those last few years of the Society's first half-century and the early years of its next, any explicit claim for bibliography as a discipline defined by the full range of historical and analytical studies appearing at that time, one would seek it in vain.

The nearest we come to a conceptual framework of the kind offered by *histoire du livre* may be found perhaps in Pollard's earlier development of the book-trade sections of the *Cambridge Bibliography of English Literature* (Cambridge, 1940) and his other contributions to that work.[6] In later years, as President of the Society, he sought to set up a publishing programme more sensitive to the primacy of trade documents as historical evidence. It would be wrong to rank his achievement higher than Greg's, for they were of quite different kinds, but it could be argued that Pollard's example speaks to the future in ways that Greg's does not. It does so simply because he addressed more fundamental and more diversely complex conditions of text production, and a wider range of evidence (in its forms, dispersal, and chronology), than were entertained by those whose attention was confined mainly to the early printed drama. Quite apart from the range of his learning, Pollard had an unrivalled ability to find the telling detail and then to extend it in a sketch of the broader patterns of production and distribution. Being concerned for the trade, he was unconstrained by canon and could range with ease from early to late, major to minor, manuscript to print. In those ways he surpassed the insights of *L'Apparition du livre* with what now must seem its misplaced emphasis on the event of printing.

But neither Pollard nor Greg quite perceived, or at least fully expressed, their common interest in the more comprehensively inclusive terms of general history. When, for example, in *An Enquiry into the Nature of Certain Nineteenth Century Pamphlets* (1934), Pollard and Carter exposed the forgeries of Thomas J. Wise, sometime President of the Bibliographical Society, that work, informed though it was by the historical evidence of trade documents, paper technology,

---

6 The significance of the *Cambridge Bibliography* in contributing conceptually to a definition of how 'the book' must be defined for any adequate history of the rôle of print did not end there. It may also be traced in Peter Davison's contribution to section 6 ('Newspapers and Magazines') of volume IV of the *New Cambridge Bibliography of English Literature*, edited by I.R. Willison (Cambridge, 1972).

and type, was seen more as a triumph of analytical bibliography than as an exercise in book history. As the title implies, it reinforced an editorial and bibliophilic concern for authenticity. Much the same point might be made about a quite different work, the edition by Harry Carter and Herbert Davis of Moxon's 1683 *Mechanick Exercises on the Whole Art of Printing* (Oxford, 1958). However independently valuable the scholarship devoted to that edition (and it is massively so) the work itself spoke to what F.P. Wilson had called 'the new bibliography' and a then current and wholly laudable concern to inform editors about the mechanics of the transmission of texts. Such was also the focus of the most magnificent product of the Society's publishing efforts in the 1950s, Sir Walter Greg's *Bibliography of the English Printed Drama to the Restoration* (1939–59). The record of British bibliography, pragmatic and (in John Feather's word) bibliocentric, reveals a deep resistance to generality and abstraction. One might note a similar resistance in the work of such distinguished North American bibliographers as Fredson Bowers and G. Thomas Tanselle, whose formidable achievements in descriptive and analytical bibliography, in the theory of textual criticism, and in editing impressively extend the example set by Greg. As Nicolas Barker notes with reference to *L'Apparition du livre*, 'Le Livre', like German *Buchwesen*, is an abstraction: 'It does not come naturally in English, which is equally insensitive to the definite article, or to its absence, as in Martin's later grand study of the press in seventeenth-century France, *Livre, pouvoirs et société à Paris*' (Geneva, 1969).[7] 'The Book' still has a ring of an imported phrase.

Paradoxically, a convergence of the various forms of British and North American bibliographical scholarship into a more unified historical discipline, and more abstractly describable one, might be said to date, not from *L'Apparition du livre* but from a new perception, in the 1960s, of the critical relevance of the detail in book-trade archives. Two important consequences were to follow.

First, the use of archival evidence to confute many ill-informed assumptions made by analytical bibliographers about the processes of book production, if initially disconcerting and subversive, was salutary in demonstrating the interdependent nature of text production in the printing house and the extraordinarily wide range of such interdependent texts. This meant that the work of printing the sheets of one book (usually the sole concern of its later editor) entailed a complex series of relations with other jobs in concurrent production. These affected the division of labour, choice of materials, and the rate of progress. But the more significant point was the clear necessity, in reconstructing those past events, of invoking the concept of a network and the rôles within it of a great diversity of textual forms. Mobility of labour, common sources of supply, the high incidence of shared printing in earlier centuries evidenced from the study of type and paper, as well as shared investment in

7 See John Feather, 'Cross-Channel Currents: Historical Bibliography and l'histoire du livre', *Lib.* VI, 2 (1980): 1–15; and Nicolas Barker, 'Reflections on the History of the Book', *BC.* (Spring 1990): 9–26.

copyrights, merely extended the pattern to the whole community of printers and booksellers.[8]

Second, the rich diversity of authors' manuscripts, proofs, revises, and successive revisions, which had to be confronted by the editors of nineteenth- and twentieth-century works, had a slow but cumulative effect in making untenable any idea of a single authoritative version of most literary texts. Their relation one to another came to be seen less in terms of their descent from a common archetype and more as differing responses, each with its own integrity, to distinct publishing contexts. Publishers' archives themselves, like those of printers, also revealed in the multiplicity of their detail about formats, costings, edition quantities, design, and sheer range of texts, a complex matrix of conditions affecting by imputation the market for a work, the manner and range of its distribution, and the forms of its reception.

Both consequences bred a lively awareness of the value of short-title catalogues. Their prime rôle in organizing and giving access to the extant national printed archive was unaffected, but they also came to be seen as an essential condition of our understanding the nature and scale of text production, whether by author (often anonymous, pseudonymous, and multiple), printer, bookseller, format, volume, place, and time, or in the dynamics of the relationships between texts as one work co-existed with or generated others. When in 1976 planning of an eighteenth-century short-title catalogue began in earnest, it was readily seen that such enquiries could be met by the new technology of computing: with its ability to search quickly on several fields, it transformed the nature of bibliographical and historical research. Once the catalogues to 1700 are also in machine-readable form they will make feasible far more complex analyses of the forms and uses of texts across three-and-a-half centuries of British history.

From the point of view of 'history of the book', the important thing is the

---

8 The earliest British archives to give detailed accounts of composition, presswork, materials, and the organization of work in a printing house (the records of the Cambridge University Press) date from the late seventeenth century. Their testimony is at most points confirmed and at others complemented in the later eighteenth century by the records of the Bowyers, Ackers, and Strahan in Britain, and by those of the Société Typographique of Neuchâtel in Switzerland. Notwithstanding differences in date, scale, and the kind of books produced by each, they all offer more complex models of text production than had been earlier entertained. The richest archive of all is that of the Plantin-Moretus Museum at Antwerp, dating from the middle of the sixteenth century. See L. Voet, *The Golden Compasses*, 2 vols. (Amsterdam, 1969–72), for an account of the Plantin archive; Robert Darnton, *The Business of Enlightenment: A Publishing History of the 'Encyclopédie'* (Cambridge, 1979), which draws upon the Neuchâtel records; D.F. McKenzie, *The Cambridge University Press, 1696–1712: A Bibliographical Study*, 2 vols. (Cambridge, 1966); D.F. McKenzie and J.C. Ross, *A Journal of Charles Ackers, Printer of the 'London Magazine'* (Oxford, 1968); and Keith Maslen and John Lancaster, *The Bowyer Ledgers: The Printing Accounts of William Bowyer Father and Son . . . with a Checklist of Bowyer Printing 1699–1777* (London: The Bibliographical Society; New York: The Bibliographical Society of America, 1991). For a general discussion of the implications for analytical bibliography of such records, see D.F. McKenzie, 'Printers of the Mind: Some Notes on Bibliographical Theories and Printing-house Practices', *SB*, 22 (1969), 1–75.

changed perception of their use. Enumerative bibliography in Britain has opened up riches unparalleled in other countries and well beyond the dreams of descriptive and analytical bibliography. It permits the resurrection of the most marginal texts and their makers (the documents and writers who have always been excluded from the merely literary canon), and thereby the study of all who were kept from the centres of power by reason of their sex, race, religion, provincial or colonial status. In that, it opens up the possibility of a far more comprehensive reconstruction of cultural history. Since bibliography as such knows no canon, only economic expediency will limit access by such catalogues to 'books that last', whether as physical books or great works. The 'ephemera' of broadsides, notices, images, tracts – all the physically slight, evanescent, occasional, uncanonical, but prolific missives of commercial impositions, entertainment, radical protest, and state power – are also enrolled as testimony to the dense and complex nature of any culture served by print and the complexity of its reconstruction.

Such catalogues cannot, however, tell the full story: the continuing presence of manuscripts, the texts lost to history by their failure to survive in manuscript or print, the import and export trade in books, the second-hand trade, the metatextual functions of private libraries, the number and nature of successive readings and partial readings (to others in company or alone), and the eternal concurrence of graphic images and formal and informal oral texts – all of these further complicate for any history the retrieval of past practices in the use of texts, let alone of those who read, viewed, spoke, or heard them. So too do typewriters and computers. In their application to text production they could be said to be only chirographic aids, producing informal texts that escape cataloguing. By networking and the provision of multiple points of access, the computer screen (like the wireless listening post before it) is beginning to emulate the principle of replication fundamental to printing, but fully efficient access to its texts, and systems to ensure their survival, for the time being remain dependent on photo-offset printing.

Nor can a national catalogue stand alone, for such is the international trade in books and the ideas they mediate that one archive must complement another. When used with comparable national retrospective catalogues in other countries, especially those of former British dependencies, they will provide unprecedented access to evidence for documenting intertextual relations between nations, whether by direct import or export of the textual artefacts, by translation, or in the dialectic of cultural influence and response.

If those reflections suggest an explosion of bibliographical studies, a complementary (as distinct from contrary) implosion may be found in finer readings of the very physicality of the book. That relation between physical detail and intellectual history is the substance of Stanley Morison's argument in *Politics and Script*:

The bibliographer may be able, by the physical form of an inscription, manuscript, book, newspaper, or other medium of record, to reveal considerations that appertain to the history of something distinct from religion, politics, and literature, namely: the history of the use of the intellect.[9]

The investigation and demonstration are no less bibliographical because their end may be an enhanced historical understanding as distinct from a bibliographical description or an edition.

The commonsense view is that the object 'book' is like any other discrete artefact, with a stable form whose detailed features can be traced back to an author and to the materials and processes of constructing its implied content or meaning. As such, its primary witness to the events which brought it into being as an object – the customary concern of analytical bibliography – presents indispensable evidence of its history. Yet the physical signs in a book also make sense only in terms of our assumptions about the historical conditions and processes by which they were made. Meanings are not therefore inherent but are constructed by successive interpretative acts, both by those who write, design, and print books and by those who buy and read them. For confirmation, we need only note as self-evident bibliographical and historical fact the diversity of a text's most obvious physical transformations when reprinted. Its presentation in different formats and typefaces, on different papers in different bindings, and its sale at different times, places, and prices, imply distinct conditions and uses and must vary the meanings its readers make from it. In that sense, the book (or script) as an *un*stable physical form in its descent through successive versions is the more valuable in offering ubiquitous evidence – in the physical signs embedded in the documents themselves – for 'history of the book' as a study of the changing *conditions* of meaning and hence of reading.[10] In their finer forms of verbal variation and typographic presentation those conditions call for even subtler interpretation.

Still more serious for any history of 'the book' as an account of the production and reception of texts is the instability of language itself. Most books mediate verbal texts, and these are a very special product of the human mind. However predetermined their content, they remain radically unstable. For every act of reading is a new act of composition: everyone reads the same text differently; no one reads the same text twice in the same way. Because in that sense meaning is again conditional, the study of the *conditions* under which texts are generated – a study bibliographical in its central concern for the physical forms of texts – provides any 'history of the book' with its rationale as one of the most powerful means we have of recovering the past, for it is only through such signs that we gain access to those conditions.

More radically still, that truth about the instability of language is common to

---

9 *Politics and Script: Aspects of Authority and Freedom in the Development of Graeco-Latin Script from the Sixth Century B.C. to the Twentieth Century A.D.*, edited and completed by Nicolas Barker (Oxford, 1972), p. 1.
10 Roland Barthes made a similar point about language, writing, and literature in *Critique et vérité* (Paris, 1966), pp. 56–7, describing a science of literature not as a science of content but as a science of the conditions of content, that is, a science of forms.

all languages, whether verbal, visual, aural, or even tactile. What were once thought of as acts of comprehending or consuming a ready-made text in any of those forms are now seen to be further and variable acts of textual construction.

The process is perhaps most evident in oral cultures where, despite claims for the exact fidelity of memorial reconstructions, texts are in fact renewed by being reshaped to address new conditions. In literate communities books have been privileged as the dominant textual medium, one impressively (and not always benignly) efficient in constraining the fluidity of oral texts and yet immensely generative in stimulating multiple readerships into further acts of composition.

It was historically inevitable that books should have been the focus of the work of the Bibliographical Society in its *first* century. But, as Greg recognized, it was not logically compelling. In his very early paper, 'What is Bibliography?', read before the Society on 19 February 1912, he remarked:

Thus it may be called bibliography, or it may be called by any other name you please, but what I want understood is that the characteristics of the science about which I am speaking cut far deeper than the distinction between writing and printing and apply to the transmission of all symbolic representation of speech or other ordered sound or even logical thought.[11]

Certainly the word 'book' can no longer be confined by its mere physical difference from other media by virtue of its particular conjunction of format, materials, and technology, however determinative these are. If the ultimate object of any 'history of the book' is not the study of books themselves but what their production, dissemination, and reception reveal about past human life and thought, then all textual forms have a claim to comparable study within that larger plan. Even as members of the Society went about their work on manuscripts and printed books and the implications of textual variations between them, new texts were merging in visual and aural forms. Photographs and phonograph, movingly married on screen, were in their turn only a prelude to the newer texts formed for transmission by television.

The last two decades have seen a remarkable expansion of studies – too prolific to permit recital here – devoted to the production and reception of texts, terms which embrace not only the current preoccupation with writing and reading in critical theory but also the broader cultural implications of the forms in which texts are printed and marketed and the conditions of readership to which they are addressed. It has also come to be recognized that a distinctively Eurocentric notion of the book and its circulation cannot account for the rôle of such texts in other societies with different communicative traditions and widely varying standards of literacy.

Faced with such range and diversity, it is not surprising that there should be disputes about boundaries (where 'bibliography' ends and history, anthropology, the psychology of perception, and so on, begin) or genuine doubts about the effect of such a diffusion on what some would see as the more central

11 His paper appeared in the Society's *Transactions*, 12 (1914): 39–53, and is reprinted in his *Collected Papers*, ed. J.C. Maxwell (Oxford, 1966); the passage cited occurs on pp. 77–8.

bibliographical activities of description and editing. Academic bibliographers of the 1950s and 1960s, if not librarians who also thought themselves bibliographers, generally conceived their rôle to be the creation of authoritative editions as the necessary basis for a literary criticism responsible to an author's words and most likely meaning. As all criticism takes off from some form of text, reporting the bibliographical evidence about its physical construction and readings remains one highly important function of the discipline.

Yet simply in terms of utility to others, since bibliographers have much more to tell from their knowledge of the making and use of books, such a focus now seems too narrow to meet the changed needs of critical enquiry in the academy and, in the library, the vastly changed conditions of acquisition, retention, and bibliographical control of texts under which national collections are having to redefine their responsibilities to scholarship. Since no history, even in trying to retell as matters of fact what actually happened in the past, can avoid selection and interpretation, what it elects to present will usually be subjects of *current* interest questioned in ways that reflect *current* concerns.[12]

It was against such a background of recent changes in the perception of our relationships with texts that the Cambridge University Press commissioned in 1989 a multi-volume collaborative history of the book in Britain and vested responsibility for its preparation in three general editors whose own work has been more literary and bibliographical than conventionally historical. Although such a history must be responsive to the wide range of interest now in the ways in which all texts were made and used in the past, to achieve anything at all it must also set limits. In defining those limits nationally (Britain) and formally (the book) it follows the example of the French *Histoire de l'édition française*, a collaborative work embracing manuscript and printed books and a wide range of ephemeral forms, completed in four volumes in 1986. With commitment to a much shorter chronological period, Die Historische Kommission des Börsenvereins des Deutschen Buchhandels has launched a six-volume history of German publishing over the last 100 years. A history of the book in America to 1876 is also proposed and the project has already generated a substantial report, *Needs and Opportunities in the History of the Book: America, 1639–1876* edited by David R. Hall and John B. Hench (Charlottesville, 1987). Comparable if less ambitious studies of the rôle of the book in the social and cultural history of Australia and of Canada also attest its rôle in the development of distinct national cultures.

For a history of the book in Britain beginning in Roman times and covering the whole period of British imperialist expansion and contraction, however,

---

12 Noting 'the current controversy within the humanities in North America between, on the one hand, those whom one might call traditional "philologists" and, on the other, the "literary theorists" wishing to subvert the traditional rationale of the humanities to include, for example, feminist, black and "popular" studies', I.R. Willison recently suggested 'that the history of the book – or, as we might rephrase it, "text" (because it pervades all modes of discourse) – would offer an invaluable interdisciplinary, middle ground for rapprochement'. See 'The History of the Book in America: A Note', *Book Trade History Group Newsletter*, 11 (October 1990), p. 9.

even 'the nation' is a highly problematic concept, whether defined geographi-
cally or culturally, and demands to be applied flexibly. Though focused on the
book 'in' the British Isles, such a history must therefore at least acknowledge
Britain's use of books brought in from the Continent, especially during the
manuscript period and the first two centuries of printing. But the cultural
impositions brought about abroad in the last three hundred years by the export
trade of books in English is also an important dimension of the nature and
production of books in Britain itself. To call them 'books', as distinct from other
forms of inscription, is to raise questions that could be evaded by calling them
'texts', but it has its pragmatic point, not to exclude the trade in prints, maps,
music, and newspapers, or any of the other forms of printing and publishing, but
to imply an emphasis.

Such a time span also poses insoluble problems about the relation between
narrative and analysis, the long view (with all the teleological risks attendant on
discussions of influence, technological progress, and cultural regression), and
the expositions of the conditions and products of book production in particular
settings. As currently planned, the Cambridge history divides into seven
volumes. The first, which ends at about AD 1100, sees the fundamental
characteristics and principles of book production and organization established
while Britain is still part of the wider Latin culture of Europe. The second, to
about 1400, begins with book production dominated by the religious houses,
traces a shift to new patrons, the increased production of vernacular texts, and
the development of town-based book trades run mainly by laymen. The third
volume covers the period from 1400 to 1557, its central concern being the
interdependent rôles of the manuscript and printed book after the introduction of
printing. The precision of the later date marks the formal incorporation of the
Stationers' Company of London, the point at which the fourth volume begins. In
dealing with book production from 1557 to the final lapse of the Licensing Act in
1695, the concerns of the fourth volume are prescribed by the distinctive
conjunction of government policy and the monopolistic control under which
conditions England generated a national literature and experienced two
revolutions. In the fifth volume the eighteenth century is extended to take
account of the many innovations in the technologies of papermaking, printing,
and binding and their implementation in the first three decades of the nineteenth
century. By taking the years 1830 to 1914, the sixth volume can concentrate on
the effect of those technologies in creating a massive expansion of printing and
publishing for an industrialized, politically educated, increasingly literate, and
mobile society within Britain and for a great diversity of overseas markets
politically and economically secured by Britain's imperial power. For the
seventh volume, 1914 to the present day, the terms of reference remain
disturbingly imprecise, partly because the book must now share its functions
with other media with which it is complexly interdependent, partly because the
archival resources are so much richer than for earlier periods, partly because
new technologies and the emergence of multinational publishing weaken the
very premises of a national history.

Four research fellows funded by the Leverhulme Trust to work on projects related to the history are providing a vast amount of factual information not hitherto available. It opens up study into patterns in the use of books, the economics of production, and study of communities of interest among members of the trade. The first of the projects is an account of books and readers, 1400–1557, based on a survey of the ownership of books known to have been acquired in those years. The others are less specific to particular volumes: a quantitative analysis of the British book trade, 1475–1700; a biographical study of the English book trade, 1557–1830; and a quantitative survey of publishing and authorship, 1830–1939. The concurrent development of a machine-readable catalogue of all extant British books to 1800, a venture to which the Society's contribution is its *STC*, will readily permit both the more selective study of particular topics and the more reliable tracing of patterns in writing and publishing over several decades.

To say more of such an enterprise when it is still so embryonic would be to create too many hostages to fortune. But as the Society embarks on its second century, the principle that bibliography quite properly embraces 'history of the book' as one of its most important applications seems firmly rooted. It is limited still by its exclusions, but the more comprehensive account of how all *texts* work to create a culture cannot proceed until the more limited task is done. There will of course be others: it is only *a* history of the book.

If in the 1890s there was a prophetic view of other forms of text production, it might be traced in the comment of the little-known New Zealand typographer, Robert Coupland Harding:

William Morris has predicted that typography will cease to exist during the next century, and he may be right in his forecast. I see it threatened by the camera, the etching fluid, and by the (at present) harmless and inoffensive 'typewriter', in the keyboard of which lies the germ of something much greater in the future.[13]

The creation, transmission, and reconstruction of literal, graphic, and even aural texts on keyboard and screen is a reality which now complicates any notion of the book as a privileged textual medium. Logically, the physical products of any technology for the recording and communication of information are equally subject to bibliographical record and textual analysis. Greg's vision of a bibliography not limited to books but 'to the transmission of all symbolic representation of speech or other ordered sound or even logical thought' has already taken on substance and will in due course also demand an account of its history. 'The book' and its history will become something more than the history of books.

13 'A Hundred Years Hence', *Typo*, 8 (27 January 1894): 1.

ENVOI
Meditations by the Captain of the Iceberg

TERRY BELANGER

I owe thanks to Peter Graham for the title of this talk. He and I were discussing the increasingly visible results of the current round of budget cuts on academic library rare-book departments all over the United States. We agreed that one of the underlying causes of the present shortage of money was the remorselessly escalating costs of academic computing services – the sort of services, in fact, that Graham is responsible for providing at Rutgers University, where he is Associate Vice President for Information Services and Associate University Librarian. The American rare-book establishment is a large one – almost Titanic in size, one might say: but listening to rare-book librarians talk about budget reductions, Graham said, made him feel like the Captain of the Iceberg, listening to the crew members over there on the *Titanic*, arguing about what colour to paint the deck chairs.

The iceberg of my title is the future. What does the future hold, during the next decade or so, for fields relating to the art and history of the book, and for the other, related areas of interest which are represented in this volume? I thought it would be interesting to speculate on what is to become of us in the interlocking worlds of our joint concerns. So that talk – this *envoi* – is intended as an essay in futurology – or, perhaps, apocalyptology.

This does seem a good time to look ahead and in doing so to reflect on the recent past, as well. We have seen a great flowering of our joint concerns over the past two decades, but recently there have been signs of a slowing down. Of the great growth since the early seventies there can be no doubt. Think just of the new journals and newsletters that have appeared since the founding of the *Bibliography Newsletter* in 1973 (to take a date that sticks in my mind): San Francisco's (and the world's) own *Fine Print*; the newsletter of the American Printing History Association, itself founded in 1974, and its journal, *Printing History*; the newsletters of the Guild of Book Workers and of the American Typecasters Fellowship; *The Paper Conservator*; *Hand Papermaking*; *Ink and Gall*; the *Abbey Newsletter* and more recently *The Alkaline Paper Advocate*; *Conservation Administration News*; *The New Bookbinder*; *Publishing History*; *Factotum*, the

Based on a talk given to the Colophon Club, San Francisco. I am indebted to Kathryn Clark and Katharine Kyes Leab, for their comments to me about recent and forthcoming developments in hand-made paper and in the antiquarian book trade.

journal of *ESTC*; *Analytical and Enumerative Bibliography* from Northern Illinois; *Rare Books and Manuscripts Librarianship* from the Rare Book and Manuscript Section of the American Library Association, Chicago; *Matrix* – the list goes on and on.

Why this sharp increase of interest in the book arts in the 1970s, represented by such an outburst of journals? One reason may be that the book as a physical object began to become more visible in the 1960s, as non-print media became ever more important a means of communication, and as computer-generated, machine-readable information sources began for the first time to become common – machine-readable information for the most part displayed or set forth on paper, to be sure, and often in book format: but disposable – to use and to throw away, because backed by electronic originals. I am aware that students of our times have been forecasting the end of the codex book ever since McLuhan and before. But still, look around: you can now buy, and cheaply, a bible and a Shakespeare that can be read off a video screen. They are no longer laptop, they are palmtop. Surely we are soon going to be renting or buying book chips the way we now rent or buy video cassette tapes, for use in our own personal reading and viewing devices.

Codex books are going to continue to be a part of our lives, ten years from now, and an important one; but books are already a lot more visible to most people than they used to be, and they're going to be a lot more so in the near future. The fish don't see the water they swim in; but they certainly notice when the level in the tank begins to sink.

Most us have a considerable instinctive affection for the codex book. One of my own cheap party tricks in teaching descriptive bibliography at Columbia University in New York City is to take a late nineteenth- or early twentieth-century book, usually a cloth-bound one with a pictorial cover, hold it up in class and talk about its contents, design, and construction for a bit, and then, suddenly and without warning, rip it into half and systematically tear it to shreds as I accuse my horrified students of being overly sentimental about the book as a physical object. 'Books,' I say, as I toss the shards of the book I have just destroyed into the wastepaper-basket, 'are to use.' I think that our sentimentality toward the physical book has been growing, as the book becomes, slowly but surely, ever less necessary a part of our daily lives. A parallel case presents itself: as a society, we are far more sentimental about the horse since it ceased to be our major mode of transportation; we use horses now mostly for play, not work.[1] The same thing, slowly but surely, is happening with the physical book: it is becoming more an object of play – or of display – than work.

Whatever the reason, book arts and book-arts programmes of all sorts mushroomed in the period between the late sixties and the present (or the near present) – we have all learned what exponential growth is, at first hand.

---

1 I owe this analogy to Sandra Kirshenbaum, editor of *Fine Print*.

One of the results is a spectacular growth in the number of private presses. When we put together the Fine Printing Conference at Columbia in 1982, we issued invitations to attend to every North American private press we could turn up which had produced at least one book. There were no qualitative requirements for attending this invitational conference at all; all you had to have done was to have published one book. The organizing committee, whose other members were Ronald Gordon of the Oliphant Press, Sue Gosin of the Dieu Donné Press and Paper Mill, Frank Mattson of The New York Public Library, and Douglas Wolf and Carol Sturm of Nadja and the Center for Book Arts, was with hard work able to turn up a grand total of about sixty presses in the United States and Canada to invite, of which about thirty, or half, actually showed up at our little conference in New York City in May 1982.

How many private presses which have produced at least one book are there in this country now, less than a decade later? Three hundred? More? Whatever the number, it is an example of exponential growth, with the result that over the past decade the market has been flooded with a great many very nice books for which the world has no need. Private-press printers are increasingly complaining about their difficulty in selling books, and I predict that they are going to have even more trouble doing so in the coming decade.

In the old days, many libraries and individual collectors routinely placed standing orders with these presses, eager to have one of everything. In the coming years, we are going to see libraries and collectors increasingly preferring to develop what they call *representative* collections. They will want one book from your press; one book from a lot of presses – or maybe a few; but they *won't* want your whole output; there is just too much out there to buy, and the resources to buy them with are too limited.

Be that as it may, we are going to continue to see a lot of private-press books produced and published. Fewer and fewer of them, I predict, are going to be letterpress. There are so many other options now available to private-press proprietors, and cheaply so, too. Claire Van Vliet has suggested that the rise of the modern private-press movement in the 1960s is the result of the cheap availability of the commercially outmoded technology of letterpress printing.[2] Handset letterpress may not have been commercially labour-effective, but it *was* cost-effective, if the labour – your own – was free. You might not be able to find a publisher willing to take the risk of producing your books for you, but you could make them yourselves, slowly but handsomely, setting the type by hand or ordering Monotype composition, and printing them yourself on a Vandercook or other handpress which you used to be able to get almost for the asking from commercial establishments changing over from letterpress to offset. That was then.

Recent years have seen the staggeringly swift advent of the cheap, desktop laser printer coupled with effective word-processing programmes and a

2 Terry Belanger, ed., *Proceedings of the Fine Printing Conference at Columbia* (New York: Book Arts Press, 1983), p. 84.

constantly growing supply of scalable electronic typestyles and faces offering both great flexibility and ubiquitous accessibility, as well. If you are a private-press printer *simply* because you love letterpress, you will stick to letterpress in the 1990s; but our private-press printers are going to become more and more infatuated with the ever-more-available, ever-more-sophisticated machine-readable arsenals of typographic materials which surround them. It may seem extreme to predict that the Twinrocker Handmade Paper Mill will, soon enough, be making editions of handmade paper suitable for laserjet printing. But that, Kathryn Clark informs me, is exactly what she is contemplating at the moment: an edition of paper for the Walt Disney studios, with a special watermark, to be used for laser-printing souvenir stills from animated Disney films, themselves increasingly generated digitally and without the use of intermediary celluloid gels. Now here is a project for some centuries-future John Bidwell or Paul Needham: studying various examples of Twinrocker paper made for Disney, and establishing their chronological order from the way Mickey Mouse's ears change in the watermarks.

Twenty years ago, people were beginning to be frightened at the ease with which new typeface designs could be generated by such firms as Compugraphic, or by the International Typeface Corporation, or by stick-on letter firms such as Letraset. They will have far more reason to be frightened in the next decade, as we begin to have the routine capacity to become our own typeface designers. Typeface designs will multiply like mice over the next decade: but they will be electronic typefaces, and available only as such.

There will be no, or virtually no, new faces produced in hot metal. The technology for producing them still exists, both the hard way (as exemplified by Stan Nelson and hand punch-cutting), and the easy way – though not *that* easy (as exemplified by the Dale Guild, Theo Rehak, and the Benton engraving machine). But it's going to be difficult to maintain the machines necessary to cast metal type by hand. The foundry skills necessary to repair, let alone remake, broken parts are becoming increasingly rare, and – if found – increasingly expensive. The price of foundry type will thus continue to rise; and though it will continue to be possible to buy Monotype composition during the next decade or so, there will be growing problems with its quality. The chief source of hot-metal machine composition in the United States will eventually be semi-hobby producers such as Pat Taylor in Westchester, Rick Hopkins in West Virginia, and Harold Berliner in Nevada City.

Calligraphy will flourish during the coming decade. The materials needed are cheap and readily available, and there is a substantial number of competent teachers out there as well as an enormous number of self-help and instruction manuals in the field. Calligraphy will become increasingly hobby-orientated, however: diplomas and other ceremonial and commercial documents will generally be produced using sophisticated software founts which imitate various styles of handwriting but which are the product of laser printing.

There will be plenty of handmade paper around for the calligraphers to work on, though it will not be cheap. Perhaps no area of the book arts has expanded so much in the past couple of decades as papermaking. Kathryn Clark says rather grimly about the operations at Twinrocker that 'we could have made a fortune if we had had a school'. Twinrocker stopped taking apprentices years ago, preferring to have *employees* in service of the Twinrocker goal of making (or, as they call it, *editioning*) book papers in quantity; with the demise of J. Barcham Green's Hayle mill in England and the gradual using up of what once seemed to be inexhaustible stocks of English mould-made papers, there is a real need for Twinrocker's wares, as well as those of Dieu Donné and other determined American producers. There are still sources of European handmade paper, especially French, and these will continue to be available, though the continuing decline of the dollar will make them a very expensive choice indeed for American printers.

The making of marbled and decorated papers will flourish; indeed, there will be a glut of such papers on the market, and they will be progressively more difficult to sell.

Hand bookbinders are going to have a rather confused time of it in the nineties. Learning how to bind in leather is going to be more difficult, for a variety of quite different reasons. It will continue to be difficult to get first-rate instruction in designer-binding in leather, because so many of those with the necessary craft skills to teach such work have gone into conservation – and collections conservation at that, as opposed to individual-item conservation. The conservators teach, but they don't teach leather binding (even though they could) because they don't *want* to. Book conservators increasingly believe that an eighteenth-century book (for example) is not generally a suitable object for an elaborate new leather binding; those who try it are going to discover that more and more people think their endeavours are absurdly inappropriate. There will be more boxes made for everything, and less rebinding of anything. The use of paper and non-adhesive bindings on new handmade books, on the other hand, will flourish, and new styles will continue to develop, supported by a new availability of extra-strong handmade cover papers. The fields of bookbinding and conservation will continue to overlap; in private practice, there will be fewer and fewer craft bookbinders and more and more conservation bookbinders.

The big subject in conservation in the 1990s will be reformatting: reproducing original materials in sophisticated substitute forms. Microform is a fairly crude way of capturing the data offered by deteriorating or fragile paper originals; the technology of digitized imaging will rapidly supplement and eventually largely replace microform. Reproductions captured in digitized form are easily transferable from one place to another via already-existing electronic media – our present fax machines are very primitive versions of what a great many of us are going to have access to, in much better versions, in ten years. The copies we are going to get will, indeed, be so good in so many ways that their existence will threaten the continued existence of the original objects of which they are copies. Why try to keep up the deteriorating original when the copy is so good, so flexible, so cheaply made, so permanent, and so replaceable? Thus, as regards book conservation, technology will increasingly become both our salvation and our greatest threat.

Some books are always going to be desirable as physical objects, and there will continue to be a flourishing book trade to deal in them. The antiquarian book trade will go on complaining about the decline of the antiquarian book trade: how there are no more books left, and how, and especially, there are no more collectors. Accordingly, and more so than ever, we will need to remember the lament of Harry Elkins Widener, a man who certainly had reason to be interested in what the Captain of the Iceberg was thinking, since he went down on the *Titanic*. Widener once cried, 'Mr Morgan and Mr Huntington are buying up all the books, and Mr Bixby is getting the manuscripts. When my time comes – if it ever does – there will be nothing left for me – everything will be gone!' 'Our grief at this outcry', once commented the late Mr Robert Taylor of Princeton, 'can be mitigated by recalling that [Elkins] did manage to secure the Van Antwerp First Folio, the Countess of Pembroke's copy of the *Arcadia*, the dedication copy of Boswell's *Life of Johnson*, and many other similar items.'[3]

The old guard of collectors and dealers tends to view the present scene with alarm, because it sees the material it is interested in drying up. Just a few weeks ago, the *New York Times* was bemoaning the decline of the antiquarian book trade for this very reason: 'The number of good books available on the market has fallen dramatically and those that are available have shot up in price, in large part because of big acquisitions in the last two decades by academic institutions and libraries.' And: 'Even those who continue to collect rare books in the United States increasingly lack the broad knowledge that typified older collectors.' And further: 'The smaller shops, which specialized in limited numbers of books, can frequently only be visited by appointment and often do not sell lower-priced volumes that would appeal to collectors of more modest means or those who were first stepping into the market. "If you want to become a collector there are no longer many stores where you can just drop in and browse", [one bookseller] said. "The loss of the open rare-book shop is tragic. A whole culture has disappeared." '[4]

Perhaps so, but it is a culture that is being replaced by a whole other one: we will witness a significant growth of used, second-hand, general, academic, and scholarly bookstores all over the country in the 1990s, many of them carrying very substantial stocks of very interesting books, by no means all of them new or even newish. Katharine Kyes Leab of *American Book Prices Current* tells the story of an investment banker who recently asked her for advice. He had been told to collect bird books, he said; what did *she* think? 'What are you interested in?' she asked him. 'The Heisenberg principle and black holes and things like that,' he said; but (he said) 'my dealer isn't interested in that kind of stuff.' Well,

---

3 Robert Taylor, *Certain Small Works* (Princeton, 1980), p. 34.
4 Chris Hedges, 'Selling Books to be Cherished, Not Just Read,' the *New York Times*, Monday, 31 December 1990, pp. 11, 17.

increasingly there will be plenty of dealers who are. The old guard in the book trade tends to ignore the presence of the Little People – dealers who exhibit at Glendale but not at California Book Fairs, for instance.

Such dealers are already nearly ubiquitous, and they will become more so in the next decade. Mainline and smaller dealers alike will continue to move out of cities and into the suburbs and the country; as Mrs Leab says, the only city dealers with decent overheads are the ones working the streets. Book catalogues will become ever more important, as dealers increasingly use them, not as repositories of unsold stock, but as their chief sales medium. High-end interest in unique book and manuscript materials will continue, as will status-y book-buying in general: the buying of books which provide good photo-opportunities in *Architectural Digest*, for instance. Medieval manuscripts will continue to increase in price.

Again at the high end, there will be an increase in bookseller partnerships, combinations, and various sorts of cartel arrangements, as the capital require-ments of the trade become greater. Dealers with large amounts of capital will increasingly become bankers (or at least loan officers) for other dealers, serving as go-betweens in dealer-customer transactions where the short-term use of substantial amounts of capital is required.

Libraries will buy fewer antiquarian books during the next decade than they did in the seventies or eighties, a fact which will hurt dealers who make a substantial part of their living selling to institutional customers. Academic institutions as a whole are going to be hurt in the nineties, and as a result so will be both their libraries and the rare-book departments within them. The relentless contest between increasing collections and decreasing resources with which to maintain them will intensify in the nineties, and there will be a slow but steady escalation of the institutional sale of rare books, benefiting those dealers – and auction houses – able to work out purchasing arrangements with such institutions.

The retrospective conversion of cataloguing records for old books into machine-readable form will continue. The records thus produced, it will shortly be discovered, are going to be useful in determining what gets used; materials that don't get used are going to be particularly likely candidates for deaccession. We are not going to be able to continue to preserve, in their original format, a great many old books; and rare-book librarians are going to become increasingly expert at the techniques of *triage*, separating the seriously hurt from the walking wounded, and leaving the moribund behind. The old books most likely to survive are those still in good condition, and in their original or at least contemporary bindings. Old books in class A library buckram bindings with no intrinsic artistic or at least some sort of graphic appeal are going to have a hard time of it, and many of them are going to end up as sanitary landfill. Indeed, rare-book librarians are going to discover that a growing part of their jobs is to lead the procession to the dump. Put in a slightly different way, the books that are most likely to survive in special collections are those which have importance or significance or relevance *as physical objects*; there will be continuing pressure for rare-book libraries to become museums of the book, a movement which will cause increasing tensions between these rare-book libraries and the larger institutions of which they are a part: rare-book libraries may become museums of the book, but are most academic libraries going to be willing to support the expenses of such museum operations? Indeed, are most academic institutions as a whole?

Institutions that sell rare books in the 1990s will not do so from a desire to make money; they won't get that much for them, by and large. They will sell because they want to save money: to save housing costs, to save insurance costs, to save preservation costs, and – and most of all – to save staffing costs. It won't all happen in the next decade, but in the next fifty years I predict that we are going to see the wholesale transfer of old books out of academic libraries at a scale that we have not seen since the decades following the French Revolution. Ten years from now, this statement will not appear to be as far-fetched as it may seem now.

Does all of this sound unbearably grim? The picture is by no means totally bleak. Many old books are going to be in different places, a decade from now, from where they are at present; but the interesting ones are likely to be *someplace*, and possibly in a better place, than they are now. Some bibliographers are going to deplore the wholesale movement of rare books, especially those who think that no library should ever deaccession any book it ever buys, or ever throw away an original even after it has been reformatted.[5] But continually improving telecommunications will make scholarly research in the *texts* of old books ever more easy and more efficient and more effective. And there will continue to be a great affection for worthy exemplars of the book production of former ages. Indeed, there will be a continued interest in all aspects of the physical history of the book, and education programmes like those of the Rare Book School, I predict, will flourish.

5 See, for instance, *Libraries, Museums, and Reading*, by G. Thomas Tanselle (New York: Book Arts Press, 1991).

Selective index

There is a very large number of names and topics in this volume many of which make up lists or are mentioned only in passing. These tend to be grouped in particular chapters – e.g., those concerned with the study of illustration and oriental literature. It should not prove difficult to locate such references so this index lists only the more important key words, the names of those who have contributed to the volume, and those whose work is discussed. Footnotes and reading lists are not usually indexed but a few exceptions have been made if that might prove helpful. Some cross-references have been given but these are not intended to be comprehensive.

Further reading: many chapters are provided with further reading lists or footnotes designed to serve that function. See particularly: 1n2, 36, 54–6, notes to 57–68, 82, 101n5, 120–1, 128–9, notes to 161–81 and 206–14, 235, 243, 257n10, and notes to 258–69; also entries for: bibliographies; catalogues; Scotland; oriental literature; and photographic reproductions.